AF678872

No. 1888
$22.95

MASTERING THE 8088 MICROPROCESSOR

BY LANNY V. DAO

TAB BOOKS Inc.
BLUE RIDGE SUMMIT, PA 17214

CP/M-86 is a registered trademark of Digital Research, Inc.
IBM is a registered trademark of IBM Corporation.
VisiCalc is a registered trademark of VisiCorp.
WordStar is a registered trademark of MicroPro International Corp.
Intel is a registered trademark of Intel Corporation.
IBM PC-DOS is a registered trademark of IBM Corporation.

FIRST EDITION

FIRST PRINTING

Copyright © 1984 by TAB BOOKS Inc.

Printed in the United States of America

Reproduction or publication of the content in any manner, without express permission of the publisher, is prohibited. No liability is assumed with respect to the use of the information herein.

Library of Congress Cataloging in Publication Data

Dao, Lanny V.
Mastering the 8088 microprocessor.

Includes index.
1. Intel 8088 (Microprocessor) I. Title.
QA76.8.I2924D36 1984 001.64 84-16419
ISBN 0-8306-0888-5
ISBN 0-8306-1888-0 (pbk.)

Cover photograph courtesy of Intel Corporation.

Contents

Introduction

While microprocessors have been available commercially for more than a decade, only recently have they become powerful enough to make the performance of low-cost microcomputers comparable to the traditional minicomputer systems. Due to dramatic advancement in very-large-scale-integration technology (VLSI), more and more efficient and powerful microprocessors are starting to surface.

Existing applications include office word processing and general business functions, legal and medical applications, computer-aided engineering design and manufacturing (CAD/CAM), graphic animation, and many other professional applications. The Intel 8088 chip and its full 16-bit family, including the 8086, 80186, and 80286 microprocessors, represent a new generation of advanced microprocessors that fully exploits the cost/performance benefits of VLSI technology.

The purpose of this book is to introduce the detailed structure of the Intel 8088 microprocessor, its instruction repertoire, and the programming concepts and techniques for this particular silicon chip. This text can therefore serve as a reference source for any software designer developing and implementing 8088-based programs. All software applications and concepts described for the 8088 chip can be equally applied to any 8086-, 80186-, and 80286-based systems with absolutely no program modifications.

I assume that you are already familiar to some extent with programming in one of the high-level languages such as FORTRAN. If you have programming experience on other microprocessors or computers, this book will teach specific programming techniques using the specific characteristics and facilities of the 8088 chip.

This book presents many practical methods and techniques frequently employed in information processing with examples that illustrate the implementation of these techniques on the 8088 microprocessor. Among the techniques discussed are generation of pseudorandom numbers, sorting and searching, manipulation of linked lists, translation of characters from one representation to another, using the stack in recursive techniques, and conversion between the algebraic expressions and the reverse polish notations.

Chapter 1 introduces the basic concepts and definitions related to the structure of a digital computer, especially the structure of 8088-based computers and the ways information is represented in them. The IBM Personal Computer will be discussed as an example of a popular 8088-based machine.

Chapter 2 is an introduction to the machine language of the 8088 microprocessor, the architecture of the 8088 Central Processing Unit, including its general registers, segment registers, and addressing modes.

Chapter 3 introduces 8088 assembly language to help you understand the concept of machine instructions represented symbolically by assembly language. The general format of 8088 assembly language and the common coding errors are discussed.

Chapter 4 is a complete description of the characteristics and uses of individual 8088 machine instructions. Examples of assembly language coding for each instruction are provided.

Chapter 5 begins the study of several simple applications such as 32-bit arithmetic operations and number conversion using the 16-bit architecture of the 8088 chip. You should try to implement these examples on your 8088-based system to actually test your understanding. Practice plays an extremely important role in the process of learning computer programming.

Chapter 6 discusses the logical instructions, which include the Boolean operators NOT, AND, inclusive-OR, and exclusive-OR. Several examples that demonstrate the power and flexibility of the 8088 chip include character conversion techniques and data encryption and decryption methods for protection and security purposes.

Chapter 7 presents a group of instructions that perform the movements of data. Examples of manipulation of data in character strings and symbol translation using table lookup techniques are discussed. The manipulation of important data structures such as linked lists is also presented. Examples to delete and insert cells into a doubly linked list structure are provided.

Chapter 8 presents the instructions that can alter the execution sequence of the 8088 microprocessor. Applications such as software looping, sorting techniques, and the use of the stack in recursive programming are discussed in detail.

Chapter 9 deals with the applications of shift and rotate instructions. Techniques to manipulate individual bits using these instructions are presented.

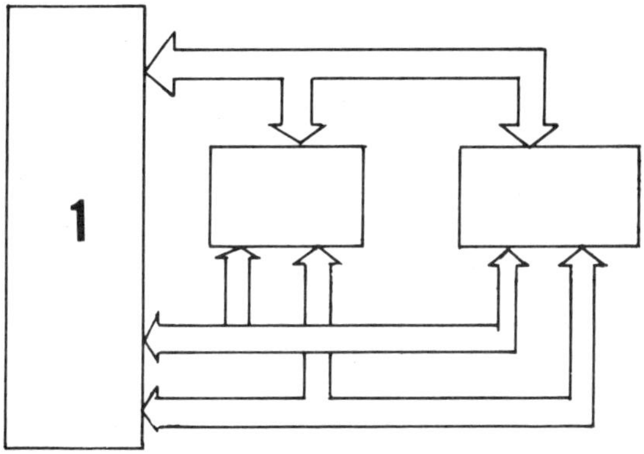

Basic Concepts

Since the first microprocessor was introduced in the early 1970s, microcomputers have become an essential tool that affects almost all sectors of today's society. From simple home applications to complex business functions, microcomputers have dramatically altered the way people think, work, and entertain.

This chapter introduces the readers to some basic concepts and definitions concerning how a microcomputer is organized and how information such as numbers and alphanumeric characters can be represented in programs and stored in the computer memory.

OVERVIEW OF A MICROCOMPUTER

The essence of a microcomputer is its simplicity: it breaks a complex problem into many smaller and simpler parts to obtain the final answers. The simplest part is represented by a machine instruction. A collection of machine instructions in a specified sequence represents the fundamental form of a computer program. A microcomputer can store a program in its memory and execute it without any human intervention.

Computer Hardware

A microcomputer consists of several basic elements that provide five essential fundamental capabilities: arithmetic-logic, control, memory, input, and output as shown in Fig. 1-1.

Central Processing Unit. The arithmetic-logic unit (ALU) and control unit (CU) are implemented on a single silicon chip that form a Central Processing Unit (CPU) or a microprocessor. Most commercial microprocessors are housed in small rectangular packages having small pins on their sides as shown in Fig. 1-2. The ALU performs basic arithmetic

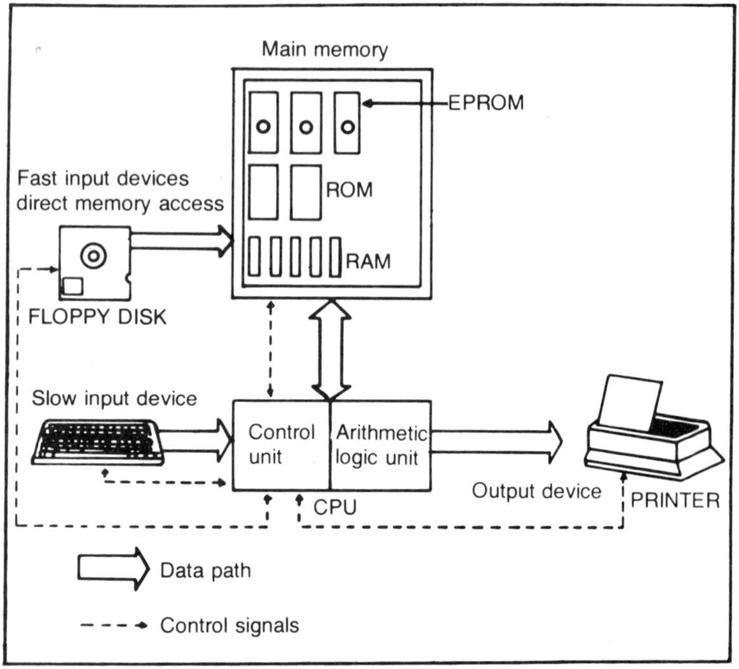

Fig. 1-1. Functional parts of a microcomputer.

Fig. 1-2. Commercial microprocessors (The 8088 and 8086 CPU).

operations such as addition and subtraction. It can also compare two given operands and indicate the result. The CU coordinates the system timing and the activities between the microprocessor and the computer memory.

In 8088-based microcomputers, the microprocessor is the 8088 chip that was developed by Intel Corporation of Santa Clara, California. Today the 8088 chip is manufactured by Intel and several other semiconductor manufacturers in several different versions.

To a software programmer, the ALU unit of the 8088 microprocessor appears as a set of registers, as shown in Fig. 1-3. The primary function of

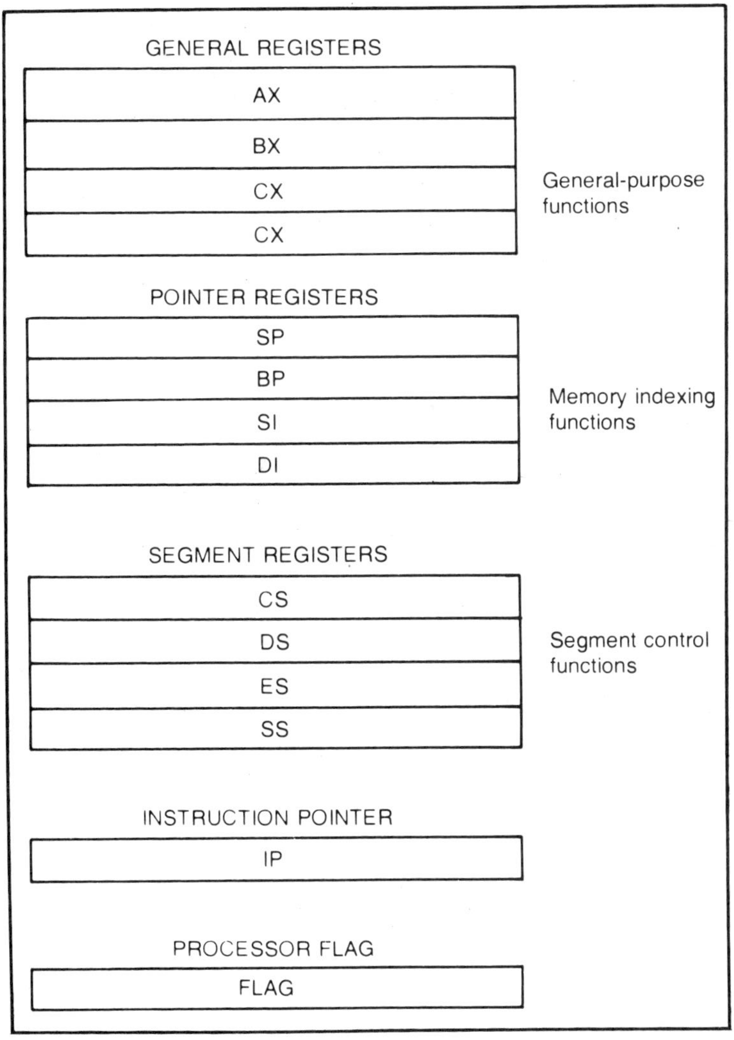

Fig. 1-3. Functional organization of the 8088 CPU.

Fig. 1-4. Read-only memories in the IBM Personal Computer.

each register is to hold information for future processing or to hold information already processed. Data can be transferred among registers, or from a register to the microcomputer memory, and vice versa. The 8088 CPU has four general-purpose registers, four pointer registers, and four segment registers. These registers are discussed in detail in Chapter 2.

Memory. Computers manipulate information in the form of numbers or in the form of characters. The main storage area of a microcomputer is its memory. Memory holds information for the job being processed by the microprocessor at a given moment. The information that is kept in the computer memory can be programs in machine language, input data, and intermediate and final results. Such information in the computer memory is always stored as groups of binary digits or bits.

A binary digit can have a value of 0 or 1 only. The binary format is used because the only practical representation of information in conventional electronics must use two-state devices (state 0 or 1, on or off, open or closed). Virtually all information-processing today is performed in the binary format. In the case of the 8088 microprocessor, these binary digits are structured into groups of eight bits. A group of eight bits is called a byte. A group of sixteen bits is called a word, and a group of thirty-two bits is called a doubleword. A word is therefore equivalent to two bytes, and a doubleword is equivalent to two words or four bytes.

The memory of the microcomputer is made up of semiconductor chips, as shown in Fig. 1-4, and can be divided into two different categories: Read-Only Memory (ROM), and Read-Write Memory or Random-Access Memory (RAM).

Read-Only Memory. Important computer programs such as operating systems and control programs to direct the microcomputer to start up and perform its basic operations are usually kept in ROM. This prevents the microcomputer from accidentally writing over the control programs and erasing or altering their contents. Read-Only Memories, therefore, are used for storage of programs, permanent constants, and tables. There are several popular forms of ROM memory: ROM, PROM, and EPROM.

ROM has its contents permanently programmed by the manufacturer at the time the chips are made. The contents of a ROM memory chip cannot be altered or reprogrammed by the user. In the IBM Personal Computer, ROM memories, as shown in Fig. 1-4, contain the machine codes of the BASIC interpreter and the basic input/output operating system (BIOS) to start up the computer and perform hardware diagnostic functions when the unit is turned on.

The contents of Programmable Read-Only Memory (PROM) can be programmed by the user with a special device called a PROM Programmer. The user can alter the contents of a PROM memory chip only once.

The contents of Erasable Programmable Read-Only Memory (EPROM) can be programmed by the user and subsequently can be erased by exposing the memory chips to high-intensity ultraviolet light. This permits an EPROM unit to be programmed, should changes be desired in the original programming. Thus, EPROM memories are convenient and flexible in the development of new systems where changes to program codes are frequent.

The capacity of a memory chip is measured in terms of K bits or K bytes where 1 K is equivalent to 1024. An EPROM memory chip is relatively inexpensive and can hold a large amount of information. The Intel 27128 chip, as shown in Fig. 1-5, can hold 128 K bits or 131,072 bits of information.

Fig. 1-5. Intel-compatible 2716, 2732, 2764, and 27128 EPROMs.

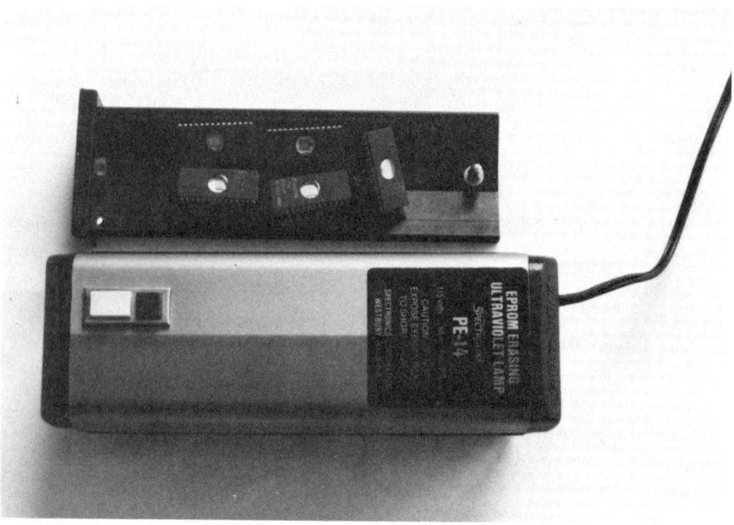

Fig. 1-6. An ultraviolet EPROM eraser unit.

The Ultraviolet Eprom Eraser in Fig. 1-6 produces the high-intensity ultraviolet light that can effectively erase the contents of an EPROM chip in a relatively short period of time (10 to 15 minutes). The EPROM Programmer in Fig. 1-7 can be used to store or program new information in an EPROM memory unit after it has been erased.

Random-Access Memory. The microcomputer uses its random-access memory as the work space to process information. There are two popular forms of RAM memory: Static RAM and Dynamic RAM.

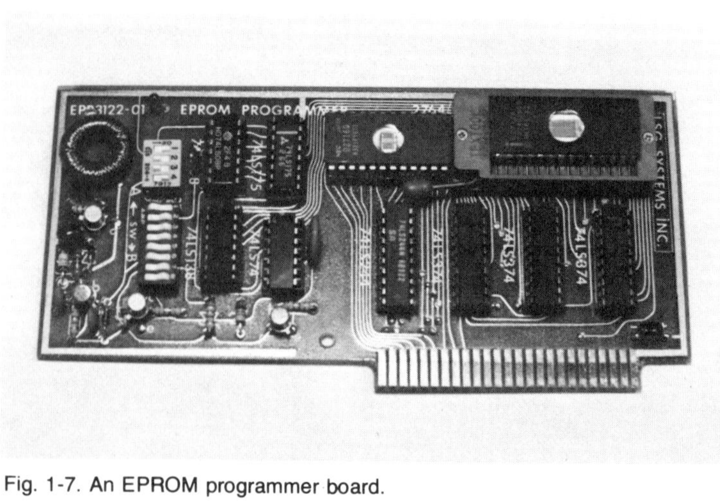

Fig. 1-7. An EPROM programmer board.

Static RAMs, as shown in Fig. 1-8, can retain their data reliably as long as power is maintained regardless of whether they will be accessed by the microprocessor or not. Static RAMs are expensive but have very fast access time. The access time refers to the time it takes to read or write information from or to a static RAM unit. Some static RAMs have their access times well within the 50-nanosecond range (1 nanosecond = 1 billionth of a second). One major disadvantage of using static RAMs is that these chips take up more space and cannot hold as much information as dynamic RAMs.

Virtually all microcomputers use dynamic RAMs as their read-write memories. Dynamic RAMs, as shown in Fig. 1-9, are much slower than static RAMs in terms of access time but they are relatively inexpensive and can contain a lot more information. Currently, the densest dynamic RAM chip can hold 256 K bits or 262,144 bits of information. The physical size of a dynamic RAM chip is smaller than that of a static RAM chip. The disadvantage of using dynamic RAMs is that these memory chips require additional circuitry on the microcomputer to perform refresh operations. Refresh operations refer to the requirements that data in dynamic RAMs must be accessed at least once during a fixed interval (for example, one memory read at every 2 milliseconds) if the data is to be retained. If refresh operations are not performed properly, data in the dynamic RAMs will be lost.

Computer Software

A complete set of instructions which can direct a microcomputer to

Fig. 1-8. Two 2 K-byte static RAM chips.

Fig. 1-9. 64 K-bit dynamic RAM chips. The larger chip is a 2 K-byte static RAM.

perform a given task or to do a specific function is called a computer program. Computer programs can be divided into two different categories because of the nature of the functions they perform. These are application programs and systems programs.

An application program is a set of complete instructions using the computer as a tool to produce the desired results for a specific application. The functions of an application program vary greatly depending on the nature of the applications. For example, an application program can be a word-processing program to create business forms and letters, a spreadsheet program to do financial calculations and forecasting, or a weather-forecasting program to collect and analyze weather-related data. In contrast, a systems program is designed to make the programming tasks of computer programmers easier and more efficient.

Editors, assemblers, debuggers, compilers, linkers, and operating system utilities are examples of the systems programs. The collection of application programs and systems programs, which make the hardware facilities of the computer more accessible to the user and easier to use, are referred to as computer software.

An operating system is a major and essential part of the computer software. It supervises internal activities in the computer hardware, responds to requests from the computer users, invokes the appropriate programs or facilities to satisfy these requests accordingly, and provides early warnings and error recovery in case there is any hardware malfunction. Therefore, a good operating system increases the efficiency of the computer and reduces the chances of undetected errors.

The MS-DOS operating system (developed by Microsoft Corp.) and the CPM-86 operating system (developed by Digital Research, Inc.) are examples of commercially available operating systems for 8086/8088-based microcomputers. These two operating systems are designed to be used in simple single-user, single-programming environment. More powerful and complex operating systems for the 8086/8088 microprocessor family are emerging which include the MPM-86 operating system (also developed by Digital Research) which can run several programs at the same time, and the Unix operating system (a version of the original Unix operating system developed by Bell Laboratories) which is a multiuser, multiprogramming operating system.

There are software tools available in each of these operating systems that greatly assist the development or modification of computer software. These include the editor, the assembler, the debugger, the linker, and interpreters and compilers.

The Editor. Editors are used to enter and modify source programs or text information. This information is normally stored on mass storage devices such as a hard disk, a floppy diskette, or a tape in the form of a file, referred to as a source file. The editor can create these files and manipulate the information contained within these files. The computer users normally request editor functions by entering commands from a keyboard and receive the desired information displayed on a video screen.

The following functions comprise a small sample of capabilities which are normally provided by a good editor in a microcomputer system.

1. The editor may be line-oriented (only one line of source program or text information can be worked on at a time). It should also have full-screen capabilities to let the users work on one page at a time (the size of a screen page is normally limited by the number of lines a video screen can display).

2. The editor may provide the users flexible control of moving the cursor on the video screen to keep track of the current character being edited. Special function keys or a combination of key sequences from the keyboard may be available to move the cursor to any place on the video screen. This includes moving the cursor to the top or bottom of the screen, to the starting or ending character of a word or a line, moving the cursor up or down one line, forward or backward.

3. The editor can bring information stored on mass storage devices, such as a hard disk or a floppy diskette, into the microcomputer memory to be viewed or modified. The editor can also write new information from the computer memory to mass storage devices with ease. The process of transferring data between the computer and its peripheral devices should be automatic and completely transparent to the computer users.

4. The editor can display the contents of source files stored on mass storage devices to the video screen. Any portion of the source file can be displayed in flexible formats as required by the users. For examples, the users may desire to display a specific number of words per line or number of lines per page at a time, or scrolling the screen display up or down by lines or by screen pages.

5. A good editor must provide many standard but flexible editing facilities so that new information and data can be entered into the microcomputer system without any effort. Existing information stored on mass storage devices can also be retrieved, maintained, and modified efficiently. Editing capabilities may include deleting and inserting text information in a source file by characters, words, lines, or paragraphs. Other important capabilities may include moving and copying information in specified blocks within a source file or from one file to another, searching and replacing certain characters, words, or phrases located at any place within a source file.

The program EDLIN.COM which is supplied as a utility of the PC-DOS operating system is an example of a simple line-oriented text editor. Figure 1-10 shows a sample session with the EDLIN editor running on an IBM Personal Computer under the PC-DOS operating system.

The Assembler. It is much more convenient to give instructions to a microcomputer in the form of mnemonics so that computer programs can be read and understood by a programmer. Symbols and labels which have suggestive names can be assigned to memory addresses. This makes a

```
New file
*i                   (insert command)
     1:*;This is the first line of a test program.
     2:*Test    Segment Para
     3:*        Assume CS:Test,DS:Test,ES:Test,SS:Test
     4:*Main    Endp
     5:*^C       (Control-C to get out entry mode)

*1l                  (listing command)
     1: ;This is the first line of a test program.
     2: Test    Segment Para
     3:         Assume CS:Test,DS:Test,ES:Test,SS:Test
     4: Main    Endp
*4d
*4i
     4:*Main    Proc Near
     5:*^C

*1l
     1: ;This is the first line of a test program.
     2: Test    Segment Para
     3:         Assume CS:Test,DS:Test,ES:Test,SS:Test
     4: Main    Proc Near
*
*
```

Fig. 1-10. A sample session with the editor, EDLIN, on the IBM Personal Computer.

machine-language program more meaningful to interpret and comprehend since it is very difficult to work directly with strings of binary digits comprising the actual machine instructions.

The assembler is a systems program that translates a machine-language program written in its symbolic form into the actual machine instructions that can be loaded into the computer memory and executed by the microprocessor. The output of an assembler which is called an object module contains the actual machine instructions. There are several available assemblers for the 8086/8088-based microcomputers such as the Macro Assembler (developed by Microsoft Corporation) and the ASM-86 Assembler (developed by Intel Corporation). Chapter 3 covers the format and syntax of the Macro Assembler in more details.

The Linker. The linker is a systems program that provides the capability to link a number of separately assembled object modules together to create another machine-language module that can be loaded into the computer memory and executed by the microprocessor.

This module is usually referred to as the load module. The linker can search and maintain libraries of useful object modules, such as math and plot functions, to be included in any desired object module. Therefore, a new program can be written to utilize all functions available in these libraries by simply requesting the linker to select the desired object modules in the libraries to be linked with the assembled object module of the new program. The program LINK.EXE which is supplied as a utility of the PC-DOS disk operating system is an example of a typical linker.

The Debugger. Because of their detailed and complex nature, machine-language programs can be very difficult to test or check out merely by running them. The Debugger is a systems program which provides a facility to scrutinize every part of every instruction of a machine-language program. Standard debugger features may include examining and modifying memory locations and/or CPU registers, running a machine-language program from a specified address and stopping its execution at a specified breakpoint, or even changing the flow of the program by modifying the contents of certain memory locations or CPU registers. Most debuggers can execute a machine-language program one instruction at a time (single step).

The most important concept of debuggers for testing a machine-language program that fails in some way is the use of breakpoints that can be set along the execution path of the program so that its execution can be monitored and completely controlled. The program DEBUG.COM which is supplied as a utility program of the PC-DOS disk operating system is an example of a standard debugger.

Interpreters and Compilers. Assembly language has several serious disadvantages. Since assembly language is a symbolic representation of machine language, it is machine dependent. For example, a program written in 8088 assembly language can be run only on microcomputers that employ microprocessors of the 8086/8088 family. It cannot be executed at all on other microcomputers that use different central processing units such as the Motorola MC68000. Even though assembly language is run-time and storage efficient, it is somewhat difficult to learn and inconvenient to program. To attack this problem, software designers in the 1950s developed several computer programs that have the capability to translate relatively English-like languages into equivalent machine instructions. These computer programs evolved into sophisticated high-level languages that can generate machine instructions comparable to programs written directly in assembly language. BASIC, FORTRAN, and Pascal are examples of popular high-level languages on today's microcomputers. These high-level languages have two different forms: interpreters and compilers.

Interpreters examine each statement of the program either exactly in its original form or in a slightly compact form, generate the equivalent machine instructions for the program statement, and execute the generated machine codes. Consequently, a statement in a program can be modified and the program can be run again immediately. The interpreters continually translate as they execute each statement of the program, therefore avoiding the need to translate the whole program at one time (as in the assembly process required in assembly language). This instantaneous modification capability makes program change and debugging a lot easier. In addition, interpreters are very easy to learn due to their interactive nature. However, interpreters have substantial run-time overhead that can significantly slow down the execution of a program by a factor of 100 or more as compared to the same program written in its equivalent assembly language. Interpreters are useful for checking out algorithms written in high-level languages. They may be suitable for tasks that do not require a large amount of number-crunching or calculations.

In contrast, compilers translate programs all the way into actual machine instructions. Many good compilers can produce machine codes as well as or even better than those written in assembly language directly by a programmer. One major disadvantage of compilers is that they require substantial amounts of time on microcomputers to perform compilation, the translation process from a high-level language to the actual machine instructions. Furthermore, modifications of programs cannot be made interactively with compilers. The most important advantage of high-level languages is their portability. For example, a program written in FORTRAN on a microcomputer can be run on any other microcomputers (including mini- and mainframe computers) with minimal or no changes.

Thus, it is useful to have both interpreters and compilers available for a given high-level language. Unfortunately, only BASIC has both the interpreter and compiler forms. All other high-level languages are available as compilers only. As an example, consider the following simple programming problem. A group of ten integers is scaled by some factors previously defined in a table. The sum and average result of the scaled integers are then calculated. Figure 1-11 and 1-12 illustrate the solution of the problem written in 8088 assembly language and the high-level language FORTRAN.

```
        MOV  CX,10              ;Initialize.
        MOV  BX,0               ;BX accumulates the resulting sum.
        LEA  SI,TABLE           ;SI points to a table containing scaled factors.
COUNT:  CALL GET                ;Get an integer in AL.
        MUL BYTE PTR AL,[SI]    ;Scale the integers.
        INC  SI                 ;Next scaled factor.
        ADD  BX,AX              ;Add another scaled integer into BX.
        LOOP COUNT              ;10 iterations.
        MOV  SUM,BX             ;Write out the resulting sum.
        MOV  CL,10
        DIV  CL                 ;Average.
        MOV  AVG,AL             ;Write out the average.
```

Fig. 1-11. An example of 8088 assembly language programming.

```
      INTEGER ITABLE(10)
      DATA ITABLE /1,2,3,4,5,6,7,8,9,0/
      NSUM = 0
C
C LOOP TO SCALE AND SUM ALL 10 INTEGERS.
C
      DO 100 I = 1,10
         CALL GET (NEW,I)
         NSUM = NSUM + NEW * ITABLE(I)
 100  CONTINUE
C
C CALCULATE THE AVERAGE NOW
C
      NAVG = NSUM/10
```

Fig. 1-12. An example of high-level language (FORTRAN) programming.

REPRESENTATION OF INFORMATION IN A MICROCOMPUTER

In 8088-based microcomputers, machine instructions are represented by a fixed sequence of binary digits that may take one or more bytes of storage. The bit patterns of each machine instruction are defined by the manufacturer and are listed in Appendix B. Any program in the computer memory will be expressed as a sequence of these binary patterns. A complete decoding and explanation of each individual instruction of the 8088 hardware instruction set is presented in Chapter 4.

Similar to the hardware instructions, numbers and alphanumeric text can also be represented inside a computer as groups of binary digits. In many cases, numbers are expressed as integers, positive or negative numbers, and floating point numbers. Alphanumeric text may be any upper- and lowercase letters of the alphabet or special symbols such as the underscore (_), the period (.), the dollar sign ($), or the asterisk (*), etc.

To understand the structure of a microcomputer, a programmer must know at least three number systems—the decimal, binary, and hexadecimal systems. The most commonly used number system is the decimal system which is based on the power of 10 (base 10 or radix 10). The binary system is based on the power of 2 (base 2) and the hexadecimal system is based on the power of 16 (base 16).

In the binary system only two symbols are used, 0 and 1. The decimal system uses 10 symbols (0, 1, 2, 3, 4, 5, 6, 7, 8, 9), and the hexadecimal systems uses 16 symbols (0, 1, 2, 3, 4, 5, 6, 7, 8, 9, A, B, C, D, E, F).

Integer Representation

An integer represented in binary format is simply the representation of the decimal value of a number in the binary system. Consider the decimal representation of the number 4896.

$$\begin{array}{rrcr} & 4 \times 1000 & = & 4000 \\ + & 8 \times 100 & = & 800 \\ + & 9 \times 10 & = & 90 \\ + & 6 \times 1 & = & 6 \\ \hline & & & 4896 \end{array}$$

This representation can also be expressed in terms of powers of 10.

$$\begin{array}{rrcr} & 4 \times 10^3 & = & 4000 \\ + & 8 \times 10^2 & = & 800 \\ + & 9 \times 10^1 & = & 90 \\ + & 6 \times 10^0 & = & 6 \\ \hline & & & 4896 \end{array}$$

Therefore, in decimal system, the rightmost digit represents 10 to the power 0. The next digit to the left represents 10 to the power 1, the next represents 10 to the power 3, and so on.

A decimal number of the form $d_3\ d_2\ d_1\ d_0$ can be expressed by the following general form:

$$(d_3 \times 10^3) + (d_2 \times 10^2) + (d_1 \times 10^1) + (d_0 \times 10^0)$$

The subscripted d's refer the position of each digit in the decimal number.

The binary representation is analogous to the decimal representation except that each digit represents a power of 2.

Consider the binary representation of the binary number 100001.

$$\begin{array}{r} 1 \times 32 = 32 \\ +0 \times 16 = 0 \\ +0 \times 8 = 0 \\ +0 \times 4 = 0 \\ +0 \times 2 = 0 \\ +1 \times 1 = 1 \\ \hline 33 \end{array}$$

This representation can also be expressed in terms of powers of two.

$$\begin{array}{r} +1 \times 2^5 = 32 \\ +0 \times 2^4 = 0 \\ +0 \times 2^3 = 0 \\ +0 \times 2^2 = 0 \\ +0 \times 2^1 = 0 \\ +1 \times 2^0 = 1 \\ \hline 33 \end{array}$$

The number 100001 is the binary representation of the decimal integer 33.

Similar to the general decimal representation, the rightmost bit of a binary number represents 2 to the power 0. The next bit to the left represents 2 to the power 1, the next represents 2 to the power 2, and so on.

In general, a binary number of the form $b_5\ b_4\ b_3\ b_2\ b_1\ b_0$ can be expressed by the following general form.

$$(b_5 \times 2^5) + (b_4 \times 2^4) + (b_3 \times 2^3) + (b_2 \times 2^2) + (b_1 \times 2^1) + (b_0 \times 2^0)$$

The maximum number of bits a microprocessor can manipulate at a moment reflects the power and flexibility of that microprocessor. The 8088 microprocessor can hold a maximum of 2 bytes or 16 bits of information at a time in one of its registers (the largest decimal integer that can be represented in 16 bits is 65,535). For this reason, the 8088 CPU is considered a 16-bit microprocessor.

Signed Integer Representation

In the previous section, only positive integers or unsigned integer

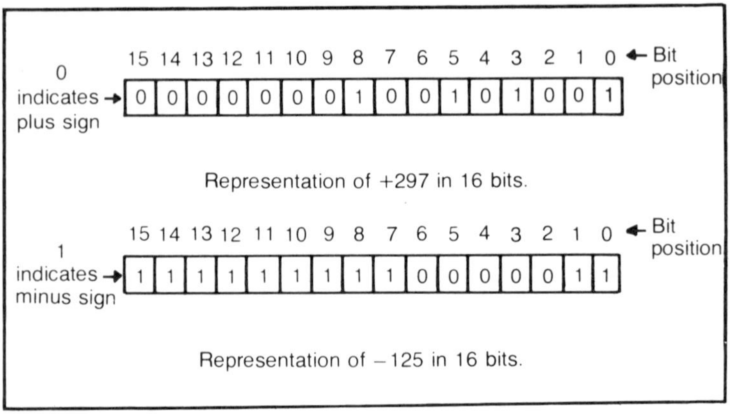

Fig. 1-13. Signed integers.

numbers are represented. Integers can be expressed as positive or negative numbers if the leftmost bit is used to indicate the sign of the number. To identify a bit in a given byte or word, the bit positions are numbered 0 to 15 from right to left. In a signed binary representation, a 0 in the leftmost bit (bit position 15) denotes a positive number while a 1 in this position indicates a negative number. Figure 1-13 illustrates the binary representation of the decimal number +297 and −125.

A negative number is represented in what is called two's-complement notation. This means that if i is positive, −i is represented by $2^{16} - i$ in 16-bit representation. For example, −125 is formed by subtracting 125 from 2^{16} in their binary forms.

$$\begin{array}{rr} 2^{16} = & 10000000000000000 \\ -125 = & 0000000001111101 \\ \hline & 1111111110000011 \end{array}$$

Hexadecimal Representations

It is awkward and difficult to work with or interpret long strings of binary digits. A shorter representation closely related to the binary system is extremely helpful. Since the hexadecimal system is a positional representation with radix 16 ($16 = 2^4$), it is equivalent to combining binary digits into groups of four. There are sixteen possible combinations in a four-digit binary number. Therefore, sixteen characters are chosen to represent them in the hexadecimal system. These characters are 0, 1, 2, 3, 4, 5, 6, 7, 8, 9, A, B, C, D, E, and F, as shown in Fig. 1-14.

Conversions between the hexadecimal and binary representations are very simple. To convert a binary integer to hexadecimal representation, the binary digits of the integer are grouped into groups of four, starting from the rightmost digit, and then each group is converted to an equivalent

Hexadecimal Digit	Binary Equivalent	Decimal Equivalent
0	0000	0
1	0001	1
2	0010	2
3	0011	3
4	0100	4
5	0101	5
6	0110	6
7	0111	7
8	1000	8
9	1001	9
A	1010	10
B	1011	11
C	1100	12
D	1101	13
E	1110	14
F	1111	15

Fig. 1-14. Hexadecimal digits.

hexadecimal digit as described in Fig. 1-14. For example, the hexadecimal equivalent of the binary number 110010010110101 is 64B5.

$$\underbrace{110}_{6}\quad\underbrace{0100}_{4}\quad\underbrace{1011}_{B}\quad\underbrace{0101}_{5}$$

It is even simpler to convert from the hexadecimal representation to its equivalent binary notation. Each hexadecimal digit is converted to binary as described in Fig. 1-14 and the binary digits are grouped together. For example, the conversion of the hexadecimal number 7F0E to its equivalent binary representation is

$$\overbrace{0111}^{7}\overbrace{1111}^{F}\overbrace{0000}^{0}\overbrace{1110}^{E}$$

Binary Integer Arithmetic

The arithmetic rules for addition and subtraction of binary numbers are straightforward.

$$\begin{aligned}0 + 0 &= 0\\ 0 + 1 &= 1\\ 1 + 0 &= 1\\ 1 + 1 &= (1)\ 0\end{aligned}$$

The (1) indicates a carry of 1 (the binary number 10 formed by the carry and the bit 0 is the representation of the decimal number 2). Binary subtraction of two numbers is performed by adding the first number with the two's complement of the second number.

Example 1. Let us try an addition of the decimal number 456 and 127 in 16-bit representation.

Decimal	Binary Equivalent
456	0000 0001 1100 1000
127	0000 0000 0111 1111
583	0000 0010 0100 0111

No Carry   No Carry

No Overflow

The above binary addition can be carried out in the equivalent hexadecimal representation.

Decimal	Hexadecimal Equivalent
456	01C8
127	007F
583	0247

Example 2. Let us try another example of finding the sum of two decimal integers 32000 and 28000 in 16-bit representation.

Decimal	Binary Equivalent
32000	0111 1101 0000 0000
28000	0110 1101 0110 0000
	1110 1010 0110 0000

No carry   Carry

Overflow

Since the sum of 32000 + 28000 is larger than the maximum permissible positive integer in 16-bit representation ($2^{16} - 1$), an overflow has occurred. The result of the addition is considered as a negative number since a carry 1 appears in the sign bit position. This result is obviously incorrect.

Example 3. Now let us try another addition of two negative decimal numbers −32700 and −4325.

Decimal	Binary Equivalent
−32700	1000 0000 0100 0100
−4325	1110 1111 0001 1011
	0100 1111 0101 1111

Carry   No carry

Underflow

Since the sum is smaller than the -32768 (-2^{16}), an underflow has occurred. The result is a positive number which is incorrect.

Example 4. Let us try again adding two negative decimal number -25 and -9 in 16-bit representation.

```
Decimal    Binary Equivalent
  -25      1111 1111 1110 0111
   -9      1111 1111 1111 0111

  -34      1111 1111 1101 1110
      Carry   Carry
         No Overflow
```

The result is a correct negative number. The carry bit (out of the sign bit) is ignored.

From the four previous examples, we may conclude that an overflow or underflow occurs in a 16-bit representation if the following conditions are met.

1. There is a carry out of the bit-position 14 but there is no carry out of the sign bit (position 15).
2. There is a carry out of the sign bit but there is no carry out of the bit position 14.

On the other hand, no overflow occurs if

3. There is a carry out of the bit position 14 and there is also a carry out of the sign bit.
4. There is no carry out of the bit position 14 and the sign bit.

BCD Representations

Binary Coded Decimal (BCD) representations are used whenever precision is required in the calculation of numbers. The principle used in representing BCD numbers is to employ four binary digits to encode each of the ten decimal digits and to use as many bits as necessary to represent the complete number exactly. Since four bits per decimal digit result in sixteen combinations and there are only ten decimal digits, the last six possible codes are not used in BCD representation, as shown in Fig. 1-15.

Since there are six of the possible codes that are not used in the BCD representation, this can cause a potential problem when the result of the standard arithmetic operations such as addition and subtraction might not produce the correct BCD representation. The 8088 microprocessor has special instructions to adjust the result to the correct BCD representation. These instructions include DAA (Decimal Adjust For Addition), DAS (Decimal Adjust For Subtraction), AAA (ASCII Adjust For Addition), AAS (ASCII Adjust For Subtraction), AAM (ASCII Adjust For Multiplication), and ADD (ASCII Adjust For Division).

Conventions to place the decimal point and the sign within a BCD

Binary Code	BCD Symbol
0000	0
0001	1
0010	2
0011	3
0100	4
0101	5
0110	6
0111	7
1000	8
1001	9
1010	Unused
1011	Unused
1100	Unused
1101	Unused
1110	Unused
1111	Unused

Fig. 1-15. BCD representation.

representation may vary. For example, the leftmost byte may be used to indicate the sign of the BCD number where a 0 indicates the plus sign and a 1 indicates the minus sign. An imaginary decimal point may be placed after the third digit from the left. Therefore, +557.2345 may be coded in the BCD representation, as shown in Fig. 1-16. This representation is also called an unpacked BCD representation.

The advantage of BCD representation is that it produces absolutely correct results. Its disadvantage is that BCD numbers require more memory space and result in slow arithmetic operations. However, BCD representations are very useful in financial and accounting applications where precision of the calculations of numbers is required. The number in Fig. 1-16 is in the unpacked BCD format because each BCD digit occupies one byte of storage. Since one byte of storage can accommodate two BCD digits, two BCD digits can be put in one single byte. If two BCD digits are

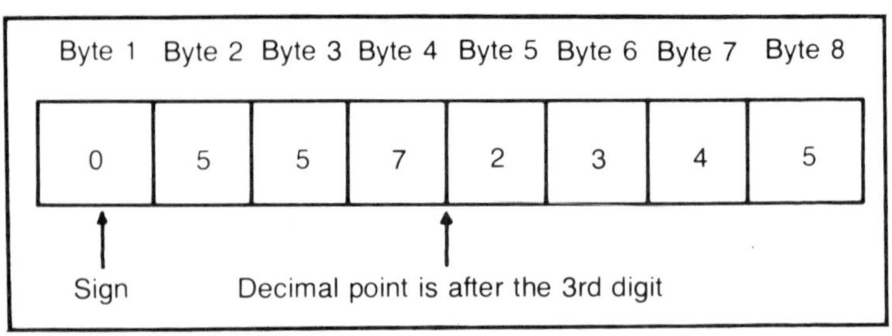

Fig. 1-16. Unpacked BCD representation.

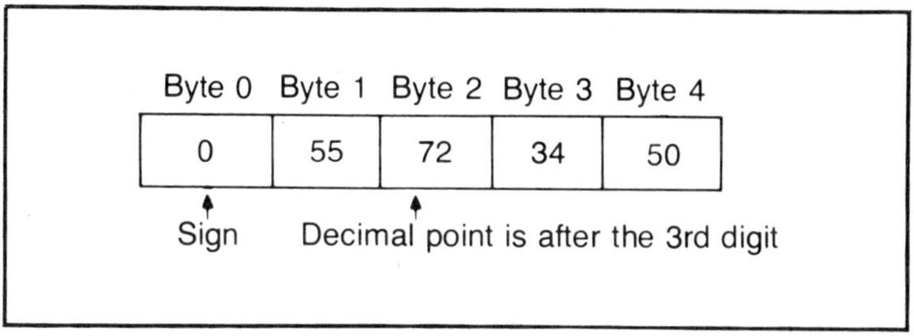

Fig. 1-17. Packed BCD representation.

packed into one byte, the representation is called packed BCD representation. For example, the decimal number +557.2345 can be represented in packed BCD representation, as shown in Fig. 1-17.

Alphanumeric Data Representation

The representation of alphanumeric data or characters is very simple. All characters are encoded in a 7-bit code if the ASCII code is used or in an 8-bit code if the EBCDIC code is used. Virtually all microcomputers use the ASCII (American Standard Code for Information Interchange) code. Figure 1-18 shows the standard 128 ASCII characters. Refer to Appendix B for explanations of abbreviated symbols.

The EBCDIC (Extended Binary Coded Decimal Interchange Code) code is used only by IBM Corporation on their large mainframe computers such as the IBM 360/370 system. The EBCDIC code is generally not used by the microcomputer world unless communication and interfacing to an IBM mainframe system is desired. Figure 1-19 shows the complete set of IBM standard 8-bit EBCDIC codes. Refer to Appendix B for explanations of abbreviated symbols.

THE IBM PERSONAL COMPUTER

Today there are many personal and business microcomputers that are designed around the 8088 microprocessor. The IBM Personal Computer is probably the most popular product among these microcomputers.

Since its introduction in 1981, the IBM Personal Computer has transformed the computer industry: it created the largest group of third-party vendors of both hardware and software to support the new machine, it enabled the microcomputers to assume a larger share of the world's computational tasks, it changed many users' views of personal computers from toys/novelties to essential tools in the corporate information system, and it stimulated tremendous growth in the personal computer market.

The IBM Personal Computer uses the Intel 8088 microprocessor as its Central Processing Unit. The tremendous commercial success of the IBM PC has helped to establish the Intel 8086/8088 microprocessor family as the personal computer industry standard.

Standard Hardware Configuration

The IBM Personal Computer consists of two basic units: the keyboard and the system unit. The detached keyboard unit is connected to the system unit via a coiled cable. It has a standard typewriter layout with ten function keys to the left and a numeric keypad to the right of the keyboard enclosure. The system unit houses the Intel 8088 microprocessor, 40 K bytes of ROM (read-only memory) containing the Microsoft BASIC interpreter and the machine codes for the basic input/output systems (BIOS), up to 256 K bytes

HEX	MSD	0	1	2	3	4	5	6	7
LSD	Bits	000	001	010	011	100	101	110	111
0	0000	NUL	DLE	SP	0	@	P	\	p
1	0001	SOH	DC1	!	1	A	Q	a	q
2	0010	STX	DC2	"	2	B	R	b	r
3	0011	ETX	DC3	#	3	C	S	c	s
4	0100	EOT	DC4	$	4	D	T	d	t
5	0101	ENQ	NAK	%	5	E	U	e	u
6	0110	ACK	SYN	&	6	F	V	f	v
7	0111	BEL	ETB	'	7	G	W	g	w
8	1000	BS	CAN	(	8	H	X	h	x
9	1001	HT	EM	)	9	I	Y	i	y
A	1010	LF	SUB	*	:	J	Z	j	z
B	1011	VT	ESC	+	:	K	[	k	{
C	1100	FF	FS	,	<	L	\	1	¦
D	1101	CR	GS	–	=	M	]	m	}
E	1110	SO	RS	.	>	N	^	n	~
F	1111	SI	US	/	?	0	–	o	DEL

Fig. 1-18. Standard 7-bit ASCII codes.

HEX LSD	MSD Bits	0	1	2	3	4	5	6	7	8	9	A	B	C	D	E	F
0	0000	NUL	DLE	DS		SP	&	−						{	}	\	0
1	0001	SOH	DC1	SOS				/		a	j	~		A	J		1
2	0010	STX	DC2	FS	SYN					b	k	s		B	K	S	2
3	0011	ETX	TM							c	l	t		C	L	T	3
4	0100	PF	RES	BYP	PN					d	m	u		D	M	U	4
5	0101	HT	NL	LF	RS					e	n	v		E	N	V	5
6	0110	LC	BS	ETB	UC					f	o	w		F	O	W	6
7	0111	DEL	IL	ESC	EOT					g	p	x		G	P	X	7
8	1000	GE	CAN							h	q	y		H	Q	Y	8
9	1001	RLF	EM						\	i	r	z		I	R	Z	9
A	1010	SMM	CC	SM		¢	!	¦	:								
B	1011	VT	CU1	CU2	CU3	.	$	,	#								
C	1100	FF	IFS		DC4	<	*	%	@								
D	1101	CR	IGS	ENQ	NAK	(	)	−	'								
E	1110	SO	IRS	ACK		+	;	>	=								
F	1111	SI	IUS	BEL	SUB	|	¬	?	"								EO

Fig. 1-19. IBM standard 8-bit EBCDIC codes.

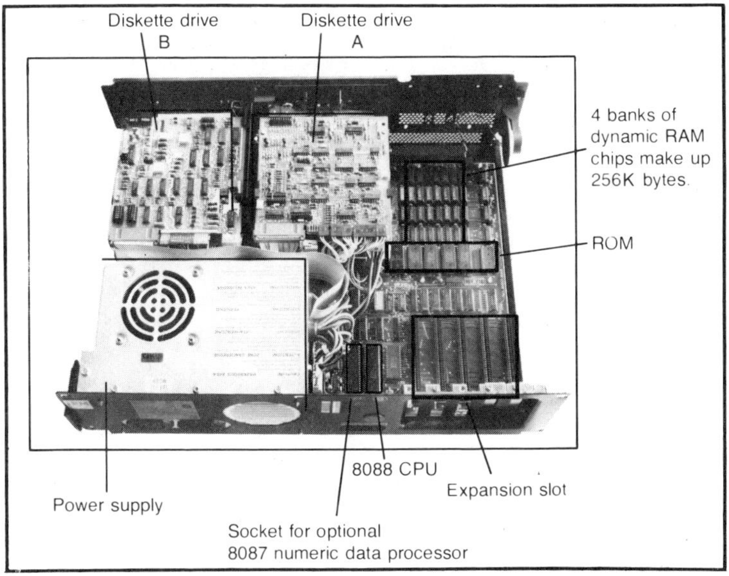

Fig. 1-20. Inside the IBM Personal Computer.

of RAM (random-access memory), up to two diskette drives, a cassette interface, a built-in speaker, and five expansion slots, as shown in Fig. 1-20.

Keyboard. The keyboard unit of the IBM Personal Computer, as shown in Fig. 1-21, is probably one of the best keyboards ever designed for a microcomputer. It is housed in a separate unit that can be moved away from the system unit. The keyboard has a total of 83 keys but it is light enough to be placed and used comfortably on the operator's lap. All keys give tactile feel and produce an audible feedback when pressed. A separate Intel 8048 microprocessor controls the keyboard and relieves the host 8088 CPU from the burden of scanning the keys. When a key is pressed, a scan code, which identifies the key being pressed or released, is sent to the system unit instead of the ASCII code of the key. The scan code is then converted to its corresponding ASCII code by the on-board ROM software or by the application program. One very nice feature of the IBM PC keyboard is its 10-character type ahead buffer, which will help fast typists not to lose keystrokes. In addition, each key will automatically repeat its functions after it is held down for more than half a second.

System Unit. Inside the IBM Personal Computer system unit, there are five expansion slots in the upper left corner (see Fig. 1-20). These slots can be used to install the Monochrome/Parallel Printer Adapter, the Color/Graphics Adapter, the Diskette Drive Adapter, and add-on controller cards such as the Asynchronous RS-232C Adapter for serial devices. The Intel 8088 microprocessor is located next to these slots and runs at 4.77 MHz. An optional 8087 Numeric Data Processor can be installed in an open socket next to the 8088 CPU to provide hardware floating-point capabilities to the system and to improve the number-crunching performance of the IBM PC significantly.

Fig. 1-21. The IBM Personal Computer keyboard.

There are four DMA (direct-memory access) channels available. One is used to refresh the dynamic memory, and the others are for high-speed data transfer between main memory and peripheral adapter cards. In addition, there are eight levels of interrupts, six of which can be programmed by users.

The system memory has eight large ROM chips that contain about 40 K bytes of code for the Microsoft BASIC Interpreter and BIOS software. There is one empty socket provided on the same row of the ROM chips so that a user's PROM or EPROM unit can be inserted. The read/write memory section has four rows of nine sockets each. One of the rows is filled in with nine 64 K-bit dynamic RAMS to make 64 K bytes of memory with parity. The ninth dynamic memory chip in a row provides the parity bit to the system. This helps to increase the overall reliability of the microcomputer. When a parity error is detected, the IBM Personal Computer issues the appropriate error messages and stops whatever program it is running. A parity error message usually indicates that there may be some malfunction in one of the memory chips.

The system unit also has a built-in cassette interface that can be connected to any good quality cassette recorder. The data transfer rate to the cassette is between 1000 and 2000 bits per second depending upon the contents of the data.

Video-Display. The IBM Personal Computer provides two separate ways of getting the video output via the Monochrome Display/Printer Adapter or the Color/Graphics Adapter. Each adapter card is a complete separate board that can be installed in one of the five expansion slots within the system unit.

The *Monochrome Display/Printer Adapter,* as shown in Fig. 1-22, produces high quality black-and-white output only. The video screen output from the monochrome adapter displays 25 lines by 80 columns of extremely readable characters (see Fig. 1-23). A 9 by 14 dot matrix is used, and each character of a 256-character set is formed within a 7 by 9 dot matrix. The

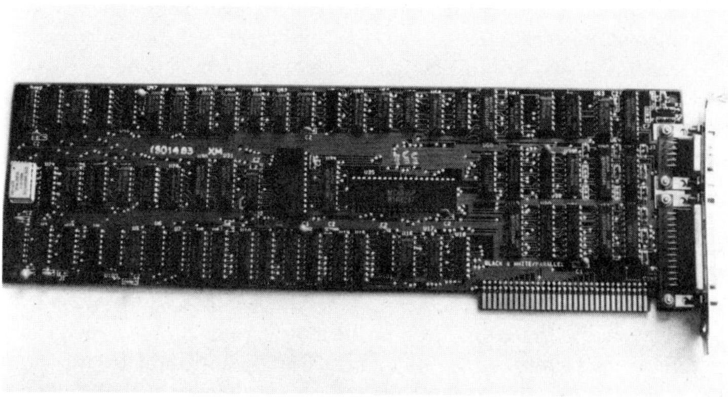

Fig. 1-22. The monochrome display/printer adapter card.

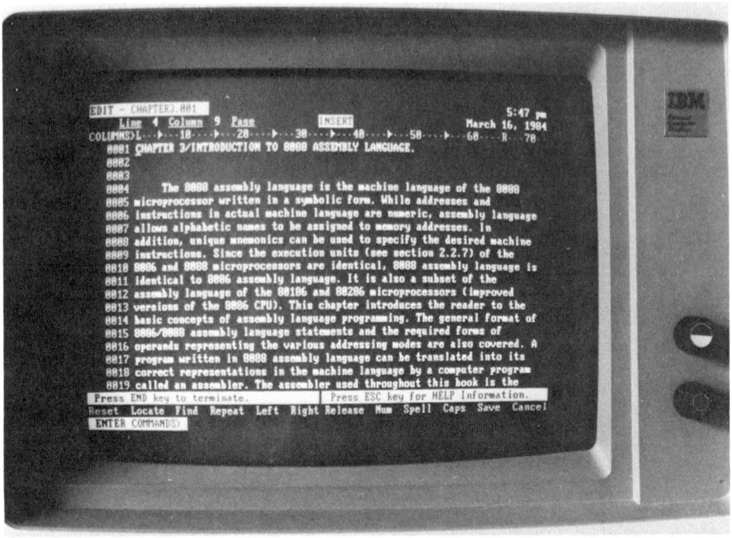

Fig. 1-23. The monochrome screen of the IBM personal computer.

screen produced by the monochrome adapter is very attractive to anyone who has to spend long periods in front of a video terminal. The Monochrome Display/Printer Adapter card contains 4096 bytes of on-board memory to hold a maximum of 2000 characters and their associated video attributes. Regardless of the type of display adapter used, the IBM Personal Computer always uses two bytes of storage to store a character: the first byte is the character's ASCII code, and the second byte is its attribute. Therefore individual characters can have any of the following characteristics: blinking, underline, half-intensity, or even invisible when using the monochrome adapter card. The 256 available video characters include all standard capital and lowercase letters, numbers, punctuation, mathematical symbols, musical notes, and many useful graphic shapes to construct charts and graphs. The Monochrome Adapter also contains the necessary interface circuitry to drive a parallel dot-matrix printer such as the Epson MX-80 printer.

The *Color/Graphics Adapter,* as shown in Fig. 1-24, has 16 K bytes of onboard memory and can display text, graphics, or both text and graphics. This adapter card displays text characters in an 8 by 8 box, with characters being formed in a 5 by 7 dot matrix, in 8 background and 8 foreground colors. Figure 1-25 shows the sixteen colors available on the color/graphics adapter. The text characters generated by this adapter do not look as well formed as those produced by the monochrome adapter card. However, these characters can be programmed by the user to create a variety of character fonts such as boldface, italics, etc., as shown in Fig. 1-26.

Color graphics are available in three different resolutions. The low-

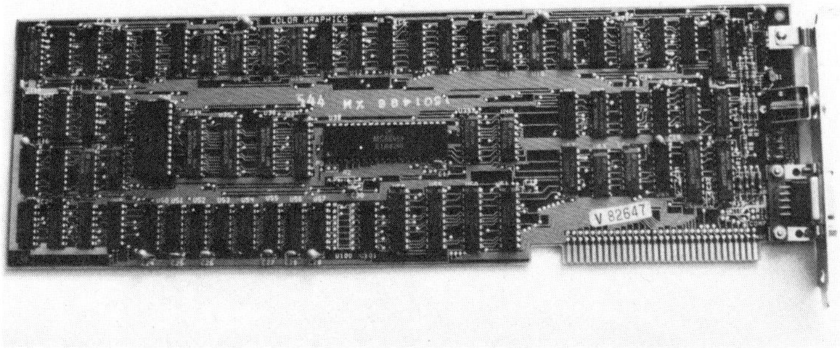

Fig. 1-24. The color/graphics adapter card.

resolution mode provides a display of 100 rows and 160 pixels (picture elements), each of which can be any of the standard 16 colors, however this low-resolution mode is not supported by IBM. The medium-resolution mode provides 200 rows and 320 pixels, each of which can have one of the four possible colors. In this mode, the background color can have any of the 16 available colors, while the foreground color must be chosen from one of two three-color sets. The first set produces cyan, magenta, and white. The second set produces green, red, and brown. The high-resolution mode uses a white-on-black image containing 200 rows of 640 pixels. Figure 1-27 shows an image produced in the high-resolution mode.

Diskette Drive. The diskette drives are soft-sectored, double-

Intensity Bit	Red Bit	Green Bit	Blue Bit	Color
0	0	0	0	Black
0	0	0	1	Blue
0	0	1	0	Green
0	0	1	1	Cyan
0	1	0	0	Red
0	1	0	1	Magenta
0	1	1	0	Brown
0	1	1	1	Light gray
1	0	0	0	Dark gray
1	0	0	1	Light blue
1	0	1	0	Light green
1	0	1	1	Light cyan
1	1	0	0	Light red
1	1	0	1	Light magenta
1	1	1	0	Yellow
1	1	1	1	White

Fig. 1-25. The 16 available colors on the IBM Personal Computer and their representation in memory.

Fig. 1-26. The color graphics screen of the IBM Personal Computer.

Fig. 1-27. A picture generated in the high-resolution graphics mode.

density, using standard MFM (modified frequency modulation) encoding. The diskette drive can be single-sided or double-sided. There are 40 tracks per side with nine 512-byte sectors per track. This results in 184,320 bytes of storage for a single-sided drive and 368,640 bytes of storage for a doubled-sided drive. Up to 4 diskette drives can be supported by the system. The diskette drive has a motor start time of 500 ms, a track-to-track seek time of 8 ms, and a data transfer rate of 250 K bits per second. The diskette drive is driven by an NEC diskette controller which is functional equivalent to an Intel 8272 diskette controller.

Software

Systems software for the IBM Personal Computer includes the Microsoft BASIC interpreter supplied in ROM (Read-Only Memory) and the PC-DOS disk operating system (a variation of the MS-DOS operating system, developed by Microsoft Corporation for IBM).

The BASIC interpreter supplied with each IBM Personal Computer contains many powerful features in addition to those normally found in the standard high-level language BASIC. The interpreter has built-in commands that allow programmers to plot points and draw lines in both the medium- and high-resolution modes, to trigger the internal speaker of the computer to make sounds, and to interface with light pens and joysticks. If PC-DOS is used, the BASIC interpreter allows many high-level disk input/output commands. The interpreter can also access the current date and time on the system.

PC-DOS provides an easy and automated way to use applications software and/or create and manage files for a particular application. The operating system is designed to work with either floppy diskette drives or hard disks. It is supplied as a group of programs that the users can select to do work on the IBM Personal Computer. The following is a small sample of essential programs that are supplied as program utilities under the PC-DOS operating system.

1. The program EDLIN.COM is a small line-oriented text editor. It can create, modify, and display standard ASCII source files. The source files can be an assembly language program or a high-level language program in the source language format. The editor also works on text files that contain text characters only. The users issue single-character commands to request the editor to perform standard editing functions such as creating and saving new source files, updating existing files and saving both the updated and original files, deleting, inserting, modifying, or displaying lines, searching and replacing text. The text files created or edited by the program EDLIN.COM are divided into lines of varying length up to 253 characters per line.

2. The program DEBUG.COM is the standard debugger supplied with the PC-DOS operating system. This debugger provides a controlled testing environment so that the execution path of a machine-language

program can be monitored and controlled. DEBUG.COM allows standard debugging functions such as loading and executing object modules or machine-language programs, setting breakpoints, displaying or modifying CPU registers and/or memory locations, and executing one instruction at a time (tracing or single stepping). The debugger can also send or receive data to or from an input/output port, and perform hexadecimal arithmetic operations. A very nice feature of DEBUG.COM is the availability of the assembly/disassembly facility. Assembly language statements can be assembled one at a time directly into machine codes and put in any memory location. Both the standard 8086/8088 assembly language syntax and the 8087 instruction are supported. Machine instructions in hexadecimal notations can also be converted to assembly-like statements with this facility.

3. The program LINK.EXE performs the tasks of a standard linker. It combines separately assembled object modules into a complete machine-language program. LINK.EXE can also search library files for definitions of names and symbols to resolve external references and produce a load module. A listing that contains all symbol references and/or error messages can also be generated.

4. The program FORMAT.COM is a utility to initialize diskettes in the designated or default diskette drive to a recording format that PC-DOS can work with. FORMAT.COM analyzes the entire diskette for defective media, and prepares a directory for the diskette. A double-sided, double-density diskette is initialized to have a total of 360 K-byte space.

The disk operating system also has commands to delete disk files (ERASE), copy or merge files (COPY), rename files (REN), list files to output devices (TYPE), and list the directory of files on the system (DIR), etc.

High-quality assemblers and compilers for high-level languages such as BASIC, FORTRAN, Pascal, and C are also available from third-party vendors. A large collection of high-quality applications software is also available for the IBM Personal Computer, and this collection of software is still growing. Popular applications software packages include WordStar (by MicroPro Inc.) to perform standard word-processing and full-screen text editing, VisiCalc (by VisiCorp) to do spreadsheet calculations, 1-2-3 (by Lotus Development Corp.) to perform spreadsheet functions and business graphics, and Peachtree accounting software (by Peachtree Software) to perform general accounting functions.

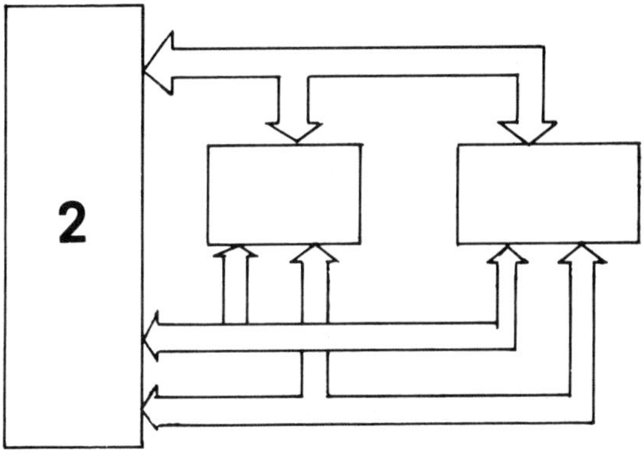

Intel 8088 Microprocessor

This chapter discusses the internal architecture of the Intel 8088 microprocessor to provide the readers a good general understanding of the internal organization of a typical 16-bit microprocessor, its addressing modes, and the execution of machine instructions. Important concepts such as the use of stack structures and interrupt procedures that take full advantage of the 8088 architecture are also presented in detail.

MACHINE LANGUAGE

In all computer systems, machine instructions are the basic units of control to give directions to the computer to perform a certain function. Machine instructions are coded numerically and kept in the computer memory during execution. A set of machine instructions which are executed in sequence is a fundamental form of a program written in machine language. Therefore, programming in machine language is simply the process of constructing these sequences of machine instructions. Each machine instruction contains an operation code which tells the computer to perform a certain operation.

A programmer who uses machine language has absolute control of the microprocessor and can access or manipulate all hardware/software facilities of the microcomputer that are usually unavailable to high-level language programs. To write effective machine language programs, a programmer must thoroughly understand the architecture of the microprocessor, the internal organization and addressing modes of the central processing unit, and the requirements and functions of each individual machine instruction.

Machine instructions can be divided into classes according to the

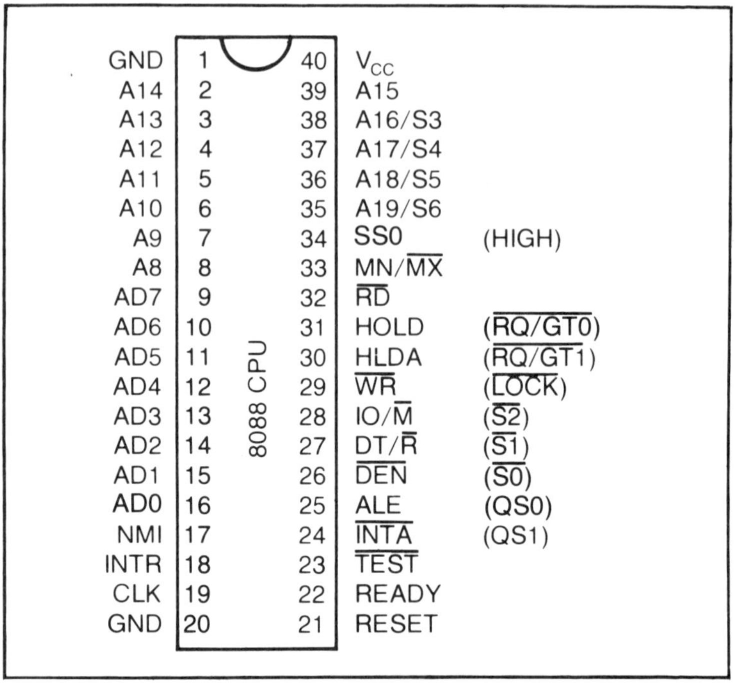

Fig. 2-1. The 8088 pin assignment.

particular operations they perform. For example, data transfer instructions move bytes and words between the computer memory and its processor registers. Input/output instructions enable the computer to communicate with external peripheral devices. Arithmetic instructions can operate on many types of number representations such as unsigned binary, signed binary, packed or unpacked decimal notations. These arithmetic operations can be performed in both 8-bit and 16-bit format. Bit manipulation instructions can perform logical, shift, and rotate functions on any bit within a byte or a word. Program transfer instructions can alter the sequence of program execution unconditionally or dependent upon certain conditions of the microprocessor. Control instructions help to coordinate and synchronize the microprocessor with occurrences of external events. A complete description of the machine-language format and functions of individual instructions in the 8088 instruction set will be presented in Chapter 4.

ARCHITECTURE

The 8088 microprocessor, as shown in Fig. 2-1, is a 16-bit third-generation Central Processing Unit (CPU) implemented on a silicon chip with an 8-bit external data path to memory and input/output devices. In other words, even though the 8088 microprocessor has 16-bit internal registers, it can read or write to the microcomputer memory only 8 bits at a time. The 8088 CPU has four 16-bit general-purpose registers (named AX, BX, CX, DX), four pointer registers (named SI, DI, BP, and SP), four 16-bit segment registers (named CS, DS, ES, and SS), and one 16-bit processor flag register, as shown in Fig. 2-2.

General-Purpose Registers

This group consists of four 16-bit registers. Each register in the group can be treated as two separate 8-bit registers which can individually be addressed for byte operations.

The Accumulator, AX. The AX register is considered to be the

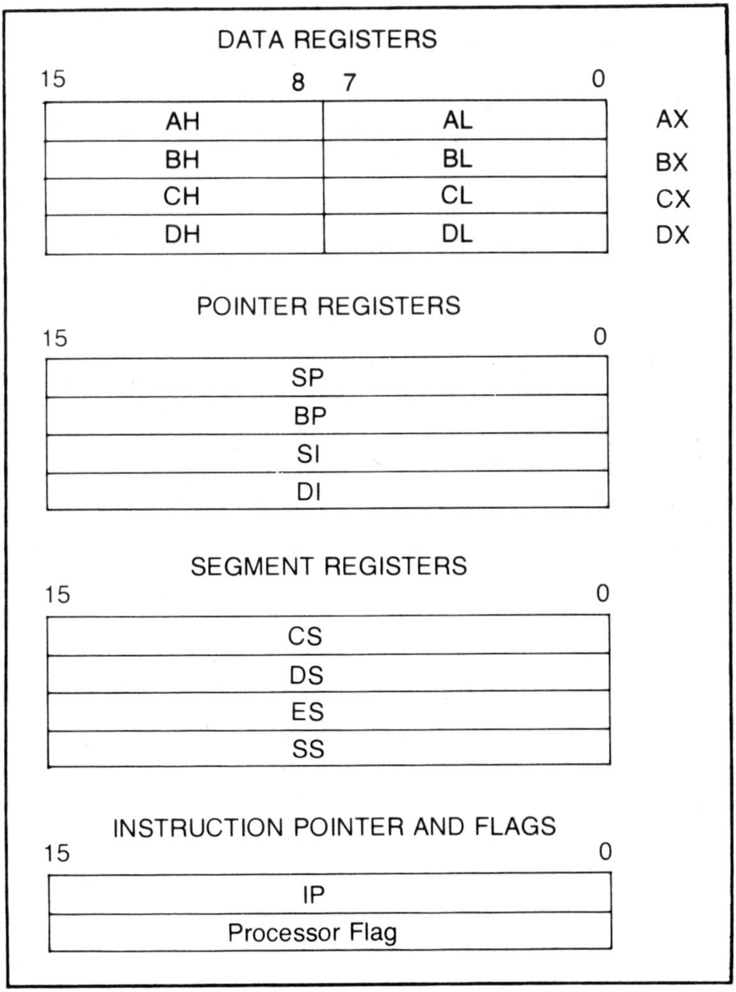

Fig. 2-2. The 8088 CPU registers.

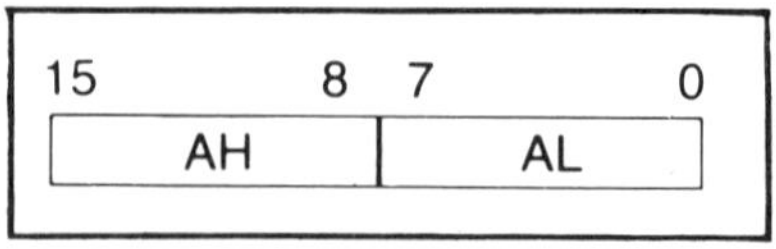

Fig. 2-3. The AX register.

CPU's principal accumulator. It is used as work space to hold intermediate data or temporary results. Instructions that are associated with the AX register are very compact and therefore take less memory space. The AX register is used to hold the quotient and the remainder of the result of a byte division. If word division is performed the AX register holds the low order 16 bits of a 32-bit dividend. The AX register can also hold a data byte or word to be referenced by string instructions. If the manipulated data is small in magnitude and 8-bit operations are sufficient, the AX register can be viewed as two completely separate 8-bit registers named AH and AL, as shown in Fig. 2-3. The AH register occupies the high-order 8 bits and the AL register occupies the low-order 8-bits.

The Base Register, BX. The BX register is called the Base register. The contents of the BX register can specify a memory location or its contents can be added to a displacement value to compute a new memory address in based addressing mode. Therefore, a single machine instruction can use the BX register to access different memory locations by simply changing the contents of the Base Register. This is the only register in the group that can be used as a pointer to a memory address. The BX register can also be used as a general-purpose register to perform most functions provided by the Accumulator, AX. If 8-bit operations are desired, the BX register can be viewed as two separate 8-bit registers named BH and BL, as shown in Fig. 2-4.

Fig. 2-4. The BX register.

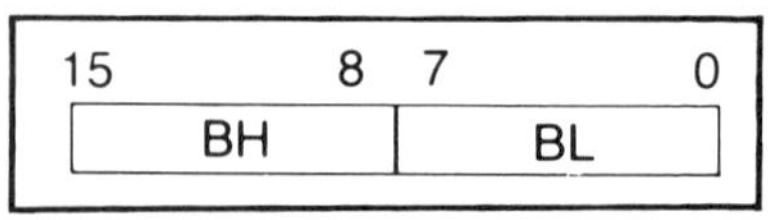

The Count Register, CX. The CX register is the Count register. Its special function is to control the number of iterations in a loop or the number of repetitions in REP (REPeat) instructions when string operations are used. It can also be used to perform most general-purpose operations provided by the Accumulator, AX. If 8-bit operation is desired, register CX can be viewed as two separate 8-bit registers named CH and CL, as shown in Fig. 2-5.

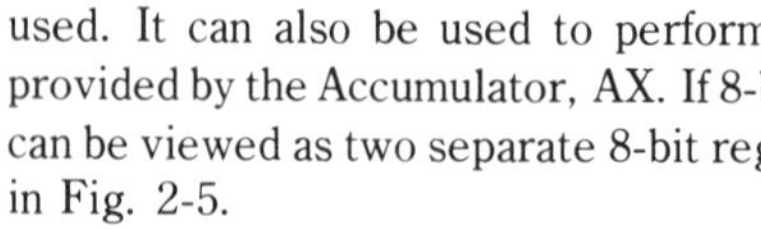

Fig. 2-5. The CX register.

The Data Register, DX. The DX register is the Data Register. It is used as a secondary accumulator to hold intermediate data and temporary results. The DX register can be combined with AX to form a 32-bit number in multiply and divide instructions where the contents of the DX register represent the high-order sixteen bits. The DX register is used to hold the remainder of the result of a 16-bit division. The DX register can also hold the address of an input/output port to send or receive information to and from peripheral devices. If 8-bit operations are desired, DX can be viewed as two separate 8-bit registers named DH and DL, as shown in Fig. 2-6.

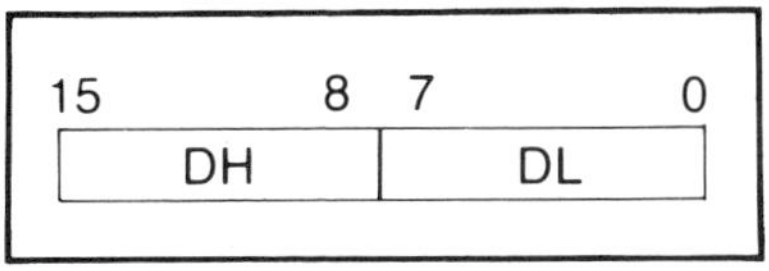

Fig. 2-6. The DX register.

Index and Pointer Registers

This group consists of four 16-bit registers. The index registers are normally used as pointers to access memory operands. The pointer registers are normally used to manipulate data on the stack. Each register in this group can also handle most arithmetic and logical operations.

The Source Index Register, SI. The SI register, as shown in Fig. 2-7, is the Source Index register. Its special function is to be used as a source pointer to a byte or a word memory address in string instructions such as LODS (Load String), CMPS (Compare String), and MOVS (Move String). In based indexed addressing mode, the contents of the SI register can be added to the contents of the BX register to form a pointer to access memory operands. The contents of the SI register can be autoincremented or autodecremented to handle string operations effectively. The Source Index register can also participate in most arithmetic and logical operations.

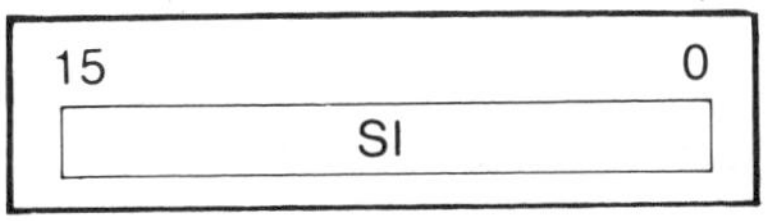

Fig. 2-7. The SI register.

The Destination Index Register, DI. The DI register, as shown in Fig. 2-8, is the Destination Index register. Its special function is to be used as a destination pointer to a byte or a word memory address in string instructions such as SCAS (Scan String), CMPS (Compare String), MOVS (Move String), and STOS (Store String). In based indexed addressing, the contents of the DI register can also be added to the contents of the BX register to form a pointer to access memory operands. The contents of the DI register can be autoincremented or autodecremented in string operations. The Destination Index register can also participate in most arithmetic and logical operations.

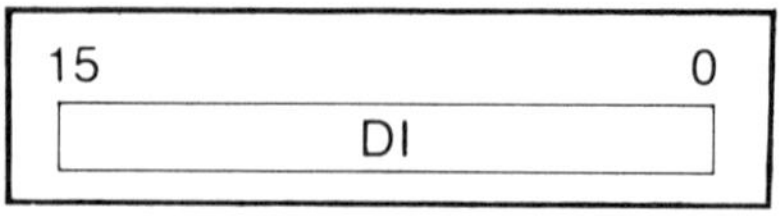

Fig. 2-8. The DI register.

The Stack Pointer Register, SP. The SP register, as shown in Fig. 2-9, is called the Stack Pointer. It is used to manipulate data on a stack structure in the computer memory. The contents of the SP register refers to the address of the top element of the stack structure. This provides a very convenient method to implement interrupts, procedure calling, or a procedure returning sequence by saving the returning address on top of the stack. Even though the SP register is capable of participating in general-purpose arithmetic and logical operations, the Stack Pointer is not normally used for this purpose.

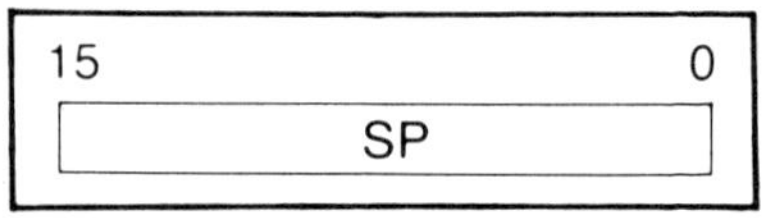

Fig. 2-9. The SP register.

The Base Pointer Register, BP. The BP register, as shown in Fig. 2-10, is the Base Pointer register. It is normally used as an additional pointer to manipulate data on a stack structure in the computer memory. The BP register can be used as a pointer to retrieve parameters or temporary data that are saved on the stack by previous PUSH instructions. In based indexed addressing mode, the contents of the BP register can be added to the contents of the SI or DI register to form a pointer to access memory operands. The BP register can also participate in most arithmetic and logical operations.

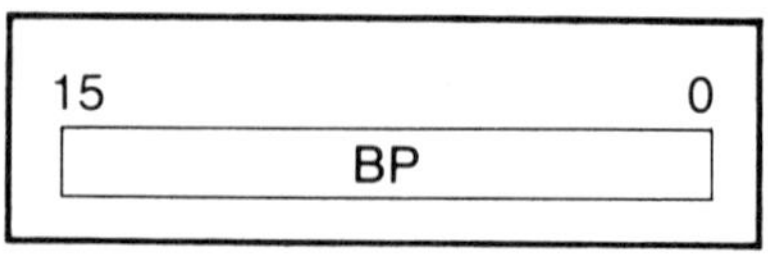

Fig. 2-10. The BP register.

Segment Registers

The 8088 microprocessor can address one megabyte (1,048,576 bytes) of memory space. However, this megabyte memory space is divided into logical segments of up to 64 K bytes each. The 8088 CPU has direct access of up to four segments at a time. The starting location of each segment is contained in one of the four segment registers. There are four 16-bit segment registers, CS, DS, ES, and SS, that are accessible to machine-language programs via instructions such as MOV (Move data), or POP (Pop from stack).

Segment registers are primarily used to identify the current 64 K-byte segment of the 8088's megabyte memory space. Thus, they cannot be used in general-purpose arithmetic and logical operations.

The Code Segment Register, CS. The Code Segment register is a 16-bit control register pointing to the segment that contains the current machine instructions. This is a 64 K-byte area of the 8088's memory space where instructions are fetched from. The contents of the CS register can only be altered by executing the JMP (Jump), CALL (Call procedures), RET (Return from procedures), or IRET (Return from interrupt) instructions to point to a different 64 K-byte code segment. Figure 2-11 shows the CS register.

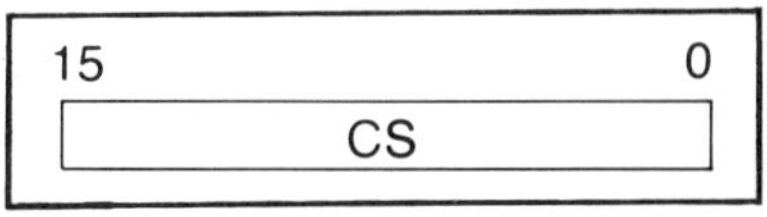

Fig. 2-11. The CS register.

The Data Segment Register, DS. The Data Segment register, as shown in Fig. 2-12, is a 16-bit control register. Its contents refer to the starting location of a 64 K-byte memory area that generally contains program variables, tables, and constants. This arrangement facilitates structure programming in the sense that program data can be grouped together in a separate segment, and these data do not have to reside in the same segment with the instruction codes. All direct memory address references or indirect memory address references using the BX, SI, or DI registers are relative to the Data Segment register. Memory address references by string instructions using the SI register such as LODS (Load String), MOVS (Move String), or CMPS (Compare String) are also computed relative to the Data Segment register.

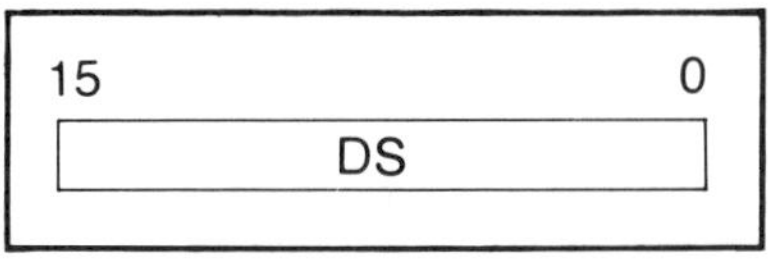

Fig. 2-12. The DS register.

The Extra Segment Register, ES. The Extra Segment register, ES, as shown in Fig. 2-13, is another 16-bit control register. Its contents refer to the starting location of a 64 K-byte memory area that is typically used for additional temporary data storage or work space. Memory address references by string instructions using the DI register such as STOS (Store String), SCAS (Scan String), MOVS (Move String), and CMPS (Compare String) are computed relative to the Extra Segment register.

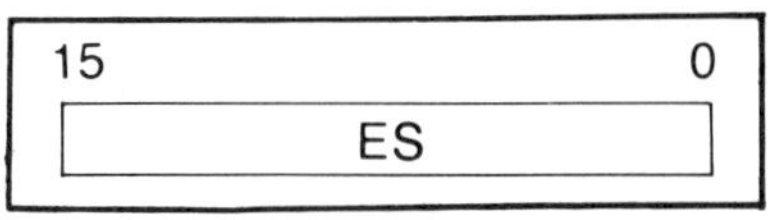

Fig. 2-13. The ES register.

The Stack Segment Register, SS. The Stack Segment register, as shown in Fig. 2-14, is the last 16-bit control register in this group. The contents of the SS register refer to the starting location of a 64 K-byte stack structure in the computer memory. The contents of the SP or BP register can be used to reflect the offset address of memory address references using the SP or BP register are computed relative to the Stack Segment register.

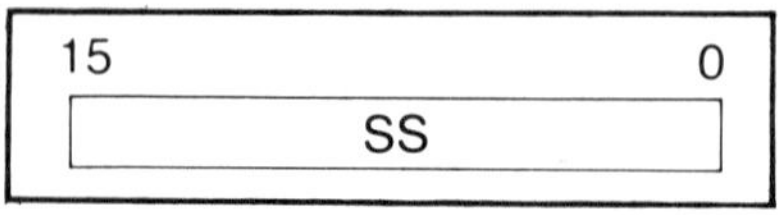

Fig. 2-14. The SS register.

The Instruction Pointer

The Instruction Pointer, IP, as shown in Fig. 2-15, is a 16-bit register which is analogous to the program counter (PC) in traditional central processing units. The contents of the instruction pointer refer to the offset address of the next machine instruction in the 64 K-byte memory segment as defined by the contents of the Code Segment register, CS. During the execution of programs, the Instruction Pointer register is updated to point to the memory address of the next instruction to be fetched.

The contents of the Instruction Pointer and the Code Segment register uniquely identify a byte location in the 8088's megabyte memory space. The physical address of this byte memory location is a 20-bit value that is generated by shifting LEFT the contents of the CS register by 4 bits and by adding the result after the shift to the contents of the IP register.

Fig. 2-15. The Instruction Pointer, IP.

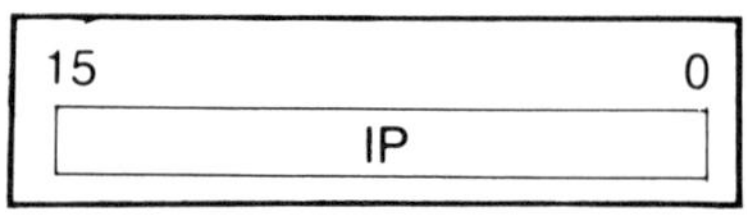

Even machine language programs do not really have direct access to the Instruction Pointer register. However, the contents of the IP register can be altered by executing instructions such as JMP (Jump), CALL (Call Procedures), RET (Return from procedures), IRET (Return from interrupt), and several jump-on-condition instructions such as JE (Jump if Equal), JO (Jump if Overflow), etc.

The Processor Flag

The Processor Flag is a 16-bit register that contains information indicating the current state of the 8088 microprocessor. The Processor Flag as shown in Fig. 2-16, has six 1-bit status flags, that indicate the result of an arithmetic or logical operation. Some machine instructions can alter the sequence of execution of a program depending upon the status of these flags. The status flags are the Auxiliary Carry Flag, AF, the Carry Flag, CF,

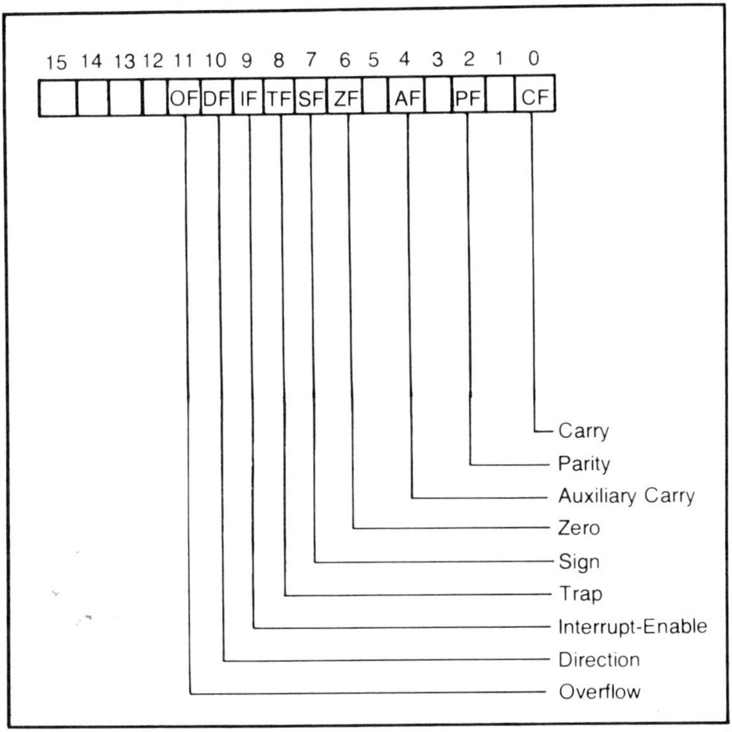

Fig. 2-16. The Processor Flag.

the Overflow Flag, OF, the Sign Flag, SF, the Parity Flag, PF, and the Zero Flag, ZF.

There are three additional control flags that can be set or cleared directly by programs to alter the state and the operations of the CPU. These control flags, which are 1-bit flags in the high-order byte of the Processor Flag, are the Direction Flag, DF, the Interrupt-Enable Flag, IF, and the Trap Flag, TF.

The Auxiliary Carry Flag, AF. The Auxiliary Carry Flag is used to indicate if there is a carry out of the low-order four bits into the high-order four bits of an 8-bit quantity. It also indicates if there is a borrow from the high-order four bits into the low-order four bits of an 8-bit quantity. This flag is very useful in decimal arithmetic. When the AF flag is set to 1, this indicates a carry or borrow has occurred. The Auxiliary Carry Flag occupies bit position 4 of the Processor Flag.

The Carry Flag, CF. The Carry Flag is used to indicate if there is a carry out of, or a borrow into, the most significant bit of a result in an 8-bit or a 16-bit operation. When the Carry Flag is 1, a carry or borrow has occurred. This flag makes possible the addition and subtraction of numbers whose magnitudes are larger than 16 bits. Rotate instructions can also use this flag to retrieve a specific bit in a byte or a word by placing the desired bit in the Carry Flag. Certain machine instructions can set the Carry Flag to 1 (STC) or clear the Carry Flag to 0 (CLC). The Carry Flag occupies the least significant bit position of the Processor Flag.

The Overflow Flag, OF. The Overflow Flag is used to indicate if an arithmetic operation results in an overflow. This flag indicates the condition that a significant bit has been lost because the magnitude of the result exceeds the 8-bit or 16-bit capacity of the 8088 CPU in byte or word operations. When the Overflow Flag is 1, an overflow has occurred. An interrupt-on-overflow procedure can be invoked to handle this condition by using the instruction INTO (Interrupt on Overflow). The Overflow Flag occupies bit position 11 of the Processor Flag.

The Sign Flag, SF. The Sign Flag is used to indicate that the most significant bit of a result in byte or word operation is 1. Since numbers in 8088-based systems are represented in standard two's complement notation, the Sign Flag indicates the sign of the result of an operation. If the Sign Flag is set to 1, the result is a negative number. If the Sign Flag is cleared to 0, the result is a positive number. The Sign Flag occupies bit position 7 of the Processor Flag.

The Parity Flag, PF. The Parity Flag is used to indicate if there is an even number of bits in an 8-bit quantity or in the low-order eight bits of a 16-bit quantity. If the Parity Flag is 1, this indicates that there is an even number of 1 bits in the result, or even parity. This flag is useful to verify the integrity of the microcomputer memory in diagnostic test or to check for parity errors during data transmission. The Parity Flag occupies bit position 2 of the Processor Flag.

The Zero Flag, ZF. The Zero Flag is used to indicate if the result of an 8-bit or 16-bit operation is 0. When the Zero Flag is 1, a result of 0 has occurred. The Zero Flag occupies bit position 6 of the Processor Flag.

The Direction Flag, DF. The Direction Flag is used primarily to control the operations of string instructions. When the DF flag is 1, the string instructions are autodecremented or are processed from high addresses to low addresses. The contents of the index registers SI and/or DI implied in the string operations are decremented by 1 or 2 accordingly depending upon byte or word operation of the instructions. If the DF flag is 0, the string instructions are autoincremented or are processed from low to high addresses. The contents of the index registers SI and/or DI implied in the string operations are incremented by 1 or 2 depending upon byte or word operation of the instructions. The Direction Flag occupies bit position 10 of the Processor Flag. The Direction Flag can be set to 1 by the instruction STD (Set Direction) or cleared to 0 by the instruction CLD (Clear Direction).

The Interrupt-Enable Flag, IF. The Interrupt-Enable Flag is used by programs to allow or to prevent external maskable interrupt appearing on the INTR line to be recognized. When the Interrupt-Enable Flag is cleared to 0, interrupt is disabled, or external maskable interrupt requests are ignored. This flag has no effect on nonmaskable external interrupts appearing on the NMI line or on software interrupts. The Interrupt-Enable Flag occupies bit position 9 of the Processor Flag. The Interrupt-Enable Flag can be set to 1 by the instruction STI (Set Interrupt) or cleared to 0 by the instruction CLI (Clear Interrupt).

The Trap Flag, TF. The Trap Flag is used primarily to enable single-step execution. When the TF flag is 1, the 8088 microprocessor automatically generates an internal interrupt after executing each instruction. This provides a convenient method to inspect a machine-language program as it executes instruction by instruction. The address of the single-step service procedure must be defined at the absolute memory locations 00004H to 00007H. The service procedure can be written to display information such as the contents of all CPU registers and certain memory locations immediately after the instruction is executed. The Trap Flag occupies bit position 8 of the Processor Flag. The instruction POPF (Pop Flag) can be used to set the value of the Trap Flag to 0 or 1.

Buses

A microcomputer system contains paths or buses so that data or information can transfer between the microprocessor and memory or input/output devices. There are three principal buses in all traditional microcomputer systems: the data bus, the address bus, and the control bus, as illustrated in Fig. 2-17.

The address bus in 8088-based microcomputers can be up to 20 bits wide. Information that appears on the address bus contains the address of a unique storage location in the 8088 memory space. This address bus

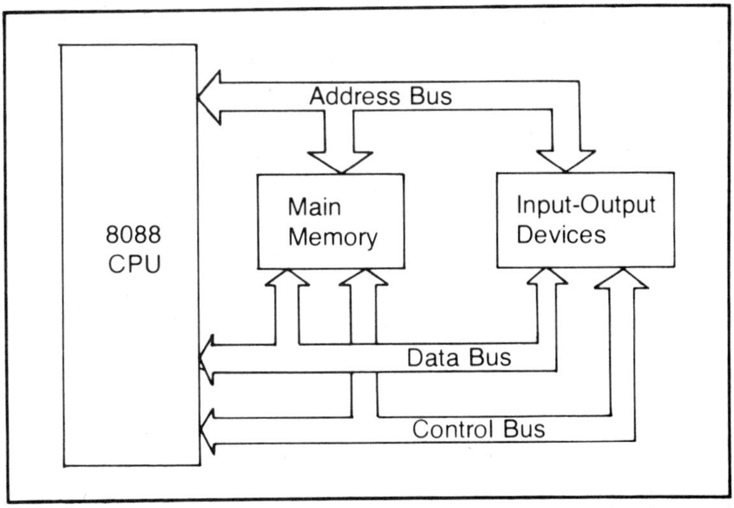

Fig. 2-17. Block diagram of a microcomputer with address bus, data bus, and control bus.

enables the 8088 microprocessor to access any location within one megabyte of its memory space.

The data bus holds the actual binary information that is generated by the 8088 CPU to be written into the computer memory. It also holds binary data (including instructions and program data) retrieved from memory units of the microcomputer such as ROM (Read-Only Memory) and RAM (Random-Access Memory) devices to be read by the CPU. The width of the data bus determines the maximum number of bytes the CPU can read or write to the computer memory at a time. Since the data bus of the 8088 chip is only 8 bits wide, the 8088 CPU is not a true 16-bit microprocessor as compared to the 8086, 80186, or 80286 CPUs in the 8086/8088 microprocessor family. The 8086, 80186, and 80286 CPUs have the data bus width of 16 bits which makes them faster than the 8088 chip, since up to two bytes can be read or written at a time. However, all internal registers of the 8088 arithmetic-logic unit are 16 bits wide. For this reason, the 8088 is considered as an 8-bit CPU with a 16-bit internal architecture.

Finally, the control bus contains signal lines that define the type of communications and coordinate the activities between the CPU and its memory or peripheral devices. For example, the RESET line of the CPU is one of the signal lines on the control bus that can initiate a predefined start-up sequence on the 8088 chip when this line is asserted.

Execution Unit and Bus Interface Unit

Traditional microprocessors execute a machine language program by repeatedly cycling through the following generalized steps:

1. Fetch the next machine instruction from the computer memory.
2. Decode the next instruction.
3. Read operands from the computer memory, if the instruction requires operands.
4. Execute the instruction.
5. Write the result to memory, if required by the machine instruction.

In traditional microcomputers, these steps have to be performed sequentially. The execution of the current instruction must be carried out to completion before another instruction fetch can be initiated. The architecture of the 8086/8088 microprocessor family also performs the steps mentioned above, but allocates these steps to two separate processing units within the CPU.

The Execution Unit (EU) performs the actual execution of machine instructions, and the Bus Interface Unit (BIU) fetches instructions, reads operands, and writes results as required. The two units can operate independently of one another. Therefore, in most cases, it is possible to perform the next instruction fetch and the execution of the current instruction at the same time. This arrangement generally helps speed up the execution cycle of a machine instruction, since the time normally required

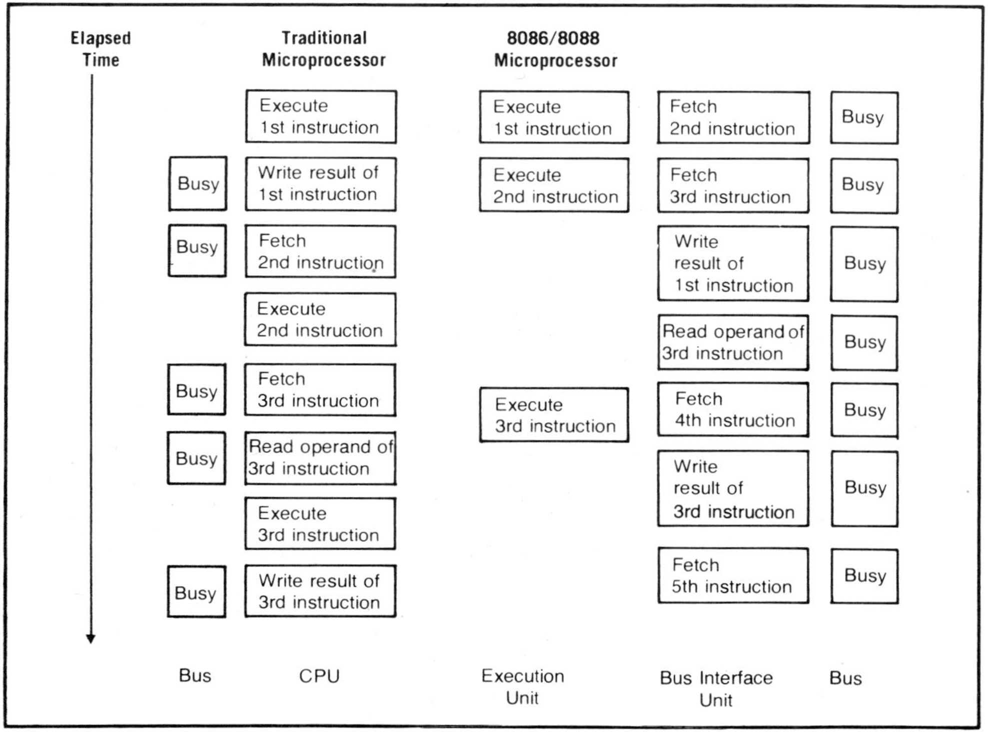

Fig. 2-18. Overlapped instruction fetch and execution.

to fetch instructions simply disappears in most circumstances. Thus, the Execution Unit can execute instructions that have already been prefetched and made available to it by the Bus Interface Unit. An example which describes this parallel operation concept and compares it with traditional microcomputer operation is illustrated in Fig. 2-18.

The Execution Unit of the 8088 CPU contains the arithmetic-logic unit (ALU) of the microprocessor that has the CPU registers and the Processor Flag. All registers and data paths in the Execution Unit are 16 bits wide for fast internal transfers. Since the Execution Unit of the 8088 and 8086 CPU are identical, these two CPUs have the same hardware instruction set.

The Execution Unit does not have access to the computer memory directly. It obtains instructions from an instruction queue provided by the Bus Interface Unit. Figure 2-19 illustrates the logical relationship between

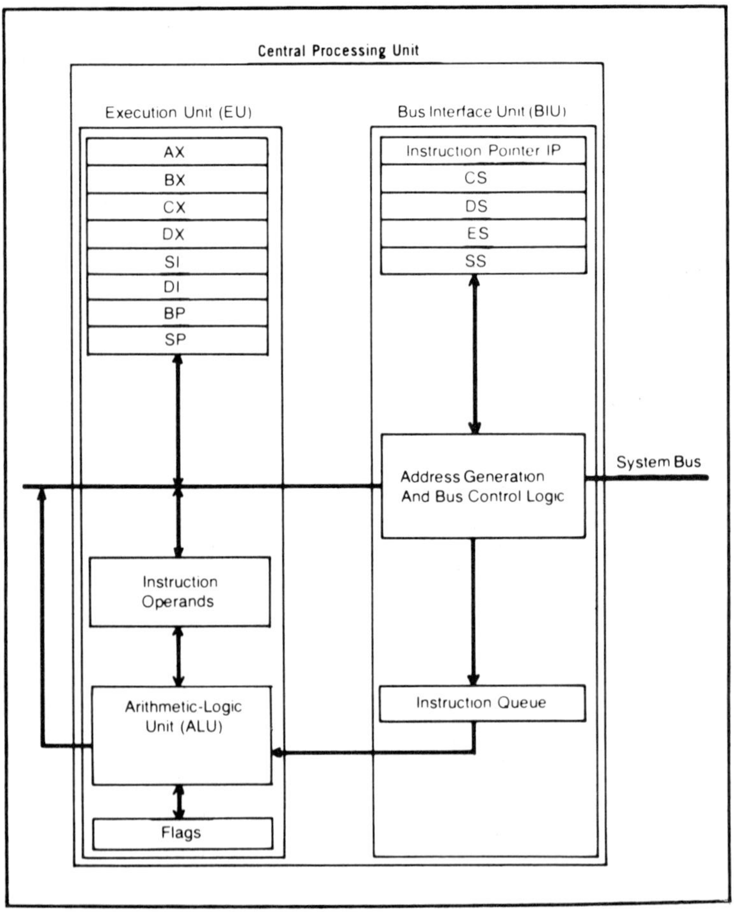

Fig. 2-19. Block diagram of the Execution Unit and the Bus Interface Unit.

the Execution Unit and the Bus Interface Unit of the 8086/8088 microprocessor family.

The Bus Interface Unit performs all memory accesses and bus operations for the Execution Unit. The BIU fetches the next instructions sequentially from a machine-language program sequence in the computer memory while the EU is busy executing the current instruction. The 8088 microprocessor has an internal RAM (Random-Access Memory) area, called the instruction queue, that can hold up to four prefetched bytes of the instruction stream. The 8088 BIU automatically fetches another instruction byte whenever one byte in the queue is empty and there is no active request for memory read or write from the EU. If the EU executes a machine instruction that transfer control to another memory location (CALL or JMP instructions, for example), the BIU resets its instruction queue and starts refilling the queue from the new location. In most cases, the EU can always get an instruction from the BIU's queue and does not have to wait for instructions to be fetched.

SEGMENTATION CONCEPTS

The 8088 microprocessor can access one megabyte of storage locations. A 20-bit pointer is required to be able to access the entire megabyte space of the 8088 memory. Since the Instruction Pointer as well as all other pointer registers in the 8088 CPU such as the BX, SI, DI, BP, and SP registers are only 16 bits wide (which limit access to 64 K-byte space), the 8088 chip microprocessor does not access the computer memory directly. It accesses memory via segmentation logic instead.

Segment Organization

The 8088 microprocessor treats its megabyte memory space as a group of segments. Each segment is a logical unit of the computer memory that can be up to 64 K (65,536) bytes long. The starting location of each segment can be defined by the application program and always begin on 16-byte memory boundaries. The base address of the segment is calculated by dividing the actual physical address of the starting location of each segment by 16. The segment registers hold these base addresses so that the 8088 microprocessor can keep track of up to four uniquely defined 64 K-byte segments at a time. There are essentially no restrictions on segment locations except that they must be on 16-byte memory boundaries (to be divisible by 16). Therefore, segments may be contiguous, separated, partially overlapped, or fully overlapped.

Figure 2-20 shows several possible segment location arrangements in the physical memory space of the microcomputer. After a segment is defined, the pointer registers can then be used to address any byte or word within the specified segment. With this addressing scheme, the 8088 microprocessor can directly access only 64 K bytes of memory space but it can address up to one million bytes using its segment registers. This is one

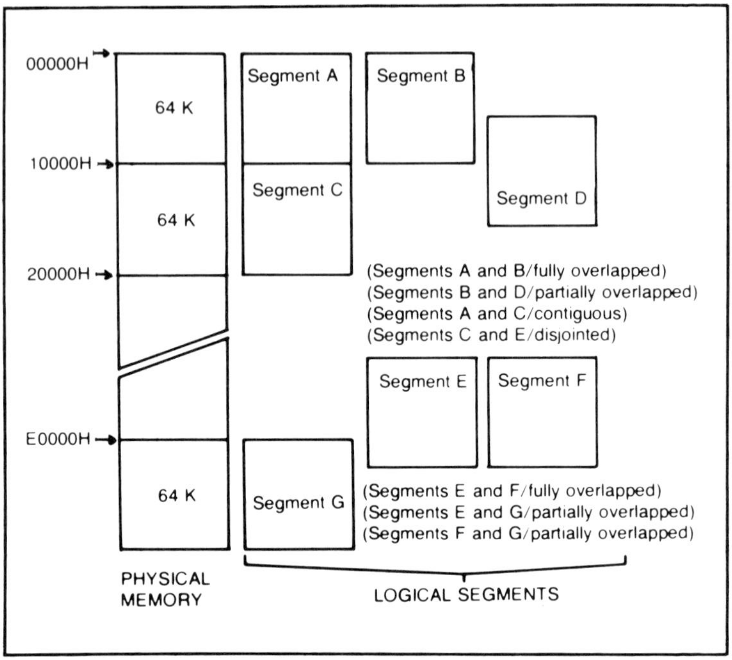

Fig. 2-20. Segment locations in physical memory.

of the inconvenient features of the 8086/8088 family of microprocessors as compared to the direct addressing schemes of other comparable 16-bit CPUs (The Motorola MC68000 microprocessor can directly access up to 16 million bytes of memory using its 32-bit internal registers as memory pointers).

Since the 8088 CPU has four segment registers, there are always four addressable segments in its memory space. These are the code segment, the data segment, the extra segment, and the stack segment whose base addresses are held in the CS, DS, ES, and SS registers, respectively. The code segment represents a 64 K-byte memory space that contains the machine instructions to be fetched by the Bus Interface Unit and executed by the Execution Unit. The contents of the Instruction Pointer corresponds to the offset address of the next instruction to be fetched within this code segment. The data segment represents another 64 K-byte memory area that is normally used to store program data, variables, and constants. The extra segment is provided as an additional 64 K-byte work space. The stack segment can hold a stack structure up to 64 K-byte within the computer memory.

It is possible to write a program that contains instructions, data, variables, constants, and a stack all within the same memory segment. This is done by assigning all segment registers the same base address so that all four memory segments overlap the same physical memory space.

The segmented structure is useful to encourage modular software design and structured programming where large programs are generally broken down into many smaller logical and modular units.

Storage Organization

The 8088 megabyte memory space can be viewed as a sequential array of 8-bit bytes starting from the physical memory address 00000H to FFFFFH as shown in Fig. 2-21. Instructions and program data in bytes or words can be freely stored at any of these byte addresses. The following convention is used to store a 16-bit word and a 32-bit doubleword in the 8088 memory space.

1. A 16-bit word is always stored with the high-order byte in the higher memory location. For example, if the hexadecimal number 0235H is stored at the memory location 2800H, the byte memory location 2800H

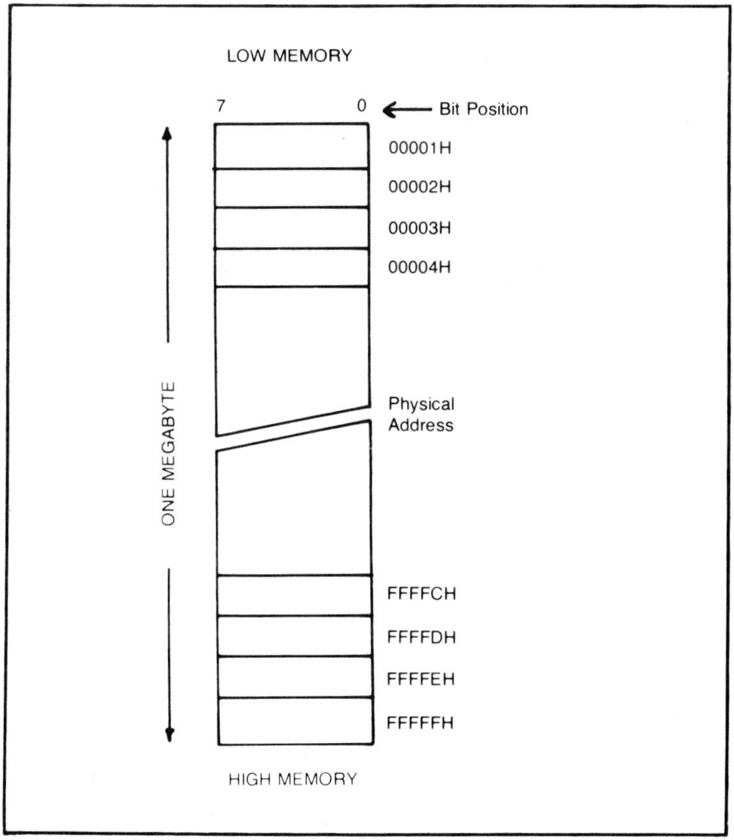

Fig. 2-21. The 8088 memory space.

Contents	Address
Hexadecimal 35H	2800H
Hexadecimal 02H	2801H

Value of word stored at 2800H: 0235H

Fig. 2-22. Storage format of a 16-bit word.

contains 35H and the byte memory location 2801H contains 02H. Figure 2-22 illustrates this method.

2. A 32-bit doubleword can be used as a pointer to address a byte or a word in any 64 K-byte segment of the computer memory. The lower-addressed word of this pointer refers to the offset address within the 64 K-byte segment, and the higher-addressed word refers to the starting location (base address) of the segment. The two bytes in each word are stored according to the same convention for a 16-bit word. Since a physical address must be uniquely identified by a 20-bit value, the 8088 Bus Interface Unit generates the actual address corresponding to the address within a segment by shifting the base address (high-order word) LEFT by four bits and adding the 16-bit offset address (low-order word) to yield the desired 20-bit physical address. Figure 2-23 shows a 32-bit pointer having a hexadecimal value of 04B54000H which refers to the physical memory address 08B50H (segment 04B5H shifting left by four bits, which is 4B50H, plus the offset address 4000H).

ADDRESSING MODES

Instruction operands of an 8088 machine language program are nor-

Contents	Address
Hexadecimal 00H	2802H
Hexadecimal 40H	2803H
Hexadecimal B5H	2804H
Hexadecimal 04H	2805H

Value of doubleword at 2802H: 04B54000H

Fig. 2-23. Storage format of a 32-bit doubleword.

mally held in a general-purpose register, a segment register, or a memory location. Instruction operands can also be specified in the form of a constant to be a part of the instruction. There are many flexible methods to access instruction operands by using the various addressing modes provided by the 8088 microprocessor. These addressing modes demonstrate the power and flexibility of the 8086/8088 microprocessor family that rival many traditional minicomputer systems.

The 8088 addressing modes can be divided into nine major categories. These modes include the register operands, immediate operands, direct addressing, indirect addressing, indirect addressing with displacement, based indexed addressing, based indexed addressing with displacement, string addressing, and input/output port addressing.

Register Operand

Instructions that have only register operands are the most compact and have the shortest execution time of all forms of instructions. This is because the operations between the specified register operands can be performed entirely within the 8088 CPU by the Execution Unit without the need to access the computer memory. General-purpose registers may serve as source operands, destination operands, or both. Segment registers may serve as either source operands or destination operands only.

For example, the machine instruction 20D0 (AND AL,DL) performs a Boolean logical AND between the AL and DL register and returns the result in the AL register. The source operand is the DL register, and the destination operand is the AL register. This instruction takes only two bytes of memory storage and can be performed completely within the CPU in 3 clocks.

Immediate Operands

Immediate operands are constant data specified as a part of the machine instruction. The data can be either 8 bits or 16 bits. Immediate operands can be accessed quickly since the CPU can retrieve them directly from the instruction queue without accessing the computer memory. Immediate operands may only be specified as source operands. The machine instruction is more compact if the destination operand is the accumulator (the AL or AX register).

For example, the machine instruction 3C02 (CMP AL,02) compares the contents of the AL register with the hexadecimal number 02 and sets the appropriate flags according to the result of the comparison. The immediate operand in this instruction is the hexadecimal constant 02. This instruction takes only two bytes of memory storage and can be performed completely within the 8088 CPU in 4 clocks.

The Effective Address, EA

The offset address within a 64 K-byte segment that the 8088 CPU calculates for a memory operand is called the effective address, EA, of the operand. Since there are 65,536 possible byte memory locations within a segment, the offset address can be represented as an unsigned 16-bit number so that access to any byte location in the segment is possible. If an instruction requires a minimum of two bytes of machine codes to access memory operands, in most cases, the bit pattern in the second byte of the instruction tells the 8088 CPU how to construct the 16-bit effective address to access the required memory operands. The general format of the second byte of an instruction that accesses memory operands is shown in Fig. 2-24.

In Fig. 2-24, XX are the two bits that form the MOD field. The MOD field is used to distinguish whether the instruction operands are CPU registers or memory locations. XX has four possible binary values: 00, 01,

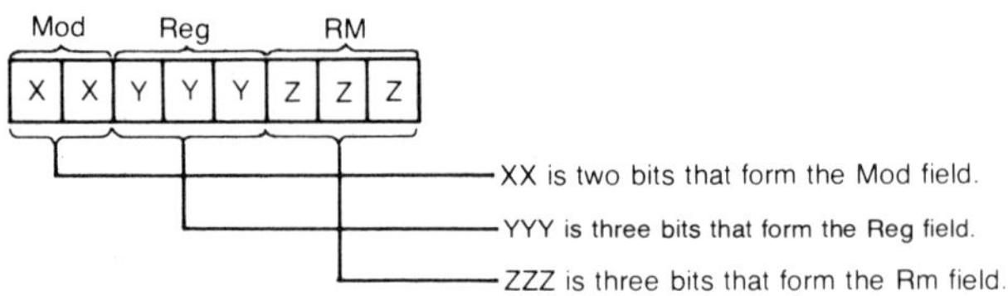

Mod= 00 No displacement bytes.
01 One signed displacement byte.

Mod Reg Rm	Displacement

10 Two displacement bytes (unsigned 16-bit).

Mod Reg Rm	Displacement	Displacement
	Low Byte	High Byte

Reg=

	Byte	Word
000	AL	AX
001	CL	CX
010	DL	DX
011	BL	BX
100	AH	SP
101	CH	BP
110	DH	SI
111	BH	DI

Rm=

	Mod=00	Mod=01 or Mod=10	Mod=11 Byte	Mod=11 Word
000	BX+SI	BX+SI+Displacement	AL	AX
001	BX+DI	BX+DI+Displacement	CL	CX
010	BP+SI	BP+SI+Displacement	DL	DX
011	BP+DI	BP+DI+Displacement	BL	BX
100	SI	SI +Displacement	AH	SP
101	DI	DI +Displacement	CH	BP
110	Direct	BP+Displacement	DH	SI
111	BX	BX+Displacement	BH	DI

Fig. 2-24. General format of the memory addressing byte.

10 and 11. The binary value 11 of the MOD field indicates the operands of the specified machine instruction are register operands. The other binary values 00, 01, or 10 specify the memory addressing mode with 0, 1, or 2 bytes of displacement, respectively. The displacement may be an 8-bit signed number or a 16-bit unsigned number which is included as a part of the machine instruction and is used in the calculation of the effective address.

YYY are the three bits that form the Reg field and are used to define the register to be used as a register operand. The Reg field identifies an 8-bit register in byte operations and a 16-bit register in word operations. In some instructions, these bits are also used to identify the machine instruction of a specific group (for example, the instruction AND in the group of logical instructions).

ZZZ are the three bits that form the Rm field. The Rm field is used in conjunction with the MOD field to identify the specific addressing mode. Any combination of the MOD and Rm field may be present in a given instruction to create a variety of 8086/8088 memory addressing modes. The following sections describe all possible ways to construct the effective address, EA.

Direct Addressing

Direct Addressing is the simplest memory addressing mode. There are no registers involved. The effective address, EA, is taken directly from the 16-bit displacement field of the machine instruction, as shown in Fig. 2-25. This direct address defines a unique byte or word memory location within a 64 K-byte segment. Direct addressing is normally used to address a single variable or constant. The 8088 CPU makes the assumption that the direct address is within the default data segment. Prefix instructions are available so that application programs can specify the direct address to be relative to any one of the four available segments. When the direct addressing mode is used, the MOD field has the binary value 00 and the Rm field has the value 110.

For example, in an assembly language program, the Data Segment register contains 04B5H, and the byte memory location 1400H in the current data segment has a symbolic name LOC1. The machine instruction C606001402 (MOV LOC1,02) stores the hexadecimal number 02 at the offset address 1400H within the data segment. The displacement field of the instruction is 1400H and is taken as the effective address, EA. The actual 20-bit physical address generated by the Bus Interface Unit which corresponds to this effective address is 05F50H (4B50H + 1400H), in this case.

There are two special formats of the direct addressing mode: relative addressing and absolute addressing.

In relative addressing, the displacement field is an 8-bit signed number. The effective address, EA, is calculated by adding this displacement field to the contents of the Instruction Pointer, IP, as shown in Fig. 2-25B. Jump-on-condition instructions such as JE (Jump if Equal), JO (Jump

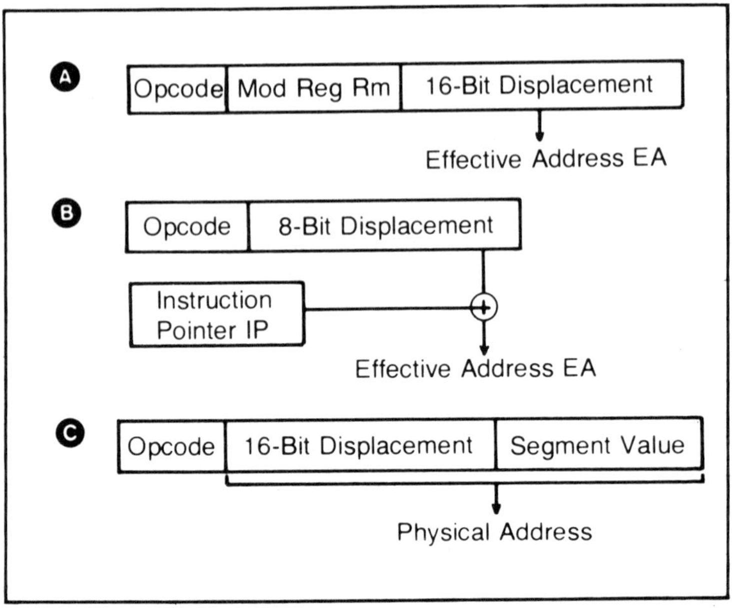

Fig. 2-25. Direct addressing. A, offset address, B, relative addressing, C, absolute addressing.

if Overflow) use the relative addressing mode. The memory addressing byte (Mod/Reg/Rm) is not required in the relative addressing mode.

In absolute addressing mode, a 32-bit pointer is specified as a part of the instruction and is taken to identify a physical address in the 8088 megabyte memory space. The low-order word of the pointer is taken as the offset address of a location in a segment whose base address is specified in the high-order word of the pointer, as shown in Fig. 2-25C. The memory addressing byte (Mod/Reg/Rm) is not required in the absolute addressing mode.

Indirect Addressing

In indirect addressing, the contents of the base or index registers (BX, SI, or DI) are taken to be the effective address, EA, as shown in Fig. 2-26. Therefore, one instruction can operate on many different memory locations by simply changing the contents of the base or index register that is used for indirect addressing. If the BX, SI, or DI registers are used, their contents are taken to be the effective address within the current data segment. Applications program may use additional prefix instructions to reassign this effective address to other segments within the 8088 memory space. This addressing mode is very effective to manipulate arrays in the computer memory.

There is one exception to the indirect addressing mode. If the machine

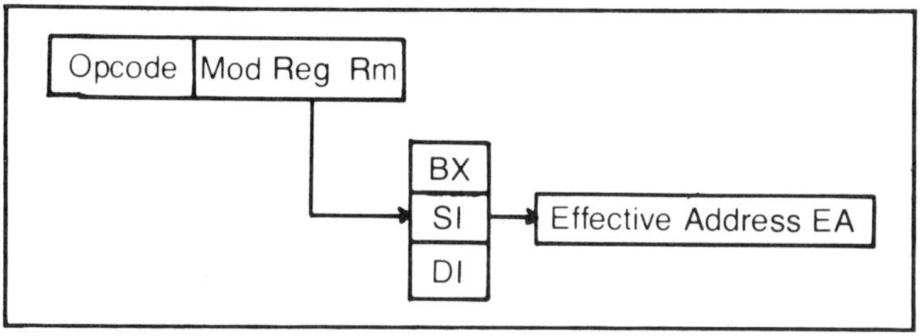

Fig. 2-26. Indirect addressing.

instruction is JMP (Jump) or CALL (Call Procedures), the contents of any 16-bit general registers (AX, BX, CX, DX, SI, DI, BP, SP) may be taken to be the effective address.

For example, in an assembly language program, the DS register contains 14C5H. If the SI register contains 28FFH, the machine instruction C60410 (MOV [SI],10H) stores the hexadecimal number 10 at the byte memory location 28FFH within the data segment. The contents of the SI register are taken to be the effective address in this case. The actual 20-bit physical memory address corresponding to offset address 28FFH is 1754FH (14C50H + 28FFH).

Indirect Addressing with Displacement

In indirect addressing with displacement, the effective address, EA, is the sum of a displacement value and the contents of one of the base or index registers (BX, BP, SI, DI), as shown in Fig. 2-27. The displacement value can be an 8-bit signed number or a 16-bit unsigned number. If the BX, SI, or DI register is used, the effective address is assumed to be an offset address within the current data segment whose base address is defined in the Data Segment, DS, register. If the BP register is used, the effective address is taken to be an offset address within the current stack segment whose base address is held in the Stack Segment, SS, register. There are prefix

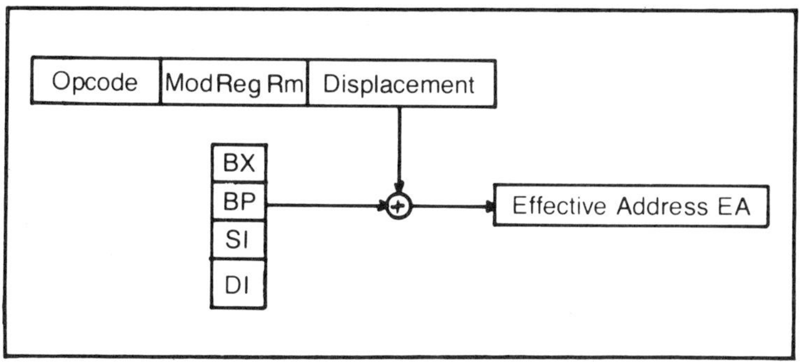

Fig. 2-27. Indirect addressing with displacement.

instructions available so that application programs can reassign the effective address to be taken relative to other segments of the 8088 memory space.

When this addressing mode is used, the MOD field has the binary value 01 or 10 depending on whether the displacement is an 8-bit or a 16-bit quantity. The Rm field has the binary value 100, 101, 110, or 111 depending on whether the SI, DI, BP, or BX register is used, respectively.

In the following example, the Stack Segment register contains 04B5H. If the BP register contains FF10H, the machine instruction C6870245 (MOV [BP+02],45H) stores in the hexadecimal number 45 at the byte memory location FF12H within the stack segment. The displacement value is an 8-bit signed number (02) and occupies the third byte of the instruction. The effective address EA is calculated by adding the displacement value to the contents of the BP register (FF10H + 02H). This corresponds to the actual physical memory location 14A62H (4B50H + FF12H) to be generated by the Bus Interface Unit. Since this addressing mode provides access to the stack segment when the BP register is used, it is very convenient to utilize this addressing mode to access data on a stack structure.

Based Indexed Addressing

The effective address in based indexed addressing mode is generated by adding the contents of a base register (BX or BP) to an index register (SI or DI), as shown in Fig. 2-28. Based indexed addressing is very powerful and flexible because the contents of the base and index registers can be varied at execution time to access different locations in the computer memory. If the BX register is used, the effective address is taken relative to the current data segment whose base address is held in the DS register. If the BP register is used, the effective address is taken relative to the stack segment whose base address is defined in the SS register. Application programs can use prefix instructions to reassign in the effective address to be taken relative to other segments of the computer memory.

In based indexed addressing mode, the MOD field has the binary value 00. The Rm field has the binary value 000, 001, 010, 011 associated with the [BX+SI], [BX+DI], [BP+SI], [BP+DI] addressing mode, respectively.

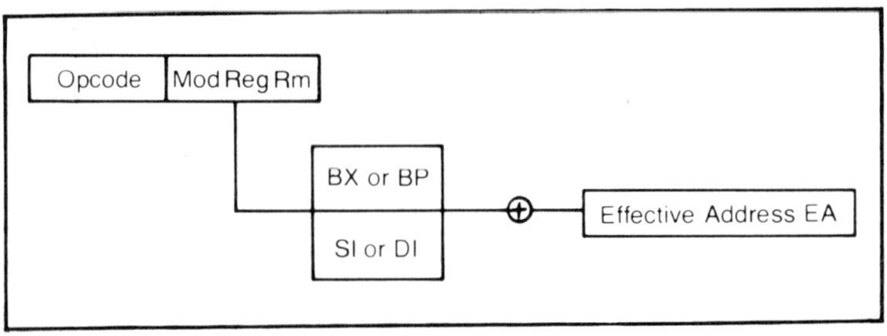

Fig. 2-28. Based indexed addressing.

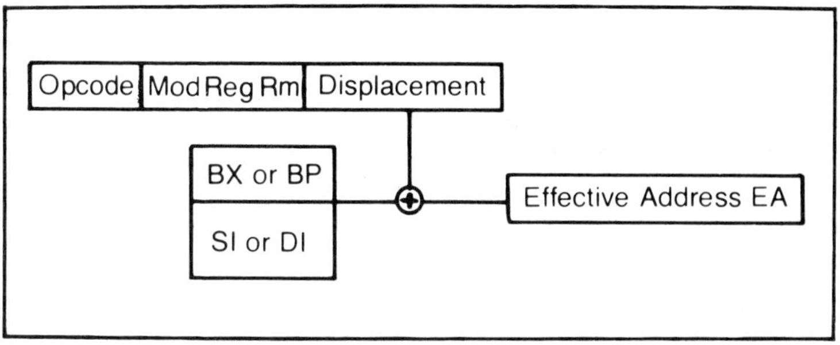

Fig. 2-29. Based indexed addressing with displacement.

In the following example, the Data Segment register contains 04B5H. If the BX and SI registers contain 1000H and 1500H, respectively, the machine instruction C60015 (MOV [BX+SI], 15H) stores the hexadecimal number 15 at the byte memory address 2500H within the data segment. The effective address 2500H is calculated by summing the contents of the BX and SI register (1000H + 1500H). This effective address corresponds to the actual physical memory location 07050H (4B50H + 2500H) to be generated by the Bus Interface Unit.

Based Indexed Addressing with Displacement

Based indexed addressing with displacement generates the effective address which is the sum of a base register (BX or BP), an index register (SI or DI), and a displacement value, as shown in Fig. 2-29. The displacement value is a part of the instruction and can be an 8-bit signed number or a 16-bit unsigned number. The effective address is taken to be an offset within the current data segment or stack segment depending on whether the BX or BP register is used, respectively. Application programs can use prefix instructions to reassign the effective address to be taken relative to other segments in the 8088 memory space.

In based indexed addressing with displacement, the MOD field has the binary value 01 or 10 depending upon whether the displacement specified in the instruction is an 8-bit or a 16-bit quantity. The Rm field has identical values as those discussed in the based indexed addressing mode.

In the following example, the Stack Segment register contains 04C5H. If the BP and SI registers contain FF00H and 0010H, respectively, the machine instruction C642200B (MOV [BP+SI], OBH) stores the hexadecimal number OB at the byte memory address FF30H in the stack segment. The displacement in this example is an 8-bit signed number (hexadecimal 20H). The effective address is calculated by adding the displacement value to the contents of the BP and SI registers (FF00H + 0010H + 20H). In this case, the effective address corresponds to the actual physical memory address 14B80H (4C50H + FF00H + 0010H + 20H) to be generated by the 8088 Bus Interface Unit.

String Addressing

String instructions such as MOVS (Move String), CMPS (Compare String), LODS (Load String), STOS (Store String), and SCAS (Scan String) do not use any of the normal memory addressing modes just mentioned to access their memory operands. The contents of the index registers (SI and/or DI) are used implicitly as pointers to access the required memory locations. Refer to Fig. 2-30. The SI register is always used as a pointer to the first byte or word of the source string.

The DI register is used as a pointer to the first byte or word of the destination string. The instruction LODS implies using the SI register as the source pointer. The instructions STOS and SCAS imply using the DI register as the destination pointer. The instructions MOVS and CMPS use both the SI and DI registers. Offset addresses implied by the DI register in STOS instructions are always taken relative to the current extra segment. With other string instructions, prefix instructions can be specified to reassign the data segment (if the instruction is LODS, MOVS, or CMPS) or the extra segment (if the instruction is SCAS) to any segment in the 8088 memory space.

When a string instruction is executed, the contents of the SI or DI register are incremented or decremented depending upon whether the Direction Flag is 0 or 1, respectively. The contents of these index registers are incremented/decremented by 1 or 2 depending on whether the machine instruction requires a byte operation or a word operation, respectively.

Input/Output Port Addressing

This addressing mode is used to access input/output devices attached to the 8088 I/O space. The 8088 I/O space provides an extra 64 K-byte area in addition to the megabyte memory space, as shown in Fig. 2-31. This I/O space is not segmented and can be designed as a separate area or as a part of the 8088 memory space. In memory-mapped I/O systems, the 64 K-byte I/O space is designed to be a part of the computer memory. This design makes the 8088 megabyte memory space to be 64 K bytes smaller but it provides additional programming flexibility since all addressing modes mentioned in previous sections can be employed to access this memory-mapped I/O space.

Each byte location in the 8088 I/O space can be assigned to be the

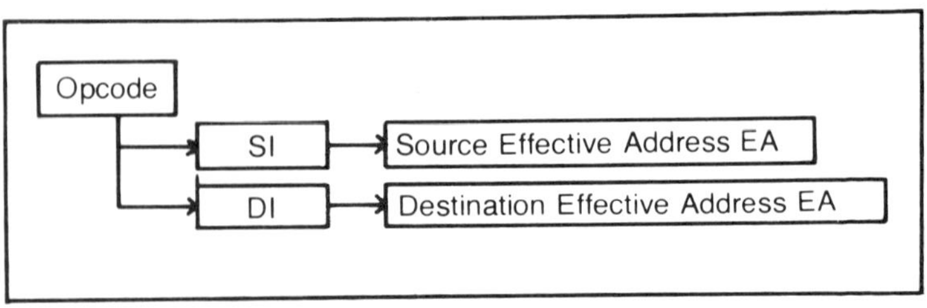

Fig. 2-30. String addressing.

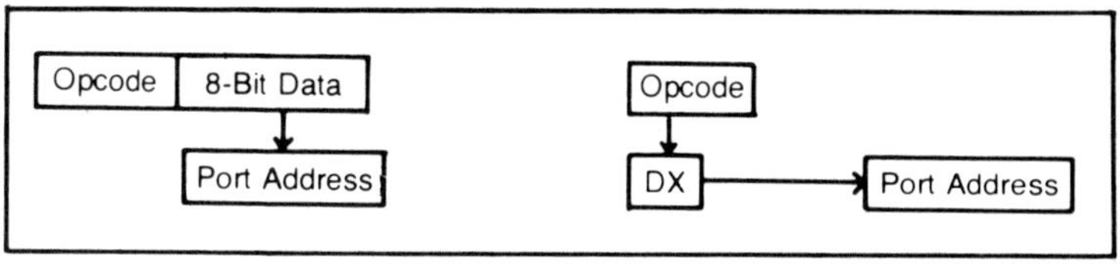

Fig. 2-31. Input/output port addressing.

address of a unique I/O port. Thus, the 8088 I/O space can accommodate up to 64 K (65,536) 8-bit I/O ports. Data can be transferred between the accumulator and any I/O port located within the 64 K-byte I/O space. The AL register is used in byte transfer, and the AX register is used in word transfer. The instructions IN (input from port) and OUT (output to port) are used for I/O port addressing. If the port number is within the decimal range 0-255, it can be specified as a part of the machine instruction. If the port number is greater than 255, the DX register is used to hold the port number.

STACK MANIPULATION

In order to produce programs which fully utilize the power and flexibility of the 8086/8088 microprocessor family, a programmer must become familiar with the concept of manipulation of data on a stack structure which is part of the design philosophy of the 8088 microprocessor. This section describes the 8088 stack structures and several typical applications of the stack.

The 8088 Stack

A *stack* in any 8088-based systems is an area of the computer memory set aside for the special purpose of temporarily storing parameters or program data to keep linkage information between programs and procedures. The stack uses the *last-in, first-out* concept. Various items may be deposited on a stack in sequential order and retrieved or removed from the stack in reverse order, as shown in Fig. 2-32. The number of stacks in the computer memory is limited only by the available memory space. The maximum size of the 8088 stack structure is 32 K (32,768) 16-bit words so that the stack can be contained within one memory segment.

Only one stack is directly addressable at a time, since there is only one register (the Stack Segment, SS, register) carrying the base address (starting location) of the stack. The contents of the Stack Pointer, SP, points to an offset address in the stack structure. This address points to a location called the *Top of Stack*. Therefore, the Stack Pointer can be used to keep track of the last item (a 16-bit word) deposited on the stack. Every item to be deposited, retrieved, or removed from a stack must be a 16-bit quantity.

In most cases, the programmer does not need to keep track of the actual locations of the program's data on the stack. Instructions such as PUSH (Push data on stack), POP (Pop data from stack), CALL (Call procedures), RET (Return from procedures), or IRET (Return from interrupt) automatically adjust the contents of the Stack Pointer, SP, to keep track of the top of the stack. Stack operations never actually move items on the stack, nor do they actually erase them. The top of stack changes only as the result of changing the contents of the Stack Pointer.

Adding an item onto the stack is called a *push* operation. When an item is pushed on the stack, the contents of the Stack Pointer is decremented by 2 to point to a new top of stack. The item is then written into the word location at the offset address specified by the SP register in the current stack segment whose base address is held in the SS register. For push operations, the stack grows toward the low-addressed portion of the stack segment. In other words, the stack grows down in memory toward the base address of the stack segment.

Removing an item from the top of stack is called a *pop* operation. When an item is popped from the stack, the contents of the Stack Pointer is incremented by 2 to point to a new top of stack. The location on the stack containing the popped item is considered free and available for other use. However, the contents of this location in the computer memory remain unchanged after the pop operation.

Figure 2-33 shows typical push and pop operations in 8088-based microcomputers. The PUSH (Push on stack) and POP (Pop from stack) instructions allow the contents of any 16-bit general registers, segment registers, or memory locations to be stored or retrieved from a stack structure.

Procedure Calling and Returning Using the Stack

Procedures or subroutines provide a facility for maintaining a single

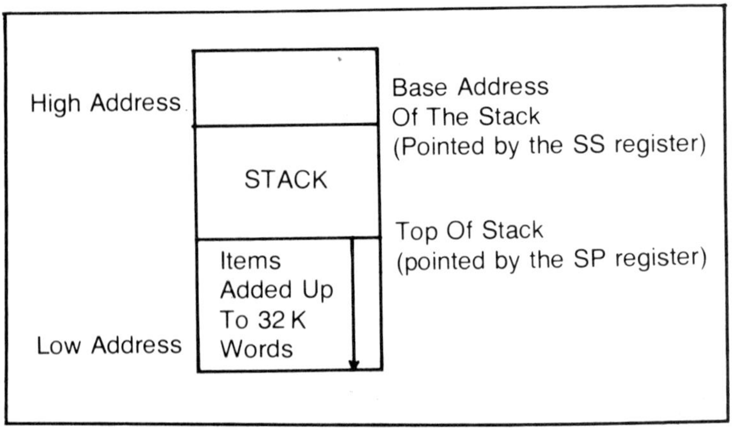

Fig. 2-32. The 8088 stack.

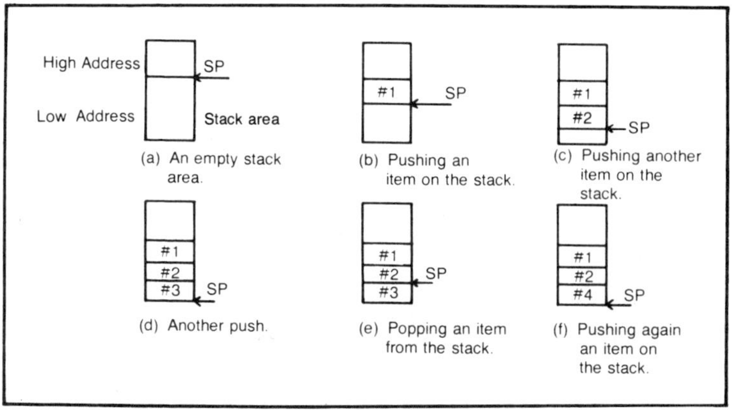

Fig. 2-33. Push and pop operations.

copy of a sequence of machine instructions and data which can be used in a repetitive manner by other programs which may be located anywhere else in the computer memory. In order to provide this facility, the machine instructions CALL (Call procedures) and RET (Return from procedures) establish a standard method to transfer control from a program to a procedure and to return control to the instruction following the CALL instruction when the execution of the procedure is completed.

Intrasegment Calling and Returning. If the physical address of the memory location containing the CALL instruction and the starting location of the procedure are within 64 K bytes, an intrasegment CALL may be used to transfer control to the procedure. The returning address (address of the next instruction following the CALL instruction) is pushed on the current stack (specified by the Stack Pointer, SP, and the SS register), as shown in Fig. 2-34. The last machine instruction to be executed before

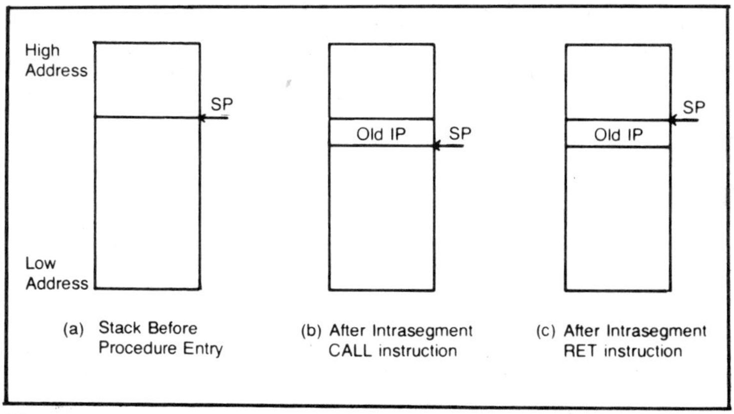

Fig. 2-34. Intrasegment procedure calling and returning.

exiting a procedure must be a RET instruction (hexadecimal number C3 in machine code) to pop the contents of the top of stack (which is the returning address) into the Instruction Pointer, IP. This will transfer control to the machine instruction following the CALL instruction. In assembly language, a procedure invoked by an intrasegment call is defined as a *near* procedure. The assembler translates all RET instructions in a *near* procedure into the hexadecimal machine code C3 (intrasegment return).

Intersegment Calling and Returning. A program can transfer control to a procedure located anywhere in the 8088 megabyte memory space by using an intersegment CALL instruction. In an intersegment CALL, the 8088 CPU automatically performs the following steps, which are also illustrated in Fig. 2-35.

1. The Stack Pointer is decremented by 2. The CS register, which holds the base address of the current code segment, is pushed on the top of stack.
2. The Stack Pointer again is decremented by 2. The offset address of the next instruction following the CALL is pushed on the stack.

The last machine instruction to be executed before exiting a procedure invoked by an intersegment CALL must be a RET instruction (the corresponding machine code is CB in hexadecimal). In assembly language, a procedure invoked by an intersegment CALL instruction is defined as a *far* procedure. The RET instruction in a *far* procedure is translated into the machine code CB in hexadecimal (intersegment return). When the intersegment RET instruction is executed, the 8088 CPU automatically performs the following steps:

1. The word at the top of stack (pointed to by the Stack Pointer, SP) is

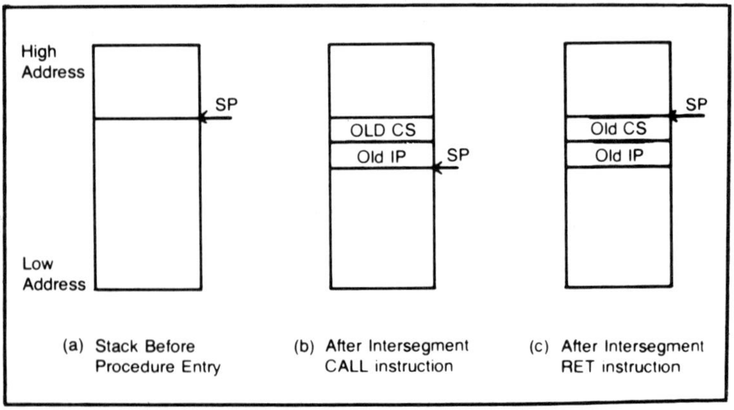

Fig. 2-35. Intersegment procedure calling and returning.

popped into the Instruction Pointer, IP. The SP register is incremented by 2 to point to a new top of stack.

2. The word at the new top of stack replaces the contents of the CS register. The SP register again is incremented by 2.

This will transfer control to the machine instruction following the CALL instruction.

Nested Procedure Calling and Returning. A program can transfer control to a procedure which can then invoke another procedure located anywhere in the computer memory. This condition is referred to as nested procedure calling. With the use of the stack, all returning addresses can be automatically restored properly without any additional programming. It is possible to nest any arbitrary mixture of intersegment and intrasegment CALLs without any confusion. The example, as shown in Fig. 2-36, demonstrates a typical sequence of the nested procedure calling and returning that can be implemented on any 8088-based microcomputers.

Argument Transmission Using the Stack. It is quite convenient to store parameters or intermediate data from a calling program on the stack to be retrieved later by a procedure. In many cases, the operations performed by the procedure can be applied directly to the data located on the stack without the need to ever actually move the data into the procedure area. The BP register is commonly used as a pointer to access data stored on the stack. A displacement can be specified with the RET instructions to allow control to be properly transferred back to the address of the instruction following the CALL by bypassing the data area on the stack, as shown in Fig. 2-37.

INTERRUPTS

Interrupts are a hardware mechanism which forces the 8088 microprocessor to suspend its current activities and to respond to an external event. Interrupts are used primarily to increase the efficiency of the central processing unit. In most 8088-based microcomputers, interrupts are also used to be a convenient method to access hardware facilities and utility programs supported by the operating system software. Interrupts enable I/O devices to proceed with input or output operations independently of the microprocessor.

Since the speed of the 8088 CPU is significantly faster than I/O devices, it is desirable that the CPU can proceed to execute other programs or to perform more useful functions without having to constantly monitor the conditions of the attached I/O devices. Whenever an input/output device needs the service of the 8088 CPU, it can signal the 8088 microprocessor via interrupts. This section presents the readers the basic concepts of interrupts in a microcomputer and discusses the structure of external and internal interrupts in the 8086/8088 microprocessor family.

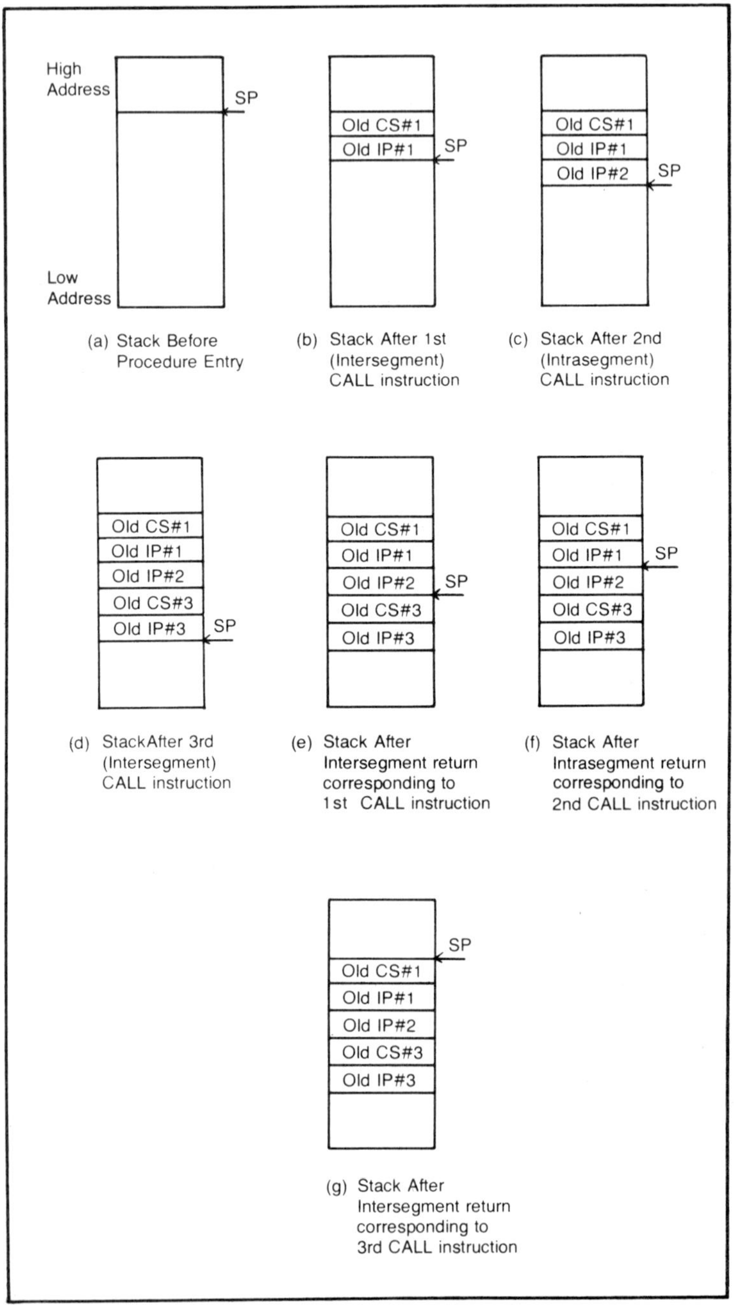

Fig. 2-36. Use of the stack in nested procedures.

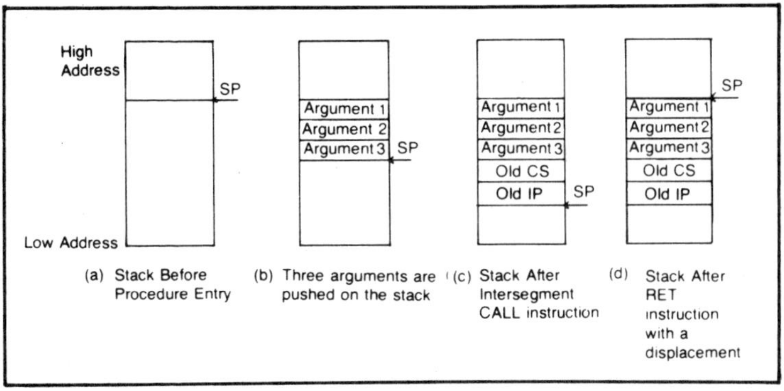

Fig. 2-37. Arguments transmitted on the stack.

Definition of an Interrupt

The concept of an interrupt can be best clarified in the following examples.

Example 1. Julie is talking to her friend on the telephone. She suddenly hears the sound of her doorbell. The following is a sample of various possibilities that Julie may respond to the sound of her doorbell:

1. Julie ignores the sound of her doorbell and continues the conversation on her telephone.
2. Julie immediately stops talking on her telephone and goes to see who might be at the door. Then she resumes the conversation on her telephone.
3. Julie continues the conversation until she finds a convenient moment that she can stop talking. Then she goes to see who might be at the door. Finally, Julie resumes the conversation on her telephone.

This simple example accurately presents the concepts of interrupts within a microcomputer system. Think of it this way. The situation in which "Julie is talking to her friend on the telephone" can be viewed as an analogy to an 8088 microprocessor executing a program. The "sound of the doorbell" is analogous to an external interrupt request (in other words, a hardware device in the 8088-based microcomputer signals the CPU that it needs the service of the 8088 microprocessor).

The first possibility ("Julie ignores the sound of her doorbell and continues the conversation on her telephone") is analogous to the situation in which the 8088 CPU ignores a maskable interrupt request and continues executing its current program. This condition happens when the Interrupt-Enable Flag, IF, of the Processor Flag is cleared to 0 (interrupt is disabled) and maskable interrupts must wait for service of the CPU.

The second possibility ("Julie immediately stops talking on her telephone and goes to see who might be at the door"), is analogous to the moment when the 8088 CPU responds to an interrupt request. The CPU suspends its execution of the current program and transfers control to an interrupt service procedure. "Going to see who might be at the door" is analogous to the operations that the interrupt service procedure must perform to satisfy the interrupt request. "Resuming the conversation on her telephone" is analogous to the moment when the interrupt service procedure returns control to the program being interrupted. The program can then continue from the point of interruption.

The third possibility ("Julie continues the conversation until she finds a convenient moment that she can stop talking"), can be viewed as an analogy to the situation in which the 8088 CPU ignores the maskable interrupt request and continues executing its current program (because the Interrupt-Enable Flag is 0). The 8088 continues executing the program until it encounters the instruction STI (Set Interrupt) which enables the CPU to acknowledge maskable interrupts. Immediately after the Interrupt-Enable Flag is set to 1, the execution of the current program is suspended, and control is then transferred to an interrupt service procedure.

The above example demonstrates the concepts of maskable interrupts. Nonmaskable interrupts can be best explained in the following example.

Example 2. A security guard is monitoring several video screens. He suddenly hears the fire alarm sound. The security guard immediately stops monitoring the screens and calls the fire department. After the phone call is completed, the security guard continues to monitor the screens.

This simple example accurately presents the concepts of nonmaskable interrupts. The "security guard" who "is monitoring several video screens" can be viewed as an analogy to an 8088 microprocessor executing a program. The "fire alarm sound" is analogous to a nonmaskable interrupt request. The moment when the CPU must suspend its execution immediately to respond to the interrupt request regardless of the status of the Interrupt-Enable Flag is analogous to the situation in which "the security guard immediately stops monitoring the screens and calls the fire department." The "fire alarm sound" simply cannot be ignored, since there is no point to continue any other activities.

Similarly, a nonmaskable interrupt normally has the highest priority on the microcomputer and must be serviced immediately by the microprocessor. In single-user microcomputers, nonmaskable interrupts normally are events which are "catastrophic" in nature such as memory parity errors, or warnings of an imminent power failure. In multiuser, multiprogramming microcomputers, nonmaskable interrupts can be signals of the system clock to switch jobs (dedicating the CPU execution time to another program), or to abort the execution of a program that violates its dedicated memory space (errors in the program that cause it to run incorrectly).

The 8088 CPU always carries out the execution of the current machine instruction to completion before it recognizes any interrupt. If the instruction must take many clock cycles to complete (for example, multiply and divide instructions), the interrupt request has to wait until the execution of the current instruction is completed before it can be acknowledged and serviced by the microprocessor. The time required for the CPU to respond to an interrupt request is known as interrupt latency.

The 8086/8088 microprocessor family has a simple but very powerful interrupt system. Every interrupt is assigned a type code that identifies itself to the microprocessor. There may be up to 256 different interrupt types. Interrupts can be generated by requests from I/O devices external to the CPU. Interrupts generated by I/O devices can be designed to be nonmaskable or maskable. Interrupts can also be generated internally by application programs depending on certain conditions such as executing the machine instruction INTO (Interrupt if Overflow) when the Overflow Flag, OF, is set to 1.

The 8088 CPU automatically generates an interrupt with a predefined interrupt type in the following cases:

1. An operation results in dividing by zero. (Divide error interrupt, type 0.)
2. An instruction is executed when the Trap Flag, TF, is set to 1. (Single-step interrupt, type 1.)
3. The machine code CC (in hexadecimal) is executed. (Breakpoint interrupt, type 3.)

External Interrupts

In a typical 8088-based microcomputer system, there are many different peripheral devices that communicate with the microprocessor. These hardware devices can be a dot-matrix printer, a CRT terminal, a floppy diskette drive, a keyboard, etc. Most of these external hardware components need the attention of the microprocessor only at certain times. At other times, they can function without any need for service provided by the 8088 CPU.

For example, consider the keyboard which is a primary input device to enter commands, instructions, and data into the microcomputer. A fast typist may be able to type 400 keystrokes per minute at the keyboard. This means that a new character may enter the microcomputer every 150 milliseconds (1 millisecond = 1/1000 second) at this typing speed from the keyboard. The 8088 microprocessor must read the new character entered at the keyboard every 150 msec and store it in the microcomputer memory.

The process required to read the character and to store it in memory may take less than 10 microseconds (1 microsecond = 1 millionth of a second). In this example the advantage of using interrupts is obvious. Each time a key is struck, the keyboard issues an interrupt request to the 8088 CPU. The microprocessor suspends whatever it is doing and transfers control to an interrupt procedure to service the keyboard request. The interrupt service procedure contains the necessary machine instructions to read the new character and to store it in the computer memory.

When this is done, the 8088 CPU continues from the point where the interrupt occurs. With this interrupt mechanism, the 8088 needs to spend less than 10 microseconds to read each keystroke. It can use the rest of the 150-msec interval between successive keystrokes to perform other functions.

The 8088 microprocessor has three interrupt lines that an external peripheral hardware device can activate to interrupt the CPU. These are the RESET, NMI, and INTR lines, as shown in Fig. 2-38.

Resetting the 8088 CPU. When the RESET line is addressed, the 8088 CPU will start executing a predefined initialization sequence. This is essential to allow an orderly start of the microprocessor when power is turned on. The predefined sequence initializes the CPU in the following way:

1. The Processor Flag is cleared to 0. This has the effect of disabling maskable interrupts and single-stepping interrupts.
2. The segment registers DS, ES, and SS are cleared to 0.
3. The Instruction Pointer, IP, is cleared to 0.
4. The Code Segment, CS, register is set to the hexadecimal value FFFF.

The 8088 CPU will start execution from the physical memory location FFFF0 (in hexadecimal). In most 8088-based microcomputers, this memory location contains a JMP (Jump) instruction to transfer control to a procedure that initializes and starts up the microcomputer.

Interrupt Vectors. Interrupt vectors are the means to identify the interrupt services procedure in the computer memory that will service the interrupt request. Each external interrupt request can be assigned an

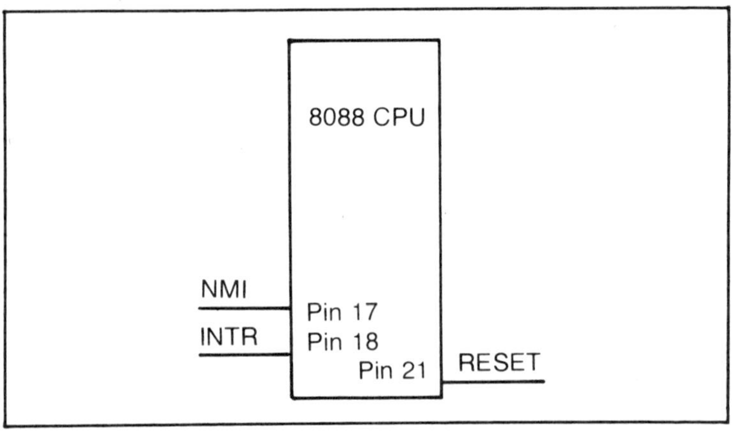

Fig. 2-38. Interrupt lines of the 8088 CPU.

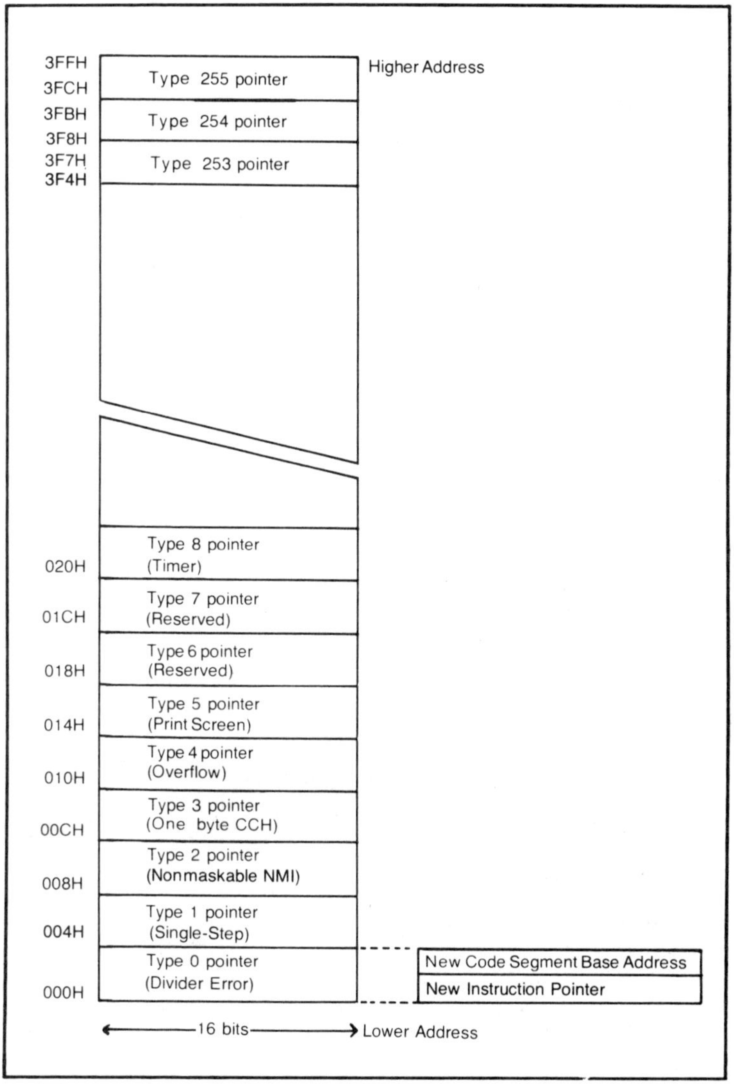

Fig. 2-39. Interrupt vector table on the IBM Personal Computer.

interrupt type code from 0 to 255 (in decimal). Thus, there are 256 interrupt vectors in an 8088-based microcomputer; one vector for each interrupt type. The interrupt vector table, as shown in Fig. 2-39, occupies 1024 bytes of low memory from the physical address 0 to 03FFH, since there may be up to 256 vectors or entries in the table.

Each entry in the interrupt vector table is a doubleword pointer containing the starting adaress of the procedure that provides service to the interrupt request of that type. The higher-addressed 16-bit word in each entry of the table contains the base address of the segment containing the procedure. The lower-addressed 16-bit word in each entry of the table contains the offset address of the service procedure within this segment. Since each entry in the table is four bytes long, the starting location of the entry for a given interrupt type can be calculated by simply multiplying the interrupt type by 4 (TYPE × 4).

Maskable Interrupts. Maskable interrupts are external requests that arrive on the INTR line of the microprocessor. Most external hardware devices synchronize with the CPU by generating maskable interrupts. When the INTR line is active, the microprocessor takes different actions depending upon the state of the Interrupt-Enable Flag. The currently executing machine instruction is always carried out to completion before any response can be given to the interrupt.

If the Interrupt-Enable Flag is 0 (interrupt is disabled), the maskable interrupt request is ignored and the CPU continues executing the next instruction of its current program. If the Interrupt-Enable Flag is 1 (interrupt is enabled), the microprocessor acknowledges the interrupt request and transfers control to an interrupt service procedure so that the interrupt request can be serviced. The 8088 CPU automatically performs the following predefined sequence of operations to respond to a maskable interrupt request:

1. An external interrupt acknowledge signal is generated. This signal tells the external hardware device that its request is honored.
2. An interrupt type code (0 to 255) is read from the data bus. The interrupt type code is placed on the data bus by the external hardware device.
3. The Processor Flag is pushed on the current top of stack as defined by the SS and SP register.
4. The Interrupt-Enable Flag, IF, is cleared to 0. This will prevent any further maskable interrupts.
5. The Trap Flag, TF, is cleared to 0 to disable single-stepping mode.
6. The contents of the Instruction Pointer, IP, are replaced by the 16-bit word at the physical byte memory locations (TYPE × 4) and (TYPE × 4) + 1 where TYPE is the interrupt type code.
7. The contents of the Code Segment, CS, register are replaced by the 16-bit word at the physical byte memory locations (TYPE × 4) + 2 and (TYPE × 4) + 3.

After steps 6 and 7 are completed, control is transferred to an interrupt service procedure that contains the necessary machine instructions to service the maskable interrupt request. The service procedure can use the instruction STI (Set Interrupt) to set the Interrupt-Enable Flag to 1 to allow further INTR requests.

Nonmaskable Interrupts. Nonmaskable interrupts are external requests that arrive on the NMI line of the microprocessor. This interrupt is normally used to signal the CPU of an extremely important external event (catastrophic in nature), such as the loss of system power, memory parity error detection, etc. Nonmaskable interrupts are always recognized by the microprocessor regardless of the status of the Interrupt-Enable Flag. Thus, nonmaskable interrupts have higher priority than interrupt requests arriving on the INTR line of the CPU. Nonmaskable interrupts are predefined as type 2. The 8088 CPU performs the following predefined sequence of operations to respond to a nonmaskable interrupt request:

1. The Processor Flag is pushed on the current top of stack as defined by the SS and SP register.
2. The Interrupt-Enable Flag, IF, is cleared to 0. This results in disabling all maskable interrupts.
3. The Trap Flag, TF, is cleared to 0 to disable single-stepping mode.
4. The contents of the Code Segment, CS, register are pushed on the stack.
5. The contents of the Instruction Pointer, IP, are pushed on the stack.
6. The 16-bit word at the physical memory location 00008H replaces the contents of the IP register.
7. The 16-bit word at the physical memory location 0000AH replaces the contents of the CS register.

After steps 6 and 7 are completed, control is transferred to an interrupt service procedure that contains the necessary machine instructions to perform the operations as required by the NMI request.

Internal Interrupts

Internal interrupts can be generated by application programs by using the INT instruction (see Chapter 4). These interrupts are also automatically generated by the microprocessor depending on certain conditions such as divide error, calculation overflow, etc. These interrupts function in exactly the same manner as the INTR requests. However, unlike the INTR requests to the microprocessor, these internal interrupts are always honored by the CPU regardless of the status of the Interrupt-Enable Flag, IF.

The interrupt type code of an internal interrupt is either predefined or can be coded as a part of the machine instruction. If the interrupt type is coded with the instruction, the internal interrupts are known as software interrupts. Since any type of code may be specified, software interrupts are very useful to test interrupt procedures written to service external hardware devices.

In the IBM Personal Computer, software interrupts are used to access facilities provided by the Basic Input/Output System (BIOS) software. For example, the instruction INT 16H (see Chapter 4) can be used to read a character from the computer's keyboard buffer. Figure 2-39 shows the interrupt vector table as implemented in the IBM Personal Computer.

Interrupt on Divide Error. The 8088 microprocessor automatically generates a type 0 interrupt immediately following the execution of a DIV (Divide) or IDIV (Integer Divide) instruction if the following conditions are met:

1. The divisor is 0.

2. The quotient result is larger than 8 bits as a result of an 8-bit division or larger than 16 bits as a result of a 16-bit division.

The address of the interrupt service procedure for a type 0 interrupt must be specified at the physical memory addresses 00000H to 00003H, as shown in Fig. 2-39.

Interrupt on Overflow. If the Overflow Flag of the Processor Flag is set to 1, executing an INTO (Interrupt If Overflow) instruction generates a type 4 interrupt immediately after the execution of INTO is completed. The address of the interrupt service procedure for a type 4 interrupt must be specified at the physical memory addresses 00010H to 00013H, as shown in Fig. 2-39.

Breakpoint Interrupt. Breakpoint interrupts are used primarily for program debugging during the development and testing of new software. The microprocessor generates a type 3 interrupt immediately upon completion of execution of the instruction INT 3 (CCH). The machine code CC (in hexadecimal) is used as a breakpoint. It can be placed at any point in the program where normal execution is stopped at the point so that crucial information such as the CPU registers and memory locations can be displayed by a breakpoint interrupt service procedure. Since the smallest 8088 instruction object code is one byte long, the machine code CCH can replace any 8088 instruction as a means of setting breakpoints.

Single-Step Interrupt. If the Trap Flag of the Processor Flag is set to 1, the single-step interrupt is generated immediately after executing an instruction. This interrupt is predefined as type 1 and is used primarily to execute programs one instruction at a time. After each program instruction is executed, a type 1 interrupt is automatically generated. When the interrupt is generated, the microprocessor automatically pushes the contents of the Processor Flag (in which the Trap Flag is 1) onto the stack and clears the Trap Flag and the Interrupt-Enable Flag to 0. Thus, the CPU is not in single-stepping mode upon entry of the interrupt service procedure. The service procedure can run normally to provide various diagnostic capabilities such as displaying the contents of CPU registers and certain memory locations, etc. The last machine instruction in the interrupt service procedure must be an IRET (Return From Interrupt) instruction. This will restore the previous Flag in which the Trap Flag is 1 and another type 1 interrupt is generated on the completion of the next instruction.

The 8088 microprocessor does not have instructions that can directly modify the status of the Trap Flag. However, the Processor Flag can be pushed onto the stack and the Trap Flag can be changed by modifying the flag-image on the stack. Instructions such as PUSHF (Push Flag On Stack) and POPF (Pop Flag From Stack) can then be used to initiate single-step mode.

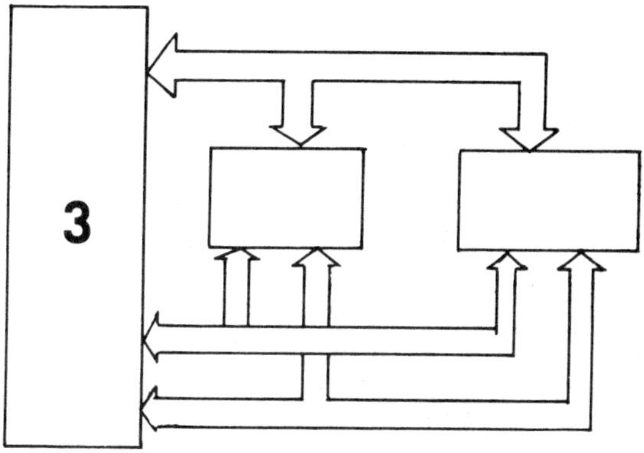

8088 Assembly Language

The 8088 assembly language is the machine language of the 8088 microprocessor written in a symbolic form. While addresses and instructions in actual machine language are numeric, assembly language allows alphabetic names to be assigned to memory addresses. In addition, unique mnemonics can be used to specify the desired machine instructions. Since the execution units of the 8086 and 8088 microprocessors are identical, 8088 assembly language is identical to 8086 assembly language. It is also a subset of the assembly language of the 80186 and 80286 microprocessors (improved versions of the 8086 CPU).

This chapter introduces the reader to the basic concepts of assembly language programming. The general format of 8086/8088 assembly language statements and the required forms of operands representing the various addressing modes are also covered. A program written in 8088 assembly language can be translated into its correct representations in the machine language by a computer program called an assembler. The assembler used throughout this book is the Microsoft Macro Assembler which runs on the IBM Personal Computer under the PC-DOS disk operating system.

There are several other assemblers available for the 8086/8088 microprocessor family. For example, the ASM-86 Assembler developed by Intel Corporation that supports standard 8086/8088 instruction mnemonics as well as floating-point instructions to the 8087 Numeric Data Processor. Even though minor differences exist among these assemblers, the structure and format of the assembly language supported by these programs are compatible in most ways. Thus, most of the subjects covered in this chapter may apply to all commercially available assemblers developed for the 8086/8088 microprocessor family.

Chapter 4 contains a complete description of each individual instruction provided by 8088 microprocessor. The use of these instructions will be discussed in the context of an assembly language program since the programs in this book are written in assembly language instead of machine language. You must try to visualize the formats of the machine language instructions as they are translated by the assembler from each assembly language statement. This is extremely important if you want to fully understand the storage organization and addressing architecture of the 8086/8088 microprocessor family.

WHY ASSEMBLY LANGUAGE?

It is extremely tedious, awkward, and sometimes difficult to write computer programs directly in machine language. A computer programmer must perform many clerical activities if he writes programs in machine language directly. The programmer must keep track of various locations in the microcomputer memory to store instructions or program data so that he can refer to or specify these memory addresses correctly later in the program. He must memorize the actual machine instructions either in binary or hexadecimal code and their associated addressing modes as required by the microprocessor. All program data must also be converted into the binary format so that they can be included in the machine language program. This process obviously can result in many clerical errors.

Assembly language is a symbolic way of writing machine language. For example, the machine instruction codes 3C02 (in hexadecimal) can be written in a symbolic form in assembly language such as CMP AL,02 (this instruction compares the contents of the AL register to the hexadecimal number 02). Thus, the clerical functions of converting machine codes and program data as mentioned previously should be delegated, as much as possible, to the assembler. After all, the principal purpose of an assembler is to translate programs written in assembly language into the machine language.

The assembler also keeps track of the memory locations used, so that instructions in the program can refer to these addresses symbolically, using names or labels suggestive of the actual meaning in the problem the program is being written for. For instance, the machine code in hexadecimal notation C606001201 can be written in assembly language as MOV BYTE_COUNT,01 where BYTE_COUNT is the symbolic name of the memory address 1200H.

The assembler also allows constants or program data to be specified symbolically. The length of the storage area in the microcomputer memory required by the constants or program data may be specified. The assembler performs all necessary conversions of the constants or program data to appropriate binary representations, calculates the correct numbers of bytes or words required for storage, and keeps a table of names or labels and their corresponding addresses.

In assembly language, a programmer can write a procedure (subroutine) as an independent and completely separate module. The assembler generates the necessary linkage information so that when the object module of the procedure is loaded into the microcomputer memory for execution, it can be linked to other object modules kept in separate libraries. These difficult and complex tasks of finding procedures and filling in the proper linkages between calling and called procedures can be performed in a standard fashion from the information generated by the assembler.

Modification of programs written in assembly language is much easier than modification of programs written directly in machine language. For instance, insertion of instructions can change the allocation of memory addresses of operands or program data after the point of insertion. If the program is written directly in machine language, the programmer must change all addresses of operands or program data that are affected. This is a very tedious and time-consuming task that can very likely produce errors. If the insertion is made in an assembly language program, the assembler automatically reassigns all memory addresses of operands and program data according to the new structure and allocation of the modified program. Therefore, many potential mistakes can be avoided.

The assembler can produce a listing of the source program which contains the original assembly language statements, the corresponding machine language instructions or data generated, and diagnostic and/or error messages that may be generated during the translation process. Therefore, many programming or clerical errors can be detected early in the assembly process. The listing of the programs contains symbols, names, or labels which symbolically represent the memory addresses, constants, or program data. This listing can serve as an invaluable tool to help the analysis and correction of logical errors that may occur during the debugging process of the program.

PROGRAM FORMAT

In general, each statement of an assembly language program is translated to one machine instruction. In most assembly languages, each statement has four unique fields which describe different aspects of the instruction to be translated. These fields are label, operation, operands, and comments. Each field is variable in length and must be separated by one or more blanks.

The first field is used to specify the name and symbol of the location containing the instruction, constant, or data area. The address of this location is kept in a table and used by the assembler so that later instructions can make references to this name or symbol. If no symbol is desired, the label field may be left blank.

The second field is the operation field. This field is required and must be specified in each assembly language statement. The operation must always be given symbolically and its functions may be one of the following:

1. Machine instructions to the 8088 microprocessor.

2. Directive statements.
3. Macro.

Instructions to the microprocessor comprise most of the codes in an assembly language program. An optional prefix instruction may also be present in the operation field. For instance, the instruction STOSB (Store String Byte) may have an instruction prefix REP (Repeat). In this case, REP STOSB can be coded together in the operation field of a single assembly language statement.

Directive statements represent other types of operations which are provided to support the assembler in the process of generating actual machine codes that can be executed by the microprocessor. Operations to define constants or character strings such as DB (Define Bytes) or DW (Define Words) supply information to the assembler to allocate appropriate memory storage for the types of constants or character strings specified. Operations such as PROC (Procedure Definition), SEGMENT (Segment Definition), ENDP (End Procedure), or ENDS (Ends Segment) are used to tell the assembler the starting and ending points of a procedure or a program segment.

These operations are called *directives* or *pseudo-opcodes* since they are used solely to supply information or directions to the assembler and will not be translated into the actual machine instructions. Some operations can also be used to direct the assembler to take certain options such as generating a program listing with references to program addresses and symbols.

Finally, a *macro* is another form of a directive statement that will be expanded into one or more assembly language statements according to some predefined patterns.

The third field contains the operands required by the machine instruction specified in the operation field. The operands within the operand field are separated by commas. In 8088-based microcomputers, if two operands are specified, the first operand is always the destination operand, and the second operand is the source operand.

The first operand may be a general register, a segment register, or a memory location. The second operand may be a general register, a segment register, a memory location, or a constant value. Operands can be an 8-bit or a 16-bit quantity. The name of a segment register can be used as a segment prefix (see the Addressing Mode section in this chapter) to force the offset address in the operand field to be taken relative to the segment specified in the segment prefix. Valid segment prefixes are CS, DS, ES, SS to indicate the code segment, data segment, extra segment, and stack segment, respectively.

The fourth field is the comment field. This field does not participate in the translation process during the assembly of the program. Comment fields are simply ignored by the assembler. The comments in the fourth field, however, are reproduced in the program listing so that they can help to document and explain the program. The comment field is an assembly language statement must begin with a semicolon (;). The entire line is treated as a comment if the first character is a semicolon.

In summary, an assembly language statement is generally written in the following form. The fields in parentheses are optional.

(Label) (Prefix) Operation (Segment Prefix) (Operands) (Comments)

Figure 3-1 shows an example of typical 8088 assembly language statements. These examples clearly show that the requirements of 8088 assembly language syntax is not as rigid as most assembly languages of minicomputers and mainframe computers. Blanks may be inserted freely within each field so that the program is more readable.

A statement does not have to begin on the first character position of the line. However, the maximum number of characters per line is limited to 132 columns. Labels and symbols can be up to 31 characters long which may include the alphabetic letters in both upper and lower case, the numeric digits 0 to 9, and the following special symbols: ? (question mark), @ (at sign), _ (underscore), $ (dollar sign), and . (period).

Fixed-Point Constants

The Macro Assembler recognizes fixed-point values or constants in binary, octal, decimal, or hexadecimal notation. Fixed-point constants must be integers and must be representable in 16 bits. Thus, a whole-number constant must be any non-fractional number between 0 and 65535. If a negative number is specified, the Macro Assembler will translate it into standard two's complement notation. The integer constant can also be coded in decimal or in other radix notation. A letter B, Q, or H is appended to the last digit of the number to indicate the number is in binary, octal, or hexadecimal notation, respectively. Octal numbers may also be ended with the letter O instead of Q. A decimal number can also have the letter D appended to the last digit of the number for program clarity in certain cases. If the hexadecimal notation is used, the first digit of the constant must be a numeric digit between 0 and 9. Examples of constants in 8088 assembly language are 100, 1257D, 11011B, 77Q, 1670, 4B5H, and 1FFFEH.

Character Constants

Any character including letters of the alphabet, numeric digits, and special symbols of the ASCII character set can be treated as a character constant. A character string of up to 255 characters long can be put in single quotes to initialize certain storage area in the computer memory. The Macro Assembler will store the appropriate ASCII value corresponding to each character of the string in the allocated storage area. When character constants are used as immediate operands, they must be one or two bytes long depending on the byte or word operation of the instruction, respec-

```
; This statement is treated as a comment line.
     MOV  DX,[BX]        ;Indirect Addressing Mode.
     MOV  AX,    [SI]    ;Blanks may be inserted freely in a statement.
NEXT_LINE:     CLC       ;The label of this statement is NEXT_LINE.
     REP  STOSB          ;Operation with a prefix.
     MOV  ES:[BX+2],AL   ;Operands may contain a segment prefix.
     MOV  AX,[BX+SI]     ;Based Indexed Addressing.
ZERO      DW 0           ;Directive DW (Define Word).
SPECIAL$  Dw 1234h       ;Upper and lower case characters and special symbols.
```

Fig. 3-1. Statements in 8088 assembly language.

tively. For example, the instruction CMP AX, 'AB' is translated into the hexadecimal sequence 3D4241 in the machine language. Since this is a 16-bit operation, the character constant must be two bytes long.

Floating-Point Constants

The 8088 microprocessor does not have any hardware floating-point instructions. However in 8088 assembly language, floating-point numbers can be specified in standard floating-point notations or scientific notations (with exponents). Examples of floating-point constants are 123.45 and 27.25E-2. The Macro Assembler converts these values to binary to be used with other floating-point processors such as the 8087 Numeric Data Processor.

Data Definition and Storage Allocation

There are several directive statements that can direct the Macro Assembler to allocate memory storage and initialize the allocated space with fixed-point constants, characters, or floating-point numbers. The storage can also be allocated without any value to be put in its space. Directives for data definition or storage allocation are DB (Define Byte), DW (Define Word), DD (Define Doubleword), DQ (Define Quadword), and DT (Define Tenbyte). Figure 3-2 shows an example of how these directives are used to allocate and initialize data storage locations in 8088 assembly language. A question mark (?) in the operand field indicates that the location is for allocation purposes only and not to be initialized with any specific value. The DUP parameter may be present in the operand field to perform repetition of the same initialized value.

Addressing Modes

The Macro Assembler supports all addressing modes of the 8088 microprocessor. It generates the correct form of machine instructions based upon the information specified in the instruction operands. The assembler also performs verification on the consistency of the use of instruction operands to catch possible clerical errors in program coding. For example, an error message is produced if an addition is performed between an 8-bit register and a 16-bit register, or an operation between a segment register and a constant. The assembler also attempts to generate optimal codes in certain situations. For instance, if a constant or displacement value is used in the operands, the assembler can calculate the required number of bytes of storage to accommodate the specified constant or displacement value.

In 8088 assembly language, any bracketed reference to the base registers (BX or BP) or the index registers (SI or DI) is interpreted to be one of the indirect addressing or based indexed addressing modes, as discussed earlier (indirect addressing, indirect addressing with displacement, based indexed addressing, or based indexed addressing with dis-

```
Offset   Machine                 8088 Assembly Language Statements
Address  Codes

0000  0A                ALPHA   DB   10                    ;One Byte Contains 0AH

0001  17                BETA    DB   17H                   ;One Byte Contains 17H

0002  00 0A 13 2F 43    GAMMA   DB   0,10D,23Q,2FH,'C'     ;Five Bytes.

0007  ??                DELTA   DB   ?                     ;Not Initialized.

0008  20 20 20 20 20    EPSI    DB   10 DUP (20H)          ;Ten "20H".
      20 20 20 20 20

0012  64 00             ONE     DW   100                   ;Two Bytes.

0014  7F 00             TWO     DW   177Q                  ;Two Bytes.

0016  00 00 FA 04 2E    THREE   DW   0,1274,0F2EH,'NO'     ;Eight bytes.
      0F 4F 4E
```

```
001E  41 42 43 44 41  FOUR   DB  3 DUP ('ABCD')       ;Twelve Bytes.
      42 43 44 41 42
      43 44
002A  00 40 B5 04     DOUBLE DD  04B54000H            ;Four Bytes.
002E  19 04 1E 81     FLOAT  DD  1.2345               ;Floating-Point Notation
0032  68 45 00 12 00  QUAD   DQ  12004568H            ;Eight Bytes.
      00 00 00
003A  00 00 00 00 00  TEN    DT  1234567890           ;Ten Bytes.
      12 34 56 78 90
```

Fig. 3-2. Data definition and storage allocation.

placement). The effective address, EA, of a memory operand in each case is constructed accordingly by the assembler. The following cases illustrate typical program coding for accessing registers and memory operands in 8088 assembly language as supported by the Macro Assembler.

1. Register operands which can be any 8-bit registers (AL, BL, CL, DL, AH, BH, CH, DH) or 16-bit registers (AX, BX, CX, DX, SI, DI, BP, SP, CS, DS, ES, SS) may be specified, as shown in Fig. 3-3.

2. Immediate operands in the forms of fixed-point constants may be specified in binary, octal, decimal, hexadecimal representation, or even in the form of a character string, as shown in Fig. 3-4. The assembler generates one or two bytes of storage for the constant to match the length of the destination operand.

3. In 8088 assembly language, a meaningful name suggestive of the problem for which the program is written is normally used as a label or a symbolic name to specify a memory location in the 8088 megabyte memory space. The assembler keeps all of these labels or symbolic names of memory locations which may be defined or referenced in an assembly language program in a symbol table.

Each symbol has at least three attributes to identify the unique memory location that it represents. These attributes are segment, offset, and type. The segment attribute identifies a 64 K-byte segment area of memory that contains the referenced location. This segment can be one of the four segments addressed by the CS, DS, ES, or SS registers. The offset attribute describes the offset address of the referenced memory location relative to the starting address of the segment which is defined by the segment attribute. The type attribute normally indicates the allocation of memory storage at an offset address.

For example, the type may have a numeric value of 1, 2, or 4 to indicate the allocation of a byte, word, or doubleword, at a referenced memory location. The type attribute also indicates if the label or symbolic name corresponding to a memory location is to be defined in the current program only (local symbol), to be defined in other procedures (external symbol), or to be known to all programs and procedures (public symbol).

In many assembly language programs, the definition of a label or symbolic name is usually deferred until the very end of a program. If an instruction operand uses a label or a symbolic name before its definition, the type of the symbolic name must be explicitly given to the assembler (because the type of the symbol is not yet defined, the assembler does not know if the instruction requires an 8-bit or a 16-bit operation to generate appropriate machine codes). The Macro Assembler provides the operators BYTE PTR, WORD PTR, and DWORD PTR to tell the assembler precisely whether the storage allocation of the referenced symbolic name is a byte, word, or doubleword.

In the direct addressing mode, a symbolic name representing a memory location is translated to a 16-bit offset address to form the displacement

```
Offset    Machine     8088 Assembly Language Statements
Address   Codes
0000      02 C3       ADD  AL,BL    ; 8-bit Source And Destination Operands.
0002      2B C2       SUB  AX,DX    ; 16-bit Source And Destination Operands.
0004      33 C9       XOR  CX,CX    ; Same Source And Destination Operands.
0006      8C D8       MOV  AX,DS    ; Source Operand Is A Segment Register.
0008      8E C1       MOV  ES,CX    ; Destination Operand Is A Segment Register.
000A      FE CB       DEC  BL       ; 8-Bit Operand.
000C      48          DEC  AX       ; 16-Bit Operand.
000D      06          PUSH ES       ; Operand Is A Segment Register.
```

Fig. 3-3. Coding examples of register operands.

```
Offset   Machine        8088 Assembly Language Statements
Address  Codes
0000     04 0C          ADD  AL,12     ;8-Bit Decimal Constant.

0002     B9 6E 00       MOV  CX,110    ;16-Bit Decimal Constant.

0005     3D FB FF       CMP  AX,-5     ;Decimal Notation.

0008     BA FA FF       MOV  DX,-6D    ;Decimal Alternate.

000B     0D 0D 00       OR   AX,1101B  ;Binary Notation.

000E     81 CD 2F 00    OR   BP,057Q   ;Octal Notation.

0012     B3 0C          MOV  BL,140    ;Octal Alternate.

0014     BB FF 0E       MOV  BX,0EFFH  ;Hexadecimal Notation.

0017     3C 41          CMP  AL,'A'    ;8-Bit Character Constant.

0019     81 F9 42 41    CMP  CX,'AB'   ;16-Bit Character Constant.
```

Fig. 3-4. Coding examples of immediate operands.

field of the instruction. This offset address is always taken relative to the data segment whose base address is defined by the DS register. However, it is perfectly possible to instruct the assembler to generate a segment prefix code so that the offset address can be taken relative to the code segment, extra segment, or stack segment.

Figure 3-5 contains some typical coding examples using the direct addressing mode in 8088 assembly language.

When the instruction of an assembly language statement is a conditional or an unconditional jump instruction, the effective address of the label or symbolic name specified in the operands will be used to generate the correct displacement as required in the relative addressing mode, or to generate a 32-bit physical address pointer as required in the absolute addressing mode. Figure 3-6 shows some coding examples of jump instructions.

4. The Macro Assembler fully supports the indirect addressing mode and the based indexed addressing mode with or without displacement. If the BP register is used, the effective address is always taken relative to the stack segment in the computer memory. Otherwise, the effective address is taken relative to the data segment. A segment prefix can be specified as a part of the instruction operands so that the effective memory address can be reassigned to any one of four memory segments. The assembly language coding of operands in this group of addressing modes is very flexible, as shown in Fig. 3-7.

A symbolic name can also be used to represent a displacement value in the operands. In many cases, if the instruction operands do not expressly define whether an 8-bit operation or a 16-bit operation is to be performed, operators such as BYTE PTR or WORD PTR must be explicitly given to the assembler.

5. String instructions such as LODS (Load String), STOS (Store String), MOVS (Move String), CMPS (Compare String), or SCAS (Scan String) do not explicitly indicate whether the string operations are performed in bytes or words. In 8088 assembly language, the letter B (Bytes) or W(Words) is appended to the mnemonic of a string instruction to tell the assembler the type of operation of the instruction so that machine codes can be generated correctly. Several coding examples using string instructions are shown in Fig. 3-8.

A prefix instruction such as LOCK (Lock The Bus), REP (Repeat), REPE (Repeat While Equal), or REPNE (Repeat While Not Equal) can be coded with a string instruction in one single assembly language statement (see Chapter 4 for a complete description of these instructions). A segment prefix can also be specified with any string instructions, except STOS, to override the default data segment containing the memory location addressed by the SI register. In the special case of the string instruction STOS, the offset address specified by the DI register is always taken relative to the extra segment.

```
Offset    Machine
Address   Codes                  8088 Assembly Language Statements

0000                         EXTRN  NEW:WORD    ;NEW Is A 16-Bit External Symbol.
0000   ??                    ALPHA   DB  ?      ;ALPHA Is An 8-Bit Local Symbol.
0001   ?? ??                 BETA    DW  ?      ;BETA Is A 16-Bit Local Symbol.
0003   C6 06 00 00 7B        MOV ALPHA,123      ;Byte Operation.
0008   C7 06 01 00 00 00     MOV BETA,OH        ;Word Operation.
000E   C6 06 2F 00 F4        MOV BYTE PTR GAMMA,-12   ;Specify Type For GAMMA.
```

```
0013  C7 06 30 00 78 12    MOV WORD PTR DELTA,1278H ;Specify Type For DELTA.
0019  2E C7 06 -- -- 01 00 MOV WORD PTR CS:NEW,01   ;Segment Prefix is CS.
0020  26 C7 06 -- -- 01 00 MOV WORD PTR ES:NEW,01   ;Segment Prefix is ES.
0027  36 C7 06 -- -- 01 00 MOV WORD PTR SS:NEW,01   ;Segment Prefix is SS.
002E  C3                   RET
002F  ??                   GAMMA   DB  ?            ;GAMMA Is An 8-Bit Local Symbol.
0030  ?? ??                DELTA   DW  ?            ;DELTA Is A 16-Bit Local Symbol.
```

Fig. 3-5. Coding examples using the direct addressing modes.

```
Offset  Machine          8088 Assembly Language Statements
Address Codes

0000                     EXTRN FAR_PROC:FAR       ;Name Of A FAR Procedure.

0000                     EXTRN NEXT_SYMBOL:WORD

0000    74 0D            JE    NEXT_LINE          ;Relative Addressing.

0002    EB 0C            JMP SHORT NEXT_CHAR      ;Relative Addressing.

0004    EA -- -- -- --   JMP FAR PTR NEXT_SYMBOL ;Absolute Addressing.

0009    9A -- -- -- --   CALL  FAR_PROC           ;Absolute Addressing.

000E    C3               RET

000F    90               NEXT_LINE: NOP

0010    90               NEXT_CHAR: NOP
```

Fig. 3-6. Coding examples using the relative addressing mode and the absolute addressing mode.

```
Offset   Machine        8088 Assembly Language Statements
Address  Codes
0000     02 17          ADD DL,[BX]        ;Indirect Addressing Using BX.

0002     13 47 02       ADC AX,[BX+02]     ;Indirect Addressing With 8-bit Displacement.

0005     3B 9C 21 00    CMP BX,FLAG[SI]    ;Indirect Addressing With 16-bit Displacement.

0009     C6 04 02       MOV BYTE PTR [SI],02 ;Indirect Addressing Using SI.

000C     26 F7 15       NOT WORD PTR ES:[DI] ;Indirect Addressing With Segment Prefix.

000F     8B 6E 02       MOV BP,[BP+02]     ;Indirect Addressing Using BP.

0012     0A 46 00       OR  AL,[BP]        ;Indirect Addressing With Displacement Using BP.

0015     02 30          ADD DH,[BX+SI]     ;Based Indexed Addressing.

0017     84 0B          TEST [BP+DI],CL ;Based Indexed Addressing.

0019     36 80 21 01    AND BYTE PTR SS:[BX+DI],01 ;Based Indexed Addressing With Segment Prefix

001D     22 80 47 12    AND AL,[BX+SI+1247H] ;Based Indexed Addressing With Displacement.

0021     90             FLAG: NOP
```

Fig. 3-7. Coding examples of the indirect addressing and the based indexed addressing modes.

Offset Address	Machine Codes	8088 Assembly Language Statements
0000	AC	LODSB ;Load String (Byte).
0001	AD	LODSW ;Load String (Word).
0002	A4	MOVSB ;Move String (Byte).
0003	A5	MOVSW ;Move String (Word).
0004	AA	STOSB ;Store String (Byte).
0005	AB	STOSW ;Store String (Word).
0006	F3/AB	REP STOSW ;String instruction with REP prefix.
0008	F3/A6	REPE CMPSB ;String instruction with REPE prefix.
000A	F2/AF	REPNE SCASW ;String instruction with REPNE prefix.

Fig. 3-8. Coding examples of string addressing.

Segments and Procedures

A program written in 8088 assembly language may be organized into one or more logical segments. Each logical segment must have a unique name and is eventually mapped into the 8088 memory segments when the program is loaded for execution. The Macro Assembler provides the directive SEGMENT and ENDS (End Segment) to define the starting and ending location of a logical segment. Instructions and/or data coded between the SEGMENT and ENDS directives form a logical segment of a program.

A well designed and documented assembly language program should be divided into several different segments. Program codes to solve a specific problem should be grouped into a segment which can be considered as the code segment of the program. Program variables, constants, tables, or data should be grouped into a second segment which is equivalent to the data segment of the program. Stack space for temporary data or procedure communications should be allocated into a third segment. A fourth segment should be used for storing output data of the program which can be viewed as the extra segment of the program.

Figure 3-9 shows a typical 8088 assembly language program that contains four logical segments. The ASSUME directive is used to tell the assembler which segment register a segment belongs to. It is also possible to write a complete program in one segment only. If this is done, all four segments addressed by the segment registers are completely overlapped since the segment registers contain the same base address.

Figure 3-10 shows an example of an assembly language program coded completely in only one segment. In this example, the ASSUME directive tells the assembler that all segment registers address the same segment.

It is sometimes difficult to write or maintain large assembly language programs. For the sake of program clarity and documentation, large logical segments in a program should be broken into as many smaller logical procedures as possible. A procedure should reflect the part of codes in a segment that is used to perform an independent or specific function. A sequence of codes that is repetitively invoked by CALL instructions should be grouped into a procedure. A block of data that has some important meanings to the application program should also be grouped into a procedure with some meaningful names so that the program can be easier to comprehend.

The Macro Assembler provides the directives PROC (Procedures) and ENDP (End Procedures) to indicate the starting and ending location of a procedure. The parameter FAR or NEAR can be specified with the directive PROC so that the assembler can keep track of whether the procedure is considered to be intersegment or intrasegment, as shown in Fig. 3-11.

COMMON ERRORS

This section presents some common errors along with coding exam-

```
;
; The following program has four logical segments:
; The code segment has the symbolic name MAIN.
; The data segment has the symbolic name DATA_SEG.
; The extra segment has the symbolic name EXTRA_SEG.
; The stack segment has the symbolic name STACK_SEG.
;
MAIN    SEGMENT
        ASSUME  CS:MAIN,DS:DATA_SEG,ES:EXTRA_SEG,SS
                  :STACK_SEG
;
; This is the beginning of the program.
;
        MOV AX,DATA_SEG
        MOV DS,AX
        MOV AX,EXTRA_SEG
        MOV ES,AX
        MOV AX,STACK_SEG
        MOV SS,AX
        MOV SP,OFFSET TOP_OF_STACK
;
; Codes of the main program should be written in
  this area.
;
```

```
MAIN    ENDS
;
; Beginning of the Data Segment.
;
DATA_SEG SEGMENT BYTE
        DB 25 DUP(0)
DATA_SEG ENDS
;
; Beginning of the Extra Segment.
;
EXTRA_SEG SEGMENT
DATA_AREA DB 2000 DUP(0)
EXTRA_SEG ENDS
;
; Following is the Stack Segment.
;
STACK_SEG SEGMENT
        DB 64 DUP('STACK   ')
TOP_OF_STACK DW ?
STACK_SEG ENDS
        END
```

Fig. 3-9. A 8088 assembly language program with four logical segments.

```
MAIN    SEGMENT
        ASSUME  CS:MAIN,DS:MAIN,ES:MAIN,SS:MAIN
        MOV     AX,CS
        MOV     DS,AX   ;Overlap Data Segment and Code Segment.
        MOV     ES,AX   ;Overlap Extra Segment and Code Segment.
        MOV     SS,AX   ;Overalp Stack Segment and Code Segment.
        LEA     SP,TOP_OF_STACK
;
; Program codes should go here.
;
 DW 256 DUP(0)          ;Stack Area.
TOP_OF_STACK DW 0
MAIN    ENDS
```

Fig. 3-10. A 8088 assembly language program with one logical segment.

ples of incorrect 8088 assembly language programming. These are not logical errors but consist principally of an incorrect sequence of instructions. Furthermore, misspelling errors are commonplace in program coding that can sometimes cause serious problems in the assembly process.

Open Procedure or Open Segment

For each PROC (Procedure Definition) directive, there must be a corresponding ENDP (End Procedure) directive. If the ENDP directive is missing or the name of the procedure on the ENDP statement is coded incorrectly, the Macro Assembler generates a message to warn the programmer that the procedure is not closed properly. Similarly, an ENDS (End Segment) directive must be specified for each SEGMENT (Segment Definition) directive in an assembly language program. If the ENDS statement is missing or the segment name on the ENDS statement is incorrect, a warning message is generated indicating that the segment is open. A misspelled segment name or procedure name is most likely the cause of this error.

```
SAMPLE   SEGMENT
PROC1    PROC     NEAR
         AND      AL,00
         RET
PROC     ENDP
PROC2    PROC     NEAR
         OR       AL,OFFH
         RET
PROC2    ENDP
         END
```

Incorrect codes.

a) No corresponding ENDP statement for procedure PROC1 (The name PROC1 on the ENDP statement is misspelled).

b) No corresponding ENDS statement.

The following is a corrected version of the previous example.

```
SAMPLE   SEGMENT
PROC1    PROC     NEAR
         AND      AL,00
         RET
PROC1    ENDP
```

```
MAIN SEGMENT

ASSUME CS:MAIN,DS:NOTHING,ES:NOTHING,SS:NOTHING

;

; The procedure CONVERSION contains three other
  procedures

; CONASC1, CONASC2, and CONVERT to perform the
  conversion of

; a hexadecimal number into its ASCII
  representation.

; All of these procedures are defined in the
  segment MAIN.

;

CONVERSION PROC NEAR

;

; First Procedure CONASC1

;

CONASC1 PROC NEAR

        MOV  AH,AL    ;Convert contents Of AL into 2
        Ascii Bytes.

        CALL CONVERT

        XCHG AL,AH

        MOV  CL,4

        SHR  AL,CL

        CALL CONVERT

        RET

CONASC1 ENDP
```

```
;
; Second Procedure CONVERT
;
CONVERT PROC NEAR
        AND  AL,0FH
        CMP  AL,9
        JBE  NEXT
        ADD  AL,7
NEXT:   ADD  AL,0B0H
        RET
CONVERT ENDP
;
; Third Procedure CONASC2
;
CONASC2 PROC NEAR           ;Convert contents Of AX
                             into 4 Ascii Bytes.
        MOV  DX,AX
        CALL CONASC1
        XCHG AX,DX
        XCHG AH,AL
        CALL CONASC1
        RET
CONASC2  ENDP
CONVERSION ENDP
MAIN    ENDS
```

Fig. 3-11. Procedures in a segment.

```
SAMPLE    SEGMENT
PROC2     PROC       NEAR
          OR         AL,0FFH
          RET
PROC2     ENDP
SAMPLE    ENDS
          END
```

Undefined Symbol

An undefined symbol is one of the most common errors that frequently occur in the coding of programs. The assembler generates this error message if the symbol has not been defined in the label field of any statement in the assembly language program. If the symbol is not a local symbol (its definition is in another program), it must be declared to be an external symbol by using the directive EXTRN (External). Misspelling is most likely the cause of this error, especially in statements where a hexadecimal constant is coded without a starting numeric digit.

```
SECOND    PROC       NEAR          Incorrect Codes.
          MOV        AX,CS
          MOV        DS,AX         a) The symbol VALUE is not
          MOV        ES,AX            defined.
          MOV        AX,VALUE      b) The hexadecimal notation
          MOV        BX,FFE2H         is incorrect. The assem-
          MOV        CX,CODE1         bler assumes that FFE2H
          MOV        DX,CODE2         is a symbol.
          MOV        SI,CODE       c) The symbol CODE is not
          RET                         defined.
CODE1     DW         100
CODE2     DW         200
CODE3     DW         300
SECOND    ENDP
```

The following is a corrected version of the previous example. The symbol VALUE is declared as a 16-bit external symbol. The hexadecimal notation is coded with a starting numeric digit and the misspelled symbol CODE is changed to the correct name CODE3.

```
SECOND    PROC      NEAR
          EXTRN     VALUE:WORD
          MOV       AX,CS
          MOV       DS,AX
          MOV       ES,AX
          MOV       AX,VALUE
          MOV       BX,0FFE2H
          MOV       CX,CODE1
          MOV       DX,CODE2
          MOV       SI,CODE3
          RET
CODE1     DW        100
CODE2     DW        200
CODE3     DW        300
SECOND    ENDP
```

Redefinition of Symbol

The Macro Assembler generates a redefinition of symbol error message whenever the same symbol or label is defined in the label field of two or more statements in a program.

```
CASE1:    DEC       AX          Incorrect Codes.
          LOOP      CASE1
          AND       DX,BX
          CMP       DX,00
CASE1:    JE        CASE1       The symbol CASE1 has
                                already been defined.
```

The following is a corrected version of the previous example.

```
CASE1:    DEC     AX
          LOOP    CASE1
          AND     DX,BX
          CMP     DX,00
CASE2:    JE      CASE1
```

Execution Error Due To Incorrect Code Generation

In 8088 assembly language, it is possible to defer the definition of a label or a symbol until the very end of a program so that all symbols used in the program can be grouped together into a segment or a procedure. This coding practice makes the program easier to understand since the definition of each symbol in the program can be quickly found in a procedure or segment near the end of the program. If an instruction refers to a symbol which is defined later in the program, the type of the symbol (byte or word) must be explicitly given to the assembler so that the correct machine codes can be generated.

If no information is available to define the type of the symbol, the assembler will make some default assumptions about the symbol which may or may not be correct. This potentially causes errors to occur during the execution of the program even though there is no error during the assembling of the program, as illustrated in the following example.

```
            MOV  NEXT_COUNT,12
            ..
            Other instructions
            ..
            RET
NEXT_COUNT  DB ?
NEXT_CHECK  DB 100
```

When the assembly language statement MOV NEXT_COUNT,12 is translated into the machine codes, the symbolic name NEXT_COUNT has not been defined yet. The assembler must know whether the symbol NEXT_COUNT represents a byte memory location or a word memory location so that it can generate a correct sequence of machine codes (5 bytes of object codes are generated if the symbol NEXT_COUNT represents a byte memory location; 6 bytes, otherwise). Since there is no other information in the statement that can expressly define the type of the symbol NEXT_COUNT, the assembler assumes that NEXT_COUNT represents a word memory location (6 bytes of object codes are generated) which is incorrect in this case.

During the program execution, the statement MOV NEXT_COUNT,12 will destroy the contents of the byte memory location NEXT_CHECK. This type of error is very difficult to locate since there has been no error messages generated in the assembling of the source program. In order to make sure the type of the symbol NEXT_COUNT is defined correctly, the directive BYTE PTR must be used, as illustrated in the following corrected version of the previous example.

```
        MOV BYTE PTR NEXT_COUNT,12

        ..

        Other instructions

        ..

        RET

NEXT_COUNT   DB ?

NEXT_CHECK   DB 100
```

Illegal Use Of Registers

The following three rules must be observed when using a register as operands in an assembly language statement.

1. It is not possible to specify an 8-bit register and a 16-bit register as two operands of an instruction. The Macro Assembler generates an error message if such combination is attempted in an assembly language statement.
2. Stack operations must be performed in 16-bit quantities only. If an 8-bit register is specified with stack instructions (PUSH/POP), an error message is generated.
3. Segment registers cannot directly participate in arithmetic calculations, logical operations, or transferring of immediate data. Furthermore, segment registers may serve as source operands only or destination operands only, not both.

```
ADD        AX,DL                        Incorrect Codes.

PUSH       BL
```

```
ADD     DS,100
MOV     ES,200
MOV     SS,CS
```

a) Mixture of an 8-bit register (DL) and a 16-bit register (AX).
b) The segment register DS participates in an addition.
c) An immediate data value is transferred directly to the segment register ES.
d) Both operands are segment registers.

The following is one of the possible corrected versions of the previous example.

```
ADD     AX,DX
PUSH    BX
MOV     CX,100
ADD     DS,CX
MOV     CX,200
MOV     ES,CX
MOV     CX,CS
MOV     SS,CX
```

Relative Jump Out Of Range

All jump-on-condition instructions use the relative addressing mode with an 8-bit displacement value. If the offset address of the symbol used as the target operand of the instruction is not within +127 bytes or −128 bytes of the end of the jump-on-condition instruction an error message is generated.

```
           AND       AL,7FH
           JE        NEXT_PROC
END_PROC:  RET
DATA       DW   300 DUP(?)
NEXT_PROC:
           CLC
```

Incorrect Codes.

There are more than 127 bytes between the symbolic address NEXT_PROC and END_PROC.

The following is one way to correct the previous example.

```
            AND  AL,7FH

            JNE  END_PROC

            JMP  NEXT_PROC

END_PROC:   RET

DATA        DW   300 DUP(?)

NEXT_PROC:

            CLC
```

Incorrect Usage Of Operands

In 8088 assembly language, the first operand is always used as the destination operand which must be a general register, a segment register, or a memory location. The Macro Assembler generates an error message if an immediate data value is specified as a destination operand as illustrated in the following example.

```
CMP   3,AL          Incorrect Code.

CMP   AL,3          Correct Code.
```

MACROS

In a large assembly language program, there are certain sequences of instructions which are repeated often with some minor variations. The basic patterns of these instruction sequences are defined as macros, and the minor variations of the sequences can be constructed by supplying the appropriate parameters to the macros. During the assembling of the assembly language program, macros are expanded into actual sequences of assembly language statements. Thus macros provide a convenient way to be able to generate a given sequence of assembly language statements from various places in a program even though different parameters may be required each time the sequence is invoked. A macro is generally formed by the following elements:

1. A name entry which defines the name of the macro. After the macro is defined, it can be invoked at any place in the assembly language program as if it were a machine instruction or a pseudo-opcode.
2. An optional parameter list that contains the specific variations required each time the macro is invoked. The parameter list can have one or more parameters to be substituted in the sequence of statements that are expanded by the macro during the assembling of the program.
3. A body which defines the basic sequence of assembly language

statements that the macro generates.

4. A trailer statement that terminates the macro.

The following is a typical example of the definition of a macro:

```
SAMPLE MACRO P1,P2,P3

         MOV    AX,P1

         ADD    AX,P2

         MOV    P3,AX

         ENDM
```

The name entry of the above macro is SAMPLE. The parameter list has three arguments P1, P2, and P3. The body of the macro has three assembly language statements. The trailer statement contains ENDM (End Macro) to terminate the macro. An assembly language program invokes this macro with the following statement:

SAMPLE CASE1,TEST_LOCATION,FLAG

The Macro Assembler generates the following assembly language statements after the expansion of the macro SAMPLE:

```
MOV   AX,CASE1

ADD   AX,TEST_LOCATION

MOV   FLAG,AX
```

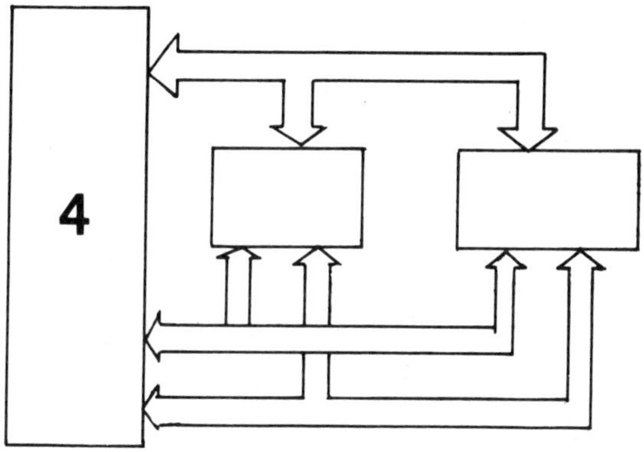

Instruction Set

This chapter gives detailed information on the 8088 instruction set. The instructions are listed alphabetically by opcodes with the opcode in boldface type.

Each instruction is defined, and its function is explained. A concise description of how the instruction works is also included. Then a typical example is given for each instruction followed by an illustration of the affected flags. Use Fig. 4-1 to interpret the abbreviations used in the affected flags section. The clock periods that are required for effective address calculation time are given in Fig. 4-2.

A decoding guide for the machine instruction is given for both hex and binary. Field bit assignments are shown in Fig. 4-3. Assembly language coding examples for each instruction are given last.

Refer to Appendix B for explanations of abbreviations used in this chapter.

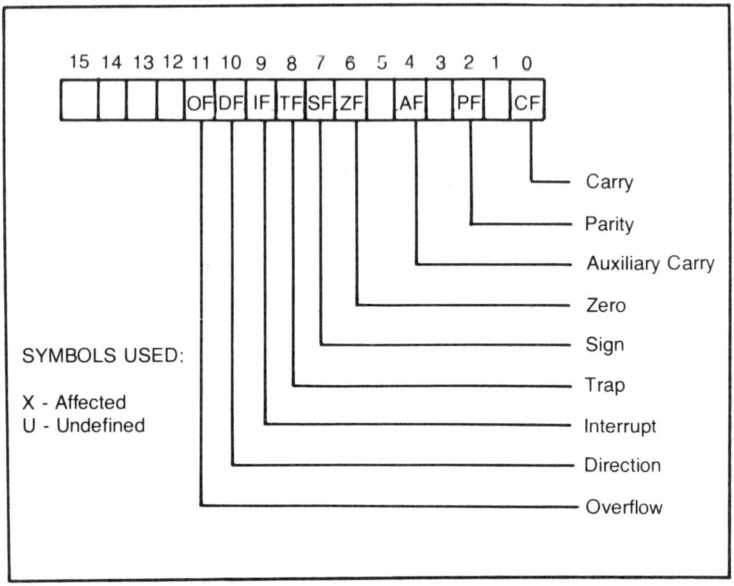

Fig. 4-1. Processor flag arrangement and abbreviations.

Addressing Modes		Clocks*
Displacement Only		6
Base Or Index Only	(BX,BP,SI,DI)	5
Base Or Index + Displacement	(BX,BP,SI,DI)	9
Base + Index	BX+SI, BP+DI	7
	BX+DI, BP+SI	8
Base + Index + Displacement	BX+SI+Disp	11
	BP+DI+Disp	11
	BP+SI+Disp	12
	BX+DI+Disp	12

*Note: Add 2 clocks for segment override

Fig. 4-2. Effective address calculation time.

REG Field Bit Assigments

16-Bit		8-Bit		Segment	
000	AX	000	AL	00	ES
001	CX	001	CL	01	CS
010	DX	010	DL	10	SS
011	BX	011	BL	11	DS
100	SP	100	AH		
101	BP	101	CH		
110	SI	110	DH		
111	DI	111	BH		

RM Field Bit Assignments

RM	Operand Address
000	(BX) + (SI) + DISP
001	(BX) + (DI) + DISP
010	(BP) + (SI) + DISP
011	(BP) + (DI) + DISP
100	(SI) + DISP
101	(DI) + DISP
110	(BP) + DISP
111	(BX) + DISP

MOD Field Bit Assignments

MOD	Displacement
00	No displacement bytes. Except if MOD=00 and RM=110 then EA = disp-low:disp-high
01	One displacement byte. DISP= Disp-low sign-extended to 16 bits, disp-high is absent
10	Two displacement bytes. DISP= Disp-low:Disp-high
11	RM is treated as "REG" field.

Fig. 4-3. Field bit assignments.

AAA

Definition: ASCII Adjust for addition.
Function: If ((AL) AND OFH) > 9 or (AF) = 1 then

```
(AL) <---- (AL) + 6

(AH) <---- (AH) + 1

(CF) <---- 1

(AF) <---- 1

(AL) <---- (AL) AND OFH
```

Description: This instruction works with unpacked BCD representations. It changes the contents of the AL register to a valid unpacked BCD number with the high-order four bits zeroed. This instruction assumes that the contents of the AL register are the result of adding two unpacked BCD numbers. The Auxiliary Carry Flag, AF and the Carry Flag, CF are updated. The Overflow Flag, OF, the Sign Flag, SF, the Zero Flag, ZF, and the Parity Flag, PF, are undefined.

Example: Consider the case where the AX and CL register contain 0008H and 04H, respectively, and the following sequence of instructions is executed.

```
ADD  AL,CL

AAA
```

After the instruction ADD AL,CL is executed, the AX register contains 000CH (decimal number 12) which is not a valid BCD representation. Executing AAA restores the contents of the AX register to a valid unpacked BCD number (0102H which is the BCD representation of the decimal number 12).

Affected Flags:

15	14	13	12	11	10	9	8	7	6	5	4	3	2	1	0
				U				U	U		X		U		X
				OF	DF	IF	TF	SF	ZF		AF		PF		CF

Machine Instruction Decoding Guide:

1st Byte Hex Binary	2nd byte	Bytes 3,4,5,6	Operand Format
37 0011 0111			No operand

Assembly Language Coding Examples:

Machine Code	Assembly Instructions	Operand Format	Bytes	Clocks
D50A	AAD	No operand	2	60

AAD

Definition: ASCII adjust for division.

Function:

```
(AL) <---- (AH) x 10 + (AL)

(AH) <---- 0
```

Description: This instruction assumes that the AX register contains a valid unpacked BCD representation. AAD converts the BCD number into the normal unsigned integer representation before dividing with an unpacked BCD denominator to produce a quotient in valid unpacked BCD format. The AH register must always be 0 for the subsequent DIV instruction to produce the correct result. The Parity Flag, PF, the Sign Flag, SF, and the Zero Flag are updated. The Auxiliary Carry Flag, AF, the Carry Flag, CF, and the Overflow Flag, OF, are undefined.

Example: Consider the case where the AX and DL register contain 0205H and 06H, respectively, and the following sequence of instructions is executed.

```
AAD
DIV  DL
```

Since the AX register contains a valid unpacked BCD number, the instruction AAD changes the contents of the AX register into 0019H (25 in decimal) which is the equivalent unsigned integer representation of the unpacked BCD number 0205H. Therefore, executing DIV DL correctly produces the quotient 04H in the AL register and the remainder 01H in the AH registers which are valid BCD numbers.

Affected Flags:

15	14	13	12	11	10	9	8	7	6	5	4	3	2	1	0
				U				X	X		U		X		U
				OF	DF	IF	TF	SF	ZF		AF		PF		CF

Machine Instruction Decoding Guide:

1st Byte Hex Binary	2nd byte	Bytes 3,4,5,6	Operand Format
D5 1101 0101	0A		No operand

Assembly Language Coding Examples:

Machine Code	Assembly Instructions	Operand Format	Bytes	Clocks
D50A	AAD	No operand	2	60

AAM

Definition: ASCII adjust for multiplication.
Function:

```
(AH) <---- Quotient of (AL):10

(AL) <---- Remainder of (AL):10
```

Description: This instruction works with unpacked BCD representations. It changes the contents of the AX register to a valid unpacked BCD number. This instruction assumes that the contents of the AX register are the result of multiplying two valid unpacked BCD numbers. The high-order half-bytes of the multiplied operands must be 0 for AAM to produce correct results. The Sign Flag, SF, the Zero Flag, ZF, and the Parity Flag, PF are updated. The Overflow Flag, OF, the Auxiliary Carry Flag, AF, and the Carry Flag, CF, are undefined.

Example: Consider the case where the AL and CL register contain 08H and 09H, respectively, and the following sequence of instructions is executed.

```
MUL  CL

AAM
```

After the instruction MUL CL is executed, the AL register contains 48H (72 in decimal) which is not a valid unpacked BCD representation. Executing AAM restores the contents of the AX.register to 0702H which is a valid unpacked BCD number (0702H is the equivalent unpacked BCD representation of the decimal number 72).

Affected Flags:

15	14	13	12	11	10	9	8	7	6	5	4	3	2	1	0
				U				X	X		U		X		U
				OF	DF	IF	TF	SF	ZF		AF		PF		CF

Machine Instruction Decoding Guide:

1st Byte Hex Binary	2nd byte	Bytes 3,4,5,6	Operand Format
D4 1101 0100	0A		No operand

Assembly Language Coding Examples:

Machine Code	Assembly Instructions	Operand Format	Bytes	Clocks
D40A	AAM	No operand	2	83

AAS

Definition: ASCII adjust for subtraction.
Function: If ((AL) AND OFH) > 9 or (AF) = 1 then

```
(AL) <---- (AL) - 6
(AH) <---- (AH) - 1
(CF) <---- 1
(AF) <---- 1
(AL) <---- (AL) AND OFH
```

Description: This instruction works with unpacked BCD representations. It changes the contents of the AL register to a valid unpacked BCD number with the high-order four bits zeroed. This instruction assumes that the contents of the AL register are the result of subtracting two unpacked BCD numbers. The Auxiliary Flag, AF, and the Carry Flag, CF, and updated. The Overflow Flag, OF, the Sign Flag, SF, the Zero Flag, ZF, and the Parity Flag, PF, are undefined.

Example: Consider the case where the AX and CL register contain 0105H and 08H, which are the BCD respresentations of the decimal number 15 and 8, respectively, and the following sequence of instructions is executed.

```
SUB  AL,CL
AAS
```

After the instruction SUB AL,CL is executed, the AX register contains 01FDH which is not a valid BCD representation. Executing AAA restores the contents of the AX register to 0007H which is a valid unpacked BCD number.

Affected Flags:

15	14	13	12	11	10	9	8	7	6	5	4	3	2	1	0
				U				U	U		1		U		1
				OF	DF	IF	TF	SF	ZF		AF		PF		CF

Machine Instruction Decoding Guide:

1st Byte Hex Binary	2nd byte	Bytes 3,4,5,6	Operand Format
3F 0011 1111			No operand

Assembly Language Coding Examples:

Machine Code	Assembly Instructions	Operand Format	Bytes	Clocks
3F	AAS	No operand	1	4

ADC

Definition: Add with carry.
Function:

(First Operand) <--- (First Operand) + (Second Operand) + (Carry Flag)

Description: The arithmetic sum of the original contents of the first and second operand and the content of the Carry Flag, CF, (0 or 1) is performed. The result replaces the contents of the first operand. The previous contents of the first operand are lost. The contents of the second operand remain unchanged.

The first operand may be a register or a memory location. The second operand may be a register, a memory location, or an immediate data value. It is not allowed to specify any operand as a segment register or to specify both operands at the same time as memory locations. Either 8-bit or 16-bit operations can be performed. Both operands may be signed or unsigned numbers. Since this instruction incorporates the Carry Flag, CF, from a previous operation, it can be used to add numbers whose magnitudes are longer than 16 bits.

Example: Consider the case where the AX register contains 4803H, and the Processor Flag contains F047H (1111 0000 0100 0111) in which the Carry Flag is 1. After the instruction ADC AX,2517H is executed, the AX register will contain 6D1BH and the Flag has a new value of F006H.

```
   Contents of AX    0100 1000 0000 0011 = 4803H
                     0010 0101 0001 0111 = 2517H
    Carry Flag CF                      1

New contents of AX   0110 1101 0001 1011 = 6D1BH
```

There are four 2 bits in the low-order 8 bits of register AX, which is an even number, so the Parity Flag, PF, is set to 1. The Sign Flag, SF, and the Zero Flag, ZF, are cleared to 0 since the result of the operation is a positive non-zero value. The Carry Flag, CF, and the Overflow Flag, OF, are cleared to 0 since there is no carry or overflow condition. The Auxiliary Carry Flag, AF, is cleared to 0 since there is no carry out of bit 3.

Affected Flags:

15	14	13	12	11	10	9	8	7	6	5	4	3	2	1	0
				X				X	X		X		X		X
				OF	DF	IF	TF	SF	ZF		AF		PF		CF

Machine Instruction Decoding Guide:

1st Byte Hex Binary	2nd byte	Bytes 3,4,5,6	Operand Format
10 0001 0000	Mod-Reg-Rm	Disp-Lo,Disp-Hi	Reg8/Mem8,Reg8
11 0001 0001	Mod-Reg-Rm	Disp-Lo,Disp-Hi	Reg16/Mem16,Reg16
12 0001 0010	Mod-Reg-Rm	Disp-Lo,Disp-Hi	Reg8,Reg8/Mem8
13 0001 0011	Mod-Reg-Rm	Disp-Lo,Disp-Hi	Reg16,Reg16/Mem16
14 0001 0100	Data8		AL,Immed8
15 0001 0101	Data-Lo	Data-Hi	AX,Immed16
80 1000 0000	Mod-010-Rm	Disp-Lo,Disp-Hi, Data8	Reg8/Mem8,Immed8
81 1000 0001	Mod-010-Rm	Disp-Lo,Disp-Hi, Data-Lo,Data-Hi	Reg16/Mem16,Immed16
82 1000 0010	Mod-010-Rm	Disp-Lo,Disp-Hi, Data8	Reg8/Mem8,Immed8
83 1000 0011	Mod-010-Rm	Disp-Lo,Disp-Hi, Data-SX	Reg16/Mem16,Immed8

Assembly Language Coding Examples:

Machine Code	Assembly Instructions	Operand Format	Bytes	Clocks
101F	ADC [BX],BL	Mem8,Reg8	2-4	16+EA
10D6	ADC DH,DL	Reg8,Reg8	2	3
11540C	ADC [SI+12],DX	Mem16,Reg16	2-4	24+EA

Machine Code	Assembly Instructions	Operand Format	Bytes	Clocks
11F2	ADC DX,SI	Reg16,Reg16	2	3
120E0020	ADC CL,NEXT_BYTE	Reg8,Mem8	2-4	9+EA
1315	ADC DX,[DI]	Reg16,Mem16	2-4	13+EA
1403	ADC AL,03	AL,Immed8	2	4
15FFFF	ADC AX,-1	AX,Immed16	3	4
80D60A	ADC DH,10	Reg8,Immed8	3	4
8095230F01	ADC BYTE PTR [DI+0F23H],1	Mem8,Immed8	3-5	17+EA
81D51122	ADC BP,2211H	Reg16,Immed16	4	4
81150123	ADC WORD PTR [SI],2301H	Mem16,Immed16	4-6	25+EA
82D50A	ADC CH,10	Reg8,Immed8	3	4
83D301	ADC BX,01	Reg16,Immed8	3	4
8316000003	ADC WORD PTR NEW,03	Mem16,Immed8	3-5	25+EA

ADD

Definition: Addition.
Function:

(First Operand) <--- (First Operand) + (Second Operand)

Description: The arithmetic sum of the original contents of the first and second operand is performed. The result replaces the contents of the first operand. The previous contents of the first operand are lost. The contents of the second operand remain unchanged.

The first operand may be a register or a memory location. The second operand may be a register, a memory location, or an immediate data value. It is not allowed to specify any operand as a segment register, or to specify both operands at the same time as memory locations. Both operands may be signed or unsigned numbers. Either 8-bit or 16-bit operations can be performed by this instruction.

Example: Consider the case where the DL register contains 58H, the byte memory location TEST_BYTE contains 27H, and the Processor Flag has a value of F046H. After the instruction ADD TEST_BYTE,DL is executed, the byte memory location TEST_BYTE contains 7FH, and the Processor Flag contains F002H.

```
         Contents of DL   0101 1000 = 58H
  Contents of TEST_BYTE   0010 0111 = 27H

New contents of TEST_BYTE   0111 1111 = 7FH
```

There are seven 1 bits in the new content of the byte at memory location TEST_BYTE, which is an odd number, so the Parity Flag, PF, is cleared to 0. The Sign Flag, SF, and the Zero Flag, ZF, are cleared to 0 since the result of the operation is a positive nonzero value. The Carry Flag, CF, and the Overflow Flag, OF, are cleared to 0 since there is no carry or overflow condition. The Auxiliary Carry Flag, AF, is cleared to 0 since there is no carry out of bit 3.

Affected Flags:

15	14	13	12	11	10	9	8	7	6	5	4	3	2	1	0
				X				X	X		X		X		X
				OF	DF	IF	TF	SF	ZF		AF		PF		CF

Machine Instruction Decoding Guide:

1st Byte Hex Binary	2nd byte	Bytes 3,4,5,6	Operand Format
00 0000 0000	Mod-Reg-Rm	Disp-Lo,Disp-Hi	Reg8/Mem8,Reg8
01 0000 0001	Mod-Reg-Rm	Disp-Lo,Disp-Hi	Reg16/Mem16,Reg16
02 0000 0010	Mod-Reg-Rm	Disp-Lo,Disp-Hi	Reg8,Reg8/Mem8
03 0000 0011	Mod-Reg-Rm	Disp-Lo,Disp-Hi	Reg16,Reg16/Mem16
04 0000 0100	Data8		AL,Immed8
05 0000 0101	Data-Lo	Data-Hi	AX,Immed16
80 1000 0000	Mod-000-Rm	Disp-Lo,Disp-Hi, Data8	Reg8/Mem8,Immed8
81 1000 0001	Mod-000-Rm	Disp-Lo,Disp-Hi, Data-Lo,Data-Hi	Reg16/Mem16,Immed16
82 1000 0010	Mod-000-Rm	Disp-Lo,Disp-Hi, Data8	Reg8/Mem8,Immed8
83 1000 0011	Mod-000-Rm	Disp-Lo,Disp-Hi, Data-SX	Reg16/Mem16,Immed8

Assembly Language Coding Examples:

Machine Code	Assembly Instructions	Operand Format	Bytes	Clocks
002C	ADD [SI],CH	Mem8,Reg8	2-4	16+EA
00F6	ADD DH,DH	Reg8,Reg8	2	3
014412	ADD [SI+12H],AX	Mem16,Reg16	2-4	24+EA
01EB	ADD BX,BP	Reg16,Reg16	2	3
021E0020	ADD BL,TEST_BYTE	Reg8,Mem8	2-4	9+EA

Machine Code	Assembly Instructions	Operand Format	Bytes	Clocks
0305	ADD AX,[DI]	Reg16,Mem16	2-4	13+EA
0403	ADD AL,03	AL,Immed8	2	4
052589	ADD AX,8925H	AX,Immed16	3	4
80C40B	ADD AH,11	Reg8,Immed8	3	4
8086230F09	ADD BYTE PTR [BP+0F23H],9	Mem8,Immed8	3-5	17+EA
81C10EFF	ADD CX,FF0EH	Reg16,Immed16	4	4
81040010	ADD WORD PTR [SI],1000H	Mem16,Immed16	4-6	25+EA
82C410	ADD AH,10H	Reg8,Immed8	3	4
83C201	ADD DX,01	Reg16,Immed8	3	4
8306000003	ADD WORD PTR LOC,3	Mem16,Immed8	3-5	25+EA

AND

Definition: Logical AND.
Function:

```
(First Operand) <--- (First Operand)  AND  (Second Operand)
           (CF) <---  0
           (OF) <---  0
```

Description: The Boolean logical AND of the original contents of the first operand and the contents of the second operand is performed. The result replaces the contents of the first operand. The previous contents of the first operand are lost. The contents of the second operand remain unchanged. The first operand may be a register or a memory location. The second operand may be a register, a memory location, or an immediate data value. It is not allowed to specify any operand as a segment register, or to specify both operands at the same time as memory locations. Either 8-bit or 16-bit operations can be performed. The Carry Flag, CF, and the Overflow Flag, OF, are always cleared to 0 by this instruction.

Example: Consider the case where the BX register contains 024DH, and BP register contains F007H, and the Flag contains F046H. After the instruction AND BX,BP is executed, the BX register contains 0005H and the Processor Flag contains F006H.

```
    Contents of BX    0000 0010 0100 1101 = 024DH
    Contents of BP    1111 0000 0000 0111 = F007H
New contents of BX    0000 0000 0000 0101 = 0005H
```

There are two 1 bits in the low-order 8 bits of the BX register, which is an even number, so the Parity Flag, PF, is set to 1. Since the result of the

Boolean AND operation is a positive nonzero value in two's complement notation, the Sign Flag, SF, and the Zero Flag, ZF, are cleared to 0. The Carry Flag, CF, and Overflow Flag, OF, are always cleared to 0 since there is no carry or overflow condition. The Auxiliary Carry Flag, AF, is undefined.

Affected Flags:

15	14	13	12	11	10	9	8	7	6	5	4	3	2	1	0
				0				X	X		U		X		0
				OF	DF	IF	TF	SF	ZF		AF		PF		CF

Machine Instruction Decoding Guide:

1st Byte Hex Binary	2nd byte	Bytes 3,4,5,6	Operand Format
20 0010 0000	Mod-Reg-Rm	Disp-Lo,Disp-Hi	Reg8/Mem8,Reg8
21 0010 0001	Mod-Reg-Rm	Disp-Lo,Disp-Hi	Reg16/Mem16,Reg16
22 0010 0010	Mod-Reg-Rm	Disp-Lo,Disp-Hi	Reg8,Reg8/Mem8
23 0010 0011	Mod-Reg-Rm	Disp-Lo,Disp-Hi	Reg16,Reg16/Mem16
24 0010 0100	Data8		AL,Immed8
25 0010 0101	Data-Lo	Data-Hi	AX,Immed16
80 1000 0000	Mod-100-Rm	Disp-Lo,Disp-Hi, Data8	Reg8/Mem8,Immed8
81 1000 0001	Mod-100-Rm	Disp-Lo,Disp-Hi, Data-Lo,Data-Hi	Reg16/Mem16,Immed16

Assembly Language Coding Examples:

Machine Code	Assembly Instructions	Operand Format	Bytes	Clocks
2028	AND [BX+SI],CH	Mem8,Reg8	2-4	16+EA
20D3	AND BL,DL	Reg8,Reg8	2	3
211E0060	AND WORD PTR SUM,BX	Mem16,Reg16	2-4	24+EA
21E9	AND CX,BP	Reg16,Reg16	2	3
220D	AND CL,[DI]	Reg8,Mem8	2-4	9+EA
23570C	AND DX,[BX+12]	Reg16,Mem16	2-4	13+EA
2401	AND AL,01	AL,Immed8	2	4
250748	AND AX,4807H	AX,Immed16	3	4
80E701	AND BH,01	Reg8,Immed8	3	4

Machine Code	Assembly Instructions	Operand Format	Bytes	Clocks
80640200	AND BYTE PTR [SI+2],0	Mem8,Immed8	3-5	17+EA
81E6FFFF	AND SI,0FFFFH	Reg16,Immed16	4	4
81260010FFFE	AND WORD PTR TEST,0FEFFH	Mem16,Immed16	4-6	25+EA

CALL

Definition: Call procedures.

Function: If Intersegment:

```
(SP) <---- (SP) - 2
(Top Of Stack) <---- (CS)
(SP) <---- (SP) - 2
(Top Of Stack) <---- (IP)
(CS) <---- Segment Of Procedure
(IP) <---- Offset Address Of Procedure
```

If Intrasegment:

```
(SP) <---- (SP) - 2
(Top Of Stack) <---- (IP)
(IP) <---- Offset Address Of Procedure
```

Description: This instruction transfers control unconditionally to a procedure (subroutine) in a standard fashion. The returning address is stored on top of the stack to permit a RET (Return From Procedure) instruction in the procedure to return control to the instruction following the CALL.

This instruction has four different formats: intrasegment direct, intrasegment indirect, intersegment direct, and intersegment indirect. An intrasegment CALL transfers control within 64 K bytes of the current code segment only. Thus, the address of the target procedure must be within +32,767 or −32,768 bytes of the address of the instruction following the CALL. On the other hand, an intersegment CALL can transfer control to any procedure within the 8088 megabyte memory space.

In intersegment CALLS, the contents of the CS and IP registers are saved on the stack. In intrasegment CALLS, only the contents of the IP register is saved on the stack. The 8088 microprocessor automatically adjusts the Instruction Pointer, IP, to point to the instruction following the CALL before saving it on the stack.

In an intrasegment direct CALL, a 16-bit displacement value is added to the Instruction Pointer, IP, to generate the address of the target procedure. In an intrasegment indirect CALL, a 16-bit general register (AX, BX, CX, DX, SI, DI, BP, SP) or a memory location may be used as an operand whose contents specify the address of the target procedure.

An intersegment direct CALL contains the values of the code segment and offset address of the target procedure as a part of the CALL instruction which will replace the contents of the CS and IP registers after the CALL instruction is executed. A memory location can also be used as operands of an intersegment indirect CALL. A doubleword at this memory location replaces the contents of the CS and IP registers after the CALL instruction is executed.

Example: In 8088 assembly language, a CALL to a NEAR procedure is translated into an intrasegment CALL, whereas a CALL to a FAR procedure is translated into an intersegment CALL, as follows:

Intersegment CALL

```
        MOV AL,00
        CALL FAR PTR CONVERT
        ..
        Instructions in calling program
        ..
CONVERT PROC   FAR
        ..
        Instructions in procedure
        ..
CONVERT ENDP
```

Intrasegment CALL

```
        MOV AL,00
        CALL CHECK
        ..
        Instructions in calling program
        ..
CHECK   PROC     NEAR
        ..
        Instructions in procedure
        ..
CHECK   ENDP
```

Affected Flags: None.

Machine Instruction Decoding Guide:

1st Byte Hex Binary	2nd byte	Bytes 3,4,5,6	Operand Format
9A 1001 1010	Offset-Lo	Offset-Hi Seg-Lo,Seg-Hi	Far-Proc
E8 1110 1000	IP-Inc-Lo	IP-Inc-Hi	Near-Proc
FF 1111 1111	Mod-010-Rm		Reg16/Mem16 (Intrasegment)
FF 1111 1111	Mod-011-Rm		Mem16 only (Intersegment)

Assembly Language Coding Examples:

Machine Code	Assembly Instructions	Operand Format	Bytes	Clocks*
9A001200F0	CALL FAR PTR TICK	Far-Proc	5	28(36)
E80020	CALL NEXT_PROC	Near-Proc	3	19(23)

Machine Code	Assembly Instructions	Operand Format	Bytes	Clocks*
FFD6	CALL SI	Reg16 (Intra)	2	16(24)
FF570C	CALL WORD PTR [BX+12]	Memp16 (Intra)	2-4	21(29)+EA
FF1D	CALL DWORD PTR [DI]	Mem16 (Inter)	2-4	37(57)+EA
*Note: Number of clock cycles in parentheses are for word operands.				

CBW

Definition: Convert byte to word.
Function:

```
If (AL) < 80H  then  (AH) <--- 0
If (AL) ≥ 80H  then  (AH) <--- FFH
```

Description: This instruction extends the most significant bit (the sign bit) of the byte in the AL register throughout the AH register. If the sign bit of the AL register is 0, a 0 is stored in the AH register to make the contents of the AX register a positive number. If the sign bit of the AL register is 1, the hexadecimal number FF is stored in the AH register to make the contents of the AX register a negative number in standard two's complement notation. This instruction does not affect any flags and requires no operands. It can be used to convert an 8-bit dividend to a 16-bit dividend prior to performing byte division.

Example: IF the AX register contains 02D3H, after the instruction CBW is executed, the AX register has a new content of FFD3H.

Affected Flags: None.

Machine Instruction Decoding Guide:

1st Byte Hex Binary	2nd byte	Bytes 3,4,5,6	Operand Format
98 1001 1000			No operand

Assembly Language Coding Examples:

Machine Code	Assembly Instructions	Operand Format	Bytes	Clocks
98	CBW	No operand	1	2

CLC

Definition: Clear carry flag.

Function: (CF) <--- 0.

Description: This instruction clears the Carry Flag to 0 and does not affect any other flags or registers. No operand is required by this instruction.

Example: If the Processor Flag contains F047H, after the instruction CLC is executed, the Processor Flag contains F046H.

Affected Flags:

15	14	13	12	11	10	9	8	7	6	5	4	3	2	1	0
															0
				OF	DF	IF	TF	SF	ZF		AF		PF		CF

Machine Instruction Decoding Guide:

1st Byte Hex Binary	2nd byte	Bytes 3,4,5,6	Operand Format
F8 1111 1000			No operand

Assembly Language Coding Examples:

Machine Code	Assembly Instructions	Operand Format	Bytes	Clocks
F8	CLC	No operand	1	2

CLD

Function: Clear direction flag.

Function: (DF) <--- 0.

Description: This instruction clears the Direction Flag, DF, to 0 does not affect any other flags or registers. No operand is required by this instruction. The pointer registers SI and/or DI will be autoincremented if they are implied by the string instructions (CMPS, LODS, MOVS, SCAS, STOS). The contents of the SI and/or DI registers are incremented by 1 or 2 depending on byte or word operation, respectively.

Example: If the Processor Flag contains F446H, after the instruction CLD is executed, the Processor Flag will contain F046H.

Affected Flags

15	14	13	12	11	10	9	8	7	6	5	4	3	2	1	0
					0										
				OF	DF	IF	TF	SF	ZF		AF		PF		CF

Machine Instruction Decoding Guide:

1st Byte Hex Binary	2nd byte	Bytes 3,4,5,6	Operand Format
FC 1111 1100			No operand

Assembly Language Coding Examples:

Machine Code	Assembly Instructions	Operand Format	Bytes	Clocks
FC	CLD	No operand	1	2

CLI

Definition: Clear interrupt flag.

Function: (IF) <--- 0.

Description: This instruction clears the Interrupt-Enable Flag, IF, to 0 and does not affect any other flags or registers. No operand is required by this instruction. When the Interrupt-Enable Flag is 0, the 8088 microprocessor ignores any maskable interrupt requests that appear on its INTR line. Only software interrupts and nonmaskable interrupts appearing on the NMI line are honored. This instruction is used by interrupt service procedures to prevent themselves from further interrupts so that they may have sufficient time to complete some of their essential functions before allowing themselves to be interrupted.

Example: If the Processor Flag contains F246H, after the instruction CLI is executed, the Processor Flag will contain F046H.

Affected Flags:

15	14	13	12	11	10	9	8	7	6	5	4	3	2	1	0
						0									
				OF	DF	IF	TF	SF	ZF		AF		PF		CF

Machine Instruction Decoding Guide:

1st Byte Hex Binary	2nd byte	Bytes 3,4,5,6	Operand Format
FA 1111 1010			No operand

Assembly Language Coding Examples:

Machine Code	Assembly Instructions	Operand Format	Bytes	Clocks
FA	CLI	No operand	1	2

CMC

Definition: Complement carry flag.

Function:

If (CF) = 0 then (CF) <--- 1
IF (CF) = 1 then (CF) <--- 0

Description: This instruction reverses the Carry Flag, CF, to its opposite state and does not affect any other flags or registers. No operand is required by this instruction.

Example: If the Processor Flag contains F047H, after the instruction CMC is executed, the Processor Flag will contain F046H.

Affected Flags:

15	14	13	12	11	10	9	8	7	6	5	4	3	2	1	0
															X
				OF	DF	IF	TF	SF	ZF		AF		PF		CF

Machine Instruction Decoding Guide:

1st Byte Hex Binary	2nd byte	Bytes 3,4,5,6	Operand Format
F5 1111 0101			No operand

Assembly Language Coding Examples:

Machine Code	Assembly Instructions	Operand Format	Bytes	Clocks
F5	CMC	No operand	1	2

CMP

Definition: Compare operands.

Function: (First Operand) - (Second Operand).

Description: The contents of the second operand are subtracted from the contents of the first operand. The result of the operation only updates the Auxiliary Carry Flag, AF, the Carry Flag, CF, the Overflow Flag, OF, the Parity Flag, PF, the Sign Flag, SF, and the Zero Flag, ZF. The contents of both operands remain unchanged. The first operand may be a register or a memory location. The second operand may be a register, a memory location, or an immediate data value. It is not allowed to specify any operand as a segment register, or to specify both operands at the same time as memory locations. Both 8-bit and 16-bit operations are allowed.

Example: Consider the case where the AX register contains 024DH, the CX register contains 1823H, and the Processor Flag contains F046H. After the instruction CMP AX,CX is executed, the Processor Flag has a new value of F083H.

Affected Flags:

15	14	13	12	11	10	9	8	7	6	5	4	3	2	1	0
				X				X	X		X		X		X
				OF	DF	IF	TF	SF	ZF		AF		PF		CF

Machine Instruction Decoding Guide:

1st Byte Hex Binary	2nd byte	Bytes 3,4,5,6	Operand Format
38 0010 0000	Mod-Reg-Rm	Disp-Lo,Disp-Hi	Reg8/Mem8,Reg8
39 0010 0001	Mod-Reg-Rm	Disp-Lo,Disp-Hi	Reg16/Mem16,Reg16
3A 0010 0010	Mod-Reg-Rm	Disp-Lo,Disp-Hi	Reg8,Reg8/Mem8
3B 0010 0011	Mod-Reg-Rm	Disp-Lo,Disp-Hi	Reg16,Reg16/Mem16
3C 0010 0100	Data8		AL,Immed8
3D 0010 0101	Data-Lo	Data-Hi	AX,Immed16

1st Byte Hex	Binary	2nd byte	Bytes 3,4,5,6	Operand Format
80	1000 0000	Mod-111-Rm	Disp-Lo,Disp-Hi, Data8	Reg8/Mem8,Immed8
81	1000 0001	Mod-111-Rm	Disp-Lo,Disp-Hi, Data-Lo,Data-Hi	Reg16/Mem16,Immed16
82	1000 0010	Mod-111-Rm	Disp-Lo,Disp-Hi, Data8	Reg8/Mem8,Immed8
83	1000 0011	Mod-111-Rm	Disp-Lo,Disp-Hi, Data-SX	Reg16/Mem16,Immed8

Assembly Language Coding Examples:

Machine Code	Assembly Instructions	Operand Format	Bytes	Clocks
3828	CMP [BX+SI],CH	Mem8,Reg8	2-4	9+EA
38D3	CMP BL,DL	Reg8,Reg8	2	3
391E0060	CMP WORD PTR SUM,BX	Mem16,Reg16	2-4	13+EA
39E9	CMP CX,BP	Reg16,Reg16	2	3
3A0D	CMP CL,[DI]	Reg8,Mem8	2-4	9+EA
3B570C	CMP DX,[BX+12]	Reg16,Mem16	2-4	13+EA
3C7F	CMP AL,7FH	AL,Immed8	2	4
3D0748	CMP AX,4807H	AX,Immed16	3	4
80FF09	CMP BH,09	Reg8,Immed8	3	4
807C0200	CMP BYTE PTR [SI+2],0	Mem8,Immed8	3-5	10+EA
81FE0090	CMP SI,9000H	Reg16,Immed16	4	4
813E00100080	CMP WORD PTR TEST,8000H	Mem16,Immed16	4-6	14+EA
82FA02	CMP DL,02	Reg8,Immed8	3	4
83FAFE	CMP DX,-2	Reg16,Immed8	3	4

CMPS

Definition: Compare string.
Function: (Operand addressed by SI) – (Operand addressed by DI).

```
If (DF) = 0  then  (SI) <---- (SI) + 1 (byte)
                   (DI) <---- (DI) + 1 (byte)
                             or
                   (SI) <---- (SI) + 2 (word)
                   (DI) <---- (DI) + 2 (word)
```

```
If (DF) = 1  then  (SI) <---- (SI) - 1 (byte)
                   (DI) <---- (DI) - 1 (byte)
                               or
                   (SI) <---- (SI) - 2 (word)
                   (DI) <---- (DI) - 2 (word)
```

Description: The contents of the memory location addressed by the DI register are subtracted from the contents of the memory location addressed by the SI register. The result of the subtraction updates the Processor Flag but does not alter the contents of the memory locations addressed by the SI and DI registers. In assembly language, the instruction CMPS is coded as CMPSB in byte operation or as CMPSW in word operation. If the Direction Flag DF is 0, the contents of the SI and DI registers are incremented by 1 after CMPSB is executed, or by 2 after CMPSW is executed. If the Direction Flag is 1, the contents of the SI and DI registers are decremented by 1 after CMPSB is executed, or by 2 after CMPSW is executed.

If CMPS is prefixed with REP/REPE/REPZ, the repetition sequence is performed while the CX register is not 0 and the string elements are equal (the Zero Flag, ZF, is 1). If CMPS is prefixed with REPNE/REPNZ the repetition sequence is performed while the XC register is not 0 and the string elements are not equal (the Zero Flag is 0).

Example: Consider the case where the SI register contains 7F00H, the byte memory location 7F00H contains 41H, and DI register contains B800H, the byte memory location B800H contains 53H, the Processor Flag contains F046H, and the following sequence of instructions is executed.

```
CLD     ;Clear the Direction Flag DF to 0.
CMPSB
```

After CMPSB is executed, the SI and DI registers will contain 7F01H and B801H, respectively. Since the result of the CMPS operation (41H – 53H = F0H) is a negative nonzero value, the Sign Flag is set to 1 and the Zero Flag is cleared to 0. The Processor Flag has a new value F097H.

Affected Flags:

15	14	13	12	11	10	9	8	7	6	5	4	3	2	1	0
				X				X	X		X		X		X
				OF	DF	IF	TF	SF	ZF		AF		PF		CF

Machine Instruction Decoding Guide:

First Byte Hex Binary	2nd byte	Bytes 3,4,5,6	Operand Format
A6 1010 0110			No Operand
A7 1010 0111			No Operand

Assembly Language Coding Examples:

Machine Code	Assembly Instructions	Operand Format	Bytes	Clocks
A6	CMPSB	No Operand	1	22
A7	CMPSW	No Operand	1	30

CWD

Definition: Convert word to doubleword.
Function:

```
If (AX) < 8000H  then  (DX) <--- 0

If (AX) ≥ 8000H  then  (DX) <--- FFFFH
```

Description: This instruction extends the most significant bit (the sign bit) of the word in the AX register throughout the DX register. If the sign bit of the AX register is 0, a 0 is stored in the DX register to make the contents of the register pair DX, AX a positive 32-bit number. If the sign bit of the AX register is 1, a hexadecimal FFFF is stored in the DX register to make the contents of the register pair DX, AX a negative 32-bit number. This instruction does not affect any flags and requires no operands. It can be used to convert a 16-bit dividend to a 32-bit dividend prior to performing word division.

Example: Consider the case where the AX register contains 9432H and the DX register contains C241H. After the instruction CWD is executed, the DX register has a new value FFFFH, and the AX register remains unchanged. The register pair DX, AX then represents the 32-bit hexadecimal number FFFF9432.

Affected Flags: None.

Machine Instruction Decoding Guide:

1st Byte Hex Binary	2nd byte	Bytes 3,4,5,6	Operand Format
99 1001 1001			No operand

Assembly Language Coding Examples:

Machine Code	Assembly Instructions	Operand Format	Bytes	Clocks
99	CWD	No operand	1	5

DAA

Definition: Decimal adjust for addition.
Function: If ((AL) and 0FH) > 9 or (AF) = 1 then:

```
(AL) <---- (AL) + 6

(AF) <---- 1
```

If (AL) > 9FH or (CF) = 1 then:

```
(AL) <---- (AL) + 60H

(CF) <---- 1
```

Description: This instruction works with packed BCD representations. It changes the contents of the AL register to a valid packed BCD number. This instruction assumes that the contents of the AL register are the result of adding two packed BCD numbers. The Auxiliary Carry Flag, AF, the Parity Flag, PF, the Zero Flag, ZF, the Sign Flag, SF, and the Carry Flag, CF, are updated. The Overflow Flag, OF, is undefined.

Example: Consider the case where the AL and BL register contain 29H and 13H, which are the packed BCD representations of the decimal number 29 and 13, respectively, and the following sequence of instructions is executed.

```
ADD  AL,BL

DAA
```

After the instruction ADD AL, BL is executed, the AL register contains 3CH which is not a valid BCD representation. Executing DAA restores the contents of the AL register to 42H which is a valid packed BCD representation of the decimal number 42.

Affected Flags:

15	14	13	12	11	10	9	8	7	6	5	4	3	2	1	0
				U				X	X		X		X		X
				OF	DF	IF	TF	SF	ZF		AF		PF		CF

Machine Instruction Decoding Guide:

1st Byte Hex Binary	2nd byte	Bytes 3,4,5,6	Operand Format
27 0010 0111			No operand

Assembly Language Coding Examples:

Machine Code	Assembly Instructions	Operand Format	Bytes	Clocks
27	DAA	No operand	1	4

DAS

Definition: Decimal adjust for subtraction.

Function: If ((AL) AND OFH) > 9 or (AF) = 1 then:

```
(AL) <---- (AL) - 6

(AF) <---- 1
```

If (AL) > 9FH or (CF) = 1 then:

```
(AL) <---- (AL) - 60H

(CF) <---- 1
```

Description: This instruction works with packed BCD representations. It changes the contents of the AL register to a valid packed BCD number. This instruction assumes that the contents of the AL register are the result of subtracting two packed BCD numbers. The Auxiliary Carry Flag, AF, the Parity Flag, PF, the Zero Flag, ZF, the Sign Flag, SF, and the Carry Flag, CF, are updated. The Overflow Flag, OF, is undefined.

Example: Consider the case where the AL and BL register contain 44H and 27H, which are the packed BCD representations of the decimal number 44 and 27, respectively, and the following sequence of instructions is executed.

```
SUB  AL,BL

DAS
```

After the instruction SUB AL, BL is executed, the AL register contains 1DH which is not a valid BCD representation. Executing DAA restores the contents of the AL register to 17H which is a valid packed BCD representation of the decimal number 17.

Affected Flags:

15	14	13	12	11	10	9	8	7	6	5	4	3	2	1	0
				U				X	X		X		X		X
				OF	DF	IF	TF	SF	ZF		AF		PF		CF

Machine Instruction Decoding Guide:

1st Byte Hex Binary	2nd byte	Bytes 3,4,5,6	Operand Format
2F 0010 1111			No operand

Assembly Language Coding Examples:

Machine Code	Assembly Instructions	Operand Format	Bytes	Clocks
2F	DAS	No operand	1	4

DEC

Definition: Decrement.

Function: (Operand) <--- (Operand) – 1.

Description: The original contents of the specified operand are decremented by 1. The operand can be a general register or a memory location. No segment register may be specified as operands. Both 8-bit and 16-bit operations can be performed. The contents of the operand are treated as an unsigned number. The Carry Flag, CF, is not affected by this instruction.

Example: Consider the case where the BL register contains 00 and the following instruction DEC BL is executed. The new content of the BL register is FFH. Since the result of the instruction is a negative non-zero number in two's complement form, the Sign Flag, SF, is set to 1 and the Zero Flag, ZF, is cleared to 0. There are eight 1 bits in the new content of the BL register, which is an even number, therefore the Parity Flag, PF, is set to 1.

Affected Flags:

15	14	13	12	11	10	9	8	7	6	5	4	3	2	1	0
				X				X	X		X		X		
				OF	DF	IF	TF	SF	ZF		AF		PF		CF

Machine Instruction Decoding Guide:

1st Byte Hex Binary	2nd byte	Bytes 3,4,5,6	Operand Format
FE 1111 1110	Mod-001-Rm	Disp-Lo,Disp-Hi	Reg8/Mem8
FF 1111 1111	Mod-001-Rm	Disp-Lo,Disp-Hi	Reg16/Mem16
0100 1reg			Reg16 only*

*Note: The instruction format FF Mod-001-Rm should not be used if the operand is a 16-bit register. The alternate format 0100 1reg is more efficient.

Assembly Language Coding Examples:

Machine Code	Assembly Instructions	Operand Format	Bytes	Clocks
48	DEC AX	Reg16	1	2
FEC8	DEC AL	Reg8	2	3
FE0E0010	DEC BYTE PTR TESTB	Mem8	2-4	15+EA
FF4C12	DEC WORD PTR [SI+18]	Mem16	2-4	23+EA

DIV

Definition: Divide.

Function: If byte operation then perform (AX):(Operand). If ((AX):(Operand) > FFH) then perform type 0 interrupt.

(AL) <---- Quotient

(AH) <---- Remainder

If word operation then perform (DX,AX):(Operand). If ((DX,AX):(Operand) > FFFFH) then perform type 0 interrupt.

```
(AX) <---- Quotient

(DX) <---- Remainder
```

Description: This instruction performs an unsigned division of the accumulator by the specified operand. In byte division, the contents of the AX register are treated as an unsigned 16-bit dividend. In word division, the contents of the register pair DX,AX are treated as an unsigned 32-bit dividend where the DX register holds the higher-order sixteen bits. The specified operand may be a general register or a memory location and is treated as an unsigned 8-bit or 16-bit divisor depending upon byte or word division, respectively.

In byte division, the quotient is retuned in the AL register and the remainder is returned in the AH register. In word division, the AX and DX registers are used to hold the 16-bit quotient and remainder, respectively. Both the quotient and remainder are treated as unsigned numbers.

The Processor Flag is undefined after executing the DIV instruction. If the quotient overflows the capacity of the Accumulator (decimal 255 in byte division or decimal 65535 in word division) or when dividing by zero is attempted, a type 0 interrupt is automatically generated. The quotient and remainder are undefined if a divide overflow occurs. The absolute byte memory locations 00000H to 00003H contain a doubleword which specifies the code segment and offset address of the interrupt service procedure for the type 0 interrupt.

Example: Consider the case where the AX register contains 0047H, the CL register contains 12H, and the following instruction DIV CL is executed. The quotient of the division (03H = 47H/12H) is returned in the AL register and the remainder 11H is returned in the AH register.

Consider the case where the DX and AX registers contain 0012H and F043H representing a 32-bit hexadecimal number 0012F043H, the BP register contains 4320H, and the following instruction DIV BP is executed. The quotient of the division (0048H= 12F043H/4320H) is returned in the AX register and the remainder (0F43H) is returned in the DX register.

Affected Flags:

15	14	13	12	11	10	9	8	7	6	5	4	3	2	1	0
				U				U	U		U		U		U
				OF	DF	IF	TF	SF	ZF		AF		PF		CF

Machine Instruction Decoding Guide:

First Byte Hex Binary	2nd byte	Bytes 3,4,5,6	Operand Format
F6 1111 0110	Mod-110-Rm	Disp-Lo,Disp-Hi	Reg8/Mem8
F7 1111 0111	Mod-110-Rm	Disp-Lo,Disp-Hi	Reg16/Mem16

Assembly Language Coding Examples:

Machine Code	Assembly Instructions	Operand Format	Bytes	Clocks
F6F5	DIV CH	Reg8	2	80-90
F67401	DIV BYTE PTR [SI+01]	Mem8	2-4	(86-96)+EA
F7F1	DIV CX	Reg16	2	144-162
F7360020	DIV WORD PTR XNUM	Mem16	2-4	(154-172)+EA

ESC

Definition: Escape.

Function: If Mod # 11B then Data Bus <---- (Effective Address).

Description: This instruction provides a mechanism for other co-processors such as the 8087 Numeric Data Processor to extract their instructions from the 8088 instruction stream and make use of the 8088 memory addressing modes. The 8088 CPU performs an equivalent of a NOP (No Operation) instruction if the operand is a register. Otherwise, it performs a dummy read for each ESC instruction by simply placing on its data bus the contents of the specified memory operand.

Example: Consider the instruction ESC OFH, DX. Since the operand of this ESC instruction is a register, the 8088 CPU simply performs a NOP. If the 8087 Numeric Data Processor is present in the microcomputer, it interprets the ESC instruction as the floating-point instruction FSQRT (Square Root).

Affected Flags: None.

Machine Instruction Decoding Guide:

First Byte Hex	First Byte Binary	2nd byte	Bytes 3,4,5,6	Operand Format
	1101 1xxx	Mod-yyy-Rm		Opcode,Reg8/Mem8* Opcode,Reg16/Mem16

*Note: The xxx and yyy bits in the first two bytes of the machine instruction form the opcode of the ESC operand.

Assembly Language Coding Examples:

Machine Code	Assembly Instructions	Operand Format	Bytes	Clocks
DED9	ESC 33H,CL	Opcode,Reg8	2	2
DED9	ESC 33H,CX	Opcode,Reg16	2	2
DB6C0A	ESC BYTE PTR 1DH,[SI+10]	Opcode,Mem8	2-4	8
DB2F	ESC WORD PTR 1DH,[BX]	Opcode,Mem16	2-4	12

HLT

Definition: Halt CPU.

Function: None.

Description: The 8088 microprocessor enters the halt state after this instruction is executed. The CPU leaves its halt state whenever its RESET line is activated. If the Interrupt-Enable Flag, IF, is 0, only nonmaskable interrupts appearing on the NMI line can activate the CPU to resume execution. If the Interrupt-Enable Flag, IF, is 1, either maskable interrupts appearing on the INTR line or nonmaskable interrupts can activate the 8088 CPU. This instruction does not affect any flags and has no operands.

Example: Many microcomputers today have self-diagnostic facilities to test themselves during system start-up to ensure that there is no malfunction in any of the system hardware components. The following sequence of instructions tests the internal registers of the 8088 CPU and will attempt to halt program execution if the microprocessor is defective.

```
           MOV  AH,0C5H     ;Prepare the new Processor Flag.
           SAHF             ;Set SF,ZF,PF,CF to 1.
           JNC  ERROR       ;Check Carry Flag.
           JNP  ERROR       ;Check Parity Flag.
           JNS  ERROR       ;Check Sign Flag.
           JNE  ERROR       ;Check Zero Flag.
NO_ERROR:  JMP  CONTINUE    ;Continue execution
ERROR:     HLT              ;Attempt to halt the defective CPU.
```

Affected Flags: None.

Machine Instruction Decoding Guide:

1st Byte Hex Binary	2nd byte	Bytes 3,4,5,6	Operand Format
F4 1111 0100			No operand.

Assembly Language Coding Examples:

Machine Code	Assembly Instructions	Operand Format	Bytes	Clocks
F4	HLT	No operand.	1	2

IDIV

Definition: Integer divide.

Function: If byte operation then perform (AX):(Operand)

```
If ( (AX):(Operand) > +127 ) then perform type 0 interrupt.

If ( (AX):(Operand) < -127 ) then perform type 0 interrupt.

(AL) <---- Quotient

(AH) <---- Remainder
```

If word operation then perform (DX, AX):(Operand)

```
If ( (DX,AX):(Operand) > +32767 ) then perform type 0 interrupt.

If ( (DX,AX):(Operand) < -32767 ) then perform type 0 interrupt.

(AX) <---- Quotient

(DX) <---- Remainder
```

Description: This instruction performs a signed division of the accumulator by the specified operand. In byte division, the contents of the AX register are treated as a signed 16-bit dividend. In word division, the contents of the register pair DX, AX are treated as a signed 32-bit dividend where the DX register holds the high-order sixteen bits. The specified operand may be a general register or a memory location and is treated as a signed 8-bit or 16-bit divisor depending upon byte or word division, respectively.

In byte division, the quotient is returned in the AL register and the remainder is returned in the AH register. In word division, the AX and DX registers are used to hold the 16-bit quotient and remainder, respectively. Both the quotient and remainder are treated as signed numbers.

The Processor Flag is undefined after executing a IDIV instruction. If the quotient is positive and exceeds the maximum (decimal 127 in byte division, or decimal 32767 in word division), or is negative and is less than the minimum (decimal −127 in byte division, or decimal −32767 in word division), or when dividing by zero is attempted, a type 0 interrupt is automatically generated. The quotient and remainder are undefined if a type 0 interrupt is generated. The absolute byte memory locations 00000H to 00003H contain a doubleword which specifies the code segment and offset address of the interrupt service procedure for the type 0 interrupt. Nonintegral quotients are truncated to whole integers. The remainder has the same sign as the dividend.

Example: Consider the case where the AX register contains 0049H, the BL register contains 12H, and the instruction IDIV BL is executed. The quotient of the division (04H = 49H/12H) is returned in the AL register and the remainder 01H is returned in the AH register.

Consider the case where the DX and AX registers contain FFFFH and F043H representing a 32-bit hexadecimal number FFFFF043H, the BP register contains 0240H, and the instruction IDIV BP is executed. The quotient of the division (FFFAH= FFFFF043H/0240H) is returned in the AX register and the remainder (FDC3H) is returned in the DX register.

Affected Flags:

15	14	13	12	11	10	9	8	7	6	5	4	3	2	1	0
				U				U	U		U		U		U
				OF	DF	IF	TF	SF	ZF		AF		PF		CF

Machine Instruction Decoding Guide:

First Byte Hex Binary	2nd byte	Bytes 3,4,5,6	Operand Format
F6 1111 0110	Mod-111-Rm	Disp-Lo,Disp-Hi	Reg8/Mem8
F7 1111 0111	Mod-111-Rm	Disp-Lo,Disp-Hi	Reg16/Mem16

Assembly Language Coding Examples:

Machine Code	Assembly Instructions	Operand Format	Bytes	Clocks
F6FD	IDIV CH	Reg8	2	101-112
F63D	IDIV BYTE PTR [DI]	Mem8	2-4	(107-118)+EA
F7FA	IDIV DX	Reg16	2	165-184
F73E0020	IDIV WORD PTR XNUM	Mem16	2-4	(175-194)+EA

IMUL

Definition: Integer multiply.
Function: If byte operation then:

```
(AX) <---- (AL) * (Operand)

If (AH) = sign extension of (AL)   then   (CF) <---- 0
                                          (OF) <---- 0
If (AH) # sign extension of (AL)   then   (CF) <---- 1
                                          (OF) <---- 1
```

If word operation then:

```
(DX,AX) <---- (AX) * (Operand)

If (DX) = sign extension of (AX)   then   (CF) <---- 0
                                          (OF) <---- 0
If (DX) # sign extension of (AX)   then   (CF) <---- 1
                                          (OF) <---- 1
```

Description: This instruction performs a signed multiplication of the accumulator and the specified operand. If the operand is an 8-bit quantity, it is multiplied by the AL register, and the 16-bit product is returned in the AX register. If the operand is a 16-bit quantity, it is multiplied by the AX register, and the 32-bit product is returned in the register pair DX, AX where the DX register holds the high-order sixteen bits. The specified operand can be a general register, or a memory location, and is treated as a signed number.

If the contents of the AH register are not the sign extension of the AL register after a byte multiplication, or the contents of the DX register are not the sign extension of the AX register after a word multiplication, the Carry Flag, CF, and the Overflow Flag, OF, are set to 1. Otherwise, they are cleared to 0. The Auxiliary Carry Flag, AF, the Parity Flag, PF, the Sign Flag, SF, and the Zero Flag, ZF are undefined following the execution of the IMUL instruction. When the Carry Flag, CF, and the Overflow Flag, OF, are set to 1, they indicate that the AH or DX register contains significant digits of the result.

Example: If the AL register contains 30H, the CL register contains 02H, and the instruction IMUL CL is executed. The product of the multiplication (60H = 30H * 2H) is returned in the AX register. Since the contents of the AH register represent the extension of the sign bit of the AL register, the Carry Flag, CF, and the Overflow Flag, OF, are cleared to 0.

If the AX register contains 0240H, the BX register contains F202H, and the instruction IMUL BX is executed. The 32-bit product of the multiplication (FFE08480H = 240H * F202H) is returned in the DX and AX register. Since the new contents of the DX register (FFE0H) do not represent the extension of the sign bit of the AX register (8480H), the Carry Flag, CF, and the Overflow Flag, OF, are set to 1.

Affected Flags:

15	14	13	12	11	10	9	8	7	6	5	4	3	2	1	0
				X				U	U		U		U		X
				OF	DF	IF	TF	SF	ZF		AF		PF		CF

Machine Instruction Decoding Guide:

First Byte Hex Binary	2nd byte	Bytes 3,4,5,6	Operand Format
F6 1111 0110	Mod-101-Rm	Disp-Lo,Disp-Hi	Reg8/Mem8
F7 1111 0111	Mod-101-Rm	Disp-Lo,Disp-Hi	Reg16/Mem16

Assembly Language Coding Examples:

Machine Code	Assembly Instructions	Operand Format	Bytes	Clocks
F6ED	IMUL CH	Reg8	2	80-98
F62C	IMUL BYTE PTR [SI]	Mem8	2-4	(86-104)+EA
F7ED	IMUL BP	Reg16	2	128-154
F72E0010	IMUL WORD PTR COUNT	Mem16	2-4	(138-164)+EA

IN

Definition: Input from port.

Function: (Accumulator) <--- (Input/Output port).

Description: This instruction transfers a byte or a word from an input/

output port to the AL or AX register, respectively. The specified input/output port can be an immediate byte constant which allows access to ports numbered from 0 to 255. If the DX register is used to specify the input/output port, up to 65536 different ports can be accessed by simply changing the contents of the DX register. This instruction does not affect any flags.

Example: If the current status byte of the printer is available at the input port 37AH, the microprocessor can determine whether the printer is ready to receive new characters to be printed based upon the information in the status byte retrieved from the input/output port. If the printer is ready when the most significant bit of the input status byte is 0, the following sequence of instructions decides whether it is time for the 8088 microprocessor to send a character to the printer port.

```
        MOV    DX,37AH     ;Get the input-output port number in DX.
WAIT:   IN     AL,DX       ;Get the status byte at this port.
        TEST   AL,80H      ;Check whether printer is busy (Bit 7 is 1).
        JNE    WAIT        ;Printer is still busy.
READY:  CLC
```

Affected Flags: None.

Machine Instruction Decoding Guide:

1st Byte Hex Binary	2nd byte	Bytes 3,4,5,6	Operand Format
E4 1110 0100	Data8		AL,Immed8
E5 1110 0101	Data8		AX,Immed8
EC 1110 1100			AL,DX
ED 1110 1101			AX,DX

Assembly Language Coding Examples:

Machine Code	Assembly Instructions	Operand Format	Bytes	Clocks
E420	IN AL,20H	AL,Immed8	2	10
E520	IN AX,20H	AX,Immed8	2	14
EC	IN AL,DX	AL,DX	1	8
ED	IN AX,DX	AX,DX	1	12

INC

Definition: Increment.

Function: (Operand) <--- (Operand) + 1.

Description: The original contents of the specified operand are incremented by 1. The operand can be a general register or a memory location. No segment register may be specified as operands. Both 8-bit and 16-bit operation can be performed. The operand is treated as an unsigned number. This instruction updates the Auxiliary Carry Flag, AF, the Overflow Flag, OF, the Parity Flag, PF, and Sign Flag, SF, and the Zero Flag, ZF.

Example: Consider the case where the word memory location specified by the BX register contains FE00H, and the instruction INC WORD PTR [BX] is executed. The new contents of the word memory location specified by the BX register will be FE01H. Since the result of the instruction is a negative nonzero number in two's complement form, the Sign Flag, SF, is set to 1 and the Zero Flag, ZF, is cleared at 0. There is only one 1 bit in the low-order byte of this word memory location, which is an odd number, so the Parity Flag, PF, is cleared to 0.

Affected Flags:

15	14	13	12	11	10	9	8	7	6	5	4	3	2	1	0
				X				X	X		X		X		
				OF	DF	IF	TF	SF	ZF		AF		PF		CF

Machine Instruction Decoding Guide:

1st Byte Hex Binary	2nd byte	Bytes 3,4,5,6	Operand Format
FE 1111 1110	Mod-000-Rm	Disp-Lo,Disp-Hi	Reg8/Mem8
FF 1111 1111	Mod-000-Rm	Disp-Lo,Disp-Hi	Reg16/Mem16
0100 Oreg			Reg16 only*

*Note: The instruction format FF Mod-000-Rm should not be used if the specified operand is a 16-bit register. The alternate format 0100 Oreg is more efficient.

Assembly Language Coding Examples;

Machine Code	Assembly Instructions	Operand Format	Bytes	Clocks
FEC5	INC CH	Reg8	2	3
FE04	INC BYTE PTR [SI]	Mem8	2-4	15+EA
45	INC BP	Reg16	1	2
FF4701	INC WORD PTR [BX+01]	Mem16	2-4	23+EA

INT

Definition: Software interrupt.

Function:

```
              (SP) <---- (SP) - 2
    (Top Of Stack) <---- (Processor Flag)
              (SP) <---- (SP) - 2
    (Top Of Stack) <---- (CS)
              (SP) <---- (SP) - 2
    (Top Of Stack) <---- (IP)
              (IF) <---- 0
              (TF) <---- 0
              (CS) <---- (Interrupt Type * 4 + 2)
              (IP) <---- (Interrupt Type * 4)
```

Description: This instruction transfers control to an interrupt service procedure whose address is generated based upon the specified interrupt type. The current machine status of the microprocessor is pushed on the stack which includes the contents of the Processor Flag, the Code Segment register, and the Instruction Pointer, IP. This arrangement permits an IRET (Return from Interrupt) instruction in the interrupt service procedure to transfer control back to the instruction following the INT instruction. The Interrupt-Enable Flag, IF, and the Trace Flag, TF, are cleared to 0 to prevent any maskable and single-step interrupts.

The absolute memory address of the interrupt vector corresponding to the interrupt type specified in the instruction's operand is calculated by multiplying the interrupt type by 4. The contents of the doubleword at this memory location replace the current contents of the Instruction Pointer, IP and the Code Segment, CS register, respectively.

Example: Consider the case where the Code Segment register contains 04B5H, the Instruction Pointer, IP, contains 32D0H, the Stack Pointer, SP, contains FFDDH, the absolute word memory locations 0048H and 004AH contain 1000H and 04C5H, respectively, and the following sequence of instructions is executed:

```
       INT 12H
NEXT:  CLC
```

Upon entry of the interrupt service procedure, the Stack Pointer contains FFD7H, the Code Segment register contains 04C5H, and the Instruction Pointer has a new value of 1000H.

Affected Flags:

15	14	13	12	11	10	9	8	7	6	5	4	3	2	1	0
						0	0								
				OF	DF	IF	TF	SF	ZF		AF		PF		CF

Machine Instruction Decoding Guide:

1st Byte Hex Binary	2nd byte	Bytes 3,4,5,6	Operand Format
CC 1100 1100			Type 3
CD 1100 1101	Type		Immed8*

Assembly Language Coding Examples:

Machine Code	Assembly Instructions	Operand Format	Bytes	Clocks*
CC	INT 3	Type 3	1	52(72)
CD21	INT 21H	Immed8	2	51(71)

*Notes:

1) If the interrupt type is 3, the alternate machine code CCH (1100 1100) is more efficient.

2) Clock cycles in parentheses are for word operands.

INTO

Definition: Interrupt on overflow.
Function:

```
           (SP) <---- (SP) - 2
(Top Of Stack) <---- (Processor Flag)
           (SP) <---- (SP) - 2
(Top Of Stack) <---- (CS)
           (SP) <---- (SP) - 2
(Top Of Stack) <---- (IP)
           (IF) <---- 0
           (TF) <---- 0
           (CS) <---- (12H)
           (IP) <---- (10H)
```

Description: This instruction transfers control to an interrupt service procedure (type 4) through the interrupt vector at the absolute memory location 00010H if the Overflow Flag, OF, is set to 1. The current machine status of the microprocessor is pushed on the stack which includes the contents of the Processor Flag, the Code Segment register, and the Instruction Pointer, IP. This arrangement permits an IRET (Return from Interrupt) instruction in the interrupt service procedure to transfer control back to the instruction following the INTO instruction. The Interrupt-Enable Flag, IF, and the Trace Flag, TF, are cleared to 0 to prevent any maskable and single-step interrupts.

Example: Consider the case where the AL register contains 30H, the CL register contains 20H, and the following sequence of instructions is executed.

```
MUL  CL
INTO
```

The result of the multiplication sets the Overflow Flag, OF, to 1. Executing the instruction INTO will generate a type 4 interrupt.

Affected Flags:

15	14	13	12	11	10	9	8	7	6	5	4	3	2	1	0
						0	0								
				OF	DF	IF	TF	SF	ZF		AF		PF		CF

Machine Instruction Decoding Guide:

1st Byte Hex Binary	2nd byte	Bytes 3,4,5,6	Operand Format
CE 1100 1110			No Operand

Assembly Language Coding Examples:

Machine Code	Assembly Instructions	Operand Format	Bytes Clocks*
CE	INTO	No Operand	1 53(73) or 4

*Notes:

1) 4 clocks if the interrupt does not occur.

2) Clock cycles in parentheses are for word operands.

IRET

Definition: Return from interrupt.

Function:

```
             (IP) <---- (Top Of Stack)
             (SP) <---- (SP) + 2
             (CS) <---- (Top Of Stack)
             (SP) <---- (SP) + 2
(Processor Flag) <---- (Top Of Stack)
             (SP) <---- (SP) + 2
```

Description: This instruction returns control to the point of interruption by restoring the Instruction Pointer, IP, the Code Segment register, and the Processor Flag from the stack to their previously saved values. Any interrupt service procedure must use this instruction to terminate the procedure properly.

Affected Flags:

15	14	13	12	11	10	9	8	7	6	5	4	3	2	1	0
				X	X	X	X	X	X		X		X		X
				OF	DF	IF	TF	SF	ZF		AF		PF		CF

Machine Instruction Decoding Guide:

1st Byte Hex Binary	2nd byte	Bytes 3,4,5,6	Operand Format
CF 1100 1111			No Operand

Assembly Language Coding Examples:

Machine Code	Assembly Instructions	Operand Format	Bytes	Clocks*
CF	IRET	No Operand	1	32(44)
*Note: Clock cycles in parentheses are for word operands.				

JA/JNBE

Definition: Jump if above/Jump if not below or equal.

Function: If (CF) = 0 and (ZF) = 0 then (IP) <---- (IP) + Disp8.

Description: Control is transferred to the address specified by the target operand if both the Carry Flag, CF, and the Zero Flag, ZF, are 0. Otherwise, the next instruction in the sequence is executed. The target operand address is generated by adding the displacement byte to the address of the next instruction. Since the displacement byte is an 8-bit signed integer, this instruction can branch to a new memory address within +127 bytes or −128 bytes of the end of the instruction. It is useful in the comparison of unsigned numbers.

Example: Consider the case where the AL register contains 62H, and the following sequence of instructions is executed.

```
        CMP  AL,60H
        JA   UPPER
        RET
UPPER:  AND  AL,5EH
```

The instruction CMP AL,60H clears the Carry Flag, CF, and the Zero Flag, ZF, to 0. After the instruction JA UPPER is executed, control is transferred to the address UPPER where the next instruction to be executed is AND AL,5EH. This reflects the condition that the contents of all AL register AL are above (not below or equal to) the hexadecimal number 60H.

If the AL register contains 41H, and the sequence of instructions is executed, the Carry Flag, CF, is set to 1 and the instruction RET takes place instead.

Affected Flags: None.

Machine Instruction Decoding Guide:

First Byte Hex Binary	2nd byte	Bytes 3,4,5,6	Operand Format
77 0111 0111	Disp8		Short-Label

Assembly Language Coding Examples:

Machine Code	Assembly Instructions	Operand Format	Bytes	Clocks*
7709	JA UPPER_CASE	Short-Label	2	4 or 16
77F1	JNBE CONVERSION	Short-Label	2	4 or 16

JAE/JNB/JNC

Definition: Jump if above or equal/Jump if not below/Jump if not carry.

Function: If (CF) = 0 then (IP) <---- (IP) + Disp8.

Description: Control is transferred to the address specified by the target operand if the Carry Flag, CF, is 0. Otherwise, the next instruction in the sequence is executed. The target operand address is generated by adding the displacement byte to the address of the next instruction. Since the displacement byte is an 8-bit signed integer, this instruction can branch to a new memory address within +127 bytes or −128 bytes of the end of the instruction. This instruction is useful in the comparison of unsigned numbers.

Example: Consider the case where the BX register contains D823H and the following sequence of instructions is executed.

```
        SUB  BX,100H
        JAE  ERROR
        CALL NEW
        RET
ERROR:  ADD  DL,125
```

The instruction SUB BX,100H clears the Carry Flag, CF, to 0. After the instruction JAE ERROR is executed, control is transferred to the address ERROR where the next instruction to be executed is ADD DL,125. This reflects the condition that the contents of the BX register is above or equal to (not below) the number 100H.

If the BX register contains 0047H, and the sequence of instructions is executed, the Carry Flag, CF, is set to 1, and the instruction CALL NEW takes place instead.

Affected Flags: None.

Machine Instruction Decoding Guide:

First Byte Hex Binary	2nd byte	Bytes 3,4,5,6	Operand Format
73 0111 0011	Disp8		Short-Label

Assembly Language Coding Examples:

Machine Code	Assembly Instructions	Operand Format	Bytes	Clocks*
7309	JAE SAVE_DATA	Short-Label	2	4 or 16
73F1	JNB PROGRAM	Short-Label	2	4 or 16
73E0	JNC END	Short-Label	2	4 or 16
*Notes: 16 clocks if the jump is performed.				

JB/JNAE/JC

Definition: Jump if below/Jump if not above or equal/Jump if carry.

Function: If (CF) = 1 then (IP) <---- (IP) + Disp8.

Description: Control is transferred to the address specified by the target operand if the Carry Flag, CF, is 1. Otherwise, the next instruction in the sequence is executed. The target operand address is generated by adding the displacement byte to the address of the next instruction. Since the displacement byte is an 8-bit signed integer, this instruction can branch to a new memory address within +127 bytes or −128 bytes of the end of the instruction. This instruction is useful in the comparison of unsigned numbers.

Example: Consider the case where the AL register contains 00, the byte memory location TEST_BIT contains 1, and the following sequence of instructions is executed.

```
        CMP  AL,TEST_BIT
        JB   PARITY
        AND  DL,AL
        RET
PARITY: HLT
```

The instruction CMP AL,TEST_BIT sets the Carry Flag, CF, to 1. After the instruction JB PARITY is executed, control is transferred to the address PARITY where the next instruction to be executed is HLT. This reflects the condition that the contents of the AL register are below (not above or equal to) the contents of the byte memory location TEST_BIT.

If the AL register contains 00, the byte memory location TEST_BIT also contains 00, and the sequence of instructions is executed, the Carry Flag, CF, will be cleared to 0 and the instruction AND AL,DL takes place instead.

Affected Flags: None.

Machine Instruction Decoding Guide:

First Byte Hex Binary	2nd byte	Bytes 3,4,5,6	Operand Format
72 0111 0010	Disp8		Short-Label

Assembly Language Coding Examples:

Machine Code	Assembly Instructions	Operand Format	Bytes	Clocks*
7209	JB CHECK_ERROR	Short-Label	2	4 or 16
72F1	JNAE END_NOW	Short-Label	2	4 or 16
72E0	JC QUIT	Short-Label	2	4 or 16

JBE/JNA

Definition: Jump if below or equal/Jump if not above.

Function: If (CF) = 1 or (ZF) = 1 then (IP) <---- (IP) + Disp8.

Description: Control is transferred to the address specified by the target operand if the Carry Flag, CF, is 1 or the Zero Flag, ZF, is 1. Otherwise, the next instruction in the sequence is executed. The target operand address is generated by adding the displacement byte to the address of the next instruction. Since the displacement byte is an 8-bit signed integer, this instruction can branch to a new memory address within +127 bytes or −128 bytes of the end of the instruction. This instruction is useful in the comparison of unsigned numbers.

Example: Consider the case where the word memory location NEW_DATA contains 0001H, and the following sequence of instructions is executed.

```
        CMP WORD PTR NEW_DATA,01
        JBE   FOUND
        CLD
        RET
FOUND:  AND  AL,00
```

Since both operands of the first instruction have the same value, executing CMP WORD PTR NEW_DATA,01 sets the Zero Flag, ZF, to 1. After the instruction JBE FOUND is executed, control is transferred to the address FOUND where the next instruction to be executed is AND AL,00. This reflects the condition that the contents of the word memory location

NEW_DATA are below or equal to (not above) the value of the second operand (1 in this case).

If the word memory NEW_DATA contains 0024H and the sequence of instructions is executed, the instruction CLD will take place instead.

Affected Flags: None.

Machine Instruction Decoding Guide:

First Byte Hex Binary	2nd byte	Bytes 3,4,5,6	Operand Format
76 0111 0110	Disp8		Short-Label

Assembly Language Coding Examples:

Machine Code	Assembly Instructions	Operand Format	Bytes	Clocks*
7609	JBE SAVE_DATA	Short-Label	2	4 or 16
76F0	JNA PROGRAM	Short-Label	2	4 or 16
Notes: 16 clocks if the jump is performed.				

JCXZ

Definition: Jump if the CX register is zero.

Function: If (CX) = 0 then (IP) <---- (IP) + Disp8.

Description: Control is transferred to the address specified by the target operand if the content of the CX register is 0. Otherwise, the next instruction in the sequence is executed. The target operand address is generated by adding the displacement byte to the address of the next instruction. Since the displacement byte is an 8-bit signed integer, this instruction can branch to a new memory address within +127 bytes or −128 bytes of the end of the instruction.

Example: Consider the case where the CX register contains 0001H, and the following sequence of instruction is executed.

```
              DEC   CX
              JCXZ  SKIP_REPEAT
              CALL  REPEAT
              RET
SKIP_REPEAT:  STD
```

The instruction DEC CX reduces the contents of the CX register to 0. After the instruction JCXZ SKIP_REPEAT is executed, control is transferred to the address SKIP_REPEAT where the instruction STD will be executed.

Affected Flags: None.

Machine Instruction Decoding Guide:

First Byte Hex Binary	2nd byte	Bytes 3,4,5,6	Operand Format
E3 1110 0011	Disp8		Short-Label

Assembly Language Coding Examples:

Machine Code	Assembly Instructions	Operand Format	Bytes	Clocks*
E3D0	JCXZ SKIP_LOOP	Short-Label	2	6 or 18
*Notes: 18 clocks if the jump is performed.				

JE/JZ

Definition: Jump if equal/Jump if zero.

Function: If (ZF) = 1 then (IP) <---- (IP) + Disp8.

Description: Control is transferred to the address specified by the target operand if the Zero Flag, ZF, is 1. Otherwise, the next instruction in the sequence is executed. The target operand address is generated by adding the displacement byte to the address of the next instruction. Since the displacement byte is an 8-bit signed integer, this instruction can branch to a new memory address within +127 bytes or –128 bytes of the end of the instruction.

Example: Consider the case where the AX register contains FFFFH, and the following sequence of instruction is executed.

```
         INC  AX
         JE   OUTPUT
         ADD  AX,4000H
         RET
OUTPUT:  CLD
```

The instruction INC AX sets the Zero Flag, ZF, to 1. After the instruction JE OUTPUT is executed, control is transferred to the address OUTPUT where the next instruction to be executed is CLD. This reflects the condition that the new content of the AX register is zero.

Affected Flags: None.

Machine Instruction Decoding Guide:

First Byte Hex Binary	2nd byte	Bytes 3,4,5,6	Operand Format
74 0111 0100	Disp8		Short-Label

Assembly Language Coding Examples:

Machine Code	Assembly Instructions	Operand Format	Bytes	Clocks*
7420	JE NO_ERROR	Short-Label	2	4 or 16
74D1	JZ NOT_WRANING	Short-Label	2	4 or 16
*Notes: 16 clocks if the jump is performed.				

JG/JNLE

Definition: Jump if greater than/Jump if not less than or equal.

Function: If ((SF) = (OF) AND (ZF) = 0 then (IP) <---- (IP) + Disp8.

Description: Control is transferred to the address specified by the target operand if the Sign Flag, SF, is equal to the Overflow Flag, OF, and the Zero Flag, ZF, is 0. Otherwise, the next instruction in the sequence is executed. The target operand address is generated by adding the displacement byte to the address of the next instruction. Since the displacement byte is an 8-bit signed integer, this instruction can branch to a new memory address within +127 bytes or −128 bytes of the end of the instruction. This instruction is useful in the comparison of signed numbers.

Example: Consider the case where the SI register contains 0020H, the DX register contains FF23H, and the following sequence of instructions is executed.

```
        CMP  SI,DX
        JG   SAME
        STD
        RET
SAME:   CLD
```

After the instruction CMP SI,DX is executed, the Sign Flag, SF, the Zero Flag, ZF, and the Overflow Flag, OF, are cleared to 0. After the instruction JG SAME is executed, control is transferred to the address SAME where the next instruction to be executed is CLD. This reflects the condition that the contents of the SI register (positive hexadecimal number 20H) are greater than (not less than or equal to) the contents of the DX register (negative hexadecimal number FF23H).

Affected Flags: None.

Machine Instruction Decoding Guide:

First Byte Hex Binary	2nd byte	Bytes 3,4,5,6	Operand Format
7F 0111 1111	Disp8		Short-Label

Assembly Language Coding Examples:

Machine Code	Assembly Instructions	Operand Format	Bytes	Clocks*
7F0C	JG NEXT_LINE	Short-Label	2	4 or 16
7FB0	JNLE NEXT_ARGUMENT	Short-Label	2	4 or 16
*Notes: 16 clocks if the jump is performed.				

JGE/JNL

Definition: Jump if greater or equal/Jump if not less than.

Function: If (SF) = (OF) then (IP) <---- (IP) + Disp8.

Description: Control is transferred to the address specified by the target operand if the Sign Flag, SF, is equal to the Overflow Flag, OF, Otherwise, the next instruction in the sequence is executed. The target operand address is generated by adding the displacement byte to the address of the next instruction. Since the displacement byte is an 8-bit signed integer, this instruction can branch to a new memory address within +127 bytes or −128 bytes of the end of the instruction. This instruction is useful in the comparison of signed numbers.

Example: Consider the case where the AX register contains 0020H, and the following sequence of instructions is executed.

```
         DEC  AX
         JGE  UNSIGN
         CLC
         RET
UNSIGN:  INC  BP
```

The result of the instruction DEC AX is a positive nonzero value in the AX register. Therefore, the Sign Flag, SF, and the Overflow Flag, OF, are cleared to 0. After the instruction JGE UNSIGN is executed, control is transferred to the address UNSIGN where the next instruction to be executed is INC BP. This reflects the condition that the contents of the AX register are not less than (greater than or equal to) 0.

Consider the case where the AX register contains FF00H, and the sequence of instructions is executed. The Sign Flag, SF, is set to 1, and the instruction CLC will take place instead.

Affected Flags: None.

Machine Instruction Decoding Guide:

First Byte Hex Binary	2nd byte	Bytes 3,4,5,6	Operand Format
7D 0111 1101	Disp8		Short-Label

Assembly Language Coding Examples:

Machine Code	Assembly Instructions	Operand Format	Bytes	Clocks*
7DOC	JGE NOW	Short-Label	2	4 or 16
7DB2	JNL NEXT_ARGUMENT	Short-Label	2	4 or 16
*Notes: 16 clocks if the jump is performed.				

JL/JNGE

Definition: Jump if less than/Jump if not greater than or equal.

Function: If (SF) # (OF) then (IP) <---- (IP) + Disp8.

Description: Control is transferred to the address specified by the target operand if the Sign Flag, SF, is not equal to the Overflow Flag, OF. Otherwise, the next instruction in the sequence is executed. The target operand address is generated by adding the displacement byte to the address of the next instruction. Since the displacement byte is an 8-bit signed integer, this instruction can branch to a new memory address within +127 bytes or −128 bytes of the end of the instruction. This instruction is useful in the comparison of signed numbers.

Example: Consider the case where the AX register contains FFFFH, the DX register contains 0002H, and the following sequence of instructions is executed.

```
        CMP  AX,DX
        JL   CHECK
        CLC
        RET
CHECK:  AND_ AX,00
```

The instruction CMP AX,DX sets the Sign Flag, SF, to 1 and clears the Overflow Flag, OF, to 0. After the instruction JL CHECK is executed, control is transferred to the address CHECK where the next instruction to be executed is AND AX,00. This reflects the condition that the contents of the AX register are less than (not greater than or equal to) the contents of the DX register.

If the AX register contains 0124H, the DX register contains 0020H, and the sequence of instructions is executed, the Sign Flag, SF, and the Overflow Flag, OF, are cleared to 0 and the instruction CLC takes place instead.

Affected Flags: None.

Machine Instruction Decoding Guide:

First Byte Hex Binary	2nd byte	Bytes 3,4,5,6	Operand Format
7C 0111 1100	Disp8		Short-Label

Assembly Language Coding Examples:

Machine Code	Assembly Instructions	Operand Format	Bytes	Clocks*
7CD2	JL LAST_OPTION	Short-Label	2	4 or 16
7C05	JNGE NEXT_SECTION	Short-Label	2	4 or 16
*Notes: 16 clocks if the jump is performed.				

JLE/JNG

Definition: Jump if less than or equal/Jump if not greater than.

Function: If (SF) # (OF) or (ZF) = 1 then (IP) <---- (IP) + Disp8.

Description: Control is transferred to the address specified by the target operand if the Sign Flag, SF, is not equal to the Overflow Flag, OF, or if the Zero Flag, ZF, is 1. Otherwise, the next instruction in the sequence is executed. The target operand address is generated by adding the displacement byte to the address of the next instruction. Since the displacement byte is an 8-bit signed integer, this instruction can branch to a new memory address within +127 bytes or −128 bytes of the end of the instruction. This instruction is useful in the comparison of signed numbers.

Example: Consider the case where the CX register contains D700H, the BP register contains 0124H, and the following sequence of instructions is executed.

```
        CMP  CX,BP
        JLE  NEXT
        AND  AL,00
        RET
NEXT:   ADD  AX,127
```

The instruction CMP CX,BP sets the Sign Flag, SF, to 1 and clears the Overflow Flag, OF, to 0. After the instruction JLE NEXT is executed, control is transferred to the address NEXT where the next instruction to be executed is ADD AX,127. This reflects the condition that the contents of the CX register are not greater than (less than or equal to) the contents of the BP register.

If the CX register contains 0125H, the BP register contains 0124H, and the sequence of instructions is executed, the Sign Flag, SF, and the Overflow Flag, OF, are cleared to 0 and the instruction AND AL,00 takes place instead.

Affected Flags: None.

Machine Instruction Decoding Guide:

First Byte Hex Binary	2nd byte	Bytes 3,4,5,6	Operand Format
7E 0111 1110	Disp8		Short-Label

Assembly Language Coding Examples:

Machine Code	Assembly Instructions	Operand Format	Bytes	Clocks*
7E25	JLE LAST_CHAR	Short-Label	2	4 or 16
7ED3	JNG NEXT_LETTER	Short-Label	2	4 or 16
*Notes: 16 clocks if the jump is performed.				

JMP

Definition: Jump unconditionally
Function: If intersegment then:

(CS) <---- Segment Of Target Operand
(IP) <---- Offset Address Of Target Operand

If intrasegment then:

(IP) <---- Offset Address Of Target Operand

Description: This instruction transfers control unconditionally to a target location in one of five different formats: intrasegment direct, intrasegment direct short, intrasegment indirect, intersegment direct, and intersegment indirect.

An intrasegment JMP instruction transfers control to a target address within the current 64 K-byte code segment only. In other words, the target address must be within 32767 or −32768 bytes of the JMP.

An intersegment JMP can transfer control to any target address within the 8088 megabyte memory space.

In an intrasegment direct JMP, the 16-bit displacement value in the instruction is added to the contents of the Instruction Pointer, IP, to generate the address of the target operand. If the target address is within 127 bytes or −128 bytes of the JMP instruction, the alternate intrasegment direct short format can be used. In this format, an 8-bit displacement value in the instruction is added to the contents of the IP register to generate the address of the target operand. In an intrasegment indirect JMP, a 16-bit general register (AX, BX, CX, DX, SI, DI, BP, SP) or a memory location may be used as an operand whose contents specify the address of the target operand.

An intersegment direct JMP contains the values of the code segment and offset address of the target operand as a part of the JMP instruction which will replace the contents of the CS and IP registers after the JMP instruction is executed. The previous contents of the CS and IP registers are lost. A memory location can also be used as operands of an intersegment indirect JMP. A doubleword at this memory location replaces the contents of the CS and IP registers after the JMP instruction is executed (see section 2.3.2 for the standard format of a doubleword in the computer memory).

Example: In 8088 assembly language, the operator FAR PTR or DWORD PTR is used to indicate an intersegment direct JMP, or an intersegment indirect JMP, respectively. If no attribute operator is specified in the JMP instruction, the assembler attempts to generate the machine codes in the intrasegment format. The operator SHORT can also be used to expressly define an intrasegment direct short JMP.

```
Intersegment JMP

        MOV AL,00
        JMP FAR PTR NEXT_PAGE
        ..
        Other instructions
        ..
        JMP DWORD PTR [BX]
        ..
        Other instructions
        ..
NEXT_PAGE:    CMP AX,00
        ..
        Other instructions
```

```
Intrasegment JMP

        MOV AL,00
        JMP SHORT NEXT_LINE
        ..
        Other instructions
        ..
NEXT_LINE: CLC
        ..
        Other instructions
        ..
SAME_LINE: AND AL,00
        ..
        Other instructions
        ..
        JMP  SAME_LINE
```

Affected Flags: None.

Machine Instruction Decoding Guide:

1st Byte Hex Binary	2nd byte	Bytes 3,4,5,6	Operand Format
E9 1110 1001	IP-Inc-Lo	IP-Inc-Hi	Near-Label
EA 1110 1010	Offset-Lo	Offset-Hi Seg-Lo,Seg-Hi	Far-Label
EB 1110 1011	IP-Inc8		Short-Label
FF 1111 1111	Mod-100-Rm		Reg16/Mem16 (Intrasegment)
FF 1111 1111	Mod-101-Rm		Mem16 only (Intersegment)

Assembly Language Coding Examples:

Machine Code	Assembly Instructions	Operand Format	Bytes	Clocks
E90020	JMP NEXT_PROC	Near-Label	3	15

Machine Code	Assembly Instructions	Operand Format	Bytes	Clocks
EA001200F0	JMP FAR PTR TICK	Far-Label	5	15
EB22	JMP SHORT NEXT	Short-Label	2	15
FFE3	JMP BX	Reg16 (Intra)	2	11
FF6404	JMP WORD PTR [SI+04]	Memp16 (Intra)	2-4	18+EA
FF6E01	JMP DWORD PTR [BP+1]	Memp16 (Inter)	2-4	24+EA

JNE/JNZ

Definition: Jump if not equal/Jump if not zero.

Function: If (ZF) = 0 then (IP) <---- (IP) + Disp8.

Description: Control is transferred to the address specified by the target operand if the Zero Flag, ZF, is 0. Otherwise, the next instruction in the sequence is executed. The target operand address is generated by adding the displacement byte to the address of the next instruction. Since the displacement byte is an 8-bit signed integer, this instruction can branch to a new memory address within +127 bytes or −128 bytes of the end of the instruction.

Example: Consider the case where the BX register contains 0457H, and the following sequence of instruction is executed.

```
         DEC  BX
         JNE  OUTPUT
         ADD  AX,4000H
         RET
OUTPUT:  CLD
```

The instruction DEC BX clears the Zero Flag, ZF, to 0. After the instruction JNE OUTPUT is executed, control is transferred to the address OUTPUT where the next instruction to be executed is CLD. This reflects the condition that the new contents of the BX register are not zero.

Affected Flags: None.

Machine Instruction Decoding Guide:

First Byte Hex Binary	2nd byte	Bytes 3,4,5,6	Operand Format
75 0111 0101	Disp8		Short-Label

Assembly Language Coding Examples:

Machine Code	Assembly Instructions	Operand Format	Bytes	Clocks*
7508	JNE ERROR_CODE	Short-Label	2	4 or 16
75E2	JNZ ERROR_CHECK	Short-Label	2	4 or 16
*Notes: 16 clocks if the jump is performed.				

JNO

Definition: Jump if not overflow.

Function: If (OF) = 0 then (IP) <---- (IP) + Disp8.

Description: Control is transferred to the address specified by the target operand if the Overflow Flag, OF, is 0. Otherwise, the next instruction in the sequence is executed. The target operand address is generated by adding the displacement byte to the address of the next instruction. Since the displacement byte is an 8-bit signed integer, this instruction can branch to a new memory address within +127 bytes or −128 bytes of the end of the instruction.

Example: Consider the case where the AX register contains 6800H, the BX register contains 1000H, and the following sequence of instructions is executed.

```
          ADD  AX,BX
          JNO  NOT_YET
          ADD  AX,256
          RET
NOT_YET:  CLD
```

The instruction ADD AX,BX clears the Overflow Flag, OF, to 0. After the instruction JNO NOT_YET is executed, control is transferred to the address NOT_YET where the next instruction to be executed is CLD. This reflects the condition that the result of the addition does not overflow the 16-bit capacity of the AX register.

Affected Flags: None.

Machine Instruction Decoding Guide:

First Byte Hex Binary	2nd byte	Bytes 3,4,5,6	Operand Format
71 0111 0001	Disp8		Short-Label

Assembly Language Coding Examples:

Machine Code	Assembly Instructions	Operand Format	Bytes	Clocks*
719D	JNO SUM_CHECK	Short-Label	2	4 or 16
*Notes: 16 clocks if the jump is performed.				

JNP/JPO

Definition: Jump if not parity/Jump if parity odd.

Function: If (PF) = 0 then (IP) <---- (IP) + Disp8.

Description: Control is transferred to the address specified by the target operand if the Parity Flag, PF, is 0. Otherwise, the next instruction in the sequence is executed. The target operand address is generated by adding the displacement byte to the address of the next instruction. Since the displacement byte is an 8-bit signed integer, this instruction can branch to a new memory address within +127 bytes or −128 bytes of the end of the instruction.

Example: Consider the case where the BP register contains 7E07H (0111 1110 0000 0111 in binary), and the following sequence of instruction is executed.

```
            CMP  BP,00
            JNP  NEXT_WORD
            CLC
            RET
NEXT_WORD:  CALL ROTATE_BIT
```

The instruction CMP BP,00 clears the Parity Flag, PF, to 0. After the instruction JNP NEXT_WORD is executed, control is transferred to the address NEXT_WORD where the next instruction to be executed is CALL ROTATE_BIT. This indicates that there is an odd number of 1 bits in the low-order eight bits of the BP register (three 1 bits in this example).

Affected Flags: None.

Machine Instruction Decoding Guide:

First Byte Hex Binary	2nd byte	Bytes 3,4,5,6	Operand Format
7B 0111 1011	Disp8		Short-Label

Assembly Language Coding Examples:

Machine Code	Assembly Instructions	Operand Format	Bytes	Clocks*
7B47	JNP BAD_PARITY	Short-Label	2	4 or 16
7BF2	JPO CHECK_BIT	Short-Label	2	4 or 16
*Notes: 16 clocks if the jump is performed.				

JNS

Definition: Jump if not sign.

Function: If (SF) = 0 then (IP) <---- (IP) + Disp8.

Description: Control is transferred to the address specified by the target operand if the Sign Flag, SF, is 0. Otherwise, the next instruction in the sequence is executed. The target operand address is generated by adding the displacement byte to the address of the next instruction. Since the displacement byte is an 8-bit signed integer, this instruction can branch to a new memory address within +127 bytes or −128 bytes of the end of the instruction.

Example: Consider the case where the AX register contains 7800H, and the following sequence of instructions is executed.

```
          CMP  AX,00
          JNS  POSITIVE
          CLD
          IRET
POSITIVE: STD
```

The instruction CMP AX,00 clears the Sign Flag, SF, to 0. After the instruction JNS POSITIVE is executed, control is transferred to the address POSITIVE where the next instruction to be executed is STD. The Sign Flag, SF, indicates that the contents of the AX register represent a positive binary number (the most significant bit of the word in the AX register is 0).

Affected Flags: None.

Machine Instruction Decoding Guide:

First Byte Hex Binary	2nd byte	Bytes 3,4,5,6	Operand Format
79 0111·1001	Disp8		Short-Label

Assembly Language Coding Examples:

Machine Code	Assembly Instructions	Operand Format	Bytes	Clocks*
7945	JNS REAL_ADJUST	Short-Label	2	4 or 16
*Notes: 16 clocks if the jump is performed.				

JO

Definition: Jump if overflow.

Function: If (OF) = 1 then (IP) <---- (IP) + Disp8.

Description: Control is transferred to the address specified by the target operand if the Overflow Flag is 1. Otherwise, the next instruction in the sequence is executed. The target operand address is generated by adding the displacement byte to the address of the next instruction. Since the displacement byte is an 8-bit signed integer, this instruction can branch to a new memory address within +127 bytes or −128 bytes of the end of the instruction.

Example: Consider the case where the AX register contains 7800H, the BX register contains 7627H, and the following sequence of instructions is executed.

```
              ADD  AX,BX
              JO   NEXT_FRAME
              AND  DL,00
              RET
NEXT_FRAME:   ADD  AX,4000H
```

The instruction ADD AX,BX sets the Overflow Flag, OF, to 1. After the instruction JO NEXT_FRAME is executed, control is transferred to the address NEXT_FRAME where the next instruction to be executed is ADD AX,4000H. This indicates that the result of the addition overflows the 16-bit capacity of the AX register.

Affected Flags: None.

Machine Instruction Decoding Guide:

First Byte Hex Binary	2nd byte	Bytes 3,4,5,6	Operand Format
70 0111 0000	Disp8		Short-Label

Assembly Language Coding Examples:

Machine Code	Assembly Instructions	Operand Format	Bytes	Clocks*
7023	JO NOT_YET	Short-Label	2	4 or 16
*Notes: 16 clocks if the jump is performed.				

JP/JPE

Definition: Jump if parity/Jump if parity even.

Function: If (PF) = 1 then (IP) <---- (IP) + Disp8.

Description: Control is transferred to the address specified by the target operand if the Parity Flag, PF, is 1. Otherwise, the next instruction in the sequence is executed. The target operand address is generated by adding the displacement byte to the address of the next instruction. Since the displacement byte is an 8-bit signed integer, this instruction can branch to a new memory address within +127 bytes or −128 bytes of the end of the instruction.

Example: Consider the case where the AX register contains 007EH (0000 0000 0111 1110 in binary), and the following sequence of instruction is executed.

```
            CMP  AX,00
            JP   NEXT_BIT
            CLC
            RET
NEXT_BIT:   CALL ROTATE_BIT
```

The instruction CMP AX,00 sets the Parity Flag, PF, to 1. After the instruction JP NEXT_BIT is executed, control is transferred to the address NEXT_BIT where the next instruction to be executed is CALL ROTATE_BIT. This indicates that there is an even number of 1 bits in the low-order eight bits of register AX (six 1 bits in this example).

Affected Flags: None.

Machine Instruction Decoding Guide:

First Byte Hex Binary	2nd byte	Bytes 3,4,5,6	Operand Format
7A 0111 1010	Disp8		Short-Label

Assembly Language Coding Examples:

Machine Code	Assembly Instructions	Operand Format	Bytes	Clocks*
7A20	JP GOOD_PARITY	Short-Label	2	4 or 16
7AD0	JPE PARITY_CHECK	Short-Label	2	4 or 16
*Notes: 16 clocks if the jump is performed.				

JS

Definition: Jump if sign.

Function: If (SF) = 1 then (IP) <---- (IP) + Disp8.

Description: Control is transferred to the address specified by the target operand if the Sign Flag, SF, is 1. Otherwise, the next instruction in the sequence is executed. The target operand address is generated by adding the displacement byte to the address of the next instruction. Since the displacement byte is an 8-bit signed integer, this instruction can branch to a new memory address within +127 bytes or −128 bytes of the end of the instruction.

Example: Consider the case where the byte memory location FIRST_BYTE contains 0, and the following sequence of instruction is executed.

```
           DEC BYTE PTR FIRST_BYTE
           JS   COMPLETE
           STD
           RET
COMPLETE:  ADD  AX,4000H
```

The instruction DEC BYTE PTR FIRST_BYTE produces a new value FFH at the byte memory location FIRST_BYTE, and sets the Sign Flag, SF, to 1. After the instruction JS COMPLETE is executed, control is transferred to the address COMPLETE where the next instruction to be executed is ADD AX,4000H. This indicates that the contents of the byte memory location FIRST_BYTE represents a negative binary number (the most significant bit of the byte is 1).

Affected Flags: None.

Machine Instruction Decoding Guide:

First Byte Hex Binary	2nd byte	Bytes 3,4,5,6	Operand Format
78 0111 1000	Disp8		Short-Label

Assembly Language Coding Examples:

Machine Code	Assembly Instructions	Operand Format	Bytes	Clocks*
789D	JS SIGN_NUMBERS	Short-Label	2	4 or 16
*Notes: 16 clocks if the jump is performed.				

LAHF

Definition: Load the AH register from flag.

Function: (AH) <--- (Low-order 8 bits of Processor Flag).

Description: The low-order 8 bits of the Processor Flag replaces the original contents of the AH register. These eight bits include the Sign Flag, SF, the Zero Flag, ZF, the Auxilary Carry Flag, AF, the Parity Flag, PF, and the Carry Flag, CF. The Processor Flag itself is not updated. This instruction is used primarily to facilitate the upward compatibility between the 8088 microprocessor and its predecessors such as the 8088/8085 CPUs.

Example: If the AX register contains 4420H, the Processor Flag contains F046H, and the instruction LAHF is executed, the AX register has a new value of 4620H. The Processor Flag remains unchanged.

Affected Flags: None.

Machine Instruction Decoding Guide:

First Byte Hex Binary	2nd byte	Bytes 3,4,5,6	Operand Format
9F 1001 1111			No Operand

Assembly Language Coding Examples:

Machine Code	Assembly Instructions	Operand Format	Bytes	Clocks
9F	LAHF	No Operand	1	4

LDS

Definition: Load pointer using the DS register.

Function:

```
(First Operand) <---- (Effective Address)

(Data Segment DS Register) <---- (Effective Address + 2)
```

Description: The low-order 16 bits of a doubleword at the memory location specified by the second operand replace the original contents of a 16-bit general register specified in the first operand. The high-order 16 bits of the doubleword replace the contents of the current DS register. The first operand of this instruction must be a 16-bit general register. No segment register may be specified as operands. The second operand must be a memory location. This instruction does not affect any flags. It is very useful to initialize memory pointers to be used in string operations such as LODS (Load String), MOVS (Move String), and CMPS (Compare String).

Example: If the DS register contains 04B5H, the SI register contains 2400H, the absolute word memory locations 6F50H and 6F52H contain F000H and 04C5H, respectively, and the instruction LDS AX,[SI] is executed. The AX and DS register will contain new contents of F000H and 04C5H, respectively.

Affected Flags: None.

Machine Instruction Decoding Guide:

First Byte Hex Binary	2nd byte	Bytes 3,4,5,6	Operand Format
C5 1100 0101	Mod-Reg-Rm*	Disp-Lo,Disp-Hi	Reg16,Mem16
*Note: If the bit pattern for the Mod field is 11, the operation is undefined.			

Assembly Language Coding Examples:

Machine Code	Assembly Instructions	Operand Format	Bytes	Clocks
C51F	LDS BX,[BX]	Reg16,Mem16	2-4	24+EA
C56D17	LDS BP,[DI+23]	Reg16,Mem16	2-4	24+EA
C50E0020	LDS CX,L_POINTER	Reg16,Mem16	2-4	24+EA

LEA

Definition: Load effective address.

Function: (First Operand) <---- Effective Address of Second Operand

Description: The 16-bit offset address of the second operand rather than its contents replaces the contents of the first operand. The first operand must be a 16-bit general register. No segment registers may be specified as operands. The second operand must be a memory location.

This instruction does not affect any flags.

Example: Consider the case where the word memory location TEST_WORD, located at the memory offset 8200H, contains 124H and the following sequence of the instruction is executed.

```
MOV  AX,TEST_WORD
LEA  SI,TEST_WORD
```

The AX and SI registers will contain 124H and 8200H, respectively.

Affected Flags: None.

Machine Instruction Decoding Guide:

First Byte Hex Binary	2nd byte	Bytes 3,4,5,6	Operand Format
8D 1000 1101	Mod-Reg-Rm*	Disp-Lo,Disp-Hi	Reg16,Mem16
*Note: If the bit pattern for the Mod field is 11, the operation is undefined.			

Assembly Language Coding Examples:

Machine Code	Assembly Instructions	Operand Format	Bytes	Clocks
8D07	LEA AX,[BX]	Reg16,Mem16	2-4	2+EA
8D6F0C	LEA BP,[BX+12]	Reg16,Mem16	2-4	2+EA
8D16091F	LEA DX,MEM_LOC	Reg16,Mem16	2-4	2+EA

LES

Definition: Load pointer using the ES register.

Function:

```
          (First Operand) <---- (Effective Address Of Second Operand)
(Extra Segment ES Register) <---- (Effective Address Of Second Operand + 2)
```

Description: The low-order 16 bits of a doubleword at the memory location specified by the second operand replace the original contents of a 16-bit general register specified in the first operand. The high-order 16 bits of the doubleword replace the contents of the current ES register. The first operand of this instruction must be a 16-bit general register. No segments register may be specified as operands. The second operand must be a memory location. This instruction does not affect any flags. It is very useful to initialize memory pointers in certain string operations such as MOVS (Move String), SCAS (Scan String), CMPS (Compare String), and STOS (Store String).

Example: If the DS register contains 04B5H, the Extra Segment register contains 04C5H, the SI register contains 2400H, the absolute word memory locations 6F50H and 6F52H contain B800H and F000H, respectively, and the following instruction LES DI, [SI] is executed, then the DI and ES register will have new contents of B800H and F000H, respectively. The Data Segment register DS remains unchanged.

Affected Flags: None.

Machine Instruction Decoding Guide:

```
C4    1100 0100    Mod-Reg-Rm* Disp-Lo,Disp-Hi      Reg16,Mem16
```

```
*Note: If the bit pattern for the Mod field is 11, the operation is
undefined.
```

Assembly Language Coding Examples:

Machine Code	Assembly Instructions	Operand Format	Bytes	Clocks
C407	LES AX,[BX]	Reg16,Mem16	2–4	24+EA
C4550F	LES DX,[DI+15]	Reg16,Mem16	2–4	24+EA
C43EFE10	LES DI,D_POINTER	Reg16,Mem16	2–4	24+EA

LOCK

Definition: Lock the bus.

Description: This instruction is a one-byte prefix that causes the 8088 microprocessor (in a microcomputer system configured to have multiple processors) to assert its bus LOCK signal while the following instruction executes. This is to ensure that the referenced memory locations can be accessed by the 8088 microprocessor without any interference from any other coprocessors present in the microcomputer system. This instruction has no operands and does not affect any flags.

Example: In 8088 assembly language, the instruction LOCK can be used as a prefix instruction to be coded with other instructions in one single assembly language statement as the following example:

```
LOCK XCHG  AL,TEST_LOCATION
```

Affected Flags: None.

Machine Instruction Decoding Guide:

First Byte Hex Binary	2nd byte	Bytes 3,4,5,6	Operand Format
F0 1111 0000			No Operand

Assembly Language Coding Examples:

Machine Code	Assembly Instructions	Operand Format	Bytes	Clocks
F0C606001000	LOCK MOV BYTE PTR X,0	No Operand	1	2

LODS

Definition: Load String
Function: (Accumulator) <---- (Operand addressed by SI).

```
If (DF) = 0  then  (SI) <---- (SI) + 1 (byte)
                                  or
                   (SI) <---- (SI) + 2 (word)


If (DF) = 1  then  (SI) <---- (SI) - 1 (byte)
                                  or
                   (SI) <---- (SI) - 2 (word)
```

Description: The contents of the memory location addressed by the SI register replace the original contents of the AL or AX register depending upon byte or word operation. In assembly language, the instruction LODS is coded as LODSB for byte operation and as LODSW for word operation. If the Direction FLAG DF is 0, the contents of the SI register are incremented by 1 after LODSB is executed, or by 2 after LODSW is executed. If the Direction Flag DF is 1, executing LODSB or LODSW will decrement the contents of the SI register by 1 or 2, respectively. This instruction requires no operands and does not affect any flags.

Example: Consider the case where the SI register contains B000H, the byte memory locations B000H and B001H contain 41H and 53H, respectively, the AX register contains 02FEH, and the following sequence of instructions is executed.

```
CLD     ;Clear the Direction Flag DF to 0.
LODSW
```

After LODSW is executed, the AX and SI registers will contain 5341H and B002H, respectively.

Consider the case where the SI register contains B000H, the byte memory location B00H contains 52H, the AL register contains FFH, and the following sequence of instructions is executed.

```
STD     ;Set the Direction Flag DF to 1.
LODSB
```

After LODSB is executed, the AL and SI register will contain 52H and AFFFH, respectively.

Affected Flags: None.

Machine Instruction Decoding Guide:

First Byte Hex	Binary	2nd byte	Bytes 3,4,5,6	Operand Format
AC	1010 1100			No Operand
AD	1010 1101			No Operand

Assembly Language Coding Examples:

Machine Code	Assembly Instructions	Operand Format	Bytes	Clocks
AC	LODSB	No Operand	1	12
AD	LODSW	No Operand	1	16

LOOP

Definition: Loop instruction.
Function:

```
(CX) <----  (CX) - 1
If (CX) # 0  then  (IP) <---- (IP) + Disp8
```

Description: The original contents of the CX register are decremented by 1. Control is transferred to the address specified by the target operand if the contents of the CX register are not 0. Otherwise, the next instruction in the sequence is executed. The target operand address is generated by adding the displacement byte to the address of the next instruction. Since the displacement byte is an 8-bit signed integer, this instruction can branch to a new memory address within +127 bytes or −128 bytes of the end of the instruction. Since the contents of the CX register are treated as an unsigned integer, this instruction can be used to repeat a sequence of codes up to 65,536 iterations using the CX register as the iteration counter.

Example: The following sequence of instruction clears the most significant bit of every byte in a 1000-byte array starting at the memory address ARRAY_ONE.

```
            MOV  CX,1000           ;Initialize the loop counter.
            LEA  SI,ARRAY_ONE      ;Starting address of the array.
CLEAR_LOOP: LODSB                  ;Get a byte in the array.
            AND  AL,7FH            ;Clear bit 7 to 0.
            LOOP CLEAR_LOOP        ;Iterate 1000 times.
```

Affected Flags: None.

Machine Instruction Decoding Guide:

First Byte Hex Binary	2nd byte	Bytes 3,4,5,6	Operand Format
E2 1110 0010	Disp8		Short-Label

Assembly Language Coding Examples:

Machine Code	Assembly Code	Operand Format	Bytes	Clocks*
E2D4	LOOP NEXT_LOOP	Short-Label	2	5 or 17
*Note: 5 clocks if the next instruction in the sequence is performed.				

LOOPE/LOOPZ

Definition: Loop while equal/Loop while zero
Function:

```
(CX)  <----   (CX) - 1

If ( (CX) # 0  AND  (ZF) = 1 )   then   (IP) <---- (IP) + Disp8
```

Description: The original contents of the CX register are decremented by 1. Control is transferred to the address specified by the target operand if the contents of the CX register are not 0 and the Zero Flag, ZF, is 1. Otherwise, the next instruction in the sequence is executed. The target operand address is generated by adding the displacement byte to the address of the next instruction. Since the displacement byte is an 8-bit signed integer, this instruction can branch to a new memory address within +127 bytes or −128 bytes of the end of the instruction. Since the contents of the CX register are treated as an unsigned integer, this instruction can be used to repeat a sequence of codes up to 65,536 iterations using the CX register as the iteration counter.

Example: The following sequence of codes searches for the first nonblank characters in a string starting at the memory location addressed by the SI register.

```
           MOV  CX,128      ;Maximum number of characters in the string.

 SEARCH:   LODSB            ;Get the character.

           CMP  AL,20H      ;Check for a blank (ASCII code 20H).

           LOOPE  SEARCH    ;Skip all heading blanks.

 NON_BLANK: MOV DI,SI
```

Affected Flags: None.

Machine Instruction Decoding Guide:

First Byte Hex Binary	2nd byte	Bytes 3,4,5,6	Operand Format
E1 1110 0010	Disp8		Short-Label

Assembly Language Coding Examples:

Machine Code	Assembly Code	Operand Format	Bytes	Clocks*
E1D2	LOOP CONVERSION	Short-Label	2	6 or 18
*Note: 6 clocks if the next instruction in the sequence is performed.				

LOOPNE/LOOPNZ

Definition: Loop while not equal/Loop while not zero.
Function:

```
(CX)  <----   (CX) - 1

If ( (CX) # 0  AND  (ZF) = 0 )  then   (IP) <---- (IP) + Disp8
```

Description: The original contents of the CX register are decremented by 1. Control is transferred to the address specified by the target operand if the contents of the CX register are not 0 and the Zero Flag, ZF, is 0. Otherwise, the next instruction in the sequence is executed. The target operand address is generated by adding the displacement byte to the address of the next instruction. Since the displacement byte is an 8-bit signed integer, this instruction can branch to a new memory address within +127 bytes or −128 bytes of the end of the instruction. Since the contents of the CX register are treated as an unsigned integer, this instruction can be used to repeat a sequence of codes up to 65,536 iterations using the CX register as the iteration counter.

Example: The following sequence of instructions converts a string of lower case letters (starting at the memory location addressed by the SI register) to upper case. The conversion process must stop if a zero value is encountered.

```
         MOV  CX,100      ;Maximum number of characters in the string.
         MOV  DI,SI       ;Pointers to the character string.
GETC:    LODSB            ;Get a character in lower case.
         AND  AL,5FH      ;Conversion factor.
         STOSB            ;Put the character in upper case in the string.
         LOOPNE GETC      ;Stop when done or a 0 is encountered.
         RET
```

Affected Flags: None.

Machine Instruction Decoding Guide:

First Byte Hex Binary	2nd byte	Bytes 3,4,5,6	Operand Format
E0 1110 0010	Disp8		Short-Label

Assembly Language Coding Examples:

Machine Code	Assembly Code	Operand Format	Bytes	Clocks*
E0D2	LOOPNE CONVERSION	Short-Label	2	5 or 19
E006	LOOPNZ NEXT BYTE	Short-Label	2	5 or 19

*Note: 5 clocks if the next instruction in the sequence is performed.

MOV

Definition: Move.

Function: (First Operand) <--- (Second Operand).

Description: The contents of the second operand replace the original contents of the first operand. The previous contents of the first operand are lost. The contents of the second operand remain unchanged. This instruction does not affect any flags.

The first operand may be a general register, a segment register (except the CS register), or a memory location. The second operand may be a general register, a segment register, a memory location, or an immediate data value. Both 8-bit and 16-bit operations can be performed.

Example: If the CX register contains 04C5H, the BP register contains 2312H, and the instruction MOV CX,BP is executed, the CX register will contain 2312H. The contents of the BP register remain unchanged.

Affected Flags: None.

Machine Instruction Decoding Guide:

1st Byte Hex Binary	2nd byte	Bytes 3,4,5,6	Operand Format
88 1000 1000	Mod-Reg-Rm	Disp-Lo,Disp-Hi	Reg8/Mem8,Reg8
89 1000 1001	Mod-Reg-Rm	Disp-Lo,Disp-Hi	Reg16/Mem16,Reg16
8A 1000 1010	Mod-Reg-Rm	Disp-Lo,Disp-Hi	Reg8,Reg8/Mem8
8B 1000 1011	Mod-Reg-Rm	Disp-Lo,Disp-Hi	Reg16,Reg16/Mem16
8C 1000 1100	Mod-OSR-Rm	Disp-Lo,Disp-Hi	Reg16/Mem16,Segreg
8E 1000 1110	Mod-OSR-Rm	Disp-Lo,Disp-Hi	Segreg,Reg16/Mem16
A0 1010 0000	Disp-Lo	Disp-Hi	AL,Mem8
A1 1010 0001	Disp-Lo	Disp-Hi	AX,Mem16
A2 1010 0010	Disp-Lo	Disp-Hi	Mem8,AL

1st Byte Hex Binary	2nd byte	Bytes 3,4,5,6	Operand Format
A3 1010 0011	Disp-Lo	Disp-Hi	Mem16,AX
1011 0Reg	Data8		Reg8,Immed8
1011 1Reg	Data16		Reg16,Immed16
C6 1100 0110	Mod-000-Rm	Disp-Lo,Disp-Hi Data8	Reg8/Mem8,Immed8
C7 1100 0111	Mod-000-Rm	Disp-Lo,Disp-Hi Data-Lo,Data-Hi	Reg16/Mem16,Immed16

Notes:

1) If the operands of the MOV instruction are the accumulator and a direct offset address, the formats AL,Mem8, AX,Mem16, Mem8,AL, or Mem16,AX should be used to be more efficient.
2) If the operand format 8E Mod-0SR-Rm is used, the operation is undefined if the SR field is specified as the binary 001.
3) The operand format C6 Mod-000-Rm or C7 Mod-000-Rm should not be used if the Mod field is the binary number 11. The alternate operand format 1011 0Reg or 1011 1Reg should be used to be more efficient.

Assembly Language Coding Examples:

Machine Code	Assembly Instructions	Operand Format	Bytes	Clocks
8817	MOV [BX],DL	Mem8,Reg8	2-4	9+EA
88EA	MOV DL,CH	Reg8,Reg8	2	2
894412	MOV [SI+12H],AX	Mem16,Reg16	2-4	13+EA
89E1	MOV CX,SP	Reg16,Reg16	2	2
8A1E3500	MOV BL,TEST_BYTE	Reg8,Mem8	2-4	8+EA
8B35	MOV SI,[DI]	Reg16,Mem16	2-4	12+EA
8ED8	MOV DS,AX	Segreg,Reg16	2	2
8E063800	MOV ES,NEW	Segreg,Mem16	2-4	8(12)+EA
8CC8	MOV AX,CS	Reg16,Segreg	2	2
8C1E3A00	MOV OLDSEG,DS	Mem16,Segreg	2-4	9(13)+EA
A03500	MOV AL,TESTB	AL,Mem8	3	10
A13600	MOV AX,TESTW	AX,Mem16	3	14
A23500	MOV TESTB,AL	Mem8,AL	3	10

Machine Code	Assembly Instructions	Operand Format	Bytes	Clocks
A33600	MOV TESTW,AX	Mem16,AX	3	14
B40B	MOV AH,11	Reg8,Immed8	2	4
B9FBFF	MOV CX,-5	Reg16,Immed16	3	4
C686230F09	MOV BYTE PTR [BP+OF23H],9	Mem8,Immed8	3-5	10+EA
C7040010	MOV WORD PTR [SI],1000H	Mem16,Immed16	4-6	14+EA
* Note: Clock cycles in parentheses are for word operands.				

MOVS

Definition: Move string.

Function: (Operand addressed by DI) <---- (Operand addressed by SI).

```
If (DF) = 0  then  (SI) <---- (SI) + 1 (byte)
                   (DI) <---- (DI) + 1 (byte)
                             or
                   (SI) <---- (SI) + 2 (word)
                   (DI) <---- (DI) + 2 (word)
If (DF) = 1  then  (SI) <---- (SI) - 1 (byte)
                   (DI) <---- (DI) - 1 (byte)
                             or
                   (SI) <---- (SI) - 2 (word)
                   (DI) <---- (DI) - 2 (word)
```

Description: The contents of the byte or word memory location addressed by the SI register (taken relative to the data segment) replace the original contents of the byte or word memory location addressed by the DI register (taken relative to the extra segment) depending on byte or word operation. The contents of the location addressed by the SI register remains unchanged. In assembly language, the instruction MOVS is coded as MOVSB for byte operation or as MOVSW for word operation. If the Direction Flag, DF, is 0, the contents of the SI and DI registers are incremented by 1 after MOVSB is executed, or by 2 after MOVSW is executed. If the Direction Flag, DF, is 1, the contents of the SI and DI registers are decremented by 1 after MOVSB is executed, or by 2 after MOVSW is executed. This instruction requires no operands and does not affect any flags.

Example: Consider the case where the SI register contains 7F00H, the word memory location 7F00H contains 0D0AH, the DI register contains

B800H, the word memory location B800H contains 2020H, and the following sequence of instructions is executed.

```
CLD    ;Clear the Direction Flag DF to 0.
MOVSW
```

After the instruction MOVSW is executed, the SI and DI registers will contain 7F02H and B802H, respectively. The word memory location B800H is updated with a new content of 0D0AH.

Consider the case where the SI register contains 2400H, the byte memory location 2400H contains 41H, the DI register contains B800H, the byte memory location B800H contains 00H, and the following sequence of instructions is executed.

```
STD    ;Set the Direction Flag DF to 1.
MOVSB
```

After the instruction MOVSB is executed, the SI and DI registers will contain 23FFH and B7FFH, respectively. The byte memory location B800H is updated with a new content of 41H.

Affected Flags: None.

Machine Instruction Decoding Guide:

First Byte Hex Binary	2nd byte	Bytes 3,4,5,6	Operand Format
A4 1010 0100			No Operand
A5 1010 0101			No Operand

Assembly Language Coding Examples:

Machine Code	Assembly Instructions	Operand Format	Bytes	Clocks
A4	MOVSB	No Operand	1	18
A5	MOVSW	No Operand	1	26

MUL

Definition: Multiply.

Function: If byte operation then:

```
(AX) <---- (AL) * (Operand)
If (AH) = 0   then   (CF) <---- 0
                     (OF) <---- 0
If (AH) # 0   then   (CF) <---- 1
                     (OF) <---- 1
```

If word operation then:

```
(DX,AX) <---- (AX) * (Operand)

If (DX) = 0   then   (CF) <---- 0

                     (OF) <---- 0

If (DX) # 0   then   (CF) <---- 1

                     (OF) <---- 1
```

Description: This instruction performs an unsigned multiplication of the accumulator and the specified operand. If the operand is an 8-bit quantity, it is multiplied by the AL register, and the 16-bit product is returned in the AX register. if the operand is a 16-bit quantity, it is multiplied by the AX register, and the 32-bit product is returned in the register pair DX, AX where the DX register holds the high-order sixteen bits. The specified operand can be a general register, or a memory location, and is treated as an unsigned number.

If the contents of the AH register are not 0 after a byte multiplication, or the contents of the DX register are not 0 after a word multiplication, the Carry Flag, CF, and the Overflow Flag, OF, are set to 1. Otherwise they are cleared to 0. The Auxiliary Carry Flag, AF, the Parity Flag, PF, the Sign Flag, SF, and the Zero Flag, ZF, are undefined following the execution of the MUL instruction. When the Carry Flag, CF, and the Overflow Flag, OF, are set to 1, they indicate that the AH or DX register contains significant digits of the result.

Example: If the AL register contains 30H, the byte memory location NEXT_L contains 12H, and the instruction MUL NEXT_L is executed. The product of the multiplication (360H = 30H * 12 H) is returned in the AX register. Since the contents of the AH register are not 0, the Carry Flag, CF, and the Overflow Flag, OF, are set to 1.

If the AX register contains 1000H, the BX register contains 550H, and the instruction MUL BX is executed. The 32-bit product of the multiplication (550000H = 1000H * 550H) is returned in the DX and AX register. Since the new contents of the DX register (0055H) are a nonzero value, the Carry Flag, CF, and the Overflow Flag, OF, are set to 1.

Affected Flags:

15	14	13	12	11	10	9	8	7	6	5	4	3	2	1	0
				X				U	U		U		U		X
				OF	DF	IF	TF	SF	ZF		AF		PF		CF

Machine Instruction Decoding Guide:

First Byte Hex Binary	2nd byte	Bytes 3,4,5,6	Operand Format
F6 1111 0110	Mod-100-Rm	Disp-Lo,Disp-Hi	Reg8/Mem8
F7 1111 0111	Mod-100-Rm	Disp-Lo,Disp-Hi	Reg16/Mem16

Assembly Language Coding Examples:

Machine Code	Assembly Instructions	Operand Format	Bytes	Clocks
F6E5	MUL CH	Reg8	2	70-77
F6A70012	MUL BYTE PTR [BX+1200H]	Mem8	2-4	(76-83)+EA
F7E5	MUL BP	Reg16	2	118-133
F7260037	MUL WORD PTR COUNT	Mem16	2-4	(128-143)+EA

NEG

Definition: Negate.

Function: (Operand) <--- – (Operand).

Description: This instruction subtracts the contents of the specified operand from 0. The result of the subtraction replaces the original contents of the operand. Previous contents of the operand are lost. Operands can be a general register or a memory location. Either byte or word operations can be performed. This instruction updates the Auxiliary Carry Flag, AF, the Carry Flag, CF, the Overflow Flag, OF, the Parity Flag, PF, the Sign Flag, SF, and the Zero Flag, ZF.

Example: Consider the case where the BX register contains the value 2, and the instruction NEG BX is executed. The new contents of the BX register will be FFFEH, which is the representation of the decimal number −2 in two's complement notation.

Affected Flags:

15	14	13	12	11	10	9	8	7	6	5	4	3	2	1	0
				X				X	X		X		X		X
				OF	DF	IF	TF	SF	ZF		AF		PF		CF

Machine Instruction Decoding Guide:

1st Byte Hex	Binary	2nd byte	Bytes 3,4,5,6	Operand Format
F6	1111 0110	Mod-010-Rm	Disp-Lo,Disp-Hi	Reg8/Mem8
F7	1111 1111	Mod-010-Rm	Disp-Lo,Disp-Hi	Reg16/Mem16

Assembly Language Coding Examples:

Machine Code	Assembly Instructions	Operand Format	Bytes	Clocks
F6DD	NEG CH	Reg8	2	3
F61C	NEG BYTE PTR [SI]	Mem8	2-4	16+EA
F7D8	NEG AX	Reg16	2	3
F75F01	NEG WORD PTR [BX+01]	Mem16	2-4	24+EA

NOP

Definition: No operation

Function: None.

Description: This instruction requests the microprocessor to do nothing. No flags are affected and no operands are required by this instruction. This instruction is useful in the implementation of controlled delay loop in situations where the CPU must wait for a certain period of time before it can begin processing some specific functions. The machine code of this instruction is identical to that of the instruction XCHG AX, AX which indicates no operation.

Example: The following sequence of instructions illustrates one of the typical delay techniques frequently implemented on microcomputer systems.

```
            MOV  CX,0      ;Initialize delay counter.
    DELAY:  NOP            ;Do nothing.
            LOOP DELAY     ;Execute 65536 NOP instructions.
```

Affected Flags: None.

Machine Instruction Decoding Guide:

1st Byte Hex Binary	2nd byte	Bytes 3,4,5,6	Operand Format
90 1001 0000			No operand.

Assembly Language Coding Examples:

Machine Code	Assembly Instructions	Operand Format	Bytes	Clocks
90	NOP	No operand.	1	3

NOT

Definition: Logical not.

Function: (Operand) <--- Invert all bits of (Operand).

Description: This instruction inverts the bits of the contents of the specified operand. The result of the inversion replaces the original contents of the operand. Previous contents of the operand are lost. Operands can be a general register or a memory location. Either byte or word operations can be performed. This instruction does not affect any flags.

Example: Consider the case where the BL register contains the value 0, and the instruction NOT BL is executed. The new contents of the BL register will be FFH (inverting all 0 bits).

Affected Flags: None.

Machine Instruction Decoding Guide:

1st Byte Hex Binary	2nd byte	Bytes 3,4,5,6	Operand Format
F6 1111 0110	Mod-010-Rm	Disp-Lo,Disp-Hi	Reg8/Mem8
F7 1111 1111	Mod-010-Rm	Disp-Lo,Disp-Hi	Reg16/Mem16

Assembly Language Coding Examples:

Machine Code	Assembly Instructions	Operand Format	Bytes	Clocks
F6D2	NOT DL	Reg8	2	3
F6160A00	NOT BYTE PTR TESTB	Mem8	2-4	16+EA
F7D2	NOT DX	Reg16	2	3
F714	NOT WORD PTR [SI]	Mem16	2-4	24+EA

OR

Definition: Logical OR
Function: (First Operand) <--- (First Operand) OR (Second Operand).

(CF) <--- 0

(OF) <--- 0

Description: The Boolean logical OR of the original contents of the first operand and the contents of the second operand are performed. The result replaces the contents of the first operand. The previous contents of the first operand are lost. The contents of the second operand remain unchanged. The first operand may be a register or a memory location. The second operand may be a register, a memory location, or an immediate data value. It is not allowed to specify any operand as a segment register, or to specify both operands at the same time as memory locations. Either 8-bit or 16-bit operations can be performed. The Carry Flag, CF, and the Overflow Flag, OF, are always cleared to 0 by this instruction.

Example: Consider the case where the AX register contains 1468H, the DX register contains 8553H, and the Flag contains F046H. After the instruction OR AX,DX is executed, the AX register contains 957BH and the Processor Flag contains F086H.

Contents of AX	0001 0100 0110 1000 = 1468H
Contents of DX	1000 0101 0101 0011 = 8553H
New contents of AX	1001 0101 0111 1011 = 957BH

There are six 1 bits in the low-order 8 bits of the AX register, which is an even number, so the Parity Flag, PF, is set to 1. Since the result of the

Boolean OR operation is a negative nonzero value in two's complement notation, the Sign Flag, SF, is set to 1, and the Zero Flag, ZF, is cleared to 0. The Carry Flag, CF, and Overflow Flag, OF, are always cleared to 0 since there is no carry or overflow condition. The Auxiliary Carry Flag, AF, is undefined.

Affected Flags:

15	14	13	12	11	10	9	8	7	6	5	4	3	2	1	0
				0				X	X		U		X		0
				OF	DF	IF	TF	SF	ZF		AF		PF		CF

Machine Instruction Decoding Guide:

1st Byte Hex Binary	2nd byte	Bytes 3,4,5,6	Operand Format
08 0000 1000	Mod-Reg-Rm	Disp-Lo,Disp-Hi	Reg8/Mem8,Reg8
09 0000 1001	Mod-Reg-Rm	Disp-Lo,Disp-Hi	Reg16/Mem16,Reg16
0A 0000 1010	Mod-Reg-Rm	Disp-Lo,Disp-Hi	Reg8,Reg8/Mem8
0B 0000 1011	Mod-Reg-Rm	Disp-Lo,Disp-Hi	Reg16,Reg16/Mem16
0C 0000 1100	Data8		AL,Immed8
0D 0000 1101	Data-Lo	Data-Hi	AX,Immed16
80 1000 0000	Mod-001-Rm	Disp-Lo,Disp-Hi, Data8	Reg8/Mem8,Immed8
81 1000 0001	Mod-001-Rm	Disp-Lo,Disp-Hi, Data-Lo,Data-Hi	Reg16/Mem16,Immed16

Assembly Language Coding Examples:

Machine Code	Assembly Instructions	Operand Format	Bytes	Clocks
0823	OR [BP+DI],AH	Mem8,Reg8	2-4	16+EA
08F6	OR DH,DH	Reg8,Reg8	2	3
090E0010	OR WORD PTR SUM,CX	Mem16,Reg16	2-4	24+EA
09F8	OR AX,DI	Reg16,Reg16	2	3
0A8D0001	OR CL,[DI+100H]	Reg8,Mem8	2-4	9+EA
0B5C0C	OR BX,[SI+12]	Reg16,Mem16	2-4	13+EA
0CFF	OR AL,-1	AL,Immed8	2	4
0DFF7F	OR AX,7FFFH	AX,Immed16	3	4
80CB01	OR BL,01	Reg8,Immed8	3	4
804C0290	OR BYTE PTR [SI+2],90H	Mem8,Immed8	3-5	17+EA

Machine Code	Assembly Instructions	Operand Format	Bytes	Clocks
81CEFF7F	OR SI,7FFFH	Reg16,Immed16	4	4
810E0020FFFE	OR WORD PTR TEST,0FEFFH	Mem16,Immed16	4-6	25+EA

OUT

Definition: Output to port.

Function: (Input-Output Port) <---- (Accumulator).

Description: This instruction transfers a byte or a word to an input/output port from the AL or AX register, respectively. The specified input/output port can be an immediate byte constant which allows access to ports numbered from 0 to 255. If the DX register is used to specify the input/output port, up to 65536 different ports can be accessed by simply changing the contents of the DX register. This instruction does not affect any flags.

Example: If the printer buffer can be accessed through the output port 3D5H, the following sequence of instructions will send the ASCII ESC code to the printer buffer.

```
MOV    DX,3D5H        ;Load the port number into the DX register.
MOV    AL,1BH         ;ASCII ESC code.
OUT    AL,DX          ;Send the code to the printer buffer.
```

Affected Flags: None.

Machine Instruction Decoding Guide:

1st Byte Hex Binary	2nd byte	Bytes 3,4,5,6	Operand Format
E6 1110 0110	Data8		AL,Immed8
E7 1110 0111	Data8		AX,Immed8
EE 1110 1110			AL,DX
EF 1110 1111			AX,DX

Assembly Language Coding Examples:

Machine Code	Assembly Instructions	Operand Format	Bytes	Clocks
E62D	OUT AL,2DH	AL,Immed8	2	10
E72E	OUT AX,2EH	AX,Immed8	2	14
EE	OUT AL,DX	AL,DX	1	8
EF	OUT AX,DX	AX,DX	1	12

PUSHF

Definition: Push processor flag on stack.

Function:

(SP <---- (SP) – 2
(Top Of Stack) <---- (Processor Flag)

Description: The Stack Pointer, SP, is decremented by 2 to point to the new top of stack. The current contents of the Processor Flag are placed on the top of stack. This instruction does not affect any flags and can be used to save the current state of the 8088 CPU.

Example: Consider the case where the Processor Flag contains F046H, the Stack Pointer SP contains FFC2H, and the instruction PUSHF is executed. The Stack Pointer, SP, will contain FFC0H, and the hexadecimal number F046H is placed on top of the stack as in the following illustration.

```
                          Low  High                                  Low  High
Low Memory Address        Byte Byte                                  Byte Byte

                  0000H   00   0A                            0000H   00   0A
                  0002H   0D   0D                            0002H   0D   0D
                    ..                                         ..
                    ..                                         ..
                  FFBEH   80   10                            FFBEH   80   10
                  FFC0H   20   20          New Top Of Stack  FFC0H   46   F0
Top Of Stack      FFC2H   41   52                            FFC2H   41   52
                    ..                                         ..
                    ..                                         ..
                  FFFEH   00   28                            FFFEH   00   28

High Memory Address

                  Before PUSHF                            After PUSHF
```

Affected Flags: None.

Machine Instruction Decoding Guide:

First Byte	2nd byte	Bytes 3,4,5,6	Operand Format
Hex Binary 9C 1001 1100			No Operand

Assembly Language Coding Examples:

Machine Code	Assembly Instructions	Operand Format	Bytes	Clocks
9C	PUSHF	No Operand	1	14

POPF

Definition: Pop processor flag from stack.
Function:

```
(Processor Flag) <---- (Top Of Stack)

           (SP) <---- (SP) + 2
```

Description: The current contents of the top of stack replace the contents of the Processor Flag. The Stack Pointer, SP, is incremented by 2 to point to the new top of stack. This instruction affects every specific flag of the Processor Flag including the Trace Flag, TF. It can be used to restore the previous state of the 8088 CPU upon returning to a calling procedure.

Example: Consider the case where the Processor Flag contains F046H, the Stack Pointer, SP, contains FFC0H, the word at the offset address FFC0H taken relative to the stack segment is F047H, and the instruction POPF is executed. The Stack Pointer, SP, will contain FFC2H, and the Processor Flag has a new value F047H.

```
                          Low  High                                       Low  High
 Low Memory Address       Byte Byte                                       Byte Byte

                  0000H   00   0A                               0000H     00   0A
                  0002H   0D   0D                               0002H     0D   0D
                    ..                                            ..
                    ..                                            ..
                  FFBEH   80   10                               FFBEH     80   10
 Top Of Stack     FFC0H   47   F0                               FFC0H     47   F0
                  FFC2H   41   52          New Top Of Stack     FFC2H     41   52
                    ..                                            ..
                    ..                                            ..
                  FFFEH   00   28                               FFFEH     00   28

 High Memory Address

                Before PUSHF                                   After PUSHF
```

Affected Flags:

15	14	13	12	11	10	9	8	7	6	5	4	3	2	1	0
				X	X	X	X	X	X		X		X		X
				OF	DF	IF	TF	SF	ZF		AF		PF		CF

Machine Instruction Decoding Guide:

First Byte Hex Binary	2nd byte	Bytes 3,4,5,6	Operand Format
9D 1001 1101			No Operand

Assembly Language Coding Examples:

Machine Code	Assembly Instructions	Operand Format	Bytes	Clocks
9D	POPF	No Operand	1	12

PUSH

Definition: Push on stack.
Function:

```
              (SP) <---- (SP) - 2
(Top Of Stack) <---- (Operand)
```

Description: The operand of this instruction must be a 16-bit register or a memory location. Any general register or segment register can be specified. The Stack Pointer is decremented by 2 to point to a new top of stack. The contents of the specified operands are then placed on the top of stack. This instruction does not affect any flags and is very useful to save temporary data on the stack.

Example: Consider the case where the DS register contains 04B5H, the Stack Pointer, SP, contains FFC2H, and the following instruction PUSH DS is executed. The Stack Pointer, SP, will contain FFC0H and the hexadecimal number 04B5H is placed on top of the stack as in the following instruction.

Low Memory Address	Low Byte	High Byte		Low Byte	High Byte
0000H	00	0A	0000H	00	0A
0002H	0D	0D	0002H	0D	0D
..			..		
..			..		

	FFBEH	80	10		FFBEH	80	10
	FFC0H	20	20	New Top Of Stack	FFC0H	B5	04
Top Of Stack	FFC2H	41	52		FFC2H	41	52
	..				..		
	..				..		
	FFFEH	00	28		FFFEH	00	28

High Memory Address

Before PUSH DS — After PUSH DS

Affected Flags: None.
Machine Instruction Decoding Guide:

First Byte Hex Binary	2nd byte	Bytes 3,4,5,6	Operand Format
FF 1111 1111	Mod-110-Rm	Disp-Lo,Disp-Hi	Mem16/Reg16*
0101 0Reg			Reg16
000Reg110			Segreg

*Note: The operand format FF Mod-110-Rm should not be used to specify a 16-bit general register, the alternate format 0101 0Reg is more efficient.

Assembly Language Coding Examples:

Machine Code	Assembly Instructions	Operand Format	Bytes	Clocks
52	PUSH DX	Reg16	1	15
1E	PUSH DS	Segreg	1	14
FF7703	PUSH WORD PTR [BX+03]	Mem16	2-4	24+EA

POP

Definition: Pop from stack.
Function:

```
(Operand) <---- (Top Of Stack)

(SP) <---- (SP) + 2
```

Description: The operand of this instruction must be a 16-bit register or a memory location. Any general register or segment register (except the

CS register) can be specified. The contents of the top of stack replace the contents of the specified operand. The Stack Pointer is incremented by 2 to point to a new top of stack. This instruction does not affect any flags and is very useful to retrieve temporary data previously saved on the stack by PUSH instructions.

Example: Consider the case where the AX register contains 000FH, the Stack Pointer, SP, contains FFC2H, the word at the offset address FFC2H taken relative to the stack segment is 04C5H, and the instruction POP AX is executed. The Stack Pointer, SP, will contain FFC4H and the AX register has the new value 04C5H.

```
                         Low  High                                      Low  High
Low Memory Address       Byte Byte                                      Byte Byte

                 0000H   00   0A                               0000H    00   0A
                 0002H   0D   0D                               0002H    0D   0D
                  ..                                            ..
                  ..                                            ..
                 FFBEH   80   10                               FFBEH    80   10
                 FFC0H   20   20                               FFC0H    20   20
Top Of Stack     FFC2H   C5   04                               FFC2H    C5   04
                 FFC4H   42   00   New Top Of Stack            FFC4H    42   00
                  ..                                            ..
                 FFFEH   00   28                               FFFEH    00   28

High Memory Address

                 Before POP  AX                          After POP AX
```

Affected Flags: None.

Machine Instruction Decoding Guide:

First Byte Hex Binary	2nd byte	Bytes 3,4,5,6	Operand Format
8F 1111 1111	Mod-000-Rm	Disp-Lo,Disp-Hi	Mem16/Reg16*
0101 1Reg			Reg16
000Reg111			Segreg

*Note: The operand format 8F Mod-000-Rm should not be used to specify a 16-bit general register, the alternate format 0101 1Reg is more efficient.

Assembly Language Coding Examples:

Machine Code	Assembly Instructions	Operand Format	Bytes	Clocks
5B	POP BX	Reg16	1	12
1F	POP DS	Segreg	1	12
8F060B00	POP WORD PTR TEST	Mem16	2-4	25+EA

RCL

Definition: Rotate through carry left.
Function:

```
(Temporary Bit) <---- (CF)
           (CF) <---- (High-order bit of operand)
      (Operand) <---- (Operand) * 2 + (Temporary Bit)
```

Description: This instruction rotates the bits in the byte or word of the operand. If the operand format Reg/Mem,1 is used, only one bit is rotated. If the operand format Reg/Mem,CL is used, the contents of the CL register specify the number of bits to be rotated. The Carry Flag, CF, is also a part of the rotation, its value is rotated into the low-order bit of the destination operand, and itself is replaced by the high-order bit of the destination operand. If only one bit is rotated (without using the CL register), the Overflow Flag, OF, is set to 1 if the value of the Carry Flag, CF, is different from the most significant bit of the destination operand. The Overflow Flag, OF, is undefined if the number of bits rotated is greater than 1. Operands in this instruction can be a general register or a memory location. Either 8-bit or 16-bit operations can be performed.

Example: Consider the case where the BX register contains 4231H, the CL register contains 04H, the Carry Flag, CF, is 0, the Processor Flag contains F046H, and the instruction RCL BX,CL is executed. The execution of this instruction is illustrated as follows:

Carry Flag CF	Contents of the BX register.	
0	0100 0010 0011 0001 = 4231H	Original contents.
0	1000 0100 0110 0010 = 8432H	After 1st rotation.
1	0000 1000 1100 0100 = 08C4H	After 2nd rotation.
0	0001 0001 1000 1001 = 1189H	After 3rd rotation.
0	0010 0011 0001 0010 = 2312H	After 4th rotation.

After the instruction RCL BX,CL is executed, the BX register contains 2312H, the Carry Flag CF is 0, and the Processor Flag contains F046H.

Affected Flags:

15	14	13	12	11	10	9	8	7	6	5	4	3	2	1	0
				X											X
				OF	DF	IF	TF	SF	ZF		AF		PF		CF

Machine Instruction Decoding Guide:

1st Byte Hex Binary	2nd byte	Bytes 3,4,5,6	Operand Format
D0 1101 0000	Mod-010-Rm	Disp-Lo,Disp-Hi	Reg8/Mem8,1
D1 1101 0001	Mod-010-Rm	Disp-Lo,Disp-Hi	Reg16/Mem16,1
D2 1101 0010	Mod-010-Rm	Disp-Lo,Disp-Hi	Reg8/Mem8,CL
D3 1101 0011	Mod-010-Rm	Disp-Lo,Disp-Hi	Reg16/Mem16,CL

Assembly Language Coding Examples:

Machine Code	Assembly Instructions	Operand Format	Bytes	Clocks
D0D0	RCL AL,1	Reg8,1	2	2
D05701	RCL BYTE PTR [BX+01],1	Mem8,1	2-4	15+EA
D1D0	RCL AX,1	Reg16,1	2	2
D1160020	RCL WORD PTR TEST,01	Mem16,1	2-4	23+EA
D2D2	RCL DL,CL	Reg8,CL	2	8+4/bit
D214	RCL BYTE PTR [SI],CL	Mem8,CL	2-4	20+EA+4/bit
D3D3	RCL BX,CL	Reg16,CL	2	8+4/bit
D315	RCL WORD PTR [DI],CL	Mem8,CL	2-4	28+EA+4/bit

RCR

Definition: Rotate through carry right.
Function:

```
            (Temporary Bit) <---- (CF)
                       (CF) <---- (Low-order bit of operand)
                  (Operand) <---- (Operand) / 2
(High-order bit of operand) <---- (Temporary Bit)
```

Description: This instruction rotates the bits in the byte or word of the operand. If the operand format Reg/Mem,1 is used, only one bit is rotated. If the operand format Reg/Mem,CL is used, the contents of the CL register specify the number of bits to be rotated. The Carry Flag, CF, is also a part of the rotation, its value is rotated into the high-order bit of the destination operand, and itself is replaced by the low-order bit of the original operand. If the number of bits rotated is 1 (not using the CL register), the Overflow Flag, OF, is set to 1 if the values of the two most significant bits of the result operand are not the same. The Overflow Flag, OF, is undefined if the number of bits rotated is greater than 1. Operands in this instruction can be a general register or a memory location. Either 8-bit or 16-bit operations can be performed.

Example: Consider the case where the BX register contains 7F86H, the CL register contains 03H, the Carry Flag, CF, is 0, the Processor Flag contains F046H, and the instruction RCR BX,CL is executed. The execution of the instruction is illustrated as follows:

Carry Flag CF	Contents of the BX register.	
0	0111 1111 1000 0110 = 7F86H	Original contents.
0	0011 1111 1100 0011 = 3FC3H	After 1st rotation.
1	0001 1111 1110 0001 = 1FE1H	After 2nd rotation.
1	1000 1111 1111 0000 = 8FF0H	After 3rd rotation.

After the instruction RCR BX,CL is executed, the BX register contains 8FF0H, the Carry Flag CF is 1, and the Processor Flag contains F847H.

Affected Flags:

15	14	13	12	11	10	9	8	7	6	5	4	3	2	1	0
				X											X
				OF	DF	IF	TF	SF	ZF		AF		PF		CF

Machine Instruction Decoding Guide:

1st Byte Hex Binary	2nd byte	Bytes 3,4,5,6	Operand Format
D0 1101 0000	Mod-011-Rm	Disp-Lo,Disp-Hi	Reg8/Mem8,1
D1 1101 0001	Mod-011-Rm	Disp-Lo,Disp-Hi	Reg16/Mem16,1
D2 1101 0010	Mod-011-Rm	Disp-Lo,Disp-Hi	Reg8/Mem8,CL
D3 1101 0011	Mod-011-Rm	Disp-Lo,Disp-Hi	Reg16/Mem16,CL

Assembly Language Coding Examples:

Machine Code	Assembly Instructions	Operand Format	Bytes	Clocks
D0D8	RCR AL,1	Reg8,1	2	2
D05F01	RCR BYTE PTR [BX+01],1	Mem8,1	2-4	15+EA
D1D8	RCR AX,1	Reg16,1	2	2
D11E0020	RCR WORD PTR TEST,01	Mem16,1	2-4	23+EA
D2DA	RCR DL,CL	Reg8,CL	2	8+4/bit
D21C	RCR BYTE PTR [SI],CL	Mem8,CL	2-4	20+EA+4/bit
D3DB	RCR BX,CL	Reg16,CL	2	8+4/bit
D31D	RCR WORD PTR [DI],CL	Mem8,CL	2-4	28+EA+4/bit

REP/REPE/REPZ

Definition: Repeat/Repeat while equal/Repeat while zero.

Description: The REP instruction is normally used as a prefix byte for string instructions such as MOVS (Move String) and STOS (Store String). The contents of the CX register represents the number repetitions that the string operations will perform. Thus the REP prefix associated with a string instruction can be interpreted as "repeat the string operation if the CX register is not 0".

REPE and REPZ are alternate mnemonics of REP provided to improve program clarity. They are typically used as prefix bytes in string instructions such as CMPS (Compare String) and SCAS (Scan String). The Zero Flag, ZF, must be set to 1 before the next repetition is initiated. The repeat sequence is terminated if the Zero Flag is 0 even if the CX register is not 0. These repeat prefixes are interruptable and should not be used with any other instructions besides the standard string instructions.

Example: The following sequence of instructions initializes a 4096-byte buffer area with the ASCII character blank (20H) starting from the memory location INPUT_BUFFER.

```
LEA  DI,INPUT_BUFFER    ;Starting address of the buffer.
MOV  CX,4096            ;4096 repetitions.
MOV  AL,20H             ;ASCII blank space.
CLD                     ;Forward direction.
REP  STOSB              ;Repeat storing blanks.
```

Affected Flags: None.

Machine Instruction Decoding Guide:

First Byte Hex Binary	2nd byte	Bytes 3,4,5,6	Operand Format
F3 1111 0011			No Operand

Assembly Language Coding Examples:

Machine Code	Assembly Instructions	Operand Format	Bytes	Clocks
F3/AB	REP STOSW	No Operand	1	2
F3/A7	REPE CMPSW	No Operand	1	2
F3/AE	REPZ SCASB	No Operand	1	2

RET

Definition: Return from procedure.

Function:

```
(IP) <---- (Top Of Stack)
(SP) <---- (SP) + 2
```

If intersegment then:

```
(CS) <---- (Top Of Stack)
(SP) <---- (SP) + 2
```

If displacement then:

```
(SP) <---- (SP) + displacement
```

Description: RET returns control from a procedure to the instruction following the CALL that activated the procedure. The Macro Assembler generates an intrasegment RET if the procedure containing the RET instruction is defined as NEAR, or an intersegment RET if the procedure is defined as FAR. In an intrasegment return, the instruction RET pops the word at the top of the stack (pointed to by the SP register) into the Instruction Pointer, IP, and the contents of the SP register are incremented by 2 to point to a new top of stack. In an intersegment return, the word at the new top of stack is popped into the CS register, and the contents of the SP register are again incremented by 2.

A 16-bit displacement value may be used as an operand of this instruction to be added to the contents of the SP register, so that temporary data or arguments pushed on the stack before the execution of the CALL instruction can be discarded.

Example: The following example illustrates intersegment and intrasegment return as coded in 8088 assembly language.

```
Intersegment RET

TEST1 PROC FAR
      ..
      Instructions in procedure
      ..
      RET ;Intersegment.
      ..
      Instructions in procedure
      ..
      RET 10   ;Intersegment.
TEST1 ENDP
```

```
Intrasegment RET

TEST2 PROC NEAR
      ..
      Instructions in procedure
      ..
      RET ;Intrasegment.
      ..
      Instructions in procedure
      ..
      RET 4   ;Intrasegment.
TEST2 ENDP
```

Affected Flags: None.

Machine Instruction Decoding Guide:

1st Byte Hex Binary	2nd byte	Bytes 3,4,5,6	Operand Format
C3 1100 0011			No Operand (Intrasegment)
C2 1100 0010	Data-Lo	Data-Hi	Displ6 (Intrasegment)
CB 1100 1011			No Operand (Intersegment)
CA 1100 1010	Data-Lo	Data-Hi	Displ6 (Intersegment)

Assembly Language Coding Examples:

C3	RET	No Operand (Intra)	1	20
C20400	RET 4	Displ6 (Intra)	3	24
CB	RET	No Operand (Inter)	1	32
CA0A00	RET 10	Displ6 (Inter)	3	31

ROL

Definition: Rotate Left.

Function:

```
        (CF) <---- (High-order bit of operand)

   (Operand) <---- (Operand) * 2 + (CF)
```

Description: This instruction rotates the bits in the byte or word of the operand. If the operand format Reg/Mem,1 is used, only one bit is rotated. If the operand format Reg/Mem,CL is used, the contents of the CL register specify the number of bits to be rotated. The high-order bit of the original operand is rotated into the low-order bit of the destination operand. If the number of bits rotated is 1 (not using the CL register), the Overflow Flag, OF, is set to 1 if the value of the Carry Flag, CF, is different from the most significant bit of the destination operand. The Overflow Flag, OF, is undefined if the number of bits rotated is greater than 1. The operand in this instruction can be a general register or a memory location. Either 8-bit or 16-bit operations can be performed.

Example: Consider the case where the DL register contains 74H, the CL register contains 06H, the Carry Flag, CF, is 0, the Processor Flag contains F046H, and the instruction ROL DL,CL is executed. The execution of this instruction is illustrated as follows:

```
Carry Flag CF   Contents of the DL register.
   0            0111 0100 = 74H   Original contents.
   0            1110 1000 = E8H   After 1st rotation.
```

Carry Flag CF	Contents of the DL register.	
1	1101 0001 = D1H	After 2nd rotation.
1	1010 0011 = A3H	After 3rd rotation.
1	0100 0111 = 47H	After 4th rotation.
0	1000 1110 = 8EH	After 5th rotation.
1	0001 1101 = 1DH	After 6th rotation.

After ROL DL,CL is executed, the DL register contains 1DH, the Carry Flag, CF, is set to 1 and the Overflow Flag is cleared to 0. The Processor Flag contains F847H.

Affected Flags:

15	14	13	12	11	10	9	8	7	6	5	4	3	2	1	0
				X											X
				OF	DF	IF	TF	SF	ZF		AF		PF		CF

Machine Instruction Decoding Guide:

1st Byte Hex Binary	2nd byte	Bytes 3,4,5,6	Operand Format
D0 1101 0000	Mod-000-Rm	Disp-Lo,Disp-Hi	Reg8/Mem8,1
D1 1101 0001	Mod-000-Rm	Disp-Lo,Disp-Hi	Reg16/Mem16,1
D2 1101 0010	Mod-000-Rm	Disp-Lo,Disp-Hi	Reg8/Mem8,CL
D3 1101 0011	Mod-000-Rm	Disp-Lo,Disp-Hi	Reg16/Mem16,CL

Assembly Language Coding Examples:

D0C0	ROL AL,1	Reg8,1	2	2
D04701	ROL BYTE PTR [BX+01],1	Mem8,1	2-4	15+EA
D1C0	ROL AX,1	Reg16,1	2	2
D1060020	ROL WORD PTR TEST,01	Mem16,1	2-4	23+EA
D2C2	ROL DL,CL	Reg8,CL	2	8+4/bit
D204	ROL BYTE PTR [SI],CL	Mem8,CL	2-4	20+EA+4/bit
D3C3	ROL BX,CL	Reg16,CL	2	8+4/bit
D305	ROL WORD PTR [DI],CL	Mem8,CL	2-4	28+EA+4/bit

ROR

Definition: Rotate right.

Function:

```
                   (CF) <---- (Low-order bit of operand)
              (Operand) <---- (Operand) / 2
(High-order bit of operand) <---- (CF)
```

Description: This instruction rotates the bits in the byte or word of the operand. If the operand format Reg/Mem,1 is used, only one bit is rotated. If the operand format Reg/Mem,CL is used, the contents of the CL register specify the number of bits to be rotated. The high-order bit of the original operand is rotated into the low-order bit of the destination operand. If the number of bits rotated is 1 (not using the CL register), the Overflow Flag, OF, is set to 1 if the value of the Carry Flag, CF, is different from the most significant bit of the destination operand. The Overflow Flag, OF, is undefined if the number of bits rotated is greater than 1. Operands of this instruction can be a general register or a memory location. Either 8-bit or 16-bit operations can be performed.

Example: Consider the case where the BX register contains 2F74H, the Carry Flag, CF, is 0, the Processor Flag contains F046H, and the instruction ROR BX,1 is executed. The execution of this instruction is illustrated as follows:

Carry Flag CF	Contents of the BX register	
0	0010 1111 0111 0100 = 2F74H	Original contents.
0	0001 0111 1011 1010 = 17BAH	After rotation.

After the instruction ROR BX,1 is executed, the BX register contains 17BAH, the Carry Flag, CF, and the Overflow Flag, OF, are cleared to 0, and the Processor Flag contains F046H.

Affected Flags:

15	14	13	12	11	10	9	8	7	6	5	4	3	2	1	0
				X											X
				OF	DF	IF	TF	SF	ZF		AF		PF		CF

Machine Instruction Decoding Guide:

1st Byte Hex Binary	2nd byte	Bytes 3,4,5,6	Operand Format
D0 1101 0000	Mod-001-Rm	Disp-Lo,Disp-Hi	Reg8/Mem8,1
D1 1101 0001	Mod-001-Rm	Disp-Lo,Disp-Hi	Reg16/Mem16,1
D2 1101 0010	Mod-001-Rm	Disp-Lo,Disp-Hi	Reg8/Mem8,CL
D3 1101 0011	Mod-001-Rm	Disp-Lo,Disp-Hi	Reg16/Mem16,CL

Assembly Language Coding Examples:

Machine Code	Assembly Instructions	Operand Format	Bytes	Clocks
D0C8	ROR AL,1	Reg8,1	2	2
D04F01	ROR BYTE PTR [BX+01],1	Mem8,1	2-4	15+EA
D1C8	ROR AX,1	Reg16,1	2	2
D10E0020	ROR WORD PTR TEST,01	Mem16,1	2-4	23+EA
D2CA	ROR DL,CL	Reg8,CL	2	8+4/bit
D20C	ROR BYTE PTR [SI],CL	Mem8,CL	2-4	20+EA+4/bit
D3CB	ROR BX,CL	Reg16,CL	2	8+4/bit
D30D	ROR WORD PTR [DI],CL	Mem8,CL	2-4	28+EA+4/bit

REPNE/REPNZ

Definition: Repeat while not equal/Repeat while not zero.

Description: REPNE and REPNZ are interchangeable mnemonics to be used with the string instructions such as CMPS (Compare String) and SCAS (Scan String) instructions. The contents of the CX register represent the number of repetitions that the string instruction will perform. The Zero Flag, ZF, must be cleared to 0 before the next repetition is initiated. The repeat sequence is terminated if the Zero Flag, ZF, is 1 even if the CX register is not 0. These repeat prefixes are interruptable and should not be used with any other instructions besides the standard string instructions.

Example: The following sequence of instructions searches for the first comma (,) in a character string starting at the memory location CHAR_STRING.

```
LEA  DI,CHAR_STRING ;Use DI as a pointer to characters in the string.
MOV  CX,64          ;Number of characters in the string.
MOV  AL,2CH         ;ASCII code for a comma.
REPNE SCASB         ;Search to the end of the string until the comma
                    ;is found.
```

Affected Flags: None.

Machine Instruction Decoding Guide:

Hex Binary	2nd byte	Bytes 3,4,5,6	Operand Format
F2 1111 0010			No Operand

Assembly Language Coding Examples:

Machine Code	Assembly Instructions	Operand Format	Bytes	Clocks
F2/A6	REPE CMPSB	No Operand	1	2
F2/AF	REPZ SCASW	No Operand	1	2

SAHF

Definition: Store the AH register into flag.

Function: (Low-order 8 bits of Processor Flag) < ---- (AH).

Description: The contents of the AH register replace the low-order eight bits of the Processor Flag. These eight bits include the Sign Flag, SF, the Zero Flag, ZF, the Auxiliary Carry Flag, AF, the Parity Flag, PF, and the Carry Flag, CF. The Overflow Flag, OF, the Direction Flag, DF, the Interrupt-Enable Flag, IF, and the Trace Flag, TF are not affected. This instruction is used primarily to facilitate the upward compatibility between the 8088 microprocessor and its predecessors such as the 8080/8085 CPUs.

Example: If the AH register contains C7H, the Processor Flag contains F046H, and the instruction SAHF is executed. The Processor Flag will contain F0C7H. The AH register remains unchanged.

Affected Flags:

15	14	13	12	11	10	9	8	7	6	5	4	3	2	1	0
								X	X		X		X		X
				OF	DF	IF	TF	SF	ZF		AF		PF		CF

Machine Instruction Decoding Guide:

First Byte Hex Binary	2nd byte	Bytes 3,4,5,6	Operand Format
9E 1001 1110			No Operand

Assembly Language Coding Examples:

Machine Code	Assembly Instructions	Operand Format	Bytes	Clocks
	SAHF	No Operand		4

SAL/SHL

Definition: Shift Arithmetic left/Shift logical left.

Function:

```
        (CF) <---- (High-order bit of operand)

   (Operand) <---- (Operand) * 2
```

Description: This instruction shifts the bits in the byte or word of the operand. If the operand format Reg/Mem,1 is used, only one bit is shifted. If the operand format Reg/Mem,CL is used, the contents of the CL register specify the number of bits to be rotated. Zeros are shifted into the lowest-order bit positions. If the sign bit of the result operand retains its original value, the Overflow Flag, OF, is cleared to 0. The Overflow Flag, OF, is undefined if the number of bits shifted is greater than 1. Operands of this instruction can be a general register or a memory location. Either 8-bit or 16-bit operations can be performed. This instruction updates the Carry Flag, CF, the Overflow Flag, OF, the Parity Flag, PF, the Sign Flag, SF, and the Zero Flag, ZF. The Auxiliary Carry Flag, AF, is undefined.

Example: Consider the case where the BX register contains 4231H, the Carry Flag, CF, is 0, the Processor Flag contains F046H, and the instruction SHL BX,1 is executed. The execution of this instruction is illustrated as follows:

Carry Flag CF	Contents of the BX register.	
0	0100 0010 0011 0001 = 4231H	Original contents
0	1000 0100 0110 0010 = 8462H	After shift

After the instruction SHL BX,1 is executed, the BX register contains 8462H, the Carry Flag, CF, is 0, and the Processor Flag contains F882H. The Overflow Flag, OF, is set to 1 because the sign bit has changed. SHL is a fast method to multiply by 2^n where n is the number of bits to be shifted. The result of the above example can be achieved by multiplying the original value by 2 (2^1).

Affected Flags:

15	14	13	12	11	10	9	8	7	6	5	4	3	2	1	0
				X				X	X		U		X		X
				OF	DF	IF	TF	SF	ZF		AF		PF		CF

Machine Instruction Decoding Guide:

1st Byte Hex Binary	2nd byte	Bytes 3,4,5,6	Operand Format
D0 1101 0000	Mod-100-Rm	Disp-Lo,Disp-Hi	Reg8/Mem8,1
D1 1101 0001	Mod-100-Rm	Disp-Lo,Disp-Hi	Reg16/Mem16,1
D2 1101 0010	Mod-100-Rm	Disp-Lo,Disp-Hi	Reg8/Mem8,CL
D3 1101 0011	Mod-100-Rm	Disp-Lo,Disp-Hi	Reg16/Mem16,CL

Assembly Language Coding Examples:

Machine Code	Assembly Instructions	Operand Format	Bytes	Clocks
D0E0	SHL AL,1	Reg8,1	2	2
D06701	SHL BYTE PTR [BX+01],1	Mem8,1	2-4	15+EA
D1E0	SHL AX,1	Reg16,1	2	2
D1263900	SHL WORD PTR TEST,01	Mem16,1	2-4	23+EA
D2E2	SHL DL,CL	Reg8,CL	2	8+4/bit
D224	SHL BYTE PTR [SI],CL	Mem8,CL	2-4	20+EA+4/bit
D3E3	SHL BX,CL	Reg16,CL	2	8+4/bit
D325	SHL WORD PTR [DI],CL	Mem8,CL	2-4	28+EA+4/bit

SAR

Definition: Shift Arithmetic Right.
Function:

```
   (CF) <---- (Low-order bit of operand)
(Operand) <---- (Operand) / 2
```

Description: This instruction shifts the bits in the byte or word of the operand. Bits equal to the original sign bit (most significant bit) are shifted in on the left to preserve the sign of the original value. If the operand format Reg/Mem,1 is used, only one bit is shifted. If the operand format Reg/Mem, CL is used, the contents of the CL register specify the number of bits to be shifted. After the shift, if the two most significant bits of the result operand have the same value, the Overflow Flag, OF, is cleared to 0. The Overflow Flag, OF, is cleared to 0 if the number of bits shifted is greater than 1. Operands of this instruction can be a general register or a memory location. Either 8-bit or 16-bit operations can be performed. This instruction updates the Carry Flag, CF, and the Overflow Flag, OF, the Parity Flag, PF, the Sign Flag, SF, and the Zero Flag, ZF. The Auxiliary Carry Flag, AF, is undefined.

Example: Consider the case where the word memory location BIT_PATTERN contains A62FH, the CL register contains 04H, the Processor Flag contains F046H, and the following instruction is executed.

```
SAR WORD PTR BIT_PATTERN,CL
```

The execution of this instruction is illustrated as follows:

```
0    1010 0110 0010 1111 = A62FH   Original contents.
1    1101 0011 0001 0111 = D317H   After 1st shift.
1    1110 1001 1000 1011 = E98BH   After 2nd shift.
1    1111 0100 1100 0101 = F4C5H   After 3rd shift.
1    1111 1010 0110 0010 = FA62H   After 4th shift.
```

After the instruction SAR WORD PTR BIT_PATTERN is executed, the word memory location BIT_PATTERN contains FA62H, the Carry Flag, CF, is 1, the Overflow Flag is 0, and the Processor Flag contains F083H.

Affected Flags:

15	14	13	12	11	10	9	8	7	6	5	4	3	2	1	0
				X				X	X		U		X		X
				OF	DF	IF	TF	SF	ZF		AF		PF		CF

Machine Instruction Decoding Guide:

1st Byte Hex Binary	2nd byte	Bytes 3,4,5,6	Operand Format
D0 1101 0000	Mod-111-Rm	Disp-Lo,Disp-Hi	Reg8/Mem8,1
D1 1101 0001	Mod-111-Rm	Disp-Lo,Disp-Hi	Reg16/Mem16,1
D2 1101 0010	Mod-111-Rm	Disp-Lo,Disp-Hi	Reg8/Mem8,CL
D3 1101 0011	Mod-111-Rm	Disp-Lo,Disp-Hi	Reg16/Mem16,CL

Assembly Language Coding Examples:

Machine Code	Assembly Instructions	Operand Format	Bytes	Clocks
D0F8	SAR AL,1	Reg8,1	2	2
D07F01	SAR BYTE PTR [BX+01],1	Mem8,1	2-4	15+EA
D1F8	SAR AX,1	Reg16,1	2	2
D13E3900	SAR WORD PTR TEST,01	Mem16,1	2-4	23+EA
D2FA	SAR DL,CL	Reg8,CL	2	8+4/bit
D23C	SAR BYTE PTR [SI],CL	Mem8,CL	2-4	20+EA+4/bit
D3FB	SAR BX,CL	Reg16,CL	2	8+4/bit
D33D	SAR WORD PTR [DI],CL	Mem8,CL	2-4	28+EA+4/bit

SBB

Definition: Subtract with borrow.

Function: (First Operand)<--- (First Operand) – (Second Operand) – (Carry Flag)

Description: This instruction subtracts the contents of the Carry Flag, CF, and the contents of the second operand from the original contents of the first operand. The result replaces the contents of the first operand. The previous contents of the first operand are lost. The contents of the second operand remain unchanged.

The first operand may be a register or a memory location. The second operand may be a register, a memory location, or an immediate data value. It is not allowed to specify any operand as a segment register or to specify both operands at the same time as memory locations. Either 8-bit or 16-bit operations can be performed. Both operands may be signed or unsigned numbers. Since this instruction incorporates a borrow from a previous operation, it can be used to subtract numbers whose magnitudes are longer than 16 bits.

Example: Consider the case where the AX register contains 4803H, and the Processor Flag contains F047H in which the Carry Flag is 1. After the instruction SBB AX,1500H is executed, the AX register contains 3302H, and the Processor Flag contains F002H.

Affected Flags:

15	14	13	12	11	10	9	8	7	6	5	4	3	2	1	0
				X				X	X		X		X		X
				OF	DF	IF	TF	SF	ZF		AF		PF		CF

Machine Instruction Decoding Guide:

1st Byte Hex Binary	2nd byte	Bytes 3,4,5,6	Operand Format
18 0001 1000	Mod-Reg-Rm	Disp-Lo,Disp-Hi	Reg8/Mem8,Reg8
19 0001 1001	Mod-Reg-Rm	Disp-Lo,Disp-Hi	Reg16/Mem16,Reg16
1A 0001 1010	Mod-Reg-Rm	Disp-Lo,Disp-Hi	Reg8,Reg8/Mem8
1B 0001 1011	Mod-Reg-Rm	Disp-Lo,Disp-Hi	Reg16,Reg16/Mem16
1C 0001 1100	Data8		AL,Immed8
1D 0001 1101	Data-Lo	Data-Hi	AX,Immed16
80 1000 0000	Mod-011-Rm	Disp-Lo,Disp-Hi, Data8	Reg8/Mem8,Immed8
81 1000 0001	Mod-011-Rm	Disp-Lo,Disp-Hi, Data-Lo,Data-Hi	Reg16/Mem16,Immed16

1st Byte Hex Binary	2nd byte	Bytes 3,4,5,6	Operand Format
82 1000 0010	Mod-011-Rm	Disp-Lo,Disp-Hi, Data8	Reg8/Mem8,Immed8
83 1000 0011	Mod-011-Rm	Disp-Lo,Disp-Hi, Data-SX	Reg16/Mem16,Immed8

Assembly Language Coding Examples:

Machine Code	Assembly Instructions	Operand Format	Bytes	Clocks
181F	SBB [BX],BL	Mem8,Reg8	2-4	16+EA
18D6	SBB DH,DL	Reg8,Reg8	2	3
19540C	SBB [SI+12],DX	Mem16,Reg16	2-4	24+EA
19F2	SBB DX,SI	Reg16,Reg16	2	3
1A0E0020	SBB CL,NEXT_BYTE	Reg8,Mem8	2-4	9+EA
1B15	SBB DX,[DI]	Reg16,Mem16	2-4	13+EA
1C03	SBB AL,03	AL,Immed8	2	4
1DFFFF	SBB AX,-1	AX,Immed16	3	4
80DE0A	SBB DH,10	Reg8,Immed8	3	4
809D230F01	SBB BYTE PTR [DI+0F23H],1	Mem8,Immed8	3-5	17+EA
81DD1122	SBB BP,2211H	Reg16,Immed16	4	4
811C0123	SBB WORD PTR [SI],2301H	Mem16,Immed16	4-6	25+EA
82DD0A	SBB CH,10	Reg8,Immed8	3	4
83DB01	SBB BX,01	Reg16,Immed8	3	4
831E000003	SBB WORD PTR NEW,03	Mem16,Immed8	3-5	25+EA

SCAS

Definition: Scan string.

Function: (Accumulator) – (Operand addressed by DI).

```
If (DF) = 0   then   (DI) <---- (DI) + 1 (byte)
                                 or
                     (DI) <---- (DI) + 2 (word)


If (DF) = 1   then   (DI) <---- (DI) - 1 (byte)
                                 or
                     (DI) <---- (DI) - 2 (word)
```

Description: The contents of the memory location addressed by the DI register are subtracted from the original contents of the AL or AX register depending upon byte or word operation. The result of the subtraction updates the Processor Flag but does not alter the contents of the accumulator. In assembly language, the instruction SCAS is coded as SCASB for byte operation, or as SCASW for word operation. If the Direction Flag DF is 0, the contents of the DI register are incremented by 1 after SCASB is executed, or by 2 after SCASW is executed. If the Direction Flag is 1, executing SCASB or SCASW will decrement the contents of the DI register by 1 or 2, respectively. SCAS is used in conjunction with the REPE/REPZ prefix to look for departure from a given value in a string, or with the REPNE/REPNZ prefix to find a given value in a string.

Example: Consider a string of 6 characters at the memory location INPUT_CHAR (offset address 2400H in this case), and the following sequence of instructions.

```
LEA   DI,INPUT_CHAR    ;Load first byte address into register DI.
CLD                    ;Forward direction.
MOV   AL,20H           ;Code for an ASCII blank.
MOV   CX,6             ;Number of characters in the string.
REPNE SCASB            ;Search for the first blank in the string.
JE    FOUND_BLANK      ;Go to FOUND_BLANK if a blank is found.
STC                    ;No blank exists in the character string.
```

The REPNE SCASB sequence sets the Zero Flag, ZF, to 1 when the CX register contains 0002H, the DI register contains 2404H, and a jump to the address FOUND_BLANK will take place.

	String	Address
INPUT_CHAR	41H	2400H
	42H	2401H
	43H	2402H
	20H	2403H
	41H	2404H
	20H	2405H

Affected Flags:

15	14	13	12	11	10	9	8	7	6	5	4	3	2	1	0
				X				X	X		X		X		X
				OF	DF	IF	TF	SF	ZF		AF		PF		CF

Machine Instruction Decoding Guide:

First Byte Hex Binary	2nd byte	Bytes 3,4,5,6	Operand Format
AE 1010 1110			No Operand
AF 1010 1111			No Operand

Assembly Language Coding Examples:

Machine Code	Assembly Instructions	Operand Format	Bytes	Clocks
AE	SCASB	No Operand	1	15
AF	SCASW	No Operand	1	19

SHR

Definition: Shift logical right.
Function:

```
(CF) <---- (Low-order bit of operand)

(Operand) <---- (Operand) / 2
```

Description: This instruction shifts the bits in the byte or word of the operand. If the operand format Reg/Mem,1 is used, only one bit is shifted. If the operand format Reg/Mem,CL is used, the contents of the CL register specify the number of bits to be shifted. Zeros are shifted in the highest-order bit positions. After the shift, if the sign bit of the result operand retains its original value, the Overflow Flag, OF, is cleared to 0. The Overflow Flag, OF, is undefined if the number of bits shifted is greater than 1. Operands of this instruction can be a general register or a memory location. Either 8-bit or 16-bit operations can be performed. This instruction updates the Carry Flag, CF, the Overflow Flag, OF, the Parity Flag, PF, the Sign Flag, SF, and the Zero Flag, ZF. The Auxiliary Carry Flag, AF is undefined.

Example: Consider the case where the BL register contains 77H, the Processor Flag contains F046H, and the instruction SHR BL,1 is executed. The execution of this instruction is illustrated as follows:

```
Carry Flag CF          Contents of the BL register.

     0              0111 0111 = 77H   Original contents.

     1              0011 1011 = 3BH   After the shift.
```

After SHR BL,1 is executed, the BL register contains 3BH, the Carry Flag, CF, is 1, and the Processor Flag contains F003H. The Overflow Flag is cleared to 0 since the sign bit does not change after the shift.

Affected Flags:

15	14	13	12	11	10	9	8	7	6	5	4	3	2	1	0
				X				X	X		U		X		X
				OF	DF	IF	TF	SF	ZF		AF		PF		CF

Machine Instruction Decoding Guide:

1st Byte Hex Binary	2nd byte	Bytes 3,4,5,6	Operand Format
D0 1101 0000	Mod-101-Rm	Disp-Lo,Disp-Hi	Reg8/Mem8,1
D1 1101 0001	Mod-101-Rm	Disp-Lo,Disp-Hi	Reg16/Mem16,1
D2 1101 0010	Mod-101-Rm	Disp-Lo,Disp-Hi	Reg8/Mem8,CL
D3 1101 0011	Mod-101-Rm	Disp-Lo,Disp-Hi	Reg16/Mem16,CL

Assembly Language Coding Examples:

Machine Code	Assembly Instructions	Operand Format	Bytes	Clocks
DOE8	SHR AL,1	Reg8,1	2	2
D06F01	SHR BYTE PTR [BX+01],1	Mem8,1	2-4	15+EA
D1E8	SHR AX,1	Reg16,1	2	2
D12E0020	SHR WORD PTR TEST,01	Mem16,1	2-4	23+EA
D2EA	SHR DL,CL	Reg8,CL	2	8+4/bit
D22C	SHR BYTE PTR [SI],CL	Mem8,CL	2-4	20+EA+4/bit
D3EB	SHR BX,CL	Reg16,CL	2	8+4/bit
D32D	SHR WORD PTR [DI],CL	Mem8,CL	2-4	28+EA+4/bit

STC

Definition: Set carry flag.
Function: (CF) <--- 1.
Description: This instruction sets the Carry Flag, CF, to 1 and does not affect any other flags or registers. No operand is required by this instruction.
Example: If the Processor Flag contains F046H, after the instruction STC is executed, the Processor Flag will contain F047H.
Affected Flags:

15	14	13	12	11	10	9	8	7	6	5	4	3	2	1	0
															X
				OF	DF	IF	TF	SF	ZF		AF		PF		CF

Machine Instruction Decoding Guide:

1st Byte Hex Binary	2nd byte	Bytes 3,4,5,6	Operand Format
F9 1111 1001			No operand

Assembly Language Coding Examples:

Machine Code	Assembly Instructions	Operand Format	Bytes	Clocks
F9	STC	No operand	1	2

STD

Definition: Set direction flag.

Function: (DF) <--- 1.

Description: This instruction sets the Direction Flag, DF, to 1 and does not affect any other flags or registers. No operand is required by this instruction. The pointer registers SI and/or DI will be auto-decremented if they are implied by string instructions (CMPS, LODS, MOVS, SCAS, STOS). The contents of the SI and/or DI registers are decremented by 1 or 2 depending upon byte or word operation of the string instructions, respectively.

Example: If the Processor Flag contains F046H, after the instruction STD is executed, the Processor Flag will contain F446H.

Affected Flags:

15	14	13	12	11	10	9	8	7	6	5	4	3	2	1	0
								1							
				OF	DF	IF	TF	SF	ZF		AF		PF		CF

Machine Instruction Decoding Guide:

1st Byte Hex Binary	2nd byte	Bytes 3,4,5,6	Operand Format
FD 1111 1101			No operand

Assembly Language Coding Examples:

Machine Code	Assembly Instructions	Operand Format	Bytes	Clocks
FD	STD	No operand	1	2

STI

Definition: Set interrupt flag.

Function: (IF) <--- 1.

Description: This instruction sets the Interrupt-Enable Flag, IF, to 1 and does not affect any other flags or registers. No operand is required by this instruction. When the Interrupt-Enable Flag, IF, is 1, the 8088 microprocessor will recognize software interrupts and any maskable or nonmaskable interrupt requests appearing on its INTR and NMI lines.

Example: If the Processor Flag contains F046H, after the instruction STI is executed, the Processor Flag will contain F246H.

Affected Flags:

15	14	13	12	11	10	9	8	7	6	5	4	3	2	1	0
								1							
				OF	DF	IF	TF	SF	ZF		AF		PF		CF

Machine Instruction Decoding Guide:

1st Byte Hex Binary	2nd byte	Bytes 3,4,5,6	Operand Format
FB 1111 1011			No operand

Assembly Language Coding Examples:

Machine Code	Assembly Instructions	Operand Format	Bytes	Clocks
FB	STI	No Operand	1	2

STOS

Definition: Store string.

Function: (Operand addressed by DI) <---- (Accumulator).

```
If (DF) = 0   then   (DI) <---- (DI) + 1 (byte)
                                 or
                     (DI) <---- (DI) + 2 (word)

If (DF) = 1   then   (DI) <---- (DI) - 1 (byte)
                                 or
                     (DI) <---- (DI) - 2 (word)
```

Description: The contents of the AL or AX register replace the original contents of the memory location addressed by the DI register depending upon byte or word operation. In assembly language, the instruction STOS is coded as STOSB for byte operation, or as STOSW for word operation. If the Direction Flag DF is 0, the contents of the DI register are incremented by 1 after STOSB is executed, or by 2 after STOSW is executed. If the Direction Flag, DF, is 1, executing STOSB or STOSW will decrement the contents of the DI register by 1 or 2, respectively. This instruction does not require any operands and does not affect any flags. The offset address implied by the DI register in this instruction is always taken relative to the extra segment whose base address is held in the ES register. It is not possible to use segment override prefix with the instruction STOS.

Example: Consider the case where the DI register contains B000H, the AX register contains 4142H, and the following sequence instructions is executed.

```
CLD     ;Clear the Direction Flag DF to 0.
STOSW
```

After STOSW is executed, the DI register contains B002H and the byte memory locations B000H and B001H contain 42H and 41H, respectively.

Consider the case where the DI register contains B800H, and the AL register contains FFH, and the following sequence of instructions is executed.

```
STD     ;Set the Direction Flag DF to 1.
STOSB
```

After STOSB is executed, the DI register contains B7FFH and the byte memory location B800H contains FFH.

Affected Flags: None.

Machine Instruction Decoding Guide:

First Byte Hex Binary	2nd byte	Bytes 3,4,5,6	Operand Format
AA 1010 1010			No Operand
AB 1010 1011			No Operand

Assembly Language Coding Examples:

Machine Code	Assembly Instructions	Operand Format	Bytes	Clocks
AA	STOSB	No Operand	1	11
AB	STOSW	No Operand	1	15

SUB

Definition: Subtraction.

Function: (First Operand) <--- (First Operand) – (Second Operand).

Description: The contents of the second operand are subtracted from the original contents of the first operand. The result replaces the contents of the first operand. The previous contents of the first operand are lost. The contents of the second operand remain unchanged.

The first operand may be a register or a memory location. The second operand may be a register, a memory location, or an immediate data value. It is not allowed to specify any operand as a segment register, or to specify both operands at the same time as memory locations. Both operands may be signed or unsigned numbers. Either 8-bit or 16-bit operations can be performed by this instruction.

Example: Consider the case where the DL register contains 58H, the DH register 20H, and the Processor Flag contains F046H. After the instruction SUB DL,DH is executed, the DL register contains 38H, and the Processor Flag contains F002H.

Affected Flags:

15	14	13	12	11	10	9	8	7	6	5	4	3	2	1	0
				X				X	X		X		X		X
				OF	DF	IF	TF	SF	ZF		AF		PF		CF

Machine Instruction Decoding Guide:

1st Byte Hex Binary	2nd byte	Bytes 3,4,5,6	Operand Format
28 0010 1000	Mod-Reg-Rm	Disp-Lo,Disp-Hi	Reg8/Mem8,Reg8
29 0010 1001	Mod-Reg-Rm	Disp-Lo,Disp-Hi	Reg16/Mem16,Reg16
2A 0010 1010	Mod-Reg-Rm	Disp-Lo,Disp-Hi	Reg8,Reg8/Mem8
2B 0010 1011	Mod-Reg-Rm	Disp-Lo,Disp-Hi	Reg16,Reg16/Mem16
2C 0010 1100	Data8		AL,Immed8
2D 0010 1101	Data-Lo	Data-Hi	AX,Immed16
80 1000 0000	Mod-101-Rm	Disp-Lo,Disp-Hi, Data8	Reg8/Mem8,Immed8
81 1000 0001	Mod-101-Rm	Disp-Lo,Disp-Hi, Data-Lo,Data-Hi	Reg16/Mem16,Immed16
82 1000 0010	Mod-101-Rm	Disp-Lo,Disp-Hi, Data8	Reg8/Mem8,Immed8
83 1000 0011	Mod-101-Rm	Disp-Lo,Disp-Hi, Data-SX	Reg16/Mem16,Immed8

Assembly Language Coding Examples:

Machine Code	Assembly Instructions	Operand Format	Bytes	Clocks
282C	SUB [SI],CH	Mem8,Reg8	2-4	16+EA
28F6	SUB DH,DH	Reg8,Reg8	2	3

Machine Code	Assembly Instructions	Operand Format	Bytes	Clocks
29440C	SUB [SI+12],AX	Mem16,Reg16	2-4	24+EA
29EB	SUB BX,BP	Reg16,Reg16	2	3
2A1E0020	SUB BL,TEST_BYTE	Reg8,Mem8	2-4	9+EA
2B05	SUB AX,[DI]	Reg16,Mem16	2-4	13+EA
2C03	SUB AL,03	AL,Immed8	2	4
2D2589	SUB AX,8925H	AX,Immed16	3	4
80EC0B	SUB AH,11	Reg8,Immed8	3	4
80AC002405	SUB BYTE PTR [SI+2400H],5	Mem8,Immed8	3-5	17+EA
81E90EFF	SUB CX,0FF0EH	Reg16,Immed16	4	4
812C0010	SUB WORD PTR [SI],1000H	Mem16,Immed16	4-6	25+EA
82EC0A	SUB AH,10	Reg8,Immed8	3	4
83EA01	SUB DX,01	Reg16,Immed8	3	4
832E0900F7	SUB WORD PTR LOC,-9	Mem16,Immed8	3-5	25+EA

TEST

Definition: TEST

Function: (First Operand) AND (First Operand).

```
(CF) <---- 0
(OF) <---- 0
```

Description: The Boolean logical AND of the original contents of the first and second operand is performed. The result of the operation updates the flags but does not change the contents of any operands.

The first operand may be a register or a memory location. The second operand may be a register, a memory location, or an immediate data value. It is not allowed to specify any operand as a segment register, or to specify both operands at the same time as memory locations. Both operands may be signed or unsigned numbers. Either 8-bit or 16-bit operations can be performed by this instruction. The Carry Flag, CF, the Overflow Flag, OF, The Parity Flag, PF, the Sign Flag, SF, and the Zero Flag are updated. The Auxiliary Carry Flag is undefined.

Example: The TEST instruction is very useful to test the binary value of a bit in a byte or a word. Consider the case where the AX register contains 9DE0H, the following sequence of instructions tests whether the most significant bit of the word in the AX register is 1.

```
            TEST  AX,8000H
            JNE   BIT_ONE     ;The bit is 1.
BIT_ZERO:   CLC               ;The bit is 0.
```

After the instruction TEST AX,8000H is executed, the result of the AND operation is not zero which clears the Zero Flag, ZF, to 0. Control is then transferred to the symbolic address BIT_ONE which indicates that the most significant bit of the word in the AX register is 1.

Affected Flags:

15	14	13	12	11	10	9	8	7	6	5	4	3	2	1	0
				X				X	X		U		X		X
				OF	DF	IF	TF	SF	ZF		AF		PF		CF

Machine Instruction Decoding Guide:

1st Byte Hex Binary	2nd byte	Bytes 3,4,5,6	Operand Format
84 1000 0100	Mod-Reg-Rm	Disp-Lo,Disp-Hi	Reg8/Mem8,Reg8
85 1000 0101	Mod-Reg-Rm	Disp-Lo,Disp-Hi	Reg16/Mem16,Reg16
A8 1010 1000	Data8		AL,Immed8
A9 1010 1001	Data-Lo	Data-Hi	AX,Immed16
F6 1111 0110	Mod-000-Rm	Disp-Lo,Disp-Hi, Data8	Reg8/Mem8,Immed8
F7 1111 0111	Mod-000-Rm	Disp-Lo,Disp-Hi, Data-Lo,Data-Hi	Reg16/Mem16,Immed16

Assembly Language Coding Examples:

Machine Code	Assembly Instructions	Operand Format	Bytes	Clocks
840F	TEST [BX],CL	Mem8,Reg8	2-4	9+EA
84E3	TEST AH,BL	Reg8,Reg8	2	3
855420	TEST [SI+20H],DX	Mem16,Reg16	2-4	13+EA
85CB	TEST CX,BX	Reg16,Reg16	2	3
84AF4523	TEST [BX+2345H],CH	Mem8,Reg8	2-4	9+EA
852D	TEST [DI],BP	Mem16,Reg16	2-4	13+EA
A880	TEST AL,80H	AL,Immed8	2	4
A90100	TEST AX,0001H	AX,Immed16	3	4
F6C201	TEST DL,01	Reg8,Immed8	3	5
F7C10080	TEST CX,8000H	Reg16,Immed16	4	5
F606090001	TEST BYTE PTR LOC,01	Mem8,Immed8	3-5	11+EA
F7060A000200	TEST WORD PTR WRD,02	Mem16,Immed16	4-6	11+EA

WAIT

Definition: Processor wait.

Function: None.

Description: This instruction causes the 8088 microprocessor to enter the wait state while its TEST line is not active. WAIT does not affect any flags and is used primarily to ensure synchronization of activities between the 8088 microprocessor and other coprocessors such as the 8087 Numeric Data Processor.

Example: If the 8087 Numeric Data Processor is present in an 8088-based microcomputer, consider the following sequence of instructions.

```
ESC  OFH.,DX   ;8087 FSQRT instruction.

WAIT           ;Wait until the 8087 completes the FSQRT calulation.

ESC  OAH,[BX] ;8087 FST instruction.
```

The 8088 CPU performs a NOP in only two clock cycles for the instruction ESC OFH,DX. However, this ESC sequence is a FSQRT instruction for the 8087 chip (taking the square root of the 8087s top-of-stack register). It will take the 8087 Numeric Data Processor approximately 180 clock cycles to complete the task. Therefore, the WAIT instruction synchronizes the 8088 microprocessor with its 8087 chip by causing the 8088 to wait until the 8087 signals that it has completed its FSORT instruction (by activating the 8088s TEST line).

The 8088 microprocessor then proceeds to execute the instruction ESC OAH,[BX] which is another 8087 instruction to store the result of the square root at the memory location specified by the BX register. If the WAIT instruction is not issued, the instruction ESC OAH,[BX] is executed immediately in the sequence and, of course, incorrect result will occur.

Affected Flags: None.

Machine Instruction Decoding Guide:

First Byte Hex Binary	2nd byte	Bytes 3,4,5,6	Operand Format
9B 1001 1011			No Operand

Assembly Language Coding Examples:

Machine Code	Assembly Instructions	Operand Format	Bytes	Clocks
9B	WAIT	No Operand	1	3+5n*

*Note: n is the number of wait states the microprocessor performs while its TEST line is active. The CPU examines its TEST pin every five clocks. Thus the effective execution time of a WAIT can be from 3 clocks to infinity.

XCHG

Definition: Exhange.
Function:

```
       (Temporary) <---- (First Operand)
    (First Operand) <---- (Second Operand)
   (Second Operand) <---- (Temporary)
```

Description: The original contents of the first and second operand are exchanged. Operands can be a register or a memory location. No segment register or immediate data values may be specified as operands. Either 8-bit or 16-bit operations can be performed. This instruction does not affect any flags.

Example: If the AX register contains 2347H, the CX register contains FF22H, and the instruction XCHG AX,CX is executed, the new contents of the AX and CX registers are FF22H and 2347H, respectively.

Affected Flags: None.

Machine Instruction Decoding Guide:

First Byte Hex	Binary	2nd byte	Bytes 3,4,5,6	Operand Format
86	1000 0110	Mod-Reg-Rm	Disp-Lo,Disp-Hi	Reg8,Reg8/Mem8
87	1000 0111	Mod-Reg-Rm	Disp-Lo,Disp-Hi	Reg16,Reg16/Mem16
	1001 1reg			AX,Reg16*

*Notes:

1) If both operands are 16-bit registers and one of the operands is the AX register, the instruction format with Mod-Reg-Rm should not be used. The alternate format 1001 1reg is more efficient.
2) The instructions XCHG AX,AX and NOP have identical machine code (90H).

Assembly Language Coding Examples:

Machine Code	Assembly Instructions	Operand Format	Bytes	Clocks
86C3	XCHG AL,BL	Reg8,Reg8	2	4
867401	XCHG DH,[SI+01]	Reg8,Mem8	2-4	17+EA
87CB	XCHG CX,BX	Reg16,Reg16	2	4
872E0C10	XCHG BP,TEST_LOCATION	Reg16,Mem16	2-4	25+EA
92	XCHG AX,DX	AX,Reg16	1	3

XLAT

Definition: Table Translation.

Function: (AL) <--- ((BX) + (AL)).

Description: This instruction uses the contents of the AL register as the offset to a 256-byte table whose offset address is held in the BX register. The byte at the offset in the table replaces the original contents of the AL register. An offset of 0 corresponds to the starting byte in the table. XLAT does not require any operands and does not affect any flags. This instruction is useful to translate data from a table to another.

Example: If a table containing the ASCII representation of each hexadecimal digit is stored at the memory location TABLE, the following sequence of instructions retrieves the proper ASCII code for each hexadecimal number specified in the AL register.

```
      MOV  AL,03
      CALL TRANS
      CLC            ;The AL register contains 33H at this instruction.
      ..
      Other instructions
      ..
TRANS PROC NEAR
      LEA  BX,TABLE  ;Load the table address into register BX.
      XLAT           ;ASCII character is returned in the AL register.
      RET
TABLE DB   30H,31H,32H,33H,34H,35H,36H,37H,38H,39H,41H,42H,43H,44H,45H,46H
TRANS ENDP
```

Affected Flags: None.

Machine Instruction Decoding Guide:

1st Byte Hex Binary	2nd byte	Bytes 3,4,5,6	Operand Format
D7 1101 0111			No operand

Assembly Language Coding Examples:

Machine Code	Assembly Instructions	Operand Format	Bytes	Clocks
D7	XLAT	No operand	1	11

XOR

Definition: Exclusive OR.

Function: (First Operand) <--- (First Operand) XOR (Second Operand).

```
(CF) <---  0

(OF) <---  0
```

Description: The Boolean exclusive-OR of the original contents of the first operand and the contents of the second operand are performed. The result replaces the contents of the first operand. The previous contents of the first operand are lost. The contents of the second operand remain unchanged. The first operand may be a register or a memory location. The second operand may be a register, a memory location, or an immediate data value. It is not allowed to specify any operand as a segment register, or to specify both operands at the same time as memory locations. Either 8-bit or 16-bit operations can be performed. The Carry Flag, CF, and the Overflow Flag, OF, are always cleared to 0 by this instruction.

Example: Consider the case where the AX register contains 7FFFH, the DX register contains 8000H, and the Flag contains F046H. After the instruction XOR AX, DX is executed, the AX register contains FFFFH and the Processor Flag contains F086H.

```
    Contents of AX    0111 1111 1111 1111 = 7FFFH

    Contents of DX    1000 0000 0000 0000 = 8000H

New contents of AX    1111 1111 1111 1111 = FFFFH
```

There are eight 1 bits in the low-order 8 bits of the AX register, which is an even number, so the Parity Flag, PF, is set to 1. Since the result of the Boolean XOR operation is a negative nonzero value in two's complement notation, the Sign Flag, SF, is set to 1, and the Zero Flag, ZF, is cleared to 0. The Carry Flag, CF, and Overflow Flag, OF, are always cleared to 0 since there is no carry or overflow condition. The Auxiliary Carry Flag, AF, is undefined.

Affected Flags:

15	14	13	12	11	10	9	8	7	6	5	4	3	2	1	0
				0				X	X		U		X		0
				OF	DF	IF	TF	SF	ZF		AF		PF		CF

Machine Instruction Decoding Guide:

1st Byte Hex Binary	2nd byte	Bytes 3,4,5,6	Operand Format
30 0011 0000	Mod-Reg-Rm	Disp-Lo,Disp-Hi	Reg8/Mem8,Reg8
31 0011 0001	Mod-Reg-Rm	Disp-Lo,Disp-Hi	Reg16/Mem16,Reg16
32 0011 0010	Mod-Reg-Rm	Disp-Lo,Disp-Hi	Reg8,Reg8/Mem8

1st Byte Hex Binary	2nd byte	Bytes 3,4,5,6	Operand Format
33 0011 0011	Mod-Reg-Rm	Disp-Lo,Disp-Hi	Reg16,Reg16/Mem16
34 0011 0100	Data8		AL,Immed8
35 0011 0101	Data-Lo	Data-Hi	AX,Immed16
80 1000 0000	Mod-110-Rm	Disp-Lo,Disp-Hi, Data8	Reg8/Mem8,Immed8
81 1000 0001	Mod-110-Rm	Disp-Lo,Disp-Hi, Data-Lo,Data-Hi	Reg16/Mem16,Immed16

Assembly Language Coding Examples:

Machine Code	Assembly Instructions	Operand Format	Bytes	Clocks
3023	XOR [BP+DI],AH	Mem8,Reg8	2-4	16+EA
32F6	XOR DH,DH	Reg8,Reg8	2	3
310E0010	XOR WORD PTR SUM,CX	Mem16,Reg16	2-4	24+EA
33C7	XOR AX,DI	Reg16,Reg16	2	3
328D0001	XOR CL,[DI+100H]	Reg8,Mem8	2-4	9+EA
335C0C	XOR BX,[SI+12]	Reg16,Mem16	2-4	13+EA
34FF	XOR AL,-1	AL,Immed8	2	4
35FF7F	XOR AX,7FFFH	AX,Immed16	3	4
80F301	XOR BL,01	Reg8,Immed8	3	4
80740290	XOR BYTE PTR [SI+2],90H	Mem8,Immed8	3-5	17+EA
81F6FF7F	XOR SI,7FFFH	Reg16,Immed16	4	4
81360020FFFE	XOR WORD PTR TEST,0FEFFH	Mem16,Immed16	4-6	25+EA

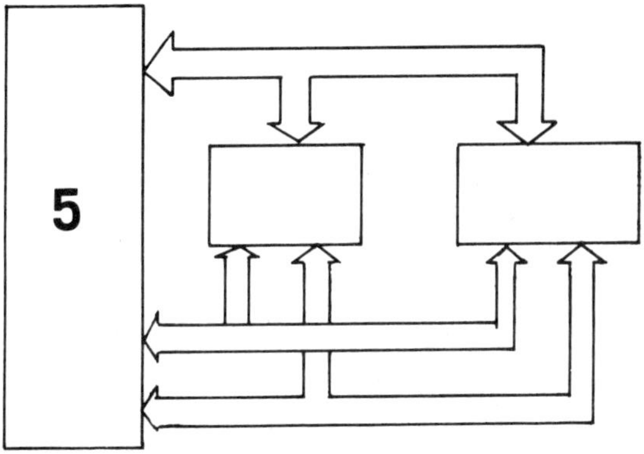

Integer Arithmetic

This chapter discusses a group of the 8088 instruction set that performs essential integer arithmetic functions. These instructions can be employed in binary and decimal arithmetic to perform the following:

Addition functions
Subtraction functions
Multiplication functions
Division functions
Comparison functions

ARITHMETIC INSTRUCTIONS

Instructions in this group consist of ADD (Addition), ADC (Add With Carry), INC (Increment), AAA (ASCII Adjust For Addition), DAA (Decimal Adjust for Addition), SUB (Subtract), SBB (Subtract With Borrow), DEC (Decrement), NEG (Negate), CMP (Comparison), AAS (ASCII Adjust For Subtraction), DAS (Decimal Adjust For Subtraction), MUL (Multiply), IMUL (Integer Multiply), AAM (ASCII Adjust For Multiplication), DIV (divide), IDIV (Integer Divide), AAD (ASCII Adjust For Division), CBW (Convert Byte To Word), and CWD (Convert Word to Doubleword).

The following section presents a brief summary of the functions that these instructions perform. Refer to Chapter 4 for a complete description of each instruction.

With these fundamental instructions, I will illustrate and discuss several examples of programs written in 8088 assembly language that perform arithmetic functions on positive and negative binary numbers represented in standard two's complement notations. These examples also show typical programming techniques to manipulate integers larger than 16 bits, to generate pseudorandom numbers in digital computers, and to convert a number in the hexadecimal representation to its equivalent decimal representation. These examples take full advantage of the powerful multiply and divide instructions of the 8088 CPU that make the 8086/8088 microprocessor family superior to many 8-bit central processing units.

ADD (Addition). This instruction produces the binary sum of two specified operands. The resulting sum replaces the destination operand, the source operand remains unchanged. Either byte or word operations can be performed. Both operands may be signed or unsigned binary numbers. ADD updates the AF, CF, OF, PF, SF, and ZF flags.

ADC (Add with Carry). This instruction produces the binary sum of two specified operands and the content of the Carry Flag, CF. The resulting sum replaces the destination operand, the source operand remains unchanged. Either byte or word operations can be performed. Both operands may be signed or unsigned binary numbers. This instruction is useful to add integer numbers whose lengths may span multiple bytes (see examples of 32-bit arithmetic in this chapter). ADC updates the AF, CF, OF, PF, SF, and ZF flags.

INC (Increment). This instruction increments the contents of the operand by one. The operand is considered an unsigned binary number and can be an 8-bit or a 16-bit quantity. INC updates the AF, OF, PF, SF, and ZF flags. The Carry Flag is not affected.

AAA (ASCII Adjust for Addition). This instruction changes the contents of the AL register to a valid unpacked BCD representation. The AF and CF flags are updated. The contents of the OF, PF, SF, and ZF are undefined after AAA is executed.

DAA (Decimal Adjust for Addition). This instruction assumes that the AL register contains the result of adding two valid packed BCD numbers. It then changes the contents of the AL register to a valid packed BCD representation. DAA updates the AF, CF, PF, SF, and ZF flags. The Overflow Flag is undefined after DAA is executed.

SUB (Subtraction). This instruction subtracts the source operand from the destination operand. The result replaces the destination operand. The source operand remains unchanged. Both operands may be signed or unsigned binary numbers. Either byte or word operations can be performed. SUB updates the AF, CF, OF, PF, SF, and ZF flags.

SBB (Subtract with Borrow). This instruction subtracts the source operand from the destination operand, and also subtracts the content of the Carry Flag from the destination operand. The result replaces the destination operand. The source operand remains unchanged. Both operands may be signed or unsigned binary numbers. Either byte or word operations can be performed. This instruction is useful to subtract integer numbers whose lengths may span multiply bytes (see the examples of 32-bit arithmetic in this chapter). SSB updates the AF, CF, OF, PF, SF, and ZF flags.

DEC (Decrement). This instruction decrements the contents of the operands by one. The operand is considered an unsigned binary number and can be an 8-bit or a 16-bit quantity. DEC updates the AF, OF, PF, SF, and ZF flags. The Carry Flag is not affected.

NEG (Negate). This instruction subtracts the contents of the specified operand from 0, and replaces the operand with the result. This operation is used to change the sign of a signed binary number from positive to negative, or from negative to positive in standard two's complement representation. NEG updates the AF, CF, OF, PF, SF, and ZF flags.

CMP (Compare). This instruction subtracts the contents of the source operands from the contents of the destination operands. The result updates the AF, CF, OF, PF, AF, and ZF flags but does not change the contents of any operands.

AAS (ASCII Adjust for Subtraction). This instruction assumes that the AL register contains the result of subtracting two valid unpacked BCD numbers. It then changes the contents of the AL register to a valid unpacked BCD representation. AAS updates the AF and CF flags. The OF, PF, SF, and ZF flags are undefined after this instruction is executed.

DAS (Decimal Adjust for Subtraction). This instruction assumes that the AL register contains the result of subtracting two valid, packed BCD numbers. It then changes the contents of the AL register to a valid packed BCD representation. DAS updates the AF, CF, PF, SF, and ZF flags. The Overflow Flag is undefined after this instruction is executed.

MUL (Multiply). This instruction performs an unsigned multiplication of the accumulator (AL in byte multiplication, AX in word multiplication) and the specified operand. The result of a byte multiplication is a 16-bit product to be stored in the AX register. The result of a word multiplication is a 32-bit product to be stored in the register pair DX,AX where the DX register contains the high-order 16 bits of the result. If the high-order part of the resulting product (AH in byte multiplication, DX in word multiplication) is not 0, the CF and OF flags are set to 1 to indicate that the AH or DX register contains significant digits of the result. Otherwise, these two flags are cleared to 0. The AF, PF, SF, and ZF flags are undefined after the MUL instruction is executed.

IMUL (Integer Multiply). This instruction performs a signed multiplication of the accumulator (AL in byte multiplication, AX in word multiplication) and the specified operand. The result of a byte multiplication is a 16-bit product to be stored in the AX register. The result of a word multiplication is a 32-bit product to be stored in the register pair DX,AX where the DX register contains the high-order 16 bits of the result. If the high-order part of the resulting product (AH in byte multiplication, DX in word multiplication) is not the sign extension of the low-order part of the result, the CF and OF flags are set to 1 to indicate that the AH or DX register contains significant digits of the result. Otherwise, these two flags are cleared to 0. The AF, PF, SF, and ZF flags are undefined after the IMUL instruction is executed.

AAM (ASCII Adjust For Multiply). This instruction assumes that the AX register contains the result of a multiplication of two valid unpacked BCD numbers. It then changes the contents of the AX register to a valid two-digit unpacked BCD representation. AAM updates the PF, SF, and ZF flags. The AF, CF, and OF flags are undefined after the instruction is executed.

DIV (Divide). This instruction performs an unsigned division of the accumulator (AX in byte division, the register pair DX,AX in word division) by the specified operand. If an 8-bit division is performed, the quotient is returned in the AL register, and the remainder is returned in the AH register. If a 16-bit division is performed, the AX register contains the quotient and the DX register contains the remainder.If the quotient exceeds the capacity of the AL register in byte division or the AX register in word division (greater than FFH in byte division, or greater than FFFFH in word division), or when division by zero is attempted, the microprocessor automatically generates a type 0 interrupt (divide error interrupt). Quotients are always truncated to integers. The AF, CF, OF, PF, SF, and ZF flags are undefined after the instruction DIV is executed.

IDIV (Integer Divide). This instruction performs a signed division of the accumulator (AX in byte division, the register pair DX,AX in word division) by the specified operand. If an 8-bit division is performed, the quotient is returned in the AL register, and the remainder is returned in the AH register. If a 16-bit division is performed, the AX register contains the quotient and the DX register contains the remainder. In byte division, the maximum positive quotient is 127 (7FH) and the minimum negative quotient is -127 (81H). In word division, the maximum positive quotient is 32767 (7FFFH) and the minimum negative quotient is −32767 (8001H). If the quotient is less than the minimum or greater than the maximum, or when division by zero is attempted, the microprocessor automatically generates a type 0 interrupt (divide error interrupt). Quotients are always truncated to integers. The AF, CF, OF, SF, and ZF flags are undefined after the DIV instruction is executed.

AAD (ASCII Adjust For Division). This instruction changes the contents of the AL register before dividing two valid unpacked BCD numbers so that the quotient of the division is a valid unpacked BCD representation. AAD updates the PF, SF, and ZF flags. The AF, CF, and OF flags are undefined after the instruction is executed.

CBW (Convert Byte To Word). This instruction extends the sign of the byte in the AL register throughout the AH register. This is useful to convert an 8-bit signed number into a 16-bit signed number. This instruction does not affect any flags.

CWD (Convert Word To Doubleword). This instruction extends the sign of the word in the AX register throughout the DX register. This is useful to convert a 16-bit signed number in the AX register into a 32-bit signed number in the register pair DX,AX. This instruction does not affect any flags.

32-BIT ADDITION

The program that follows is designed to perform the binary addition of two 32-bit integers stored at the symbolic memory locations NUMBER1 and NUMBER2. The resulting sum of the two numbers is to be stored at the symbolic memory location SUM. Figure 5-1 shows a block diagram of how the operands and result are stored in the computer memory. In this example, the contents of the doubleword representing each integer number and resulting sum are stored in the computer memory according to the standard format of a doubleword. The listing for the program performing 32-bit addition is shown in Fig. 5-2.

In this example, the instructions that perform the 32-bit addition are grouped into a procedure. The first line of the program listing declares the procedure to be intrasegment (by using the operator NEAR). Furthermore, the program makes the assumption that the code segment, the data segment, and the extra segment overlap one another (these three segments occupy the same 64 K-byte memory space).

NUMBER1 is a symbolic representation of the actual location in the computer memory that contains one of the 32-bit integers. The location NUMBER1 has been declared to contain a doubleword constant by the

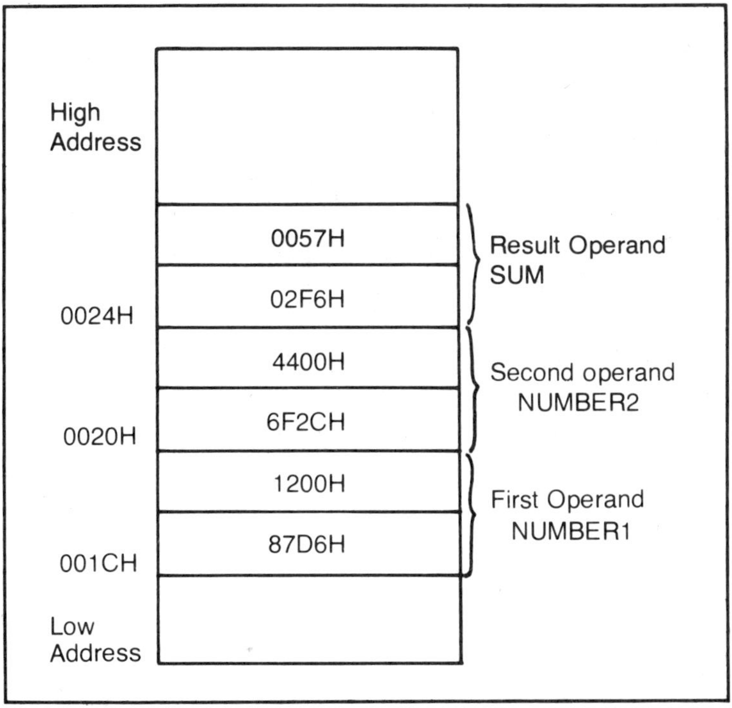

Fig. 5-1. Diagram showing how the operands and result in a 32-bit addition are stored in memory.

```
0000                ADD32     PROC  NEAR          ;Procedure to add two 32-bit integers.
0000 8D361C00                 LEA   SI,NUMBER1    ;SI has the Offset Address of NUMBER1.
0004 8D1E2000                 LEA   BX,NUMBER2    ;BX has the Offset Address of NUMBER2.
0008 8D3E2400                 LEA   DI,SUM        ;DI has the Offset Address of SUM.
000C 8B04                     MOV   AX,[SI]       ;AX has the low-order word of 1st number.
000E 0307                     ADD   AX,[BX]       ;Sum of the low-order words of two numbers.
0010 8905                     MOV   [DI],AX       ;Write out the low-order word of SUM.
0012 8B4402                   MOV   AX,[SI+2]     ;AX has the high-order word of 1st number.
0015 134702                   ADC   AX,[BX+2]     ;Sum of the high-order words of two numbers
                    ;                              plus the carry of previous addition.
0018 894502                   MOV   [DI+2],AX     ;Write out the high-order word of SUM.
001B C3                       RET
001C 87D6 1200      NUMBER1   DD    1234567       ;The first number.
0020 6F2C 4400      NUMBER2   DD    4467823       ;The second number.
0024 ??             SUM       DD    ?             ;The addition result will be stored at
                    ;                              this doubleword location.
0028                ADD32     ENDP
```

Fig. 5-2. Procedure to add 32-bit integers.

directive DD (Define Doubleword). The Macro Assembler reserves four bytes of storage to accommodate this 32-bit integer and then initializes the reserved space (offset addresses 1CH to 1FH) with the number 12D687H which is the hexadecimal representation of the decimal number 1234567. The low-order 16 bits of the 32-bit integer always occupy the lower memory address to conform with the standard storage format of a doubleword.

Similarly, NUMBER2 is another symbolic address representing the location that contains the second 32-bit integer. The Macro Assembler again reserves four bytes of memory (offset addresses 20H to 23H) to accommodate the number 442C6FH which is the hexadecimal representation of the decimal number 4467823.

The result of the addition is another 32-bit integer to be stored at the symbolic address SUM (offset addresses 24H to 27H). As you can see from the program listing, the doubleword contents of this location are left undefined initially. When the execution of the procedure is completed, the result of the 32-bit addition is stored at the symbolic address SUM which is the hexadecimal number 570F6H (5702390 in decimal). You should try to verify the result of this example as an exercise.

The first three instructions in the procedure employ the SI, BX, and DI registers as pointers to access the memory locations that hold the two 32-bit integers and the result of the addition. The instruction LEA (Load Effective Address) initializes the SI, BX, and DI registers with the values 001CH, 0020H, and 0024H, respectively. The addition is then performed by summing the low-order words of two specified integers, writing the partial result into the location addressed by the DI register, summing the high-order words of the two integers and the carry resulting from the previous add operation, and again writing the result to memory. This algorithm can easily be extended to perform addition of two binary integers whose lengths may span multiple bytes of memory storage.

32-BIT SUBTRACTION

The 8088 microprocessor provides the Carry Flag to record a carry out of or a borrow into the most significant bit of a byte or a word in an 8-bit or a 16-bit operation, respectively. Therefore, the Carry Flag in conjunction with the SBB (Subtract with Borrow) instruction can effectively manipulate the subtraction of integers longer than 16 bits.

The program that follows is designed to subtract two 32-bit integers stored at the symbolic memory locations NUMBER1 and NUMBER2. The intrasegment procedure listed in Fig. 5-3 performs the subtraction of two specified integers and stores the result at the symbolic location RESULT. Similar to the addition example, the BX, SI, and DI registers are used as memory pointers to access the 32-bit integers in the program. The code segment, data segment, and extra segment also overlap one another in this case. When the execution of the program is completed, the symbolic location RESULT contains a doubleword having the value FFCEAA18H

```
0000                SUB32    PROC  NEAR        ;Procedure to subtract two 32-bit integers.
0000 8D361C00                LEA   SI,NUMBER1  ;SI has the Offset Address of NUMBER1.
0004 8D1E2000                LEA   BX,NUMBER2  ;BX has the Offset Address of NUMBER2.
0008 8D3E2400                LEA   DI,RESULT   ;DI has the Offset Address of RESULT.
000C 8B04                    MOV   AX,[SI]     ;AX has the low-order word of 1st number.
000E 2B07                    SUB   AX,[BX]     ;Subtraction of the low-order words of two
                                                numbers.
0010 8905                    MOV   [DI],AX     ;Write out the low-order word of RESULT.
0012 8B4402                  MOV   AX,[SI+2]   ;AX has the high-order word of 1st number.
0015 1B4702                  SBB   AX,[BX+2]   ;Subtraction of the high-order words of two
                    ;                           numbers and the borrow bit of previous
0018 894502                  MOV   [DI+2],AX    subtraction.
001B C3                      RET               ;Write out the high-order word of RESULT.
001C 87D6 1200      NUMBER1  DD   1234567
0020 6F2C 4400      NUMBER2  DD   4467823     ;The first number.
0024 ??             RESULT   DD   ?           ;The second number.
                    ;                         ;The subtraction result will be stored at
0028                SUB32    ENDP              this doubleword location.
```

Fig. 5-3. Procedure to subtract 32-bit integers.

which is the correct hexadecimal representation of the negative decimal number -3233256 in standard two's complement notation. This subtraction logic can be extended to work with binary integers whose magnitudes require multiple bytes of memory storage.

32-BIT MULTIPLICATION

This section discusses a more complex arithmetic problem: the multiplication of binary integers whose magnitudes are greater than 16 bits. In order to fully comprehend the logic that is used in the algorithm to perform binary integer multiplication, consider a simple case of decimal multiplica-

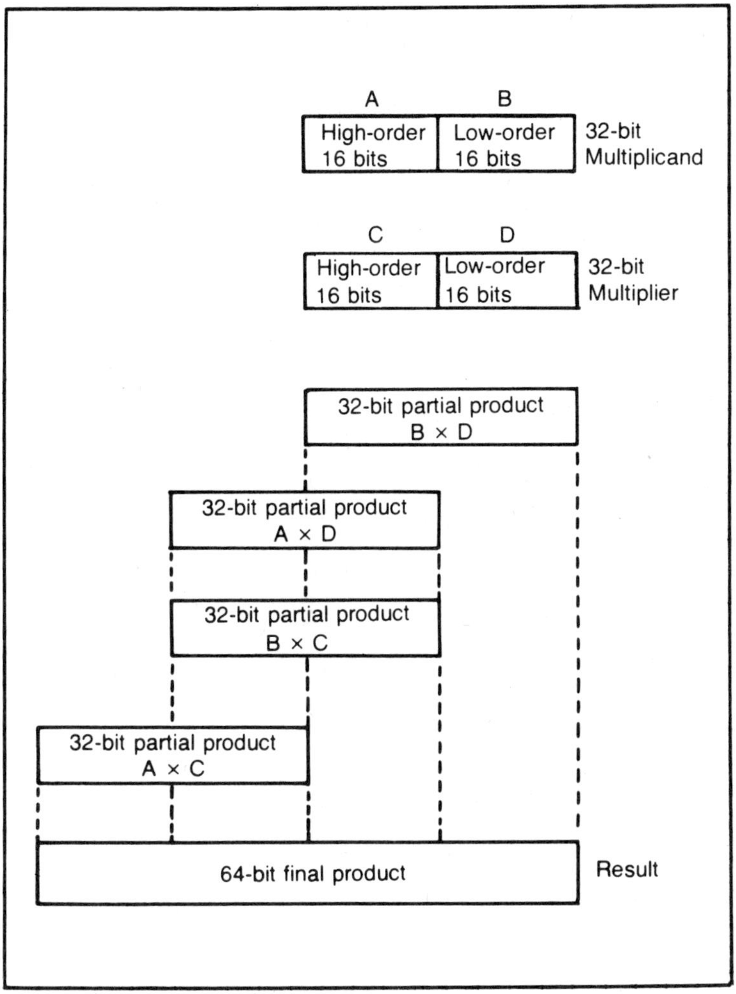

Fig. 5-4. Block diagrams of the algorithm to multiply 32-bit integers.

```
0000                 MUL32      PROC  NEAR              ;Procedure to multiply 32-bit integers.
                     ;
                     ; This procedure performs the multiplication of two unsigned
                     ; 32-bit integers. We can view the first integer as ab where
                     ; a and b represent the high-order and low-order 16 bits of the
                     ; number. Similarly, the second 32-bit integer is viewed as cd.
                     ; This procedure then performs:
                     ;
                     ;       ab
                     ;     x cd
                     ;
                     ;      ____
                     ;       bd  (b x d) First partial product
                     ;    +  ad  (a x d)
                     ;    +  bc  (b x c) Shift one position relative to 1st partial product.
                     ;    + ac   (a x c)
                     ;    -------
                     ;      mnop  (final result).
                     ;
0000 8D363800                  LEA   SI,NUMBER1        ;SI points to the first integer.
0004 8D1E3C00                  LEA   BX,NUMBER2        ;BX points to the second integer.
0008 8D3E4000                  LEA   DI,PRODUCT        ;DI points to the resulting product.
000C 8B04                      MOV   AX,[SI]
000E F727                      MUL WORD PTR [BX]       ;Calculate b x d.
0010 8905                      MOV   [DI],AX           ;Low-order word of 1st partial product.
```

```
0012 895502                MOV    [DI+02],DX     ;High-order word of 1st partial product.
0015 8B4402                MOV    AX,[SI+02]
 0018 F727                 MUL WORD PTR [BX]    ;Calculate a x d.
 001A 014502               ADD    [DI+02],AX    ;Shift the 2nd partial product.
 001D 115504               ADC    [DI+04],DX    ;High-order word of 2nd partial product.
 0020 8B04                 MOV    AX,[SI]
 0022 F76702               MUL WORD PTR [BX+02];Calculate  b x c.
 0025 014502               ADD    [DI+02],AX    ;Product with the next digit of multiplier.
 0028 115504               ADC    [DI+04],DX    ;High-order word of 3rd partial product.
 002B 8B4402               MOV    AX,[SI+02]
 002E F76702               MUL WORD PTR [BX+2] ;Calculate a x c.
 0031 014504               ADD    [DI+04],AX    ;Shift the 4th partial product.
 0034 115505               ADC    [DI+05],DX    ;High-order word of 4th partial product.
 0037 C3                   RET
 0038 4629 6900 NUMBER1 DD 6891846              ;First 32-bit integer.
 003C 0023 4600 NUMBER2 DD 4596480              ;Second 32-bit integer.
 0040 ??        PRODUCT DQ ?                    ;64-bit product of the multiplication.
 0048           MUL32   ENDP
```

Fig. 5-5. Procedure to multiply 32-bit integers.

tion. For instance, the multiplication of two decimal numbers 135 and 43 can be performed in the following manner:

	135	(multiplicand)
	43	(multiplier)
	———	
	15	(3 × 5) First partial product
Partial products with digit 3 of the multiplier	9	(3 × 3) Shift one position relative to 15
	3	(3 × 1) Shift one position relative to 9
	———	
	20	(4 × 5) Shift one position relative to 15
Partial products with digit 4 of the multiplier	12	(4 × 3) Shift one position relative to 20
	4	(4 × 1) Shift one position relative to 12
	———	
	5805	(Final Result = Sum of all partial products)

The multiplication is done by multiplying each digit of the multiplier by every digit toward the most significant one. Since the multiplicand has 3 digits and the multiplier has 2 digits, there will be six (3 × 2) partial products. In this example the first partial product which is 15 (3 × 5) is derived by multiplying the rightmost digit of the multiplier by the rightmost digit of the multiplicand.

The second partial product, which is 9 (3 × 3), is derived similarly by multiplying the next digit of the multiplicand by the same digit of the multiplier. Before adding the partial products, there is one more operation that must be performed. The partial product 9 is offset to the left by one position. In other words, the number 9 is shifted left by one digit position relative to the number 15 in this calculation. However, the first partial product of the next digit of the multiplier is shifted left by one position relative to the first partial product of the previous digit of the multiplier, as illustrated above. The six partial products in this simple decimal multiplication, correctly shifted, are then added together to produce the final result 5805.

The algorithm for multiplication of large binary integers, in general, operates exactly as the process described above the decimal multiplication. We can consider each word in a binary integer to be analogous to a decimal digit of a decimal number. Figure 5-4 illustrates the process required to multiply two 32-bit integers. The result of a 32-bit by 32-bit multiplication is a 64-bit product.

An 8088 assembly language procedure that performs the multiplication of two 32-bit integers is listed in Fig. 5-5. The two 32-bit integers are 6891846 and 4596840. They are stored at the symbolic memory locations NUMBER1 (Offset Addresses 38H to 3BH) and NUMBER2 (Offset Addresses 3CH to 3FH). The result of the multiplication will be stored at the symbolic location PRODUCT (Offset Addresses 40H to 47H). The procedure reserves an area of 8 bytes to accommodate the 64-bit product by using

```
0000        PSEUDO_RANDOM PROC NEAR          ;Generate a new random number in AX.
0000 51                   PUSH CX            ;Save previous contents of CX.
0001 52                   PUSH DX            ;Save previous contents of DX.
0002 B90501               MOV  CX,261
0005 F7E1                 MUL  CX            ;The 64-bit result is in DX,AX.
            ;                                 The contents of the AX register are the
            ;                                 same as the remainder of the division
            ;                                 (DX,AX) and 2 to the power 16.
            ;
0007 5A                   POP  DX            ;Restore previous value of DX.
0008 59                   POP  CX            ;Restore previous value of CX.
0009 C3                   RET
000A        PSEUDO_RANDOM ENDP
```

Fig. 5-6. Procedure to generate pseudorandom numbers.

the directive DQ (Define Quadword). The hexadecimal number 1CCFA9C89200H is stored at the location PRODUCT when the execution of the procedure is completed.

GENERATION OF PSEUDORANDOM NUMBERS

One of the most useful applications of microcomputers is the simulation of some actual processes or activities in the real world so that their behaviors can be emulated and studied. Processes or activities such as the flow of oil and gas in a pipeline network, the landing and takeoff of an aircraft, flows of jobs in a digital computer system, movements of graphic

200 Decimal Pseudo-Random Numbers Generated By Procedure PSEUDO_RANDOM

127	33147	615	29443	16911	22859	2423	42579	37535	31771
34695	11427	33327	47595	35991	22003	41151	58043	10407	29251
32335	50827	27575	53651	43743	13659	26055	50147	46703	65323
9944	39480	15128	16248	46424	58040	9624	21496	39896	58168
43032	24696	23128	7096	17048	58616	28888	3128	29976	24952
24408	13496	49048	22008	42456	5432	41496	17016	50264	11704
40088	42744	15064	65080	12056	888	35160	1720	55704	55288
12248	51000	7192	42104	44632	49080	30360	59640	34008	28728
26904	9592	13144	22712	29592	55800	14808	63800	5656	34424
6232	53688	53400	43768	20184	25144	8984	51064	23896	10936
36248	23544	50136	43832	36888	59512	600	25528	43672	60664
39128	54328	23832	59768	1880	31928	10136	24056	52696	56632
35352	51832	27736	30136	1176	44792	25304	50744	5912	35704
12632	20152	16792	57336	22488	36664	1048	11384	22104	1976
56984	61688	44248	14392	20760	44408	56152	41144	56216	57848
25048	49464	65048	3704	49240	6584	14488	45816	30424	10808
2840	20344	1368	29368	62872	25592	60376	29496	30744	28792
43608	43960	4760	62712	49368	39992	17688	29048	44888	50360
36760	26104	62936	42296	29208	21112	5208	48568	27800	46840
35544	36408	65304	4984	55640	38584	43416	59384	32728	22328

The Same 200 Pseudo-Random Numbers In Hexadecimal Notation.

007F	817B	0267	7303	420F	594B	0977	A653	929F	7C1B
8787	2CA3	822F	B9EB	8C97	55F3	A0BF	E2BB	28A7	7243
7E4F	C68B	6BB7	D193	AADF	355B	65C7	C3E3	B66F	FF2B
26D8	9A38	3B18	3F78	B558	E2B8	2598	53F8	9BD8	E338
A818	6078	5A58	1BB8	4298	E4F8	70D8	0C38	7518	6178
5F58	34B8	BF98	55F8	A5D8	1538	A218	4278	C458	2DB8
9C98	A6F8	3AD8	FE38	2F18	0378	8958	06B8	D998	D7F8
2FD8	C738	1C18	A478	AE58	BFB8	7698	E8F8	84D8	7038
6918	2578	3358	58B8	7398	D9F8	39D8	F938	1618	8678
1858	D1B8	D098	AAF8	4ED8	6238	2318	C778	5D58	2AB8
8D98	5BF8	C3D8	AB38	9018	E878	0258	63B8	AA98	ECF8
98D8	D438	5D18	E978	0758	7CB8	2798	5DF8	CDD8	DD38
8A18	CA78	6C58	75B8	0498	AEF8	62D8	C638	1718	8B78
3158	4EB8	4198	DFF8	57D8	8F38	0418	2C78	5658	07B8
DE98	F0F8	ACD8	3838	5118	AD78	DB58	A0B8	DB98	E1F8
61D8	C138	FE18	0E78	C058	19B8	3898	B2F8	76D8	2A38
0B18	4F78	0558	72B8	F598	63F8	EBD8	7338	7818	7078
AA58	ABB8	1298	F4F8	C0D8	9C38	4518	7178	AF58	C4B8
8F98	65F8	F5D8	A538	7218	5278	1458	BDB8	6C98	B6F8
8AD8	8E38	FF18	1378	D958	96B8	A998	E7F8	7FD8	5738

Fig. 5-7. 200 pseudorandom numbers.

images in electronic video games, to name a few, can be effectively simulated by a microcomputer. In many of these simulations, the more random and unpredictable the behaviors of the processes or activities, the more realistic the simulation becomes.

One of the techniques frequently employed to make the simulation containing actions that may occur at chance or random intervals is the use of computer-generated pseudorandom numbers. A table of values carefully produced at random could be stored in the microcomputer memory. However, it is desirable that the microprocessor can generate its own random values rather than use such a table.

A sequence of random numbers generated by a microprocessor can be duplicated if the same initial values and calculation algorithm are known. For this reason, computers can only generate pseudorandom numbers. Pseudorandom numbers are not truly random, but sequences of them have many of the characteristics of true random numbers. This becomes obvious in a large sequence of pseudorandom numbers where the next number in the sequence is almost impossible to predict.

One widely used technique for generating pseudorandom numbers is called the multiplicative congruence method. The algorithm for this method consists of the following steps:

1. A beginning value X is selected. This value is called the seed value which is the first number of the generated pseudorandom sequence.
2. X is then multiplied by a constant multiplier N to yield the product P.
3. The product P is divided by a constant M called the modulus. The remainder of the division is used as a new value for X, which is the next pseudorandom number in sequence.
4. Steps 2 and 3 are repeated for sucessive pseudorandom numbers in a sequence.

A complete proof of the multiplicative congruence method is beyond the scope of this book. For further references, see Shan S. Kuo, *Computer Applications of Numerical Methods* (Reading, Mass., Addison-Wesley, 1972).

Since the pseudorandom number generated by this method is always taken as the remainder of the division P/M, if the modulus M has a value of 2^{16}, there will be 2^{16} or 65,536 possible values for X in a complete pseudorandom sequence. This range is sufficient for most microcomputer applications. If the calculation is limited to a 16-bit range, a good value for the multiplier N should be close to a square root of the modulus M in order to achieve the maximum apparent independence of sucessive values. It can be shown that the last three bits of the multiplier X should be 011 or 101 to yield a quite uniform distribution of numbers over the possible range of generation.

The procedure listed in Fig. 5-6 assumes that register AX has a pseudorandom value. It then generates the next pseudorandom number in a sequence of up to 65536 different numbers by the multiplicative congruence

```
0000                MOVEMENT PROC NEAR
0000 B9C800                  MOV      CX,200           ;Number of pseudorandom numbers to be
                    ;                                   generated.
0003 8D3E2C00                LEA      DI,OUT_AREA      ;Random numbers are stored in this area.
0007 A12A00                  MOV      AX,SEED_VALUE    ;The starting value of the sequence.
000A                NUMBER_LOOP:
000A E8E700                  CALL     PSEUDO_RANDOM
000D 3DFF3F                  CMP      AX,16383         ;Divide the 64k possible values into
                    ;                                   four ranges for the numbers 0,1,2,3.
0010 B200                    MOV      DL,0
0012 7610                    JBE      STORE_MOVEMENT
0014 3DFF7F                  CMP      AX,32767
0017 B201                    MOV      DL,01
0019 7609                    JBE      STORE_MOVEMENT
001B 3DFFBF                  CMP      AX,49151
001E B202                    MOV      DL,02
0020 7602                    JBE      STORE_MOVEMENT
0022 B202                    MOV      DL,02
```

```
0024                STORE_MOVEMENT:
0024 8815                   MOV     [DI],DL         ;Write the simulated movement number.
0026 47                     INC     DI
0027 E2E1                   LOOP    NUMBER_LOOP
0029 C3                     RET
002A 9500           SEED_VALUE DW 149
002C                OUT_AREA DB 200 DUP(0)
00F4                MOVEMENT ENDP
                    ;
00F4                PSEUDO_RANDOM PROC NEAR             ;Generate a new random number in AX.
00F4 51                     PUSH    CX
00F5 52                     PUSH    DX
00F6 B90501                 MOV     CX,261
00F9 F7E1                   MUL     CX
00FB 5A                     POP     DX
00FC 59                     POP     CX
00FD C3                     RET
00FE                PSEUDO_RANDOM ENDP
```

Fig. 5-8. Procedure to generate random movements.

method and places the new random value in the AX register. The seed value can be any unsigned number between 0 and 65535.

The listing in Fig. 5-7 contains 200 pseudorandom numbers generated by the procedure using the multiplicative congruence method. The seed value used in this example is the decimal number 127.

In graphic applications such as the electronic video games, the movements of a graphic image on the video screen can be easily generated by using random numbers so that the next movements of the graphic image are very difficult to predict. The more random the movements, the more exciting and realistic the game will become.

Consider a video game in which a graphic image can move in four directions: up, down, left, and right. The procedure in Fig. 5-8 can generate pseudorandom numbers using the multiplicative congruence method to simulate the four possible movements of a graphic image on the video screen. The initial seed value in the procedure is taken from the symbolic location SEED_VALUE which should be initialized by some random parameters such as the current second of the time on the computer system, the hexadecimal value of the last struck key of the keyboard, etc. To simplify the example, the procedure uses an initial seed value 127 (decimal).

Since the numbers generated by this model have a very good uniform distribution, each direction of movement has an approximately 25 percent chance of occurence. The movements generated are stored in the computer memory starting from the symbolic location OUT_AREA. The output values 0, 1, 2, or 3 represent the up, down, left, and right movements, respectively. Figure 5-9 shows the first 50 possible random movements generated by the procedure described in Fig. 5-8.

CONVERSION FROM HEXADECIMAL TO DECIMAL

When numeric data initially enter a microcomputer, they are normally coded in the decimal representation in the forms of ASCII characters. The 8088 microprocessor cannot perform meaningful arithmetic operations on data in this form. Instead, it must convert these data to its internal binary format before it can perform the arithmetic on these representations. Then, if the results are to be printed or displayed in readable format on typical output devices such as a printer or video terminal, these numbers must be converted once again to the decimal representation in the forms of ASCII characters.

The procedure listed in Fig. 5-10 converts the contents of the AX register into an appropriate ASCII string representing a decimal number to be stored at the memory location addressed by the DI register. The number to be converted is treated as a signed quantity. Therefore the resultant ASCII string will have a value between +32767 and −32768.

The conversion from hexadecimal representation to decimal is done by a division process. The 8088 DIV instruction is very effective in this case. The number to be converted is divided by 10, and the remainder is the digit

```
0     2     0     1     1     1     0     2     2     1
2     0     2     2     2     1     2     3     0     1
1     3     1     3     2     0     1     3     2     3
0     2     0     0     2     3     0     1     2     3
2     1     1     0     1     3     1     0     1     1

UP    LEFT  UP    DOWN  DOWN  DOWN  UP    LEFT  LEFT  DOWN
LEFT  UP    LEFT  LEFT  LEFT  DOWN  LEFT  RIGHT UP    DOWN
DOWN  RIGHT DOWN  RIGHT LEFT  UP    DOWN  RIGHT LEFT  RIGHT
UP    LEFT  UP    UP    LEFT  RIGHT UP    DOWN  LEFT  RIGHT
LEFT  DOWN  DOWN  UP    DOWN  RIGHT DOWN  UP    DOWN  DOWN
```

Fig. 5-9. Fifty numeric values representing random movements generated by the procedure MOVEMENT.

of the number's decimal representation. The quotient is divided by 10, and the new remainder is another digit of the decimal representation. The process of dividing each new quotient by 10 continues until the quotient is smaller than 10. Each remainder is another digit of the decimal representation. The conversion of the hexadecimal 345H to the decimal 837 is illustrated in the following manner:

OAH/345H

OAH/053H with remainder 07H

OAH/008H with remainder 03H

last quotient 08H

yielding the decimal number 837

```
0000             INTEGER  PROC    NEAR            ;Procedure to convert a 16-bit signed
                 ;                                 hexadecimal number in the AX register
                 ;                                 to its equivalent ASCII representation
                 ;                                 to be stored at the memory location
                 ;                                 addressed by the DI register.
0000 51                   PUSH    CX
0001 50                   PUSH    AX
0002 52                   PUSH    DX              ;Save registers to be used.
0003 2BD2                 SUB     DX,DX
0005 3D0000               CMP     AX,0            ;Check if the number is positive.
0008 7902                 JNS     POSITIVE
000A F7D8                 NEG     AX
000C             POSITIVE:
000C E80C00               CALL    CONVERT         ;Conversion procedure.
000F 5A                   POP     DX
0010 58                   POP     AX
0011 3D0000               CMP     AX,0
0014 7903                 JNS     DONE
0016 C6052D               MOV BYTE PTR [DI],'-' ;Minus sign for negative numbers.
0019             DONE:
0019 59                   POP     CX
```

```
001A C3                RET
001B         INTEGER ENDP
             ;
001B         CONVERT PROC      NEAR              ;Conversion procedure.
001B B90A00            MOV     CX,10
001E         LOOP_COUNT:
001E F7F1              DIV     CX
0020 80CA30            OR      DL,30H            ;Convert to ASCII format.
0023 8815              MOV     [DI],DL           ;Output a decimal digit.
0025 4F                DEC     DI
0026 3D0A00            CMP     AX,10
0029 BA0000            MOV     DX,00
002C 73F0              JAE     LOOP_COUNT
002E 3C00              CMP     AL,00
0030 7405              JE      EXIT_CONVERT      ;Do not display leading zeros.
0032 0C30              OR      AL,30H
0034 8805              MOV     [DI],AL           ;Most significant digit.
0036 4F                DEC     DI                ;At the next high-order digit.
0037         EXIT_CONVERT:
0037 C3                RET
0038         CONVERT  ENDP
```

Fig. 5-10. Procedure to convert a 16-bit signed integer from the hexadecimal notation to the decimal notation.

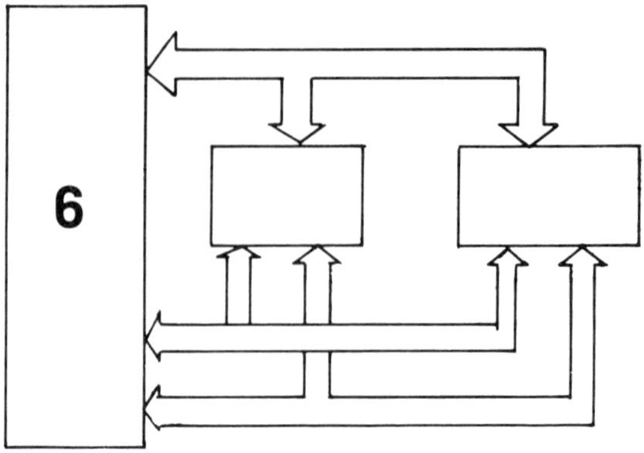

Logical Functions

This chapter discusses a group of instructions of the 8088 microprocessor that performs logical functions. Logical functions provide a convenient method to manipulate individual bits in binary representations. These functions are related to those used in logic and are quite different from the arithmetic functions discussed in the previous chapter. The 8086/8088 microprocessor family supports four standard logical functions: AND, inclusive-OR, exclusive-OR, and NOT.

DEFINITIONS

A brief definition of these four logical functions are presented in the following section before I proceed to illustrate their implementation and applications in 8088-based microcomputers.

Logical AND

Suppose that we have two operands. Each may have a value of 0 or 1. The logical AND function of the two operands has a value 1 if both operands have the value 1. Otherwise, the value of the function is 0. I have illustrated or defined the logical AND function in Fig. 6-1A. The table is called a truth table.

The number in the boxes of the table indicate the value of the logical AND function in each of the four possible cases.

Inclusive-OR

The second logical function is OR. For emphasis and clarity in certain situations, it is also called inclusive-OR. The value of the inclusive-OR

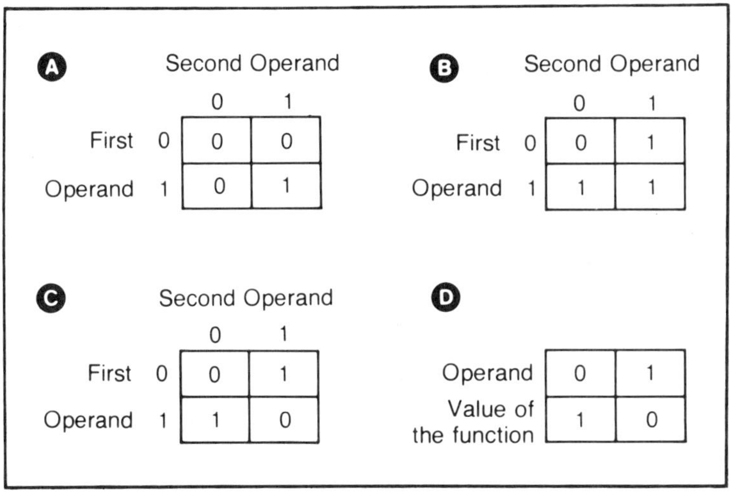

Fig. 6-1. Logic functions. A, AND; B, OR; C, exclusive-OR; D, NOT.

function of two operands is 1 if one of the operands is 1, or both of the operands are 1. The value of the function is 0 only if both operands are 0. I illustrate the inclusive-OR function in the truth table in Fig. 6-1B.

Exclusive-OR

The third logical function is exclusive-OR. The exclusive-OR function of two operands has a value 1 if either of the two operands, but not both, has the value 1. In other words, the function has a value 0 if both operands are 0 or if both are 1. The exclusive-OR function is illustrated in Fig. 6-1C.

Logical NOT

The fourth function in this group is logical NOT, which is a function of one operand only. The value of the function is the opposite of the value of the operand. In other words, the value of the function is 1 if the operand is 0, and 0 if the operand is 1. The logical NOT function is illustrated in Fig. 6-1D.

LOGICAL INSTRUCTIONS

The 8088 instruction set provides five instructions which can perform the logical functions just described. The following section is a brief summary of these logical instructions which include AND (logical AND), OR (inclusive-OR), NOT (logical NOT), TEST (test by logical AND), and XOR (exclusive-OR). Logical instructions always clear the Overflow Flag, OF, and the Carry Flag, CF, to 0. The Sign Flag, SF, the Zero Flag, ZF, and the Sign Flag, SF, are updated. The Auxiliary Carry Flag, AF, is always undefined after a logical instruction is executed.

```
0000            UPPER_CASE PROC NEAR            ;Procedure to convert the lower-case
                ;                                character in AL to upper case.
0000 3C61                  CMP   AL,61H         ;Check if the character is a valid
                ;                                lower-case character.
0002 7206                  JB    UPPER_DONE
0004 3C7A                  CMP   AL,7AH
0006 7702                  JA    UPPER_DONE
0008 245F                  AND   AL,01011111B   ;Turn the bit position 5 to 0.
000A            UPPER_DONE:
000A C3                    RET
000B            UPPER_CASE ENDP
                ;
000B            LOWER_CASE PROC NEAR            ;Procedure to convert the upper-case
                ;                                character in AL to lower case.
000B 3C41                  CMP   AL,41H         ;Check if the character is a valid
                ;                                upper-case character.
000D 7206                  JB    LOWER_DONE
000F 3C5A                  CMP   AL,5AH
0011 7702                  JA    LOWER_DONE
0013 0C20                  OR    AL,00100000B   ;Turn the bit position 5 to 1.
0015            LOWER_DONE:
0015 C3                    RET
0016            LOWER_CASE ENDP
```

Fig. 6-2. Procedure to change case of text characters.

AND (Logical AND). This instruction performs the logical AND of two specified operands. The result replaces the contents of the destination operand. The source operand remains unchanged. Either 8-bit or 16-bit operations can be performed. A bit in the result is set to 1 if both corresponding bits of the original operands are set to 1; otherwise the result bit is cleared to 0. The logical operation applies to all bits in the byte or word of the operands.

OR (Inclusive-OR). This instruction performs the logical inclusive-OR of two specified operands. The result replaces the contents of the destination operand. The source operand remains unchanged. Either 8-bit or 16-bit operations can be performed. A bit in the result is set to 1 if either or both corresponding bits in the original operands are set to 1, otherwise the result bit is cleared to 0. The logical operation applies to all bits in the byte or word of the operands.

NOT (Logical NOT). This instruction performs the logical NOT of the specified operand by inverting all the bits in the byte or word of the specified operand. The original contents of the operand are lost. Either 8-bit or 16-bit operations can be performed. A bit in the result is 1 if the corresponding bit in the original operand is 0, and vice versa. The logical operation applies to all bits in the byte or word of the specified operand.

TEST (Test by logical AND). This instruction performs the logical AND of two operands, updates the flags, but does not return the result. The contents of both operands remain unchanged. Either 8-bit or 16-bit operations can be performed. TEST is very useful in examining the binary value of a specific bit in an operand without destroying the contents of the operand to achieve the result.

XOR (Exclusive-OR). This instruction performs the logical exclusive-OR of two specified operands. The result replaces the contents of the destination operand. The source operand remains unchanged. Either 8-bit or 16-bit operations can be performed. A bit in the result is set to 1 if the corresponding bits of the original operations do not have the same value. The result bit is cleared to 0 if both corresponding bits of the original operands are 0 or 1. The logical operation applies to all bits in the byte or word of the operands.

BIT MANIPULATION

Logical instructions are very simple and straightforward in those operations performed to change selective bits in an operand. Normally, the bits to be changed are specified by the contents of the first operand (destination operand). The bits which are eligible for modification are determined by the bits specified by the contents of the second operand (source operand). Thus, the second operand is considered as a bit mask, covering and protecting certain bits while leaving other bits exposed and eligible for modifications by the logical operations.

The instruction AND (logical AND) selectively clears the bits in the first operand to 0, in bit positions where the second operand contains 0s. Thus in the bit mask, a 1 bit protects the bit in the corresponding position of the first operand from being altered, while a 0 bit in the bit mask clears the bit in the corresponding position of the first operand to 0 regardless of its previous content. Consider the following instruction as an example.

```
AND   AL,01111111B
```

The above instruction clears the most significant bit (the sign bit) of the byte in the AL register to 0. The remaining seven bits of the AL register are not altered. The status of the Zero Flag, ZF, can be used to verify whether there are any 1 bits left in the new contents of the AL register (destination operand), or whether all bits in the AL register are cleared to 0. If the Zero Flag, ZF, is 1, all bits in the AL register are cleared after the logical operation.

The instruction OR (inclusive-OR) selectively sets the bits in the first operand to 1 in bit positions where the second operand contains 1 bits. In positions where the bits of the second operand are 0, the bits in the corresponding position of the first operand remain unchanged. For example, the following instruction

```
OR DX,0000111111111111B
```

sets the last twelve bits of the contents of the DX register to 1. The four most significant bits remain unchanged. The status of the Zero Flag can also be used in this case to verify whether the new contents of the DX register contain all 0 bits.

The instruction XOR (exclusive-OR) selectively inverts the bits of the first operand in positions where the corresponding bits of the second operand are 1 bits. The bits in positions where the corresponding bits of the second operands are 0 remain unchanged. For example, the following instruction

```
XOR BYTE PTR SWITCH, 01
```

changes the last bit of the contents of the byte memory location SWITCH from 1 to 0 or from 0 to 1, and does not affect the remaining seven bits. If the number 0 or 1 is stored at the memory location SWITCH, this location can act as a toggle switch to alternate the binary value of its contents between 0 and 1 by simply repeating the above XOR instruction.

Logical instructions are also useful to extract or modify certain groups of bits in an operand. Thus, these instructions are very efficient in the conversion of alphanumeric characters from one representation to another. In the next sections, several examples are presented to illustrate some useful applications of logical instructions in the manipulation of text characters.

CHARACTER CONVERSION

In text-editing and word-processing applications, it is sometimes desirable to have a facility to convert text characters in sentences or paragraphs from the lowercase to the uppercase, or from the uppercase to the lowercase, without the need to reenter these characters from the computer keyboard. There are many possible ways to instruct the computer to perform this task. The procedure in Fig. 6-2 illustrates one of the conversion techniques utilizing logical instructions. The program codes in the procedure use the knowledge of the structure of the ASCII representations of upper- and lowercase alphabets which are shown in Fig. 6-3. Lowercase characters have a 1 bit in the bit position 5 of their ASCII representation.

When a new assembly language program is tested, it is desirable to have a debugging facility that provides some means to examine or to modify the hexadecimal contents of the CPU registers and certain memory locations. The debugger must convert each hexadecimal digit from their internal representations in memory to printable characters. It must also have the capability to accept hexadecimal digits from an input ASCII string and convert these digits to their proper binary representations to be stored in the computer memory.

The procedure listed in Fig. 6-4 provides some coding examples to

Upper Case	ASCII Representation		Lower Case	ASCII Representation	
Letters	Hexadecimal	Binary	Letters	Hexadecimal	Binary
A	41	0100 0001	a	61	0110 0001
B	42	0100 0010	b	62	0110 0010
C	43	0100 0011	c	63	0110 0011
D	44	0100 0100	d	64	0110 0100
E	45	0100 0101	e	65	0110 0101
F	46	0100 0110	f	66	0110 0110
G	47	0100 0111	g	67	0110 0111
H	48	0100 1000	h	68	0110 1000
I	49	0100 1001	i	69	0110 1001
J	4A	0100 1010	j	6A	0110 1010
K	4B	0100 1011	k	6B	0110 1011
L	4C	0100 1100	l	6C	0110 1100
M	4D	0100 1101	m	6D	0110 1101
N	4E	0100 1110	n	6E	0110 1110
O	4F	0100 1111	o	6F	0110 1111
P	50	0101 0000	p	70	0111 0000
Q	51	0101 0001	q	71	0111 0001
R	52	0101 0010	r	72	0111 0010
S	53	0101 0011	s	73	0111 0011
T	54	0101 0100	t	74	0111 0100
U	55	0101 0101	u	75	0111 0101
V	56	0101 0110	v	76	0111 0110
W	57	0101 0111	w	77	0111 0111
X	58	0101 1000	x	78	0111 1000
Y	59	0101 1001	y	79	0111 1001
Z	5A	0101 1010	z	7A	0111 1010

Fig. 6-3. ASCII representation of upper- and lowercase characters.

```
0000                CONASC1   PROC      NEAR              ;Convert the contents of AL into two
                    ;                                      ASCII bytes to be stored in AX. The
                    ;                                      previous contents of AL are lost.
0000 8AE0                     MOV       AH,AL
0002 E81600                   CALL      CONVERT           ;Conversion procedure.
0005 86C4                     XCHG      AL,AH
0007 B104                     MOV       CL,4
0009 D2E8                     SHR       AL,CL             ;Get the high-order 4 bits.
000B E80D00                   CALL      CONVERT
000F C3                       RET
000F                CONASC1   ENDP
                    ;
000F                CONASC2   PROC      NEAR              ;Convert the contents of AX into four
                    ;                                      ASCII bytes to be stored in AX and DX.
                    ;                                      Previous contents of AX and DX are lost.
000F 8BD0                     MOV       DX,AX
0011 E8ECFF                   CALL      CONASC1
0014 92                       XCHG      AX,DX
0015 86E0                     XCHG      AH,AL
0017 E8E6FF                   CALL      CONASC1
001A C3                       RET
001B                CONASC2   ENDP
                    ;
001B                CONVERT   PROC      NEAR              ;Conversion procedure.
001B 240F                     AND       AL,0FH            ;Look at the low-order four bits.
001D 3C09                     CMP       AL,09
001F 7602                     JBE       NEXT
0021 0407                     ADD       AL,07             ;Adjustment for numbers greater than 9.
0023 0430           NEXT:     ADD       AL,30H            ;Convert to the ASCII representation.
0025 80E100                   AND       CL,00             ;Set Z-flag to 1 to indicate successful
                    ;                                      operation.
```

```
0028 C3                    RET
0029           CONVERT     ENDP
               ;
0029           CONBIN0     PROC      NEAR             ;Convert the ASCII representation in AL
               ;                                       into one hexadecimal digit to be stored in AL.
0029 3C30                  CMP       AL,30H
002B 7216                  JB        ERROR            ;Check for valid range.
002D 3C46                  CMP       AL,46H
002F 7712                  JA        ERROR
0031 3C39                  CMP       AL,39H           ;Check for hexadecimal digits A to F.
0033 7706                  JA        ATOF
0035 240F                  AND       AL,0FH           ;Convert to binary.
0037 80E100                AND       CL,00            ;No error.
003A C3                    RET
003B 240F      ATOF:       AND       AL,0FH
003D 0409                  ADD       AL,09H
003F 80E100                AND       CL,00            ;No error.
0042 C3                    RET
0043 80C9FF    ERROR:      OR        CL,0FFH          ;Clear the Z-flag to 0 to indicate
               ;                                       there is an error in the conversion.
0046 C3                    RET
0047           CONBIN0     ENDP
               ;
0047           CONBIN1     PROC      NEAR             ;Convert two ASCII representations in AX
               ;                                       into two hexadecimal digits in AL.
0047 8AEC                  MOV       CH,AH
0049 E8DDFF                CALL      CONBIN0
004C 7401                  JE        NEXTD            ;Continue conversion for the next digit.
004E C3                    RET
004F 86C5      NEXTD:      XCHG      AL,CH
```

Fig. 6-4. Procedures to perform conversions of hexadecimal digits.

```
0051 E8D5FF              CALL    CONBIN0
0054 7401                JE      OK
0056 C3                  RET
0057 B104       OK:      MOV     CL,4
0059 D2E5                SHL     CH,CL           ;Move the hexadecimal digit to the
                ;                                 high-order bit positions.
005B 0AC5                OR      AL,CH
005D 80E100              AND     CL,00           ;No error.
0060 C3                  RET
0061            CONBIN1  ENDP
                ;

0061            CONBIN2  PROC    NEAR            ;Convert four ASCII representations in
                ;                                 the register pair DX,AX into four
                ;                                 hexadecimal digits in AX.
0061 E8E3FF              CALL    CONBIN1
0064 7401                JE      NEXT2
0066 C3                  RET
0067 92         NEXT2:   XCHG    AX,DX
0068 E8DCFF              CALL    CONBIN1
006B 7401                JE      OK2
006D C3                  RET
006E 86E2       OK2:     XCHG    AH,DL
0070 80E100              AND     CL,00           ;No error.
0073 C3                  RET
0074            CONBIN2 ENDP
```

Fig. 6-4. Procedures to perform conversions of hexadecimal digits (continued from page 237).

convert hexadecimal digits from their internal representations in memory to the appropriate ASCII format so that these digits can be displayed on a video terminal or printed on a printer. Logical instructions are used in the procedure to facilitate the conversion and to set the appropriate flags to indicate whether any error has occurred during the conversion process.

The procedure CONASC1 converts the contents of the AL register into two corresponding ASCII characters to be left in the AX register. The procedure CONASC2 converts the contents of the AX register into four corresponding ASCII characters to be stored in the AX and DX registers. The procedure CONBIN0 assumes that the AL register contains the ASCII representation of a hexadecimal digit and converts it into the corresponding hexadecimal value. The procedure CONBIN1 assumes that the AX register contains the ASCII representation of two hexadecimal digits. It converts the representation into two hexadecimal digits to be stored in the AL register. Similarly, the procedure CONBIN2 converts the ASCII representations in the AX and DX registers into four hexadecimal digits to be stored in the AX register.

In the procedures CONBIN0, CONBIN1, and CONBIN2, the logical instructions AND or OR are used to perform the necessary conversion and to produce the appropriate error codes to indicate whether the conversion is successful. If there is any error in the conversion, the Zero Flag is cleared to 0. The ASCII representation of the sixteen hexadecimal digits is shown in FIG. 6-5

DATA ENCRYPTION AND DECRYPTION

As computing has evolved dramatically over the past several decades, it has become more accessible to the general public. The number of

Hexadecimal	ASCII Representation		Hexadecimal	ASCII Representation	
Digits	Hexadecimal	Binary	Digits	Hexadecimal	Binary
0	30	0011 0000	8	38	0011 1000
1	31	0011 0001	9	39	0011 1001
2	32	0011 0010	A	41	0100 0001
3	33	0011 0011	B	42	0100 0010
4	34	0011 0100	C	43	0100 0011
5	35	0011 0101	D	44	0100 0100
6	36	0011 0110	E	45	0100 0101
7	37	0011 0111	F	46	0100 0110

Fig. 6-5. Hexadecimal digits and their ASCII representations.

```
0000                MAIN      SEGMENT PARA PUBLIC
                              ASSUME  CS:MAIN,DS:MAIN,ES:MAIN,SS:STACK
0000                DECRYPT   PROC    NEAR               ;Procedure to perform data decryption.
0000 9C                       PUSHF
0001 1E                       PUSH    DS
0002 2BC0                     SUB     AX,AX
0004 50                       PUSH    AX
0005 1E                       PUSH    DS                 ;Save system status to return later
0006 06                       PUSH    ES                 ;to the PC-DOS operating system.
0007 8CC8                     MOV     AX,CS              ;Program code segment.
0009 8ED8                     MOV     DS,AX              ;Overlap Data Segment with Code Segment.
000B 8EC0                     MOV     ES,AX              ;Overlap Extra Segment also.
000D 8D167500                 LEA     DX,OLD_FCB         ;File Control Block of the text file
                    ;                                     to be decrypted.
0011 B40F                     MOV     AH,0FH             ;Code to open the file.
0013 CD21                     INT     21H                ;Request DOS service.
0015 8D16C100                 LEA     DX,DATA_AREA       ;Buffer area to hold input text data.
0019 B41A                     MOV     AH,1AH             ;Code to set the Disk Transfer Address.
001B CD21                     INT     21H                ;Request DOS service.
001D 8D367500                 LEA     SI,OLD_FCB
0021 2BC0                     SUB     AX,AX
0023 894421                   MOV WORD PTR [SI+33],AX
0026 894423                   MOV WORD PTR [SI+35],AX    ;Prepare to read the encrypted information.
0029 8B4410                   MOV     AX,[SI+16]         ;Get the actual size of the encrypted file.
002C 89440E                   MOV     [SI+14],AX         ;Number of character to read.
002F A3BF00                   MOV     FILE_SIZE,AX       ;Save for later use.
0032 8BD6                     MOV     DX,SI
0034 B421                     MOV     AH,21H             ;Code to read the encrypted data.
0036 CD21                     INT     21H                ;Request DOS service.
                    ;
0038 8D169A00                 LEA     DX,NEW_FCB         ;File Control Block of decryted file.
003C B416                     MOV     AH,16H             ;Code to create a new file.
```

```
003E CD21                 INT      21H                 ;Create the decrypted file.
0040 8D16C100             LEA      DX,DATA_AREA
0044 8BF2                 MOV      SI,DX
0046 8BFA                 MOV      DI,DX
0048 8B0EBF00             MOV      CX,FILE_SIZE        ;Number of character to be decrypted.
004C             ENCRYPT_LOOP:
004C AC                   LODSB                        ;Get a text character.
004D 3438                 XOR      AL,00111000B        ;Encryption mask.
                 ;                                      Bit positions 3,4, and 5 are inverted.
004F AA                   STOSB                        ;Write out the encrypted data.
0050 E2FA                 LOOP     ENCRYPT_LOOP
0052 B41A                 MOV      AH,1AH              ;Code to set the Disk Transfer Address.
0054 CD21                 INT      21H                 ;Request DOS service.
0056 8D369A00             LEA      SI,NEW_FCB
005A 2BC0                 SUB      AX,AX
005C 894421               MOV WORD PTR [SI+33],AX
005F 894423               MOV WORD PTR [SI+35],AX ;Prepare to write the encrypted data.
0062 A1BF00               MOV      AX,FILE_SIZE
0065 89440E               MOV      [SI+14],AX          ;Number of encrypted data bytes.
0068 8BD6                 MOV      DX,SI
006A B415                 MOV      AH,15H              ;Code to write out the encrypted data.
006C CD21                 INT      21H                 ;Request DOS service.
006E B410                 MOV      AH,10H              ;Code to close files and update the
                 ;                                      disk directory.
0070 CD21                 INT      21H                 ;Request DOS service.
0072 07                   POP      ES                  ;Restore previous ES and DS.
0073 1F                   POP      DS
0074 CF                   IRET                         ;Return to the PC-DOS operating system.
0075             ENCRYPT  ENDP
```

Fig. 6-6. Procedure to perform data encryption.

```
                    ;
0075                WORK_AREA PROC NEAR
0075 00             OLD_FCB   DB     0                ;Default disk drive.
0076                          DB     'ORIGINALDAT'    ;Original data file.
0081                          DB 25 dup(0)
009A 00             NEW_FCB   DB     0                ;Encrypted file is created on the
                    ;                                  default disk drive.
009B                          DB     'ENCRYPT FIL'
00A6                          DB 25 dup(0)
00BF ??             FILE_SIZE DW ?                    ;Size of the encrypted file.
00C1                DATA_AREA DB 32767 dup(0)
80C0                WORK_AREA ENDP
80C0                MAIN      ENDS
                    ;
0000                STACK     SEGMENT STACK  PARA     ;Stack area.
          DB 32 DUP('STACK   ')
0100                STACK    ENDS
                    END
```

Fig. 6-6. Procedure to perform data encryption (continued from page 241).

```
                         Data Before Encryption

ASCII Representation                                      Text characters

57 68 65 6E 20 61 20 6E 65 77 20 61 73 73 65 6D           When a new assem
62 6C 79 20 6C 61 6E 67 75 61 67 65 20 70 72 6F           bly language pro
67 72 61 6D 20 69 73 20 74 65 73 74 65 64 2C 20           gram is tested,
69 74 20 69 73 20 64 65 73 69 72 61 62 6C 65 0D           it is desirable
0A 74 6F 20 68 61 76 65 20 61 20 64 65 62 75 67           to have a debug
67 69 6E 67 20 66 61 63 39 6C 69 74 79 20 74 68           ging facility th
61 74 20 70 72 6F 76 69 64 65 73 20 73 6F 6D 65           at provides some
20 6D 65 61 6E 73 20 74 6F 20 65 78 61 6D 69 6E           means to examin

                         Data After Encryption

6F 50 5D 56 18 59 18 56 5D 4F 18 59 4B 4B 5D 55           oP]V Y V]O YKK]U
5A 54 41 18 54 59 56 5F 4D 59 5F 5D 18 48 4A 57           ZTA TYV_MY_] HJW
5F 4A 59 55 18 51 4B 18 4C 5D 4B 4C 5D 5C 14 18           _JYU QK L]KL]\
51 4C 18 51 4B 18 5C 5D 4B 51 4A 59 5A 54 5D 35           QL QK \]KQJYZT]5
32 4C 57 18 50 59 4E 5D 18 59 18 5C 5D 5A 4D 5F           2LW PYN] Y \]ZM_
5F 51 56 5F 18 5E 59 5B 51 54 51 4C 41 18 4C 50           _QV_ ^Y[QTQLA LP
59 4C 18 48 4A 57 4E 51 5C 5D 4B 18 4B 57 55 5D           YL HJWNQ\]K KWU]
18 55 5D 59 56 4B 18 4C 57 18 5D 40 59 55 51 56           U]YVK LW ]@YUQV
```

Fig. 6-7. Text characters before and after the encryption.

major computer installations as well as the number of small personal computers has increased dramatically. With the advancement of today microprocessors, microcomputer systems can now easily access timesharing and remote-access installations. This introduces the vulnerability of data communications since there are millions of computer systems that have been tied together via communication networks, most commonly through the telephone system.

Computers are routinely programmed to handle the most sensitive information or transactions. Thus it is extremely important to implement security measures to prevent information and data files on a computer system from any unauthorized access. Data encryption is one of the means

```
0000                MAIN      SEGMENT PARA PUBLIC
                              ASSUME  CS:MAIN,DS:MAIN,ES:MAIN,SS:STACK
0000                ENCRYPT   PROC    NEAR               ;Procedure to perform data encryption.
0000 9C                       PUSHF
0001 1E                       PUSH    DS
0002 2BC0                     SUB     AX,AX
0004 50                       PUSH    AX
0005 1E                       PUSH    DS                 ;Save system status to return later
0006 06                       PUSH    ES                 ;to the PC-DOS operating system.
0007 8CC8                     MOV     AX,CS              ;Program code segment.
0009 8ED8                     MOV     DS,AX              ;Overlap Data Segment with Code Segment.
000B 8EC0                     MOV     ES,AX              ;Overlap Extra Segment also.
000D 8D167500                 LEA     DX,OLD_FCB         ;File Control Block of the text file
                    ;                                     to be encrypted.
0011 B40F                     MOV     AH,0FH             ;Code to open the file.
0013 CD21                     INT     21H                ;Request DOS service.
0015 8D16C100                 LEA     DX,DATA_AREA       ;Buffer area to hold input text data.
0019 B41A                     MOV     AH,1AH             ;Code to set the Disk Transfer Address.
001B CD21                     INT     21H                ;Request DOS service.
001D 8D367500                 LEA     SI,OLD_FCB
0021 2BC0                     SUB     AX,AX
0023 894421                   MOV WORD PTR [SI+33],AX
0026 894423                   MOV WORD PTR [SI+35],AX    ;Prepare to read in original data.
0029 8B4410                   MOV     AX,[SI+16]         ;Get the actual file size.
002C 89440E                   MOV     [SI+14],AX         ;Number of character to read.
002F A3BF00                   MOV     FILE_SIZE,AX       ;Save for later use.
0032 8BD6                     MOV     DX,SI
0034 B421                     MOV     AH,21H             ;Code to read the original text data.
0036 CD21                     INT     21H                ;Request DOS service.
                    ;
0038 8D169A00                 LEA     DX,NEW_FCB         ;File Control Block of encryted file.
003C B416                     MOV     AH,16H             ;Code to create a new file.
```

```
003E CD21               INT     21H                 ;Create the encrypted file.
0040 8D16C100           LEA     DX,DATA_AREA
0044 8BF2               MOV     SI,DX
0046 8BFA               MOV     DI,DX
0048 8B0EBF00           MOV     CX,FILE_SIZE        ;Number of character to be encrypted.
004C           DECRYPT_LOOP:
004C                    LODSB                       ;Get a text character.
004D 3438               XOR     AL,00111000B        ;Decryption mask (must be identical to
               ;                                     the encryption mask to decode the bit
               ;                                     pattern correctly).
               ;                                     Bit positions 3,4, and 5 are inverted.
004F AA                 STOSB                       ;Write out the encrypted data.
0050 E2FA               LOOP    DECRYPT_LOOP
0052 B41A               MOV     AH,1AH              ;Code to set the Disk Transfer Address.
0054 CD21               INT     21H                 ;Request DOS service.
0056 8D369A00           LEA     SI,NEW_FCB
005A 2BC0               SUB     AX,AX
005C 894421             MOV WORD PTR [SI+33],AX
005F 894423             MOV WORD PTR [SI+35],AX ;Prepare to write the decrypted data.
0062 A1BF00             MOV     AX,FILE_SIZE
0065 89440E             MOV     [SI+14],AX          ;Number of decrypted data bytes.
0068 8BD6               MOV     DX,SI
006A B415               MOV     AH,15H              ;Code to write out the decrypted data.
006C CD21               INT     21H                 ;Request DOS service.
006E B410               MOV     AH,10H              ;Code to close files and update the
               ;                                     disk directory.
0070 CD21               INT     21H                 ;Request DOS service.
0072 07                 POP     ES                  ;Restore previous ES and DS.
```

Fig. 6-8. Procedure to decrypt an encrypted file.

```
0073 1F                 POP     DS
0074 CF                 IRET                            ;Return to the PC-DOS operating system.
0075          DECRYPT   ENDP
              ;
0075          WORK_AREA PROC NEAR
0075 00       OLD_FCB   DB      0                       ;Default disk drive.
0076                    DB      'ENCRYPT FIL'           ;Name of the encrypted file.
0081                    DB 25 dup(0)
009A 00       NEW_FCB   DB      0                       ;Decrypted file is created on the
              ;                                          default disk drive.
009B 00                 DB      'DECRYPT FIL'
00A6                    DB 25 dup(0)
00BF ??       FILE_SIZE DW ?                            ;Size of the decrypted file.
00C1          DATA_AREA DB 32767 dup(0)
80C0          WORK_AREA ENDP
80C0          MAIN      ENDS
              ;
0000          STACK     SEGMENT STACK   PARA            ;Stack area.
0000                    DB 32 DUP('STACK   ')
0100          STACK     ENDS
              END
```

Fig. 6-8. Procedure to decrypt an encrypted file (continued from page 245).

to implement a security system for data or program files on a computer system.

Data encryption essentially is the use of data transformers to make the data incomprehensible to all except the intended users. The data, after being transformed or encrypted, are available on the computer system but are no longer in their normal formats or representations. They cannot be extracted, browsed, or copied by unauthorized access. When an encrypted program or data file is used, its contents must be restored by a decryption procedure so that the information can be put back together in its original unprotected representations.

The procedure listed in Fig. 6-6 performs a simple encryption of a text file stored on the IBM Personal Computer system. The ASCII representations of the characters in the file are scrambled so that the text file can no longer be displayed properly by the normal operating system utilities. Figure 6-7 lists the hexadecimal contents of the text file before and after the encryption. The procedure to perform the decryption of the protected text file is listed in Fig. 6-8. The encryption and decryption technique uses some very simple sequences of exclusive-OR instructions to scramble and restore the standard ASCII representation of characters in the text file.

For simplicity, the text files used in this example are standard ASCII files on the IBM Personal Computer under the PC-DOS operating system. Software interrupts supported by the PC-DOS disk operating system are used to perform the disk input/output functions. The bit mask pattern 00111000 is used to invert the bits in position 3, 4, and 5 of each hexadecimal representation of characters in the ASCII files.

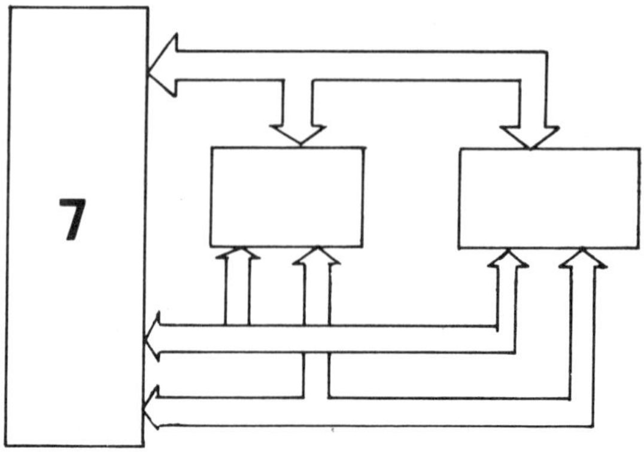

Data Movement

This chapter discusses one of the most frequently used group of instructions of the 8088 instruction set: the data movement instructions. These instructions facilitate the movements of data from registers to registers, registers to memory, memory to registers, memory to memory, and finally the movements of immediate data onto and off the stack. These instructions include LDS (Load Pointer with DS), LEA (Load Effective Address), LES (Load Pointer with ES), LAHF (Load AH with Flag), LODS (Load String), MOV (Move), MOVS (Move String), PUSH (Push on Stack), PUSHF (Push Processor Flag), POP (Pop from Stack), POPF (Pop Processor Flag), SAHF (Store AH to Flag), STOS (Store String), XCHG (Exchange), and XLAT (Translate).

The programming examples take full advantage of the capabilities of the data movement instructions. You should try to verify the results of these examples or implement the concepts described in this chapter on your 8088-based microcomputer to really understand and appreciate the power and flexibility provided by these instructions.

DATA MOVEMENT INSTRUCTIONS

The following section presents a brief summary of the principal functions that these instructions perform to move data.

LDS (Load Pointer Using the DS Register). This instruction transfers a doubleword from a memory operand to replace the contents of a 16-bit general register and the DS register.

LEA (Load Effective Address). The offset address of the source operand rather than its contents replaces the contents of the destination operand which must be a general 16-bit register.

LES (Load Pointer Using the ES Register). This instruction transfers a doubleword from a memory operand to replace the contents of a 16-bit general register and the ES register.

LAHF (Load the AH Register with Flags). This instruction replaces the contents of the AH register with the low-order 8 bits of the Processor Flag. These 8 bits include the Sign Flag, the Zero Flag, the Auxiliary Carry, the Parity Flag, and the Carry Flag.

LODS (Load String). This string instruction replaces the contents of the accumulator (AL in byte operation, AX in word operation) with the contents of the memory location addressed by the SI register. The SI register is then incremented or decremented depending upon whether the Direction Flag is 0 or 1, respectively. The incremented/decremented value is 1 or 2 depending upon byte or word operation of the instruction.

MOV (Move). This is the most useful instruction in the data movement group. Information can be moved from a register (including segment registers) to a memory location, or vice versa. An immediate data value can also be moved to a register or a memory location. Either 8-bit or 16-bit operations can be performed.

MOVS (Move String). This instruction is used primarily to move blocks of data in memory. The SI and DI register are used to hold the offset address of the source and destination operand, respectively. The SI and DI register are then incremented or decremented depending upon whether the Direction Flag is 0 or 1, respectively. The incremented/decremented value is 1 or 2 depending upon byte or word operation of the instruction.

PUSH (Push on Stack). The Stack Pointer is decremented by 2 to point to a new top of stack. This instruction then places the 16-bit contents of a register or a memory location on top of the stack.

PUSHF (Push Flag on Stack). The Stack Pointer is decremented by 2 to point to a new top of stack. This instruction then places the contents of the Processor Flag on top of the stack.

POP (Pop from Stack). This instruction replaces the contents of a register or a memory location with the word on top of the stack. The Stack Pointer is incremented by 2 to point to a new top of stack.

POPF (Pop Flag from Stack). This instruction uses the word on top of the stack as the new Processor Flag and updates all flags of the 8088 microprocessor. The Stack Pointer is incremented by 2 to point to a new top of stack.

SAHF (Store the AH Register to Flags). This instruction replaces the low-order 8 bits of the Processor Flag with the contents of the AH register. The affected flags include the Sign Flag, the Zero Flag, the Auxiliary Flag, the Parity Flag, and the Carry Flag.

STOS (Store String). The contents of the accumulator (AL in byte operation, AX in word operation) are written into the memory locations addressed by the DI register in this instruction. The DI register is incremented or decremented depending upon whether the Direction Flag is 0 or 1, respectively. The incremented/decremented value is 1 or 2 depending upon byte or word operation of the instruction.

XCHG (Exchange). This instruction exchanges the contents of a register with the contents of a memory location. Either 8-bit or 16-bit operations can be performed.

XLAT (Translate). This instruction replaces a byte in the AL register with a byte from a 256-byte table. The byte in the AL register is used as an index into the table and is replaced by the byte at the offset in the table corresponding to the original binary values in the AL register.

MOVING DATA IN OVERLAPPING STRINGS

The string instruction MOVS (Move String) is the only instruction in the 8088 instruction repertoire that allows moving information from one place to another in the computer memory without the need to use any CPU register. In assembly language, the MOVS instruction is written as MOVSB (Move String Byte) to move blocks of information in bytes. If blocks of words need to be moved, the form MOVSW (Move String Word) is used. The content of the Direction Flag can be manipulated to control the direction of the movement. When the Direction Flag is cleared to 0, the implied index registers SI and DI are in the autoincrement mode. Thus a block of data is moved from the lower addresses to the higher addresses of memory. When the Direction Flag is set to 1, the SI and DI registers are in the autodecrement mode, and data are moved from the higher addresses to the lower addresses of memory.

If the source string and the destination string contain portions that overlap one another, the MOVS instruction can also be used effectively, as

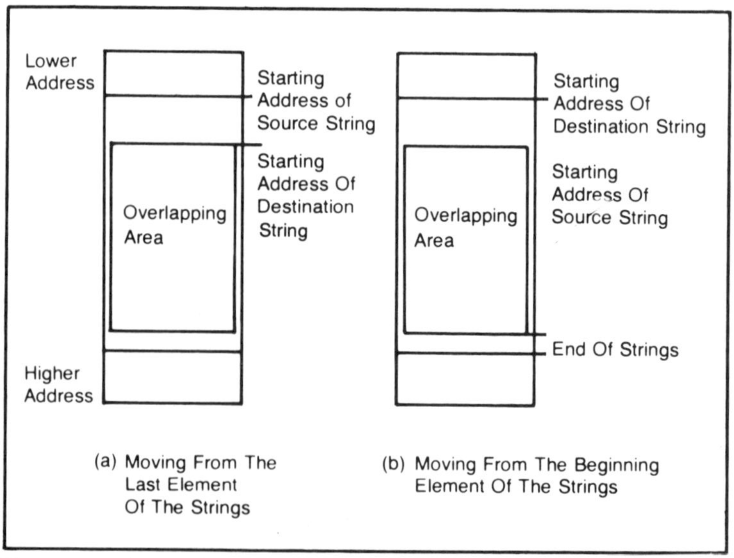

Fig. 7-1. Examples of overlapping strings in memory.

```
0000                MOVE       PROC NEAR               ;Procedure to move data between overlapping strings.
= 012C              STRING_SIZE  EQU 300               ;Number of data bytes to move.
                    ;
0000 B92C01                    MOV  CX,STRING_SIZE     ;Number of data bytes to move.
0003 BE7F00                    MOV  SI,OFFSET STRING_1 ;Starting offset address of source string.
0006 BF9800                    MOV  DI,OFFSET STRING_2 ;Starting offset address of destination string.
0009 FC                        CLD                     ;Prepare for a forward move.
000A 3BF7                      CMP  SI,DI              ;Check for forward or backward move.
000C 7309                      JAE  FORWARD
000E FD                        STD                     ;Prepare for backward move.
000F 81C62B01                  ADD  SI,STRING_SIZE-1   ;Start at the last data byte to be moved.
0013 81C72B01                  ADD  DI,STRING_SIZE-1
0017                FORWARD:
0017 F3A4                      REP  MOVSB              ;Move the data.
0019 FC                        CLD                     ;Restore the Direction Flag.
001A C3                        RET
001B                MOVE       ENDP
                    ;
001B                DATA       PROC NEAR
001B                STRING     DB   1000 DUP(?)        ;1000 bytes of overlapping strings.
= 007F              STRING_1 EQU    STRING+100
= 0098              STRING_2 EQU    STRING+125
0403                DATA       ENDP
```

Fig. 7-2. Procedure to move data between two overlapping strings.

```
0000                CONVERT1 PROC NEAR                 ;Translate source string to EBCDIC codes.
0000 8D36AE00               LEA  SI,BUFFER             ;Offset address of source string.
0004 8D1E2C00               LEA  BX,EBCDIC_TABLE       ;Translation table.
0008 8B0EAC00               MOV  CX,NO_BYTES           ;Number of bytes to translated.
000C FC                     CLD
000D AC             LOOP1:  LODSB
000E D7                     XLAT                       ;Look up the EBCDIC codes in table.
000F 8844FF                 MOV  [SI-1],AL             ;Update the source string.
0012 E2F9                   LOOP LOOP1
0014 C3                     RET
0015                CONVERT1 ENDP
                    ;
0015                CONVERT2 PROC NEAR                 ;Translate to another buffer.
0015 8D36AE00               LEA  SI,BUFFER
0019 8D1E2C00               LEA  BX,EBCDIC_TABLE
001D 8D0EAC00               MOV  CX,NO_BYTES
0021 8D3EB800               LEA  DI,OUT_BUFFER         ;Offset address of the output buffer.
0025 FC                     CLD
0026 AC             LOOP2:  LODSB
```

```
0027 D7                  XLAT
0028 AA                  STOSB                       ;Write out the EBCDIC codes to output buffer.
0029 E2FB                LOOP LOOP2
002B C3                  RET
002C              CONVERT2 ENDP
                  ;
002C              DATA   PROC NEAR
002C              EBCDIC_TABLE DB 00H,01H,02H,03H,37H,2DH,2EH,2FH,16H,05H,25H,0BH,0CH,0DH,0EH,0FH
                   DB 10H,11H,12H,00H,3CH,3DH,32H,26H,18H,19H,3FH,27H,1CH,1DH,1EH,1FH
                   DB 40H,5AH,7FH,7BH,5BH,6CH,50H,7DH,4DH,5DH,5CH,4EH,6BH,60H,4BH,61H
                   DB 0F0H,0F1H,0F2H,0F3H,0F4H,0F5H,0F6H,0F7H,0F8H,0F9H,7AH,5EH,4CH,7EH,6EH,6FH
                   DB 7CH,0C1H,0C2H,0C3H,0C4H,0C5H,0C6H,0C7H,0C8H,0C9H,0D1H,0D2H,0D3H,0D4H,0D5H,0D6H
                   DB 0D7H,0D8H,0D9H,0E2H,0E3H,0E4H,0E5H,0E6H,0E7H,0E8H,0E9H,00H,0E0H,00H,5FH,6DH
                   DB 79H,81H,82H,83H,84H,85H,86H,87H,88H,89H,91H,92H,93H,94H,95H,96H
                   DB 97H,98H,99H,0A2H,0A3H,0A4H,0A5H,0A6H,0A7H,0A8H,0A9H,0C0H,6AH,0D0H,0A1H,07H
00AC 0A00         NO_BYTES DW   10
00AE              BUFFER   DB   'ABCDEF',00H,01H,02H,7FH   ;ASCII string.
00B8              OUT_BUFFER DB 10 DUP(?)             ;EBCDIC codes translated by CONVERT2.
00C2              DATA     ENDP
```

Fig. 7-3. Procedures to convert ASCII notations to EBCDIC notations.

shown in the following programming example. The direction used to move the block of data in memory must be considered in this case so that the original contents of the overlapping portion of the source string will not be damaged by the block move operation. If the offset address of the source string is higher than that of the destination, the move can be initiated with the first byte of the source string.

Otherwise, if the offset address of the source string is higher than that of the destination string, the move must begin with the last data byte of the source string (moving backward). The situation can be best illustrated in Fig. 7-1. The procedure listed in Fig. 7-2 illustrates the use of the MOVS instruction to move a number of bytes of data between two overlapping strings in memory. The CX register is initialized to hold the number of bytes to be moved. The SI and DI register contain the offset addresses of the first data byte in the source string and destination string, respectively.

CONVERSION FROM ASCII TO EBCDIC

There are two different standards to represent information in the computing world: the ASCII representation and the EBCDIC representation. ASCII stands for American Standard Code For Information Interchange and is universally accepted in the world of microcomputers. EBCDIC stands for Extended Binary Coded Decimal Interchange Code, and is used by IBM mainframe computers ony. Because of the differences between the two representations, when data communications between a microcomputer and an IBM mainframe is desired, the translation from the ASCII codes to EBCDIC codes, or vice versa, is necessary.

Information to be translated is normally put together into a buffer. Every element in the buffer is then converted, using a translation table to make the conversion. The translation table contains a direct replacement value for every original value that an element in the buffer can have. Data in the buffer may be translated and left in the buffer, or they can be translated and moved from one buffer to another.

The procedure CONVERT1 listed in Fig. 7-3 translates data without moving it. This procedure assumes that the BX register contains the offset address of the translation table, the SI register contains the offset address of the buffer to be translated, and the CX register contains the number of data bytes to be translated. The procedure CONVER2 in Fig. 7-3 translates data while moving the converted data to another buffer. This procedure makes the same assumption as the procedure CONVERT1 does, and also assumes that the DI register contains the offset address of the buffer where the translated data will be stored.

You should try to rewrite these two procedures to convert data from EBCDIC codes back to ASCII codes as an exercise.

SEARCHING FOR A SEQUENCE OF CHARACTERS

One of the most useful features of a microcomputer is its ability to perform efficiently editing functions on standard text files. A standard text file normally contains alphanumeric information that can be displayed on an input/output device such as a printer or a video terminal. For example, a text file may be a personalized letter generated by a word-processing program, a financial report created by a data base program, or the source listing of an assembly language program.

Information recorded in a text file is usually grouped into many records of variable lengths. Normally, a Carriage Return and a Line Feed character (the hexadecimal notations of these characters are OD and OA in the ASCII representations, respectively) are appended to the end of each record to indicate the physical termination of a record. In text files that are created by a text editor, a record usually corresponds to a complete line displayed on the video screen. In text files that are created by a word-processing program, a record may include all characters of a complete sentence or an entire paragraph. The final character in the last record of a text file usually is an ASCII symbol that indicates the physical termination of the file. Text files on the IBM Personal Computer under the PC-DOS operating system use the hexadecimal number 1A to mark the end of a text file.

In word-processing and text-editing applications, it is often desirable to be able to search and locate a specified word or a sequence of characters in a text file so that modifications can be conveniently performed at specific places of interest in the file. If the specified sequence of characters is found, the particular text line that contains the desired sequence can be displayed on the video screen. If the specified sequence does not exist, an appropriate error message is generated. The sequential search technique can be used to locate the sequence of characters.

The procedure listed in Fig. 7-4 assumes that the text file has been read into the computer memory. The first character in the file can be obtained at the offset address specified by the contents of the BX register. The procedure then sequentially searches the text file for a specified sequence of characters. Control characters that indicate the physical end of a record or the end of the text file are ignored.

The procedure makes the assumption that the CX register contains the number of characters in the sequence to be searched. The SI register contains the offset address of the first character in the sequence. The content of the Carry Flag is used to indicate whether the specified sequence of characters does exist in the text file. If the character sequence is found, the Carry Flag is cleared to 0, and the DI register contains the offset address of the first character of the located sequence in the text file.

MANIPULATING A DOUBLY LINKED LIST

In a computer system there are often data items or blocks of information which cannot be easily moved. It is sometimes prohibitive to move these blocks of information due to the large amount of computing overheads involved in the required operations to perform the movements. One way to

```
0000               CHAR     PROC NEAR                    ;This procedure contains the character sequence
                   ;                                      to be searched.
0000 8D1E1000               LEA     BX,START_DATA       ;Offset address of the first character
                   ;                                      of the text file in memory.
0004 8B0EBD00               MOV     CX,NO_CHARACTER     ;Number of characters in the sequence.
0008 8D36B700               LEA     SI,SEQUENCE         ;Offset address of the sequence of characters.
000C E8B000                 CALL    SEARCH
000F C3                     RET
0010               START_DATA DB 'In word-processing and text-editing applications,'
                              DB 0DH,0AH
                              DB ' it is often desirable to be able to search and locate'
                              DB ' a specified word or a sequence of characters in a text'
                              DB 'file',0DH,0AH,1AH
00B7               SEQUENCE   DB 'locate'
00BD               NO_CHARACTER DW 6
00BF               CHAR     ENDP
                   ;
00BF               SEARCH   PROC    NEAR        ;This procedure searches for a sequence of characters.
00BF 8BD1                   MOV     DX,CX       ;Save the number of characters in the sequence.
00C1 8BEE                   MOV     BP,SI       ;Save the original offset address in SI.
00C3 8BFB          MATCH:   MOV     DI,BX       ;Keep track of current character in the text file.
00C5 AC            NEXT:    LODSB               ;Get a character in the text file.
00C6               RESTART:
00C6 803F0D                 CMP BYTE PTR [BX],0DH   ;Check for a Carriage Return.
```

```
00C9 741B                JE      CONTROL_CHAR
00CB 803F0A              CMP BYTE PTR [BX],0AH   ;Check for a Line Feed.
00CE 7416                JE      CONTROL_CHAR
00D0 803F1A              CMP BYTE PTR [BX],1AH   ;Check for the end of the text file.
00D3 7414                JE      END_FILE
00D5 3A07                CMP     AL,[BX]         ;Is it a match.
00D7 9C                  PUSHF                   ;Save the Zero Flag.
00D8 43                  INC     BX              ;Prepare to get the next character.
00D9 9D                  POPF                    ;Restore the status of previous comparison.
00DA E1E9                LOOPE   NEXT            ;Check all characters in the sequence.
00DC 7502                JNE     SKIP
00DE F8                  CLC                     ;The character sequence is found.
               ;                                  The offset address of the first character is in DI.
00DF C3                  RET
00E0 8BF5      SKIP:     MOV     SI,BP
00E2 8BCA                MOV     CX,DX
00E4 EBDD                JMP SHORT MATCH
00E6           CONTROL_CHAR:
00E6 43                  INC     BX
00E7 EBDD                JMP SHORT RESTART
00E9 F9        END_FILE: STC             ;The sequence of characters does not exist in the file.
00EA C3                  RET
00EB           SEARCH   ENDP
```

Fig. 7-4. Procedure to search for a character sequence.

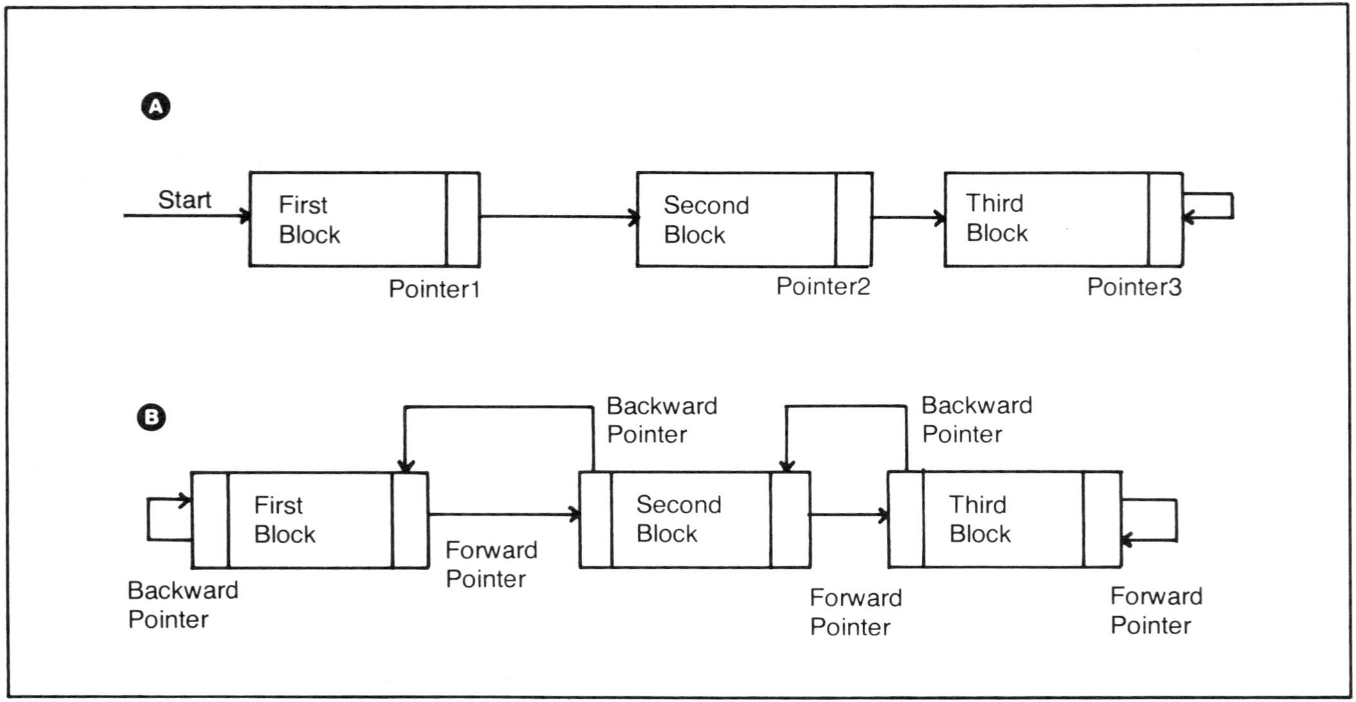

Fig. 7-5. A linked list, A, and a doubly linked list, B.

```
0000                 INSERT   PROC    NEAR     ;Insert a new block into a doubly linked list.
                     ;                          This procedure assumes that the memory location
                     ;                          INSERT_BLOCK contains the offset address of the
                     ;                          new block to be inserted. The location OLD_BLOCK
                     ;                          contains the offset address of the block where
                     ;                          the new block is inserted after.
                     ;
0000 A11700                   MOV    AX,INSERT_BLOCK   ;Offset address of the new block.
0003 8B1E1900                 MOV    BX,OLD_BLOCK      ;Offset address of the block having the insertion.
0007 FF37                     PUSH   [BX]              ;Save the original forward pointer.
0009 8907                     MOV    [BX],AX           ;New forward pointer.
000B 93                       XCHG   AX,BX             ;BX points to the block to be inserted.
000C 894702                   MOV    [BX+02],AX        ;Create the link backward pointer for the new block.
000F 58                       POP    AX                ;Offset address of the next block in the list.
0010 8907                     MOV    [BX],AX           ;Create the link forward pointer for the new block.
0012 93                       XCHG   AX,BX             ;BX points to the next block in the sequence.
0013 894702                   MOV    [BX+02],AX        ;New backward pointer.
0016 C3                       RET
0017 ??              INSERT_BLOCK DW ?
0019 ??              OLD_BLOCK    DW ?
001B                 INSERT   ENDP
```

Fig. 7-6. Procedure to insert a new block in a doubly linked list.

solve this problem is to leave the blocks of information where they are and establish some sort of pointers to keep track of the ordering relationship between these blocks. A linked list structure can be extremely effective in solving this problem.

The concept of a linked list is illustrated in Fig. 7-5A. In the illustration, a list pointer called POINTER1 points to the beginning of the first block of information. A dedicated area within the first block contains a pointer, called POINTER2, to specify the beginning of the second block. The process repeats until the last block of the list. The last block usually contains a pointer with a special vlaue or it can point to the beginning of itself so that the last block of the linked list can be detected.

This list structure has advantages in situations requiring many insertions and deletions of blocks of information. You can see that by manipulating the block pointers on the list, the relationship between these blocks are maintained without actually moving the blocks.

A linked list allows forward reference only. In other words, we can identify the position of a block of information which follows the current

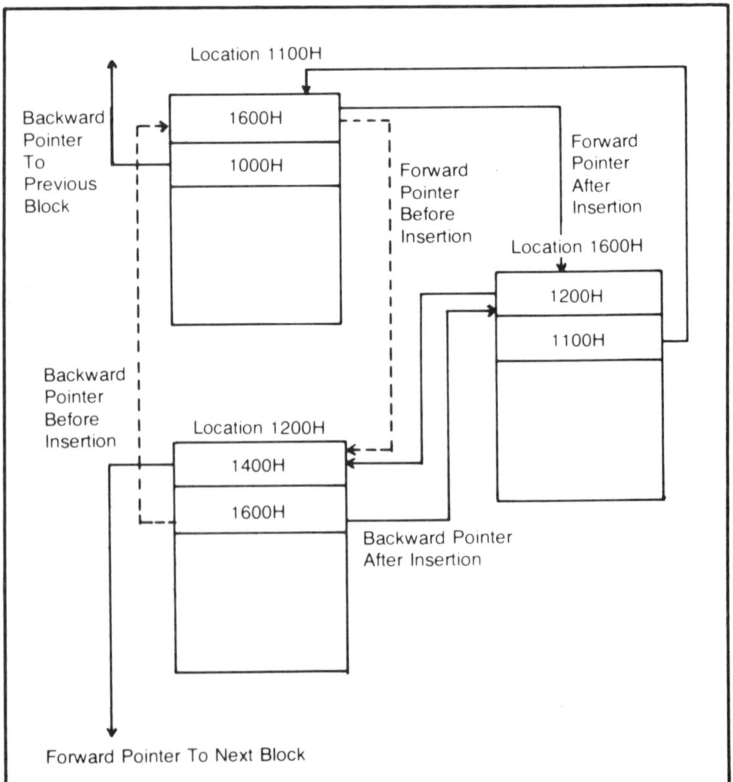

Fig. 7-7. Insertion in a doubly linked list.

```
0000                DELETE PROC NEAR          ;Delete a block in a doubly linked list.
                    ;                          This procedure assumes that the memory location
                    ;                          DELETE_BLOCK contains the offset address of the
                    ;                          block to be deleted from a doubly linked list.
                    ;
0000 8B1E1300              MOV    BX,DELETE_BLOCK       ;Offset address of the block to be deleted.
0004 8B07                  MOV    AX,[BX]               ;Offset address of the next block.
0006 8B5702                MOV    DX,[BX+02]            ;Offset address of the previous block.
0009 8BDA                  MOV    BX,DX
000B 8907                  MOV    [BX],AX               ;Update the forward pointer.
000D 8BD8                  MOV    BX,AX
000F 895702                MOV    [BX+02],DX            ;Update the backward pointer.
0012 C3                    RET
0013 ??             DELETE_BLOCK DW ?
0015                DELETE_ENDP
```

Fig. 7-8. Procedure to delete a block from a doubly linked list.

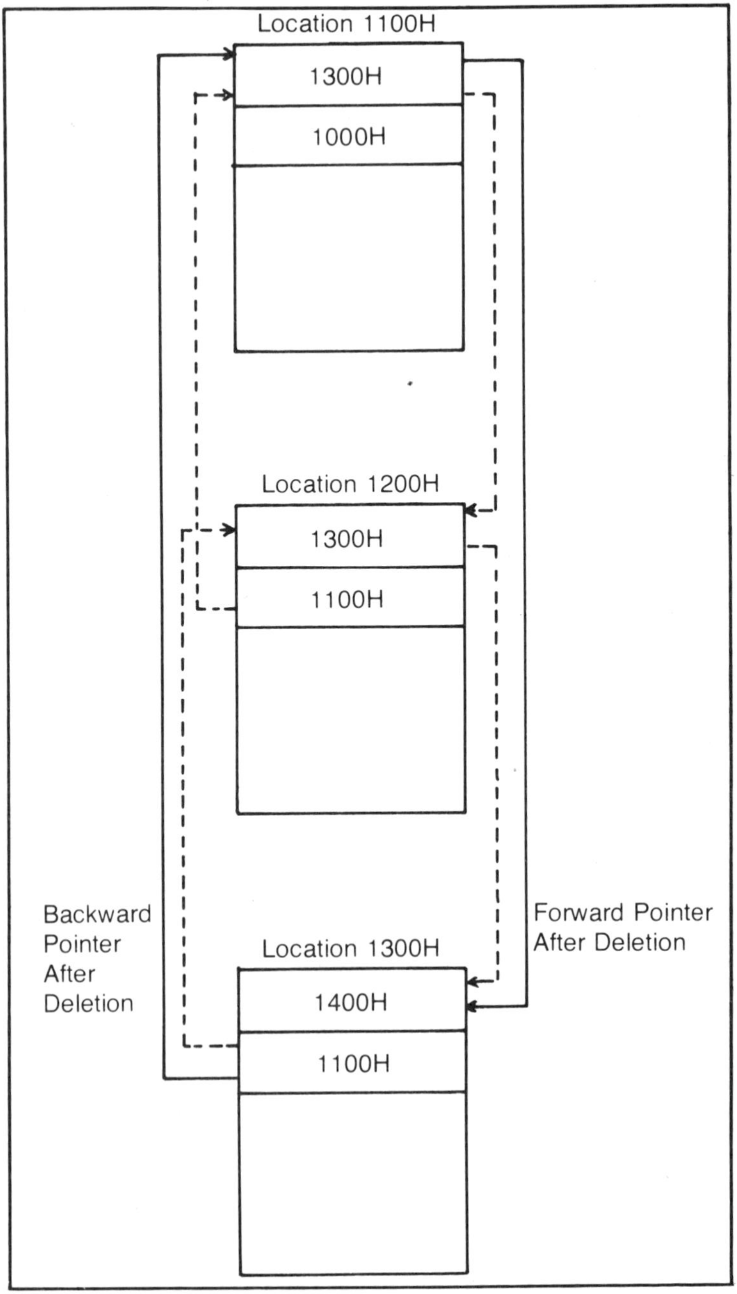

Fig. 7-9. Deletion in a doubly linked list.

block only. There are no pointers that can identify the positions of the blocks on the list that are defined before the current block. A doubly linked list structure, as shown in Fig. 7-5B, can be implemented to solve this problem.

Linked lists are very useful in text-editing applications where activities such as inserting and deleting lines of text are frequent. If the characters of a text file are stored sequentially in the computer memory, each time a new character is inserted into the file, room for insertion has to be made by moving all characters which are beyond the point at which the insertion is to be made. Similarly, deleting a character in the file causes all characters which are beyond the point of deletion to move again to fill in the vacant space of the deleted character.

This sequential organization is clearly very inefficient. A text file can be stored in the computer memory configured as a doubly linked list where each line of text is considered as a block of information on the list. Each line of the text file stored in memory may have a header to contain information about the line such as the line number, or the number of characters currently on the line, etc. The header of each text line must also include forward and backward pointers to point to the memory addresses of the text line immediately before and following the current line. When a new line is inserted or deleted, only the pointers in the headers of these text lines are modified to reflect the changes.

The procedure listed in Fig. 7-6 provides an example of inserting a new line of text in a doubly linked list structure. In this procedure, each text line has a header prepared in the following format:

Byte 0,1	Offset Address of the next line (Forward Pointer)
Byte 2,3	Offset Address of the previous line (Backward Pointer)
Byte 4,5	Low-order word of the line number
Byte 6,7	High-order word of the line number
Byte 8,9	Number of characters currently on the line

In this example, I adopt the convention that if a forward pointer of a block in the list contains the hexadecimal value FFFF, it indicates the end of the list. Similarly, a backward pointer having the hexadecimal value FFFF indicates the starting block of the list. The operations required to perform the insertion are illustrated in Fig. 7-7.

Deletion of a block of information in a doubly linked list is very simple. The procedure listed in Fig. 7-8 performs the deletion of a line of a text file configured in the computer memory as a doubly linked list structure. The operations required to perform the deletion are illustrated in Fig. 7-9. After the deletion is complete, there may be some additional operations performed to update the information in the headers of each member of the list. For example, if a text line is deleted from a file, it might be necessary to renumber all lines in the file after the line has been deleted.

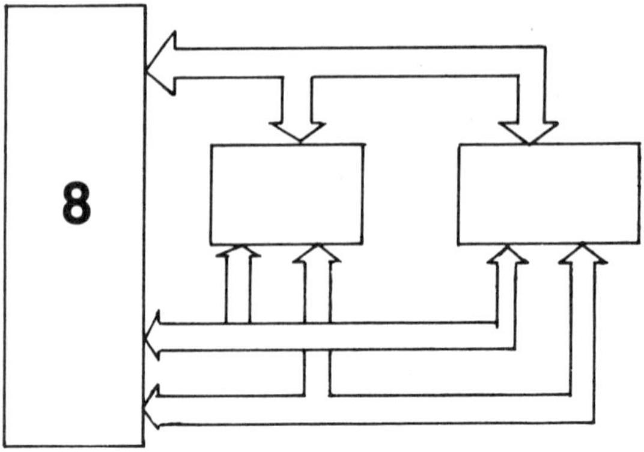

Control Transfer

The control transfer instructions of the 8088 microprocessor can alter the contents of the Instruction Pointer, and in some cases they alter the contents of the Code Segment register as well. Thus the sequence of execution of instructions in an 8088 program can be altered since the CS register contains the base address of the current code segment which is the 64 K-byte portion of memory from which instructions are fetched, and the IP register represents an offset from the beginning of the code segment. When a control transfer instruction is executed, the instruction queue of the 8088 CPU is reset. The Bus Interface Unit (BIU) obtains the next instruction from the computer memory using the new contents of the CS and IP register, passes the fetched instruction to the Execution Unit (EU), and then begins to refill the instruction queue from the new memory address.

UNCONDITIONAL TRANSFER INSTRUCTIONS

There are two groups of control transfer instructions: unconditional transfer instructions and conditional transfer instructions. Unconditional transfer instructions which include CALL (Call Procedures), JMP (Jump), and RET (Return From Procedures) are briefly discussed in the following section.

CALL (Call Procedures). CALL instructions transfer control to a procedure, saving the returning address on the stack so that executing a RET instruction in the procedure can transfer control back to the instruction following the CALL. In 8088 assembly language, if a procedure is declared as NEAR, the CALL instruction which makes reference to the procedure is assembled into an intrasegment CALL. An intersegment CALL is generated for CALL instructions which makes reference to procedures that are declared FAR. Different forms of the CALL instruction allow the address of the target procedure to be obtained from the instruction itself (direct CALL) or from a register or a memory location referenced by the instruction (indirect CALL). The intrasegment form can only transfer control to a specified target within ±32 K bytes of the instruction. The intersegment form allows transfer to any location within the 8088 megabyte memory space.

RET (Return from Procedures). RET instructions normally are the last instructions to be executed before exiting a procedure. This transfers control back to the instruction following the CALL which invokes the procedure. Thus, RET instructions that terminate a procedure operate as the inverse of the CALL that invokes the procedure. When a RET instruction is executed, the returning address on the stack is popped into the IP register (intrasegment return), or both the IP and CS registers (intersegment return). The RET instruction can optionally add a 16-bit displacement value to the contents of the SP register. This allows a RET instruction to adjust the Stack Pointer to bypass parameters previously saved on the stack.

JMP (Unconditional Jump). JMP instructions transfer control to a target location unconditionally without saving any information on the stack. Similar to CALL instructions, the address of the target location in JMP instructions can be obtained from the instruction itself (direct JMP) or from a register or a memory location (indirect JMP). In 8088 assembly language, the mnemonic JMP is normally assembled into a direct intrasegment JMP instruction. The operator FAR PTR is available to specify an intersegment JMP. The operator SHORT is also available to specify a jump within 127 bytes or −128 bytes of the instruction. The contents of the IP register are updated following execution of an intrasegment JMP instruction. The previous contents of the IP register are lost. In intersegment JMP instructions, the contents of both the IP and CS register are updated.

CONDITIONAL TRANSFER INSTRUCTIONS

Conditional transfer instructions include the jump-on-condition instructions and looping instructions. These instructions transfer control to a specified target address within 127 bytes or −128 bytes of the instruction only, depending on certain conditions of the Processor Flag and/or the contents of the CX register. A brief summary of these instructions is presented in the following section.

JA/JNBE (Jump if Above/Jump if Not Below or Equal). The jump occurs if the Carry Flag and the Zero Flag are 0.

JAE/JNB/JNC (Jump if Above or Equal/Jump if Not Below/Jump if Not Carry). The jump occurs if the Carry Flag is 0.

JB/JNAE/JC (Jump if Below/Jump if Not Above or Equal/Jump if Carry). The jump occurs if the Carry Flag is 1.

JBE/JNA (Jump if Below or Equal/Jump if Not Above). The jump occurs if the Carry Flag or the Zero Flag is 1.

JCXZ (Jump if the CX Register is 0). The jump occurs if the CX register contains 0.

JE/JZ (Jump if Equal/Jump if Zero). The jump occurs if the Zero Flag is 1.

JG/JNLE (Jump if Greater Than/Jump if Not Less Than or Equal). The jump occurs if the Sign Flag is equal to the Overflow Flag and the Zero Flag is 0.

JGE/JNL (Jump if Greater Than or Equal/Jump if Not Less Than). The jump occurs if the Sign Flag is equal to the Overflow Flag.

JL/JNGE (Jump if Less/Jump if Not Greater Than or Equal). The jump occurs if the Sign Flag is not equal to the Overflow Flag.

JLE/JNG (Jump if Less Than or Equal/Jump if Not Greater Than). The jump occurs if Sign Flag is not equal to the Overflow Flag or the Zero Flag is 1.

JNE/JNZ (Jump if Not Equal/Jump if Not Zero). The jump occurs if the Zero Flag is 0.

JNO (Jump if Not Overflow). The jump occurs if the Overflow Flag is 0.

JNS (Jump if Not Sign). The jump occurs if the Sign Flag is 0.

JNP/JPO (Jump if Not Parity/Jump if Parity Odd). The jump occurs if the Parity Flag is 0.

JO (Jump if Overflow). The jump occurs if the Overflow Flag is 1.

JP/JPE (Jump if Parity/Jump if Parity Even). The jump occurs if the Parity Flag is 1.

JS (Jump if Sign). The jump occurs if the Sign Flag is 1.

LOOP (Loop Instruction). The loop continues if the CX register is not 0.

LOOPE/LOOPZ (Loop if Equal/Loop if Zero). The loop continues if the CX register is not 0 and the Zero Flag is 1.

LOOPNE/LOOPNZ (Loop if Not Equal/Loop if Not Zero). The loop continues if the CX register is not 0 and the Zero Flag is 0.

STRUCTURE OF A LOOP

A loop in a computer program is a group of instructions to be executed repeatedly to perform the same task. The number of repetitions of the loop is normally specified in an iteration counter. In analyzing the structure of a loop in a computer program, a loop can be divided into four functional parts: initialization, the body of the program loop, adjustment logic, and a test to terminate the loop. These parts are related to one another and in certain cases, no instructions are needed to perform the functions of one of these parts. The following section discusses the nature of these functional parts of the loop.

The Body of a Loop

The body of the loop contains the necessary machine instructions to perform the task that we instruct the computer to do repetitively. The body may contain a few instructions or even a complete program which can include input/output instructions to communicate with peripheral devices, arithmetic instructions to perform computational tasks, logical instructions to test or modify certain conditions and statuses of the CPU, CALL instructions to invoke other procedures or instructions necessary to perform the repetitive task. The other functional parts of the loop are used to ensure that the body of the loop will be performed the correct number of repetitions on the appropriate data or information.

The Adjustment Logic

The adjustment logic is a functional part of the loop that normally contains instructions that modify the values of an iteration counter to keep track of the number of repetitions of the loop that has already been performed, or has yet to be performed. An iteration counter can be a register or a memory location. If an 8-bit counter is used, the number of repetitions a loop can perform is up to 256 iterations. If a 16-bit counter is used, the repetitions can be up to 65536. In LOOP instructions, the CX register is used to hold the value of the iteration counter. The adjustment logic part of the loop may also contain instructions to move information or to perform computations so that the next repetition of the loop can be performed properly.

The Test to Terminate the Loop

A loop can be terminated in several possible ways. The loop may be terminated by a jump-on-condition instruction that makes the jump out of the loop when certain conditions are met. In many simple loops, the loop is terminated when the body of the loop has been repeated a given number of times as specified in the iteration counter. The structure of the loop may also be complicated if there are several possible exits in the structure so that any of several possible conditions may force the loop to terminate. In many cases, the loop may terminate even when the number of repetitions specified in the iteration counter has not been exhausted.

Initialization

The body of the loop, the adjustment logic part, and the test to terminate the loop may be executed in many repetitions inside a loop structure. On the contrary, the initialization step normally takes place outside of the loop before the loop begins. The initialization step should be executed only once and be performed before entry to the loop. The primary functions of this step are to initialize the iteration counter of the loop, to set or clear certain flags in the CPU, and to set up or prepare initial data for certain registers or memory locations so that the execution of the body of the loop can be started properly.

After the initialization is completed, the other three functional parts of a loop structure may appear in any order. Figure 8-1 shows two common structures of a program loop. Structure (B) is employed in special cases where the body of the loop should not be executed if the test to terminate causes an exit upon the first repetition of the loop. Figure 8-2 shows a simple loop structure to perform the additions of 100 integer numbers. In the initialization step, the CX register is used as an iteration counter and is intialized with the number 100 to indicate 100 repetitions. The symbolic memory location SUM is also initialized with a value 0. The body of the loop performs the addition to the location SUM. The adjustment logic part is done by the LOOP instruction which decrements the contents of the CX register to keep track of the number of repetitions. The test to terminate the loop is implied by the contents of the CX register. The loop is terminated when the number of repetitions is completed (100 in this case). An assembly language procedure that performs this function is listed in Fig. 8-3.

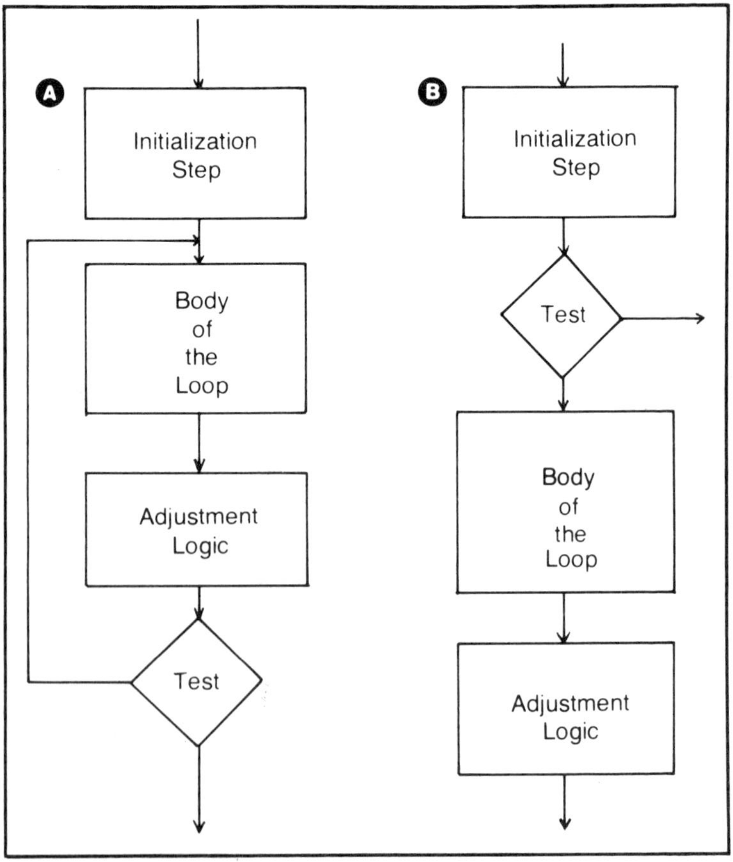

Fig. 8-1. Two loop structures.

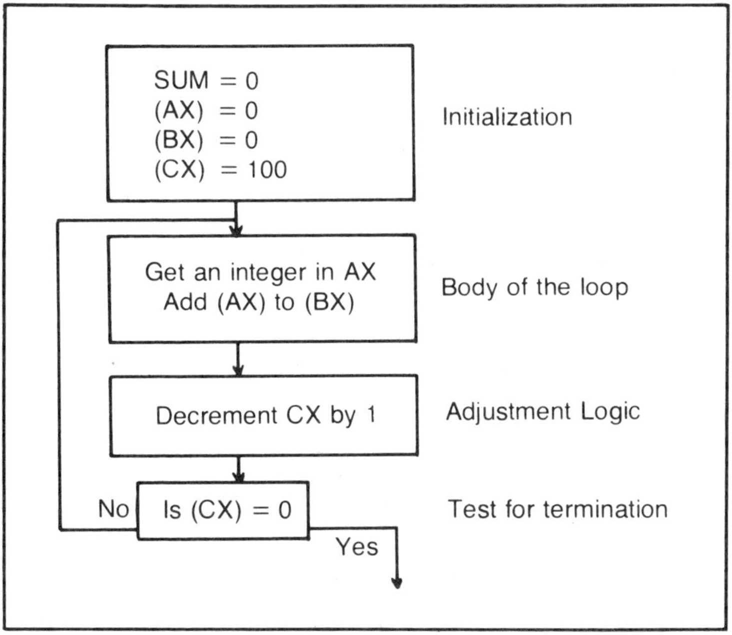

Fig. 8-2. Loop structure to add 100 integers.

STRUCTURE OF A PROCEDURE

A sequence of instructions that is to be executed at several different points in a computer program does not have to be coded in its entirety at each of these points. In fact, a computer program can be much easier to comprehend if the portions of machine codes that perform the same functions can be grouped together and called a procedure. Then at each point of the program where execution of that specific sequence is necessary, an appropriate method of transfer of control to the procedure is sufficient. However, enough information must be given to the procedure so that it knows what information to work with and where to return control when the execution of the procedure is completed. In 8088-based systems, the information to return control to the calling program is normally stored on the stack.

Parameters passing from the main program to a procedure are normally specified in the CPU registers, or are also pushed on the stack. Thus, a procedure in 8088 assembly language normally refers to a block of instructions and data with a given name so that it can be invoked by another program, or even by another procedure, to perform some specific functions in a repetitive manner.

The assembly language directives PROC (Procedure Definition) and ENDP (End Procedure) can be specified to identify the starting and ending point of the procedure. The use of a procedure is illustrated in Fig. 8-4

```
0000                  ADDITION  PROC NEAR       ;Procedure to add 100 integers.
0000 8D361B00                   LEA  SI,TABLE   ;Table contains 100 8-bit integers.
0004 FC                         CLD
0005 2BDB                       SUB  BX,BX      ;Initialize.
0007 2BC0                       SUB  AX,AX
0009 A31900                     MOV  SUM,AX
000C B96400                     MOV  CX,100     ;Iteration counter for 100 iterations.
000F AC               ADD:      LODSB           ;Get an integer in the table.
0010 03D8                       ADD  BX,AX      ;Sum all the integers.
0012 E2FB                       LOOP ADD        ;Loop until all 100 integers are added.
0014 891E1900                   MOV  SUM,BX     ;The sum of 100 integers.
0018 C3                         RET
0019 ??               SUM      DW   ?
001B                  TABLE    DB   10,12,14,16,18,17,3,3,4,2,0,0,0,1,2,1,0,0,0,0
                               DB   1,2,3,4,5,5,5,70,12,14,16,12,17,14,15,16,8,7,1,2
                               DB   2,4,5,2,3,14,32,21,12,16,18,12,11,11,11,16,17,12,19,0
                               DB   66,12,13,0,0,0,0,0,1,1,1,1,2,3,3,3,4,0,0,0
                               DB   77,8,1,2,0,0,0,0,0,1,2,121,12,12,15,16,17,18,19,20
007F                  ADDITION ENDP
```

Fig. 8-3. Procedure to add 100 integers.

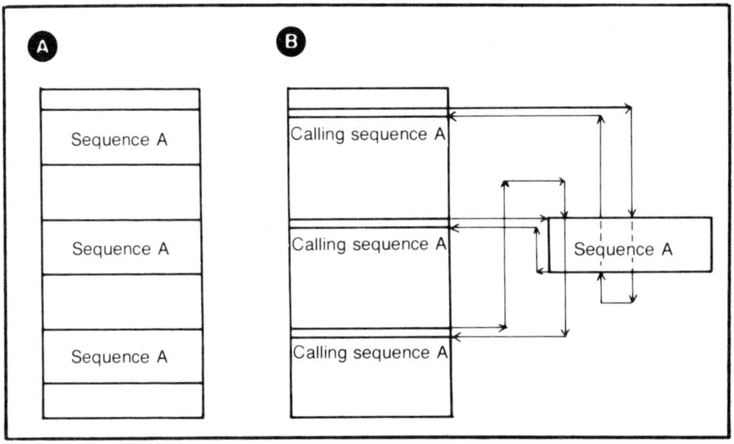

Fig. 8-4. Structure of procedures. A, without procedures, B, with procedures.

where the principal purpose of a procedure is to replace the storage and control structure of case (A) with the structure of case (B).

Invoking a procedure in 8088 assembly language is very simple. The CALL instructions are used to transfer control to a procedure. If the procedure is declared as a NEAR procedure, the assembler generates an intrasegment CALL. The offset address of the instruction following the CALL is saved on the stack so that the procedure can return properly. If the procedure is declared as a FAR procedure, the assembler generates an intersegment CALL. The contents of the CS register and the offset address of the instruction following the CALL are saved on the stack. Executing a RET instruction when exiting a procedure will return control to the calling program properly.

There are many advantages to using a procedure structure. It helps simplify the programming task by breaking down a large and complex problem into many smaller pieces, each of which may perform a unique function and has no or minimal relationships with other pieces. These small pieces or procedures can then be implemented and tested separately. This helps tremendously in the debugging of new computer software. The procedure approach also saves memory space and reduces the program size since there is no need to rewrite the procedure every time it is needed. The greatest advantage of a procedure is that a programmer designs it once and then uses it repetitively as a building block to construct larger programs. The only problem of implementing a procedure is that this structure requires some computing overheads due to the need to save and restore returning information via the stack.

A procedure can also call another procedure (nested procedures) as illustrated in Fig. 8-5, or call itself (recursive procedure). The following sections provide some examples to demonstrate the implementation and structure of procedures in 8088 assembly language.

BUBBLE SORT

Bubble sort is one of the popular techniques to sort small quantities of data or to rearrange a small number of elements in a table. The elements are sorted either in ascending or descending order. If the elements in a table are arranged in ascending order, the largest element will be placed at the bottom of the table, while the smallest element will *bubble up* to the top of the table. Bubble sort techniques are also very effective to sort text characters since the alphabetic characters are assigned sequential codes in their ASCII representations, and these codes can be manipulated very easily.

A simple example of bubble sort is shown in Fig. 8-6. The table in the example contains four numbers to be sorted in ascending order: 65, 70, 67, and 69. When the sorting process is completed, the table contains 65, 67, 69, and 70 where 65 is the top element of the table and 70 is at the bottom of the table. The algorithm of the bubble sort technique is very straightforward. The top two (or bottom two) elements in the table are compared. If the lower element has a smaller value, hence lighter, than the top one, the two elements are exchanged. Otherwise, they remain the same. The process continues until all pairs of elements in the table have been compared. Figure 8-6 illustrates a bubble sort example starting from the top two elements of the table. Figure 8-7 shows the same sorting process but starting from the bottom elements of the table. These two examples are self-explanatory and produce identical results.

If we consider the numbers in the above bubble sort examples to be the ASCII representations of text characters, we have the following characters to work with: A (65 or 41H), F (70 or 46H), C (67 or 43H), and E (69 or 45H). We can clearly see that the bubble sort technique can also be utilized to arrange characters in alphabetical order. The procedure listed in Fig. 8-8

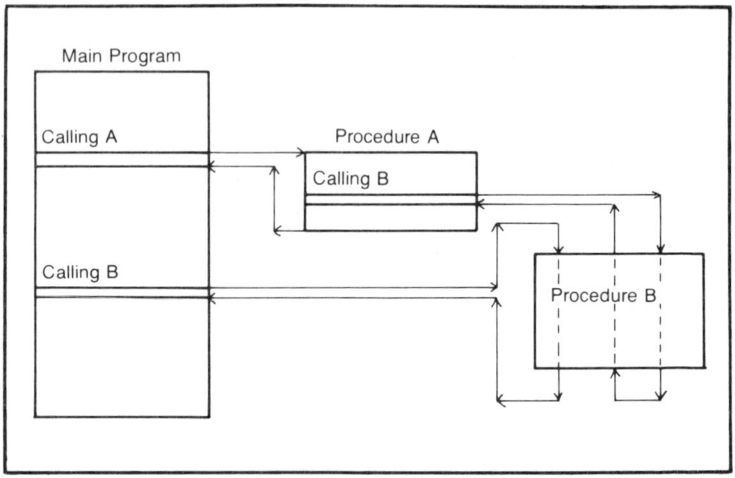

Fig. 8-5. Nested procedures.

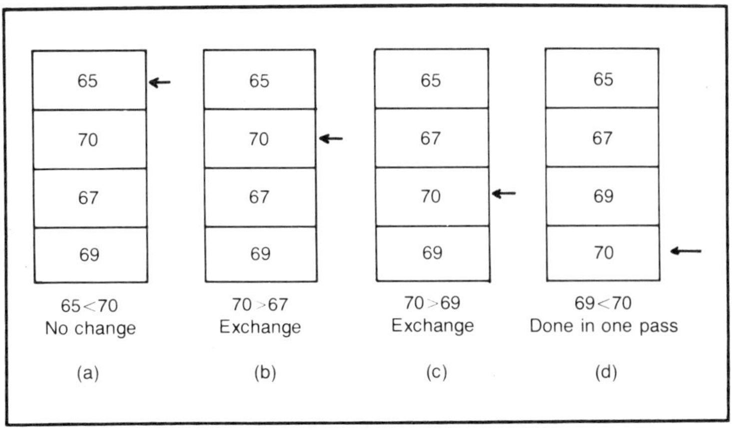

Fig. 8-6. Bubble sort example starting from the top elements.

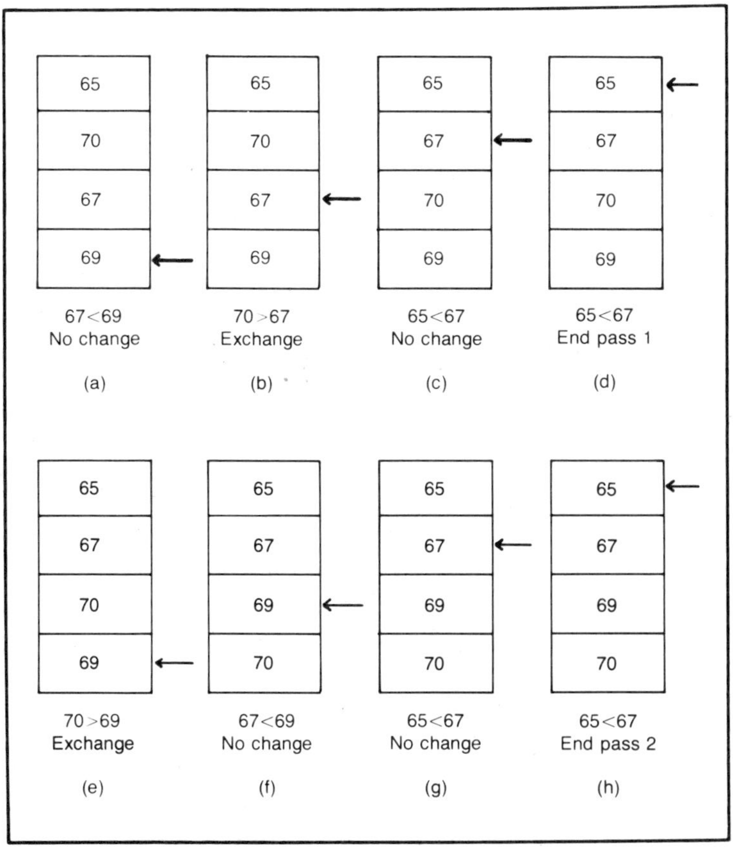

Fig. 8-7. Bubble sort example starting from the bottom elements.

```
0000                SORT     SEGMENT
                             ASSUME CS:SORT,DS:SORT,ES:SORT,SS:NOTHING
                    ;
                    ; In this programming example, we assume that the file names are stored
                    ; beginning at the memory location INPUT_BUFFER. Each file name may have
                    ; up to 11 characters. This procedure then sorts the number of file names
                    ; specified at the location NO_ENTRIES. The sorted file names are then
                    ; written to the memory location OUTPUT_BUFFER. A set of pointers is kept
                    ; at the location SORT_TABLE to keep track of the sorted position of each
                    ; file name. The bubble sort technique is then applied to all file
                    ; names defined at the buffer INPUT_BUFFER. The pointers at SORT_TABLE are
                    ; updated accordingly. Note that the pointers of SORT_TABLE are exchanged
                    ; during the bubble sort rather than the file names themselves.
                    ;
0000                MAIN     PROC     NEAR
0000 9C                      PUSHF
0001 1E                      PUSH     DS
0002 2BC0                    SUB      AX,AX
0004 50                      PUSH     AX
0005 06                      PUSH     ES
0006 1E                      PUSH     DS              ;Save registers to return to DOS later.
0007 8CC8                    MOV      AX,CS
0009 8ED8                    MOV      DS,AX
000B 8EC0                    MOV      ES,AX
000D E89A01                  CALL     BUBBLE_SORT     ;Sort the file names in alphabetical order.
0010 8B2E3700                MOV      BP,NO_ENTRIES
0014 8D3E0501                LEA      DI,OUTPUT_BUFFER
0018 8D1E3B00                LEA      BX,SORT_TABLE   ;Prepare to get the sorted pointers.
001C                CONTINUE:
001C 8BF3                    MOV      SI,BX
```

```
001E AC                         LODSB
001F B400                       MOV     AH,00
0021 B10B                       MOV     CL,11
0023 F6E1                       MUL     CL
0025 8D366000                   LEA     SI,INPUT_BUFFER
0029 03F0                       ADD     SI,AX           ;Position of the next sorted file name.
002B B90B00                     MOV     CX,11
002E F3A4                       REP     MOVSB
0030 43                         INC     BX              ;Next sorted pointer.
0031 4D                         DEC     BP              ;Check for the number of remaining file names.
0032 75E8                       JNE     CONTINUE
0034 1F                         POP     DS
0035 07                         POP     ES
0036 CF                         IRET                    ;Return to DOS.
0037               MAIN         ENDP
                   ;
0037               WORK_AREA PROC NEAR
0037 0F00          NO_ENTRIES        DW 15              ;Sort 15 file names in this example.
0039 ??            CURRENT_POINTER   DW ?               ;Current pointer in SORT_TABLE.
003B               SORT_TABLE        DB 15 DUP(?)       ;Reserved area for 15 pointers.
004A               SOURCE_STRING     DB 11 DUP(?)
0055               COMPARE_STRING    DB 11 DUP(?)
0060               INPUT_BUFFER      DB 'DRESSER    '
                                     DB 'TRW86      '
                                     DB 'RAYMOND    '
                                     DB 'INTEGER    '
                                     DB 'PARADE     '
                                     DB 'COPYN      '
                                     DB 'XEROXLONGST'
```

Fig. 8-8. Procedure to sort file names in alphabetical order.

```
                                      DB 'PENGUIN    '
                                      DB 'ELECTRONART'
                                      DB 'ORIGINAL   '
                                      DB 'RANDOM     '
                                      DB 'TEMP3      '
                                      DB 'CHAPTER3   '
                                      DB 'APPENDIX   '
                                      DB 'SORT       '
0105                  OUTPUT_BUFFER   DB 165 DUP(?)     ;Reserved area for 15 sorted file names.
01AA                  WORK_AREA ENDP
                      ;
01AA                  BUBBLE_SORT PROC NEAR             ;Sort the file names at INPUT_BUFFER.
01AA 8D363B00                  LEA     SI,SORT_TABLE
01AE 8B0E3700                  MOV     CX,NO_ENTRIES    ;Number of entries to be sorted.
01B2 2BDB                      SUB     BX,BX
01B4                  LOOP_SORT:
01B4 8818                      MOV     [BX+SI],BL       ;Initialize entry pointers.
01B6 43                        INC     BX
01B7 E2FB                      LOOP    LOOP_SORT
01B9 B90B00                    MOV     CX,11
01BC 8D3E4A00                  LEA     DI,SOURCE_STRING
01C0 B82020                    MOV     AX,2020H         ;Blank out the two buffers holding
                                                         names of two entries to be compared.
01C3 F3AB                      REP     STOSW
01C5 8D3E5500                  LEA     DI,COMPARE_STRING
01C9 8D366000                  LEA     SI,INPUT_BUFFER
01CD B90B00                    MOV     CX,11
01D0 F3A4                      REP     MOVSB
01D2 C70639000100              MOV WORD PTR CURRENT_POINTER,1  ;At least two entries.
01D8                  LOOP_CHECK:
01D8 E84900                    CALL    STRING_MOVE
```

```
01DB E87200              CALL    STRING_COMPARE
01DE 762D                JBE     NEXT_ENTRY       ;Entries are in the correct order.
01E0 FF363900            PUSH    CURRENT_POINTER
01E4           LOOP_SWAP:
01E4 8D363B00            LEA     SI,SORT_TABLE
01E8 03363900            ADD     SI,CURRENT_POINTER
01EC 8A04                MOV     AL,[SI]          ;Swap two entries in the buffer only.
01EE 8644FF              XCHG    AL,[SI-1]
01F1 8804                MOV     [SI],AL
01F3 832E390002          SUB WORD PTR CURRENT_POINTER,2  ;Skip the swapped entries.
01F8 720F                JB      EXIT_SWAP
01FA E82700              CALL    STRING_MOVE
01FD E85E00              CALL    STRING_SWAP
0200 FF063900            INC WORD PTR CURRENT_POINTER
0204 E84900              CALL    STRING_COMPARE
0207 77DB                JA      LOOP_SWAP        ;Start next pass of bubble-sort.
0209           EXIT_SWAP:
0209 8F063900            POP     CURRENT_POINTER
020D           NEXT_ENTRY:
020D A13900              MOV     AX,CURRENT_POINTER
0210 40                  INC     AX
0211 3B063700            CMP     AX,NO_ENTRIES
0215 7201                JB      CHECK_NEXT_ENTRY
0217 C3                  RET                      ;Complete sorting.
0218           CHECK_NEXT_ENTRY:
0218 A33900              MOV     CURRENT_POINTER,AX
021B 8D363A00            LEA     SI,SORT_TABLE - 1
021F E81300              CALL    STRING_RESTORE
```

Fig. 8-8. Procedure to sort file names in alphabetical order (continued from page 275).

```
0222 EBB4               JMP SHORT LOOP_CHECK
0224               BUBBLE_SORT ENDP
                   ;
0224               STRING_MOVE PROC NEAR
0224 8D365500           LEA     SI,COMPARE_STRING
0228 8D3E4A00           LEA     DI,SOURCE_STRING
022C B90B00             MOV     CX,11
022F F3A4               REP     MOVSB
0231 8D363B00           LEA     SI,SORT_TABLE   ;Get another file name.
0235               STRING_RESTORE:
0235 03363900           ADD     SI,CURRENT_POINTER
0239 AC                 LODSB
023A B400               MOV     AH,00
023C B10B               MOV     CL,11           ;11 characters per file name.
023E F6E1               MUL     CL
0240 8D366000           LEA     SI,INPUT_BUFFER
0244 03F0               ADD     SI,AX
0246 B90B00             MOV     CX,11
0249 8D3E5500           LEA     DI,COMPARE_STRING ;Get another entry.
024D F3A4               REP     MOVSB
024F C3                 RET
0250               STRING_MOVE ENDP
```

```
                      ;
0250                  STRING_COMPARE PROC NEAR
0250 B90B00                    MOV      CX,11
0253 8D364A00                  LEA      SI,SOURCE_STRING
0257 8D3E5500                  LEA      DI,COMPARE_STRING
025B F3A6                      REPE     CMPSB
025D C3                        RET
025E                  STRING_COMPARE ENDP
                      ;
025E                  STRING_SWAP PROC NEAR
025E B90B00                    MOV      CX,11
0261 8D364A00                  LEA      SI,SOURCE_STRING
0265 8D3E5500                  LEA      DI,COMPARE_STRING
0269                  SWAP_LOOP:
0269 AC                        LODSB
026A 8605                      XCHG     AL,[DI]
026C 8844FF                    MOV      [SI-1],AL
026F 47                        INC      DI
0270 E2F7                      LOOP     SWAP_LOOP
0272 C3                        RET
0273                  STRING_SWAP ENDP
                      ;
0273                  SORT     ENDS
                               END
```

Fig. 8-8. Procedure to sort file names in alphabetical order (continued from page 277).

sorts the file names of a diskette directory on an IBM Personal Computer in alphabetical order. Figure 8-9 illustrates the before and after conditions.

CONVERSION FROM ALGEBRAIC TO REVERSE POLISH

In this section we shall consider a highly practical example that fully utilizes the stack structure of the 8086/8088 microprocessor family. The example is written in the form of a procedure that can be invoked by any 8088 assembly language program. Parameters required to initialize the procedure are assumed to be held in several general registers. The example presents one of the popular techniques to translate an expression written in ordinary algebraic notation (with parentheses and operators specified among the operands of the expression) into the reverse polish notation. In the reverse polish notation, there are never any parentheses, and operators are written after the operands on which they operate.

This notation is very useful in compiler design in the sense that complex equations in high-level languages such as FORTRAN or BASIC can be converted into the equivalent and simpler reverse polish notations so that compact and efficient machine instructions can be generated to perform the functions described by the equations.

The following is an expression written in the polish notation:

AB+C/

The first operator in the notation is the plus sign which implies that the arithmetic operation add is performed on the two operands to the left of the plus sign. The plus sign is the first operator to appear if the expression is scanned in the left-to-right fashion, and thus the addition operation between the operands A and B is carried out first. After completing the addition, the expression continues to be scanned until another operator is encountered, in this case the slash sign. The division operation indicating by the slash sign is carried out to the two quantities preceding it, which now are (A+B) and the operand C. The above polish notation is thus equivalent to the ordinary algebraic expression (A+B)/C.

The procedure listed in Fig. 8-10 performs the translation of an algebraic expression to its reverse polish notation. The parameters required to invoke the procedure are as follows:

1. The SI register points to the starting address of an ASCII string that contains an algebraic expression.
2. The DI register points to the starting address of a reserved area where the output reversed polish notation is stored.
3. The CX register contains the number of characters in the input string that contains the algebraic expression.

The procedure also assumes that the syntax requirements of the ASCII

File Names Before Bubble Sort	File Names After Bubble Sort
DRESSER	APPENDIX
TRW86	CHAPTER3
RAYMOND	COPYN
INTEGER	DRESSER
PARADE	ELECTRONART
COPYN	INTEGER
XEROXLONGST	ORIGINAL
PENGUIN	PARADE
ELECTRONART	PENGUIN
ORIGINAL	RANDOM
RANDOM	RAYMOND
TEMP3	SORT
CHAPTER8	TEMP3
APPENDIX	TRW86
SORT	XEROXLONGST

Fig. 8-9. File names of a diskette directory before and after the bubble sort.

string have been verified by some other procedures. For simplicity, operands are single characters, and only the operators +, −, *, and / are supported in this procedure. Each operator is assigned a priority level to facilitate the conversion. The operators * and / have higher priority than the operators + and −. This reflects the rule that multiply and divide operations take precedence over add and subtract operations. The following algorithm is used in the procedure to implement the conversion.

1. Examine the next character in the input string.
2. If the character is an operand, write it to the output string.
3. If the character is an opening parenthesis, push it on the stack with the priority 0.
4. If the character is an operator, compare its priority with that of the operator at the top of the stack. If its priority is greater, the new operator is pushed on top of the stack. Otherwise, the operator at the top of stack is popped in the ouput string. The comparison is repeated with the new top of stack until an operator with lower priority than the current operator is found at the top of the stack or the stack is empty. Then the current operator is pushed on the top of stack.
5. If the character is a closing parenthesis, all operators on the stack are popped into the output string until an opening parenthesis appears at the top of stack. This parenthesis is simply ignored.
6. If the algebraic expression is completed, any remaining operators

```
0000                RPN   SEGMENT PARA PUBLIC
                          ASSUME CS:RPN,DS:RPN,ES:RPN,SS:Nothing
                    ;
                    ;  [SI]  Starting address of the string that contains the
                    ;        algebraic notations.
                    ;  [DI]  Starting address of the area to hold the output
                    ;        string in Reverse Polish Notation.
                    ;   CX   Number of characters in the input string.
                    ;   DX   Stack Level.
                    ;   BX   Temporary storage.
                    ;   BP   Temporary storage.
                    ;
                    ;
0000 2BD2                    SUB     DX,DX    ;Keep track of the stack level.
0002 AC             LOOP:    LODSB            ;Get a character from the input string.
0003 8BE8                    MOV     BP,AX    ;Save it.
0005 3C2A                    CMP     AL,'*'   ;Check for the multiply operator.
0007 7519                    JNE     CHECKDIV
0009 85D2           MULDIV:  TEST    DX,DX    ;Check if the stack is empty (level 0).
000B 7411                    JE      PUSHSTACK
000D 8BDC           CHECK1:  MOV     BX,SP
000F 803F2A                  CMP BYTE PTR [BX],'*' ;Check for the multiply or
                    ;                               divide operators on the stack.
0012 7405                    JE      POPSTACK
0014 803F2F                  CMP BYTE PTR [BX],'/'
```

```
0017 7505               JNE     PUSHSTACK
0019            POPSTACK:
0019 58                 POP     AX
001A 4A                 DEC     DX
001B AA                 STOSB           ;Write out the operator.
001C EBEF               JMP SHORT CHECK1
001E            PUSHSTACK:
001E 55                 PUSH    BP
001F 42                 INC     DX
0020 E2E0               LOOP    LOOP    ;Process all characters in the input string.
0022            CHECKDIV:
0022 3C2F               CMP     AL,'/'
0024 74E3               JE      MULDIV
0026 3C2B               CMP     AL,'+'
0028 7510               JNE     CHECKSUB
002A 85D2       ADDSUB: TEST    DX,DX   ;Check if the stack is empty.
002C 74F0               JE      PUSHSTACK
002E 8BDC       CHECK2: MOV     BX,SP
0030 803F28             CMP BYTE PTR [BX],'('   ;Check for an opening parenthesis.
0033 74E9               JE      PUSHSTACK
0035 58                 POP     AX
0036 4A                 DEC     DX      ;Adjust the stack level.
0037 AA                 STOSB           ;Write out this operator.
0038 EBF0               JMP SHORT ADDSUB
003A            CHECKSUB:
```

Fig. 8-10. Procedure to convert algebraic expressions into reverse polish notations.

```
003A 3C2D                CMP     AL,'-'   ;Check for the minus operator.
003C 74EC                JE      ADDSUB
003E 3C28                CMP     AL,'('   ;Check for another opening parenthesis.
0040 74DC                JE      PUSHSTACK
0042 3C29                CMP     AL,')'
0044 7509                JNE     OPERAND ;Write out the operands until a closing
                ;                          parenthesis is encountered.
0046 58         POPALL:  POP     AX
0047 4A                  DEC     DX
0048 3C28                CMP     AL,'('
004A 7404                JE      LOOP1
004C AA                  STOSB
004D EBF7                JMP SHORT POPALL
004F            OPERAND:
004F AA                  STOSB            ;Write out the operands.
0050 E2B0       LOOP1:   LOOP    LOOP
0052 8BCA                MOV     CX,DX
0054 85C9                TEST    CX,CX    ;Check if the stack is empty.
0056 7404                JE      RETURN
0058            LOOP2:
0058 58                  POP     AX
0059 AA                  STOSB
005A E2FC                LOOP    LOOP2    ;Write the rest of the stack to output string.
005C            RETURN:
005C C3                  RET
005D            RPN      ENDS
                         END
```

Fig. 8-10. Procedure to convert algebraic expressions into reverse polish notations (continued from page 283).

Algebraic Notation

A + B*C + (D + E)* F

Input String (Algebraic)	**Output String** (Reverse Polish Notations	**Stack** (Top of stack on right)
A+B*C+(D+E)*F	Empty	Empty
+B*C+(D+E)*F	A	Empty
B*C+(D+E)*F	A	+
*C+(D+E)*F	AB	+
C+(D+E)*F	AB	+*
+(D+E)*F	ABC	+*
(D+E)*F	ABC*+	+
D+E)*F	ABC*+	+(
+E)*F	ABC*+D	+(
E)*F	ABC*+D	+(+
)*F	ABC*+DE	+(+
*F	ABC*+DE+	+
F	ABC*+DE+	+*
Empty	ABC*+DE+F	+*
	ABC*+DE+F*+	Empty

Fig. 8-11. Operations performed in the conversion from the algebraic notations to the reverse polish notations.

on top of stack are popped into the output string.

Figure 8-11 summarizes the required operations to convert the following algebraic expression into polish notation.

A + B*C + (D+E)*F

RECURSIVE PROGRAMMING

A procedure that invokes itself either directly or indirectly through CALL instructions is called a recursive procedure. Some high-level programming languages, such as FORTRAN, do not allow recursive procedure calling, namely a procedure that calls itself.

When a recursive procedure is first invoked, its depth of recursion is 1, and the procedure executes itself at level 1. If the depth of recursion of a procedure is N and the procedure calls itself, it descends one level of recursion to level N+1. When the procedure returns (by executing a RET instruction), it ascends one level of recursion. Recursive programming is usually implemented by storing the return address for each level of recursion on the stack during descending and retrieving these return addresses from the stack during ascending. Care must be taken in the design of a recursive procedure in 8088 assembly language to prevent the possibility of

```
0000                 TOWER     SEGMENT
                               ASSUME   CS:TOWER,DS:TOWER,ES:TOWER,SS:TOWER
0000                 MAIN      PROC     NEAR     ;Main program.
0000 9C                        PUSHF
0001 1E                        PUSH     DS
0002 2BC0                      SUB      AX,AX
0004 50                        PUSH     AX
0005 1E                        PUSH     DS
0006 06                        PUSH     ES       ;Save registers to return to DOS later.
0007 8CC8                      MOV      AX,CS
0009 8ED8                      MOV      DS,AX    ;Overlap Code Segment And Data Segment.
000B 89265401                  MOV      SP_SAVE,SP
000F 8C165601                  MOV      SS_SAVE,SS ;Save SS and SP registers.
0013 8EC0                      MOV      ES,AX    ;Overlap Code Segment And Extra Segment.
0015 8ED0                      MOV      SS,AX    ;Overlap Code Segment And Stack Segment.
0017 8D265805                  LEA      SP,TOP_OF_STACK
001B 8D3E5400                  LEA      DI,OUT_AREA  ;Area that contains the required movements.
001F B400                      MOV      AH,00    ;From tower 0.
0021 B001                      MOV      AL,01    ;To tower 1.
0023 B602                      MOV      DH,02    ;Temporary tower 2.
0025 B205                      MOV      DL,05    ;Number of disks to be moved.
0027 E80F00                    CALL     TOWER_HANOI
002A B8FFFF                    MOV      AX,0FFFFH
002D AB                        STOSW             ;Indicator of the end of the sequence.
002E 8E165601                  MOV      SS,SS_SAVE
0032 8B265401                  MOV      SP,SP_SAVE
```

```
0036 07                 POP     ES
0037 1F                 POP     DS
0038 CF                 IRET                ;Return to the Disk Operating System.
0039            MAIN    ENDP
                ;
                TOWER_HANOI PROC NEAR       ;Recursive procedure.
                ;
                ;  AH   Tower number where the disks are move from.
                ;  AL   Tower number where the disks are moved to.
                ;  DH   Tower number to hold the disks temporarily.
                ;  DL   Number of disks to be moved.
                ;
                ; The sequence of movements are generated and terminated by the
                ; hexadecimal number FFFFH. The movements are in the format
                ; To-From, To-From, etc. For example, a sequence
                ;
                ; 01 00 02 00 02 01 means
                ;
                ; Move a disk from tower 0 to tower 1, then move another disk
                ; from tower 0 to tower 2, and then move a disk from tower 1 to tower
                ; 2, etc.
                ;
0039 80FA01             CMP     DL,01   ;Check for the last disk.
003C 7502               JNE     RECURSIVE
003E AB                 STOSW
003F C3                 RET
```

Fig. 8-12. Procedure to solve the Towers of Hanoi problem.

```
0040             RECURSIVE:
0040 50                 PUSH    AX
0041 52                 PUSH    DX
0042 FECA               DEC     DL
0044 86F0               XCHG    DH,AL   ;Move n-1 disks from tower 0 to 2.
0046 E8F0FF             CALL    TOWER_HANOI
0049             FIRST_RETURN:
0049 5A                 POP     DX
004A 58                 POP     AX
004B AB                 STOSW           ;Move 1 disk from tower 0 to 1 after n-1
                 ;                       disks on top of it have been moved to tower 2.
004C 86E6               XCHG    AH,DH   ;Move n-1 disks back to tower 1.
004E FECA               DEC     DL
0050 E8E6FF             CALL    TOWER_HANOI
0053             SECOND_RETURN:
0053 C3                 RET
0054             OUT_AREA DB 256 DUP(0)
0154             TOWER_HANOI ENDP
                 ;
0154             STACK     PROC    NEAR    ;Stack area.
0154 ??          SP_SAVE   DW ?
0156 ??          SS_SAVE   DW ?
0158                       DB 128 DUP('STACK   ')
0558             TOP_OF_STACK DW ?
055A             STACK     ENDP
055A             TOWER     ENDS
                 END
```

Fig. 8-12. Procedure to solve the Towers of Hanoi problem (continued from page 287).

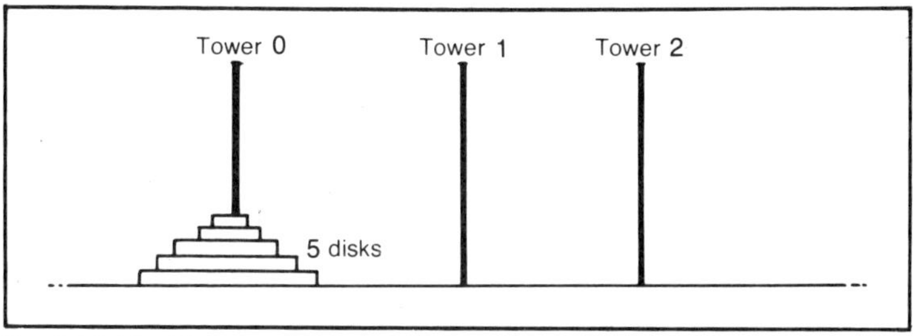

Fig. 8-13. The Towers of Hanoi.

the overflow of the stack (the maximum size of a stack structure in 8088-based systems is 32 K words).

The procedure listed in Fig. 8-12 illustrates a typical problem that is difficult to solve by conventional methods but can be solved effectively by recursive programming. The procedure provides the required solutions to a problem known as the Towers of Hanoi problem. In this problem, five disks A, B, C, D, and E and three towers 0, 1, and 2 are set up as shown in Fig. 8-13. The disks have different perimeters and are stacked on top of one

Movements Generated By The Procedure TOWER_HANOI

```
01 00 02 00 02 01 01 00 00 02 01 02 01 00 02 00
02 01 00 01 00 02 02 01 01 00 02 00 02 01 01 00
00 02 01 02 01 00 00 02 02 01 00 01 00 02 01 02
01 00 02 00 02 01 01 00 00 02 01 02 01 00 FF FF
```

Optimal Movements

From Tower	To Tower	From Tower	To Tower
0	1	2	0
0	2	2	1
1	2	0	1
0	1	2	0
2	0	1	2
2	1	1	0
0	1	2	0
0	2	2	1
1	2	0	1
1	0	0	2
2	0	1	2
1	2	0	1
0	1	2	0
0	2	2	1
1	2	0	1
0	1		

Fig. 8-14. Optimal movements to move five disks from one tower to another in the Towers of Hanoi problem.

another. Disk A is located at the top of the stack of disks and is the smallest disk. Disk E is located at the bottom of the stack and is the largest disk.

The objective is to move all five disks from tower 0 to tower 1 or from tower 0 to tower 2. A legal move consists of removing the top disk from any tower and putting it on another tower, with the restriction that no disk may rest on top of a smaller disk. The principal function of the procedure in Fig. 8-12 is to produce the optimal movements required to move all five disks from one tower to another. This is a typical example when nonrecursive programming does not even seem to provide a solution. The listed procedure solves the problem recursively and the optimal movements generated are stored starting at the memory location MOVEMENT.

Figure 8-14 lists the optimal movements required to move five disks from tower 0 to tower 1, using tower 2 to hold the disks temporarily. With five disks in this example, there is a minimum of 31 movements to move all the disks from one tower to another.

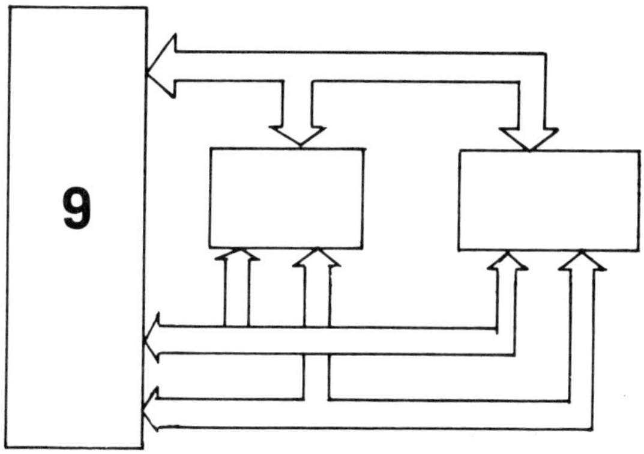

Shift and Rotate

Rotate and shift instructions provide a convenient way to perform manipulation of individual bits in a byte or a word. These instructions can be used by themselves or in conjunction with the logical instructions to modify or extract certain bit patterns in the contents of a register or a memory location.

There are seven instructions in this group which include RCL (Rotate Through Carry Left), RCR (Rotate Through Carry Right), ROL (Rotate Left), ROR (Rotate Right), SHL/SAL (Shift Logical Left/Shift Arithmetic Left), SAR (Shift Arithmetic Right), and SHR (Shift Logical Right). The number of bits to be shifted or rotated can be up to 255. The contents of the CL register are used to specify the number of bit positions to be shifted or rotated. Shift instructions move data sideways within a register or a memory location while rotate instructions move data in a circular fashion. In shift instructions, the movement from right to left is equivalent to a multiplication by a power of 2, and the movement from left to right is equivalent to a division by a power of 2. The shift and rotate functions are illustrated in Fig. 9-1.

The following section presents a brief summary of the principal functions that the shift and rotate instructions perform. Then some programming examples are presented to illustrate possible applications of these instructions.

ROTATE INSTRUCTIONS

The bits in a byte or a word can be rotated. The Carry Flag can also be treated as an extension of the rotate operation. Bits rotated out of a register or a memory location are not lost as in shift operations, but are moved in a

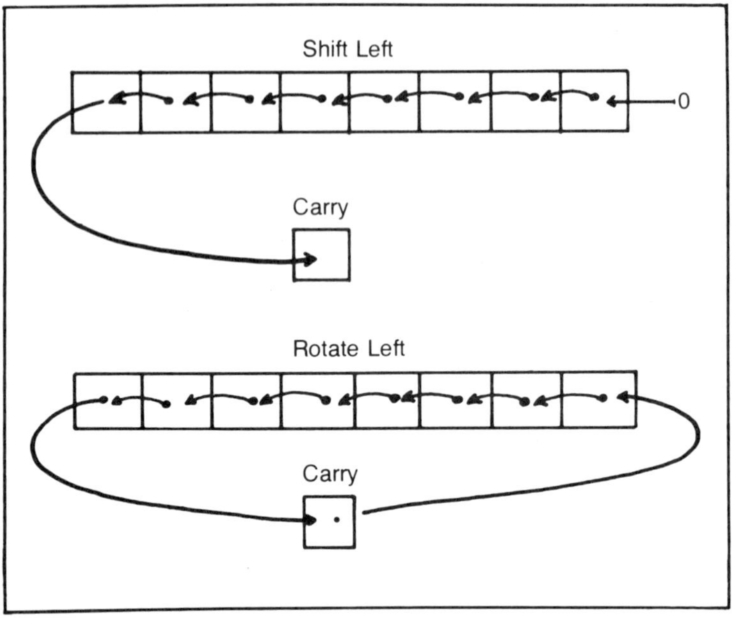

Fig. 9-1. Shift and rotate functions.

circular fashion within the operand, moving out of one end and circling back on the other end. Up to 255 rotations can be performed by specifying a count value in the CL register. If the count value is 1, it is not necessary to use the CL register since the count value can be a part of the instruction itself. Thus the use of the CL register allows the number of bits to be rotated to be changed at execution time.

Rotate instructions affect only the Carry Flag and the Overflow Flag. The Carry Flag always holds the value of the last bit rotated out of an operand. If the number of bits rotated is more than 1, the Overflow Flag is always undefined. If single-bit rotation is performed, the Overflow Flag is set to 1 if the most significant bit (the sign bit) of the operand changes its original value after the rotate operation. Otherwise, the Overflow Flag is cleared to 0 if the sign bit retains its original value.

RCL (Rotate through Carry Left). The instruction rotates the bits in a byte or word operand to the left by one bit or by the number of bits specified in the CL register. The Carry Flag is treated as an extension of the operand. The content of the Carry Flag is rotated into the least significant bit of the destination operand, and itself is replaced by the most significant bit of the destination operand.

RCR (Rotate through Carry Right). This instruction rotates the bits in a byte or word operand to the right by one bit or by the number of bits specified in the CL register. The Carry Flag is treated as an extension of the operand. The content of the Carry Flag is rotated into the most significant bit of the destination operand, and itself is replaced by the least significant bit of the destination operand.

ROL (Rotate Left). This instruction rotates the contents of a byte or word operand by one bit or by the number of bits specified in the CL register toward the left side (toward the most significant bit).

ROR (Rotate Right). This instruction rotates the contents of a byte or word operand by one bit or by the number of bits specified in the CL register toward the right side (toward the least significant bit).

SHIFT INSTRUCTIONS

The bits in a byte or a word can be shifted arithmetically or logically. Up to 255 shifts in either left or right direction can be performed by specifying a count value in the CL register. If the count value is 1, it can be specified as a part of the instruction itself. The use of the CL register allows the shift count to be variable during program execution.

Shift instructions affect the flags as follows. The Auxiliary Carry Flag is always undefined after a shift instruction is executed. The Parity Flag, the Sign Flag, and the Zero Flag are updated normally as in other logical instructions. The Carry Flag always holds the last bit shifted out of the destination operand. If the shift count is more than 1, the Overflow Flag is always undefined. If the shift count is 1, the Overflow Flag is set to 1 if the value of the most significant bit (the sign bit) is changed by the shift operation. Otherwise, the Overflow Flag is cleared to 0 if the sign bit retains its original value.

SHL/SAL (Shift Logical Left/Shift Arithmetic Left). These are two mnemonics of the same instruction. The contents of a byte or word operand are shifted left by one bit or by the number of bits specified in the CL register. Zeros are shifted in on the right (the position of the least significant bit).

SAR (Shift Arithmetic Right). This instruction shifts the bits in a byte or word operand to the right by one bit or by the number of bits specified in the CL register. The value of the most significant bit (the sign bit) is duplicated and shifted in on the left. Thus the sign bit of the original operand does not change in this shift operation.

SHR (Shift Logical Right). This instruction shifts the bits in a byte or word operand to the right by one bit or by the number of bits specified in the CL register. Zeros are shifted in on the left (the position of the most significant bit or the sign bit).

COUNTING 1-BITS IN A WORD

In this simple example, the number of 1 bits in a word is counted. This can be done very easily with the use of shift instructions. The procedure listed in Fig. 9-2 performs the counting of the 1-bits. The DX register is used as a counter. The AX register holds the word that contains the bits to be counted. Each bit is moved into the least significant bit position of the AX register, from where it is added to the contents of the DX register. Thus

```
0000             SHIFT    PROC   NEAR      ;Procedure to count 1-bits by SHIFT instruction.
0000 2BD2                 SUB    DX,DX     ;Set the bit count to 0.
0002 B91000               MOV    CX,16     ;Number of iterations.
0005 8BD8        COUNT:   MOV    BX,AX
0007 250100               AND    AX,0001H  ;Look at the least significant bit.
000A 03D0                 ADD    DX,AX     ;Add this bit to the counter.
000C 8BC3                 MOV    AX,BX
000E D1E8                 SHR    AX,1      ;Get next bit to the bit position 0.
0010 E2F3                 LOOP   COUNT
0012 C3                   RET
0013             SHIFT    ENDP
```

Fig. 9-2. Procedure to count the 1-bits in a word using shift instructions.

```
0000             ROTATE   PROC   NEAR      ;Procedure to count the 1-bits using ROTATE instructions.
0000 2BD2                 SUB    DX,DX     ;Set the bit count to 0.
0002 B91000               MOV    CX,16     ;Number of iterations.
0005             COUNT_LOOP:
0005 D1C0                 ROL    AX,1      ;Get the bit into the Carry Flag.
0007 7301                 JNC    BIT0      ;Check for bit 0 or 1.
0009 42                   INC    DX        ;Keep counting the 1-bits.
000A E2F9        BIT0:    LOOP    COUNT_LOOP
000C C3                   RET
000D             ROTATE   ENDP
```

Fig. 9-3. Procedure to count the 1-bits in a word using rotate instructions.

each 1-bit is added, forming the count. The 0-bits are also added in the process, but of course they do not affect the sum, and it is much easier to add them rather than to provide codes to decide not to. Since there are sixteen bits in a word, the loop in this example will iterate sixteen times to achieve the final result.

The procedure listed in Fig. 9-3 also performs the counting of the number of 1-bits in a word, but uses rotate instructions instead of shift instructions. The DX register is again used as a counter to hold the number of 1-bits. Each time a rotation is performed, the content of the Carry Flag indicates whether the last rotated bit is 0 or 1. Thus this can be used to update the bit count in the DX register. The procedure in this example also performs sixteen iterations to achieve the result.

DECODING A MACHINE INSTRUCTION

After an assembly language program is translated into machine language by the assembler, an object file is created that contains the actual machine instructions to perform the desired task. If the contents of the object file are to be displayed on an input/output device such as a printer or a video terminal, strings of hexadecimal digits representing the actual machine instructions are displayed instead of those meaningful mnemonics that are used in the original source program. In the development of new assembly language programs, if small modifications to the generated machine codes are desired, it is sometimes quicker and more convenient to update the object file directly rather than to go through the process of editing the source program, and reassembling the program after the corrections have been made.

It is quite difficult to work directly with the hexadecimal digits representing the machine instructions, however. Also it is extremely important that the new changes to the object codes can be verified to make sure that the new object codes introduced to the object file are valid machine instructions. Thus it is desirable to have a facility to convert the hexadecimal representations of actual machine instructions at a specific memory location to their equivalent mnemonics in assembly language. The process is known as unassembling the object codes. This is possible since the bit patterns of each byte of the object codes can uniquely identify a machine instruction and its associated addressing modes. If the machine instruction contains more than one byte, the unassembling process is valid only if the memory location containing the starting byte of the instruction is known.

The following programming example attempts to identify the mnemonic of an instruction that belongs to a group of instructions that can operate with immediate data values. In 8088 assembly language, this group of instructions includes ADD (Addition), OR (Logical OR), ADC (Add With Carry), SBB (Subtract With Borrow), XOR (Exclusive-OR), and CMP (Compare). The first byte of the actual machine instruction representing this group has a hexadecimal value between 80 and 83. The second byte which is the addressing mode byte can help to identify the particular instruction in the group. The bit pattern of the bit positions 3, 4, and 5 of the second byte that defines the mnemonic of the instruction in assembly language can be illustrated as follows.

Address Mode Byte	Corresponding Mnemonics
Mod 000 Rm	ADD
Mod 001 Rm	OR
Mod 010 Rm	ADC
Mod 011 Rm	SBB
Mod 100 Rm	AND
Mod 101 Rm	SUB
Mod 110 Rm	XOR
Mod 111 Rm	CMP

The Mod and Rm fields of the addressing mode bytes are covered in Chapter 2. The procedure listed in Fig. 9-4 assumes that the bit patterns of the addressing mode byte are held in the AL register. It then stores the required corresponding instruction mnemonics to the memory locations addressed by the DI register. Shift instructions are used in the procedure to accomplish the decoding process.

CONSTRUCTING A SEGMENT OVERRIDE PREFIX

In 8088-based microcomputers, the memory space is viewed as a group of 64 K-byte logical segments. There are four segment registers named CS, DS, ES, and SS that uniquely identify the current code segment, data segment, extra segment, and stack segment in the computer memory, respectively. These segments may or may not overlap one another.

The offset address of a memory reference using the SI register as a pointer is always taken relative to the data segment whose base address is defined by the contents of the Data Segment register. It is possible to direct the 8088 microprocessor to take this address to be an offset address relative to any of the four currently defined segments in memory by the use of a segment prefix. In machine language, a segment prefix byte can be defined and illustrated as follows:

Segment Prefix Byte 0 0 1 X X 1 1 0

XX is two bits that identify the segment which the offset address is taken relative to. The combination of the XX bits is descriped as follows:

Pattern Of XX Bits	Corresponding Segment
00	ES (Extra Segment)
01	CS (Code Segment)
10	SS (Stack Segment)
11	DS (Data Segment)

```
0000               DECODE    PROC    NEAR          ;Procedure to decode a machine instruction.
0000 2438                    AND     AL,00111000B  ;Retrieve the bits in positions 3,4,and 5.
0002 B103                    MOV     CL,3          ;Number of shifts.
0004 D2E8                    SHR     AL,CL         ;Shift the bit pattern to the right end.
0006 F6E1                    MUL     CL            ;Offset to mnemonic table.
0008 8D361300                LEA     SI,TABLE
000C 03F0                    ADD     SI,AX         ;SI points to the first character of the mnemonic.
000E B500                    MOV     CH,00
0010 F3A4                    REP     MOVSB         ;Write out the instruction mnemonics.
0012 C3                      RET
0013               TABLE     DB   'ADD','OR ','ADC','SBB'
001F                         DB   'AND','SUB','XOR','CMP'
002B               DECODE    ENDP
```

Fig. 9-4. Procedure to decode a machine instruction.

```
MOV  AX,ES:NEXT_LOCATION         ;Override with Extra Segment Prefix.

CMP  DI,CS:[SI]                  ;Override with Code Segment Prefix.

TEST BYTE PTR SS:[BP+1234H],01   ;Override with Stack Segment Prefix.

ADD  DL,DS:[DI+02]               ;Override with Data Segment Prefix.
```

Fig. 9-5. Coding examples of segment prefixes in 8088 assembly language.

```
0000               ENCODE      PROC     NEAR          ;Procedure to construct the segment prefix byte.
0000 50                        PUSH     AX            ;Save original contents of AX.
0001 FC                        CLD                    ;Clear the Direction Flag to 0.
0002 B90400                    MOV      CX,4          ;Scan four possible segment prefixes.
0005 8D3E1D00                  LEA      DI,TABLE      ;Table contains the segment name.
0009 8BD7                      MOV      DX,DI         ;Starting address of the table.
000B F2AF                      REPNE    SCASW         ;Scan the prefixes for a match.
000D 2BFA                      SUB      DI,DX
000F 8BC7                      MOV      AX,DI
0011 48                        DEC      AX
0012 48                        DEC      AX            ;XX bit pattern.
0013 D0E0                      SHL      AL,1
0015 D0E0                      SHL      AL,1          ;Move the XX bit pattern to proper position.
0017 0C26                      OR       AL,00100110B  ;Construct the segment prefix byte.
0019 8AD0                      MOV      DL,AL
001B 58                        POP  AX                ;Restore original contents of AX.
001C C3                        RET
001D               TABLE       DB   'ES','CS','SS','DS'
0025               ENCODE      ENDP
```

Fig. 9-6. Procedure to construct the segment prefix byte.

In assembly language, the name of a segment register and a colon are attached in front of the source or destination operands of an instruction to specify the appropriate override segment prefix. Figure 9-5 shows several examples of assembly language statements that contain segment prefixes. The procedure listed in Fig. 9-6 performs the part of a 8088 assembler that converts the segment prefix mnemonic to its corresponding representation in actual machine codes. The procedure assumes that the AX register holds the segment prefix name as ASCII characters. It then constructs the segment prefix byte and places the result in the DL register. Shift instructions are used in the procedure to accomplish the translation.

Appendix A
ASCII and EBCDIC Conversion Tables

IBM Standard 8-bit EBCDIC Codes

HEX LSD	MSD BITS	0	1	2	3	4	5	6	7	8	9	A	B	C	D	E	F
0	0000	NUL	DLE	DS		SP	&	-						{	}	/	0
1	0001	SOH	DC1	SOS				/		a	j	~		A	J		1
2	0010	STX	DC2	FS	SYN					b	k	s		B	K	S	2
3	0011	ETX	TM							c	1	t		C	L	T	3
4	0100	PF	RES	BYP	PN					d	m	u		D	M	U	4
5	0101	HT	NL	LF	RS					e	n	v		E	N	V	5
6	0110	LC	BS	ETB	UC					f	o	w		F	O	W	6
7	0111	DEL	IL	ESC	EOT					g	p	x		G	P	X	7
8	1000	GE	CAN							h	q	y		H	Q	Y	8
9	1001	RLF	EM						`	i	r	z		I	R	Z	9
A	1010	SMM	CC	SM		c	!	¦	:								
B	1011	VT	CU1	CU2	CU3	.	$	,	#								
C	1100	FF	IFS		DC4	<	*	%	@								
D	1101	CR	IGS	ENQ	NAK	(	)	_	'								
E	1110	SO	IRS	ACK		+	;	>	=								
F	1111	SI	IUS	BEL	SUB	|	¬	?	"								EO

Control Character Representations

ACK Acknowledge
BEL Bell
BS Backspace
BYP Bypass
CAN Cancel
CC Cursor Control
CR Carriage Return
CU1 Customer Use 1
CU2 Customer Use 2
CU3 Customer Use 3
DC1 Device Control 1
DC2 Device Control 2
DC4 Device Control 4
DEL Delete
DLE Data Link Escape
DS Digit Select
EM End of Medium
ENQ Enquiry
EO Eight Ones
EOT End of Transmission
ESC Escape
ETB End of Transmission Block
ETX End of Text
FF Form Feed
FS Field Separator
GE Graphic Escape
HT Horizontal Tab
IFS Interchange File Separator
IGS Interchange Group Separator
IL Idle
IRS Interchange Record Separator
US Interchange Unit Separator
LC Lower Case
LF Line Feed
NAK Negative Acknowledge
NL New Line
NUL Null
PF Punch Off
PN Punch On
RES Restore
RLF Referse LF
RS Reader Stop
SI Shift In
SM Set Mode
SMM Start Manual Message
SO Shift Out
SOH Start Of Heading
SOS Start Of Significance
SP Space
STX Start of Text
SUB Substitute
SYN Synchronous Idle
TM Tape Mark
UC Upper Case
VT Vertical Tab

ASCII Codes

HEX LSD	MSD BITS	0 000	1 001	2 010	3 011	4 100	5 101	6 110	7 111
0	0000	NUL	DLE	SP	0	@	P	‵	p
1	0001	SOH	DC1	!	1	A	Q	a	q
2	0010	STX	DC2	"	2	B	R	b	r
3	0011	ETX	DC3	#	3	C	S	c	s
4	0100	EOT	DC4	$	4	D	T	d	t
5	0101	ENQ	NAK	%	5	E	U	e	u
6	0110	ACK	SYN	&	6	F	V	f	v
7	0111	BEL	ETB	'	7	G	W	g	w
8	1000	BS	CAN	(	8	H	X	h	x
9	1001	HT	EM	)	9	I	Y	i	y
A	1010	LF	SUB	*	:	J	Z	j	z
B	1011	VT	ESC	+	;	K	[	k	{
C	1100	FF	FS	,	<	L	\	1	¦
D	1101	CR	GS	–	=	M	]	m	}
E	1110	SO	RS	.	>	N		n	~
F	1111	SI	US	/	?	O	_	o	DEL

Control Character Representations

NUL	Null	DLE	Data Link Escape
SOH	Start Of Heading	DC	Device Control
STX	Start Of Text	NAK	Negative Acknowledge
ETX	End Of Text	SYN	Synchronous Idle
EOT	End Of Transmission	ETB	End Of Transmission Block
ENQ	Enquiry	CAN	Cancel
ACK	Acknowledge	EM	End Of Medium
BEL	Bell	SUB	Substitute
BS	Backspace	ESC	Escape
HT	Horizontal Tabulation	FS	File Separator
LF	Line Feed	GS	Group Separator
VT	Vertical Tabulation	RS	Record Separator
FF	Form Feed	US	Unit Separator
CR	Carriage Return	SP	Space (Blank)
SO	Shift Out	DEL	Delete
SI	Shift In		

Appendix B

8086/8088 Machine Instruction Encoding and Decoding Guide

(reprinted by permission from Intel)

Table B-1. Key to Machine Instruction Encoding and Decoding.

IDENTIFIER	EXPLANATION
MOD	Mode field
REG	Register field
R/M	Register/Memory field
SR	Segment register code: 00=ES, 01=CS, 10=SS, 11=DS.
W, S, D, V, Z	Single-bit instruction fields
DATA-8	8-bit immediate constant.
DATA-SX	8-bit immediate value that is automatically sign-extended to 16-bits before use.
DATA-LO	Low-order byte of 16-bit immediate constant.
DATA-HI	High-order byte of 16-bit immediate constant.
(DISP-LO)	Low-order byte of optional 8- or 16-bit unsigned displacement; MOD indicates if present.
(DISP-HI)	High-order byte of optional 16-bit unsigned displacement; MOD indicates if present.
IP-LO	Low-order byte of new IP value.
IP-HI	High-order byte of new IP value
CS-LO	Low-order byte of new CS value.
CS-HI	High-order byte of new CS value.
IP-INC8	8-bit signed increment to instruction pointer.
IP-INC-LO	Low-order byte of signed 16-bit instruction pointer increment.
IP-INC-HI	High-order byte of signed 16-bit instruction pointer increment.
ADDR-LO	Low-order byte of direct address (offset) of memory operand; EA not calculated.
ADDR-HI	High-order byte of direct address (offset) of memory operand; EA not calculated.
——	Bits may contain any value.
XXX	First 3 bits of ESC opcode.
YYY	Second 3 bits of ESC opcode.
REG8	8-bit general register operand.
REG16	16-bit general register operand.
MEM8	8-bit memory operand (any addressing mode).
MEM16	16-bit memory operand (any addressing mode).
IMMED8	8-bit immediate operand.
IMMED16	16-bit immediate operand.
SEGREG	Segment register operand.
DEST-STR8	Byte string addressed by DI.

Table B-1 Key to Machine Instruction Encoding and Decoding (continued).

IDENTIFIER	EXPLANATION
SRC-STR8	Byte string addressed by SI.
DEST-STR16	Word string addressed by DI.
SRC-STR16	Word string addressed by SI.
SHORT-LABEL	Label within ±127 bytes of instruction.
NEAR-PROC	Procedure in current code segment.
FAR-PROC	Procedure in another code segment.
NEAR-LABEL	Label in current code segment but farther than −128 to +127 bytes from instruction.
FAR-LABEL	Label in another code segment.
SOURCE-TABLE	XLAT translation table addressed by BX.
OPCODE	ESC opcode operand.
SOURCE	ESC register or memory operand.

Table B-2. 8086 Instruction Encoding.

DATA TRANSFER	7 6 5 4 3 2 1 0	7 6 5 4 3 2 1 0	7 6 5 4 3 2 1 0	7 6 5 4 3 2 1 0	7 6 5 4 3 2 1 0	7 6 5 4 3 2 1 0
MOV = Move:						
Register/memory to/from register	1 0 0 0 1 0 d w	mod reg r/m	(DISP-LO)	(DISP-HI)		
Immediate to register/memory	1 1 0 0 0 1 1 w	mod 0 0 0 r/m	(DISP-LO)	(DISP-HI)	data	data if w = 1
Immediate to register	1 0 1 1 w reg	data	data if w = 1			
Memory to accumulator	1 0 1 0 0 0 0 w	addr-lo	addr-hi			
Accumulator to memory	1 0 1 0 0 0 1 w	addr-lo	addr-hi			
Register/memory to segment register	1 0 0 0 1 1 1 0	mod 0 SR r/m	(DISP-LO)	(DISP-HI)		
Segment register to register/memory	1 0 0 0 1 1 0 0	mod 0 SR r/m	(DISP-LO)	(DISP-HI)		
PUSH = Push:						
Register/memory	1 1 1 1 1 1 1 1	mod 1 1 0 r/m	(DISP-LO)	(DISP-HI)		
Register	0 1 0 1 0 reg					
Segment register	0 0 0 reg 1 1 0					
POP = Pop:						
Register/memory	1 0 0 0 1 1 1 1	mod 0 0 0 r/m	(DISP-LO)	(DISP-HI)		
Register	0 1 0 1 1 reg					
Segment register	0 0 0 reg 1 1 1					

Table B-2. 8086 Instruction Encoding (continued).

DATA TRANSFER (Cont'd.)						
XCHG = **Exchange:**	7 6 5 4 3 2 1 0	7 6 5 4 3 2 1 0	7 6 5 4 3 2 1 0	7 6 5 4 3 2 1 0	7 6 5 4 3 2 1 0	7 6 5 4 3 2 1 0
Register/memory with register	1 0 0 0 0 1 1 w	mod reg r/m	(DISP-LO)	(DISP-HI)		
Register with accumulator	1 0 0 1 0 reg					
IN = **Input from:**						
Fixed port	1 1 1 0 0 1 0 w	DATA-8				
Variable port	1 1 1 0 1 1 0 w					
OUT = **Output to:**						
Fixed port	1 1 1 0 0 1 1 w	DATA-8				
Variable port	1 1 1 0 1 1 1 w					
XLAT = Translate byte to AL	1 1 0 1 0 1 1 1					
LEA = Load EA to register	1 0 0 0 1 1 0 1	mod reg r/m	(DISP-LO)	(DISP-HI)		
LDS = Load pointer to DS	1 1 0 0 0 1 0 1	mod reg r/m	(DISP-LO)	(DISP-HI)		
LES = Load pointer to ES	1 1 0 0 0 1 0 0	mod reg r/m	(DISP-LO)	(DISP-HI)		
LAHF = Load AH with flags	1 0 0 1 1 1 1 1					
SAHF = Store AH into flags	1 0 0 1 1 1 1 0					
PUSHF = Push flags	1 0 0 1 1 1 0 0					
POPF = Pop flags	1 0 0 1 1 1 0 1					

Table B-2. 8086 Instruction Encoding (continued).

Instruction	Byte 1	Byte 2	Byte 3	Byte 4	Byte 5	Byte 6
ARITHMETIC						
ADD = Add:						
Reg/memory with register to either	0 0 0 0 0 0 d w	mod reg r/m	(DISP-LO)	(DISP-HI)		
Immediate to register/memory	1 0 0 0 0 0 s w	mod 0 0 0 r/m	(DISP-LO)	(DISP-HI)	data	data if s: w=01
Immediate to accumulator	0 0 0 0 0 1 0 w	data	data if w=1			
ADC = Add with carry:						
Reg/memory with register to either	0 0 0 1 0 0 d w	mod reg r/m	(DISP-LO)	(DISP-HI)		
Immediate to register/memory	1 0 0 0 0 0 s w	mod 0 1 0 r/m	(DISP-LO)	(DISP-HI)	data	data if s: w=01
Immediate to accumulator	0 0 0 1 0 1 0 w	data	data if w=1			
INC = Increment:						
Register/memory	1 1 1 1 1 1 1 w	mod 0 0 0 r/m	(DISP-LO)	(DISP-HI)		
Register	0 1 0 0 0 reg					
AAA = ASCII adjust for add	0 0 1 1 0 1 1 1					
DAA = Decimal adjust for add	0 0 1 0 0 1 1 1					

Table B-2. 8086 Instruction Encoding (continued).

ARITHMETIC (Cont'd.)						
SUB = Subtract:	7 6 5 4 3 2 1 0	7 6 5 4 3 2 1 0	7 6 5 4 3 2 1 0	7 6 5 4 3 2 1 0	7 6 5 4 3 2 1 0	7 6 5 4 3 2 1 0
Reg/memory and register to either	0 0 1 0 1 0 d w	mod reg r/m	(DISP-LO)	(DISP-HI)		
Immediate from register/memory	1 0 0 0 0 0 s w	mod 1 0 1 r/m	(DISP-LO)	(DISP-HI)	data	data if s: w=01
Immediate from accumulator	0 0 1 0 1 1 0 w	data	data if w=1			
SBB = Subtract with borrow:						
Reg/memory and register to either	0 0 0 1 1 0 d w	mod reg r/m	(DISP-LO)	(DISP-HI)		
Immediate from register/memory	1 0 0 0 0 0 s w	mod 0 1 1 r/m	(DISP-LO)	(DISP-HI)	data	data if s: w=01
Immediate from accumulator	0 0 0 1 1 1 0 w	data	data if w=1			
DEC Decrement:						
Register/memory	1 1 1 1 1 1 1 w	mod 0 0 1 r/m	(DISP-LO)	(DISP-HI)		
Register	0 1 0 0 1 reg					
NEG Change sign	1 1 1 1 0 1 1 w	mod 0 1 1 r/m	(DISP-LO)	(DISP-HI)		

Table B-2. 8086 Instruction Encoding (continued).

Instruction	Byte 1	Byte 2	Byte 3	Byte 4	Byte 5	Byte 6
CMP = Compare:						
Register/memory and register	0 0 1 1 1 0 d w	mod reg r/m	(DISP-LO)	(DISP-HI)		
Immediate with register/memory	1 0 0 0 0 0 s w	mod 1 1 1 r/m	(DISP-LO)	(DISP-HI)	data	data if s: w=1
Immediate with accumulator	0 0 1 1 1 1 0 w	data				
AAS ASCII adjust for subtract	0 0 1 1 1 1 1 1					
DAS Decimal adjust for subtract	0 0 1 0 1 1 1 1					
MUL Multiply (unsigned)	1 1 1 1 0 1 1 w	mod 1 0 0 r/m	(DISP-LO)	(DISP-HI)		
IMUL Integer multiply (signed)	1 1 1 1 0 1 1 w	mod 1 0 1 r/m	(DISP-LO)	(DISP-HI)		
AAM ASCII adjust for multiply	1 1 0 1 0 1 0 0	0 0 0 0 1 0 1 0	(DISP-LO)	(DISP-HI)		
DIV Divide (unsigned)	1 1 1 1 0 1 1 w	mod 1 1 0 r/m	(DISP-LO)	(DISP-HI)		
IDIV Integer divide (signed)	1 1 1 1 0 1 1 w	mod 1 1 1 r/m	(DISP-LO)	(DISP-HI)		
AAD ASCII adjust for divide	1 1 0 1 0 1 0 1	0 0 0 0 1 0 1 0	(DISP-LO)	(DISP-HI)		
CBW Convert byte to word	1 0 0 1 1 0 0 0					
CWD Convert word to double word	1 0 0 1 1 0 0 1					
LOGIC						
NOT Invert	1 1 1 1 0 1 1 w	mod 0 1 0 r/m	(DISP-LO)	(DISP-HI)		
SHL/SAL Shift logical/arithmetic left	1 1 0 1 0 0 v w	mod 1 0 0 r/m	(DISP-LO)	(DISP-HI)		
SHR Shift logical right	1 1 0 1 0 0 v w	mod 1 0 1 r/m	(DISP-LO)	(DISP-HI)		
SAR Shift arithmetic right	1 1 0 1 0 0 v w	mod 1 1 1 r/m	(DISP-LO)	(DISP-HI)		
ROL Rotate left	1 1 0 1 0 0 v w	mod 0 0 0 r/m	(DISP-LO)	(DISP-HI)		

Table B-2. 8086 Instruction Encoding (continued).

	7 6 5 4 3 2 1 0	7 6 5 4 3 2 1 0	7 6 5 4 3 2 1 0	7 6 5 4 3 2 1 0	7 6 5 4 3 2 1 0	7 6 5 4 3 2 1 0
LOGIC (Cont'd.)						
ROR Rotate right	1 1 0 1 0 0 v w	mod 0 0 1 r/m	(DISP-LO)	(DISP-HI)		
RCL Rotate through carry flag left	1 1 0 1 0 0 v w	mod 0 1 0 r/m	(DISP-LO)	(DISP-HI)		
RCR Rotate through carry right	1 1 0 1 0 0 v w	mod 0 1 1 r/m	(DISP-LO)	(DISP-HI)		
AND = And:						
Reg/memory with register to either	0 0 1 0 0 0 d w	mod reg r/m	(DISP-LO)	(DISP-HI)		
Immediate to register/memory	1 0 0 0 0 0 0 w	mod 1 0 0 r/m	(DISP-LO)	(DISP-HI)	data	data if w=1
Immediate to accumulator	0 0 1 0 0 1 0 w	data	data if w=1			
TEST = And function to flags no result:						
Register/memory and register	0 0 0 1 0 0 d w	mod reg r/m	(DISP-LO)	(DISP-HI)		
Immediate data and register/memory	1 1 1 1 0 1 1 w	mod 0 0 0 r/m	(DISP-LO)	(DISP-HI)	data	data if w=1
Immediate data and accumulator	1 0 1 0 1 0 0 w	data				

Table B-2. 8086 Instruction Encoding (continued).

Instruction	Byte 1	Byte 2	Byte 3	Byte 4	Byte 5	Byte 6
OR = Or:						
Reg/memory and register to either	0 0 0 0 1 0 d w	mod reg r/m	(DISP-LO)	(DISP-HI)		
Immediate to register/memory	1 0 0 0 0 0 0 w	mod 0 0 1 r/m	(DISP-LO)	(DISP-HI)	data	data if w=1
Immediate to accumulator	0 0 0 0 1 1 0 w	data	data if w=1			
XOR = Exclusive or:						
Reg/memory and register to either	0 0 1 1 0 0 d w	mod reg r/m	(DISP-LO)	(DISP-HI)		
Immediate to register/memory	0 0 1 1 0 1 0 w	data	(DISP-LO)	(DISP-HI)	data	data if w=1
Immediate to accumulator	0 0 1 1 0 1 0 w	data	data if w=1			
STRING MANIPULATION						
REP = Repeat	1 1 1 1 0 0 1 z					
MOVS = Move byte/word	1 0 1 0 0 1 0 w					
CMPS = Compare byte/word	1 0 1 0 0 1 1 w					
SCAS = Scan byte/word	1 0 1 0 1 1 1 w					
LODS = Load byte/wd to AL/AX	1 0 1 0 1 1 0 w					
STDS = Stor byte/wd from AL/A	1 0 1 0 1 0 1 w					

Table B-2. 8086 Instruction Encoding (continued).

	7 6 5 4 3 2 1 0	7 6 5 4 3 2 1 0	7 6 5 4 3 2 1 0	7 6 5 4 3 2 1 0	7 6 5 4 3 2 1 0	7 6 5 4 3 2 1 0
CONTROL TRANSFER						
CALL = Call:						
Direct within segment	1 1 1 0 1 0 0 0	IP-INC-LO	IP-INC-HI			
Indirect within segment	1 1 1 1 1 1 1 1	mod 0 1 0 r/m	(DISP-LO)	(DISP-HI)		
Direct intersegment	1 0 0 1 1 0 1 0	IP-lo	IP-hi			
		CS-lo	CS-hi			
Indirect intersegment	1 1 1 1 1 1 1 1	mod 0 1 1 r/m	(DISP-LO)	(DISP-HI)		
JMP = Unconditional Jump:						
Direct within segment	1 1 1 0 1 0 0 1	IP-INC-LO	IP-INC-HI			
Direct within segment-short	1 1 1 0 1 0 1 1	IP-INC8				
Indirect within segment	1 1 1 1 1 1 1 1	mod 1 0 0 r/m	(DISP-LO)	(DISP-HI)		
Direct intersegment	1 1 1 0 1 0 1 0	IP-lo	IP-hi			
		CS-lo	CS-hi			
Indirect intersegment	1 1 1 1 1 1 1 1	mod 1 0 1 r/m	(DISP-LO)	(DISP-HI)		

Table B-2. 8086 Instruction Encoding (continued).

Instruction	Byte 1	Byte 2	Byte 3
RET = Return from CALL: Within segment	1 1 0 0 0 0 1 1		
Within seg adding immed to SP	1 1 0 0 0 0 1 0	data-lo	data-hi
Intersegment	1 1 0 0 1 0 1 1		
Intersegment adding immediate to SP	1 1 0 0 1 0 1 0	data-lo	data-hi
JE/JZ = Jump on equal/zero	0 1 1 1 0 1 0 0	IP-INC8	
JL/JNGE = Jump on less/not greater or equal	0 1 1 1 1 1 0 0	IP-INC8	
JLE/JNG = Jump on less or equal/not greater	0 1 1 1 1 1 1 0	IP-INC8	
JB/JNAE = Jump on below/not above or equal	0 1 1 1 0 0 1 0	IP-INC8	
JBE/JNA = Jump on below or equal/not above	0 1 1 1 0 1 1 0	IP-INC8	
JP/JPE = Jump on parity/parity even	0 1 1 1 1 0 1 0	IP-INC8	
JO = Jump on overflow	0 1 1 1 0 0 0 0	IP-INC8	
JS = Jump on sign	0 1 1 1 1 0 0 0	IP-INC8	
JNE/JNZ = Jump on not equal/not zer0	0 1 1 1 0 1 0 1	IP-INC8	
JNL/JGE = Jump on not less/greater or equal	0 1 1 1 1 1 0 1	IP-INC8	
JNLE/JG = Jump on not less or equal/greater	0 1 1 1 1 1 1 1	IP-INC8	
JNB/JAE = Jump on not below/above or equal	0 1 1 1 0 0 1 1	IP-INC8	
JNBE/JA = Jump on not below or equal/above	0 1 1 1 0 1 1 1	IP-INC8	
JNP/JPO = Jump on not par/par odd	0 1 1 1 1 0 1 1	IP-INC8	
JNO = Jump on not overflow	0 1 1 1 0 0 0 1	IP-INC8	

Table B-2. 8086 Instruction Encoding (continued).

CONTROL TRANSFER (Cont'd.)						
RET = Return from CALL:	7 6 5 4 3 2 1 0	7 6 5 4 3 2 1 0	7 6 5 4 3 2 1 0	7 6 5 4 3 2 1 0	7 6 5 4 3 2 1 0	7 6 5 4 3 2 1 0
JNS = Jump on not sign	0 1 1 1 1 0 0 1	IP-INC8				
LOOP = Loop CX times	1 1 1 0 0 0 1 0	IP-INC8				
LOOPZ/LOOPE = Loop while zero/equal	1 1 1 0 0 0 0 1	IP-INC8				
LOOPNZ/LOOPNE = Loop while not zero/equal	1 1 1 0 0 0 0 0	IP-INC8				
JCXZ = Jump on CX zero	1 1 1 0 0 0 1 1	IP-INC8				
INT = Interrupt:						
Type specified	1 1 0 0 1 1 0 1	DATA-8				
Type 3	1 1 0 0 1 1 0 0					
INTO = Interrupt on overflow	1 1 0 0 1 1 1 0					
IRET = Interrupt return	1 1 0 0 1 1 1 1					

Table B-2. 8086 Instruction Encoding (continued).

PROCESSOR CONTROL

Instruction	Byte 1	Byte 2	Byte 3	Byte 4
CLC = Clear carry	1 1 1 1 1 0 0 0			
CMC = Complement carry	1 1 1 1 0 1 0 1			
STC = Set carry	1 1 1 1 1 0 0 1			
CLD = Clear direction	1 1 1 1 1 1 0 0			
STD = Set direction	1 1 1 1 1 1 0 1			
CLI = Clear interrupt	1 1 1 1 1 0 1 0			
STI = Set interrupt	1 1 1 1 1 0 1 1			
HLT = Halt	1 1 1 1 0 1 0 0			
WAIT = Wait	1 0 0 1 1 0 1 1			
ESC = Escape (to external device)	1 1 0 1 1 x x x	m o d y y y r / m	(DISP-LO)	(DISP-HI)
LOCK = Bus lock prefix	1 1 1 1 0 0 0 0			
SEGMENT = Override prefix	0 0 1 reg 1 1 0			

1ST BYTE		2ND BYTE	BYTES 3, 4, 5, 6	ASM-86 INSTRUCTION FORMAT	
HEX	BINARY				
00	0000 0000	MOD REG R/M	(DISP-LO),(DISP-HI)	ADD	REG8/MEM8,REG8
01	0000 0001	MOD REG R/M	(DISP-LO),(DISP-HI)	ADD	REG16/MEM16,REG16
02	0000 0010	MOD REG R/M	(DISP-LO),(DISP-HI)	ADD	REG8,REG8/MEM8
03	0000 0011	MOD REG R/M	(DISP-LO),(DISP-HI)	ADD	REG16,REG16/MEM16
04	0000 0100	DATA-8		ADD	AL,IMMED8
05	0000 0101	DATA-LO	DATA-HI	ADD	AX,IMMED16
06	0000 0110			PUSH	ES
07	0000 0111			POP	ES

Table B-3. Machine Instruction Decoding Guide.

1ST BYTE HEX	1ST BYTE BINARY	2ND BYTE	BYTES 3,4,5,6	ASM-86 INSTRUCTION FORMAT	
08	0000 1000	MOD REG R/M	(DISP-LO),(DISP-HI)	OR	REG8/MEM8,REG8
09	0000 1001	MOD REG R/M	(DISP-LO),(DISP-HI)	OR	REG16/MEM16,REG16
0A	0000 1010	MOD REG R/M	(DISP-LO),(DISP-HI)	OR	REG8,REG8/MEM8
0B	0000 1011	MOD REG R/M	(DISP-LO),(DISP-HI)	OR	REG16,REG16/MEM16
0C	0000 1100	DATA-8		OR	AL,IMMED8
0D	0000 1101	DATA-LO	DATA-HI	OR	AX,IMMED16
0E	0000 1110			PUSH	CS
0F	0000 1111			(not used)	
10	0001 0000	MOD REG R/M	(DISP-LO),(DISP-HI)	ADC	REG8/MEM8,REG8
11	0001 0001	MOD REG R/M	(DISP-LO),(DISP-HI)	ADC	REG16/MEM16,REG16
12	0001 0010	MOD REG R/M	(DISP-LO),(DISP-HI)	ADC	REG8,REG8/MEM8
13	0001 0011	MOD REG R/M	(DISP-LO),(DISP-HI)	ADC	REG16,REG16/MEM16
14	0001 0100	DATA-8		ADC	AL,IMMED8
15	0001 0101	DATA-LO	DATA-HI	ADC	AX,IMMED16
16	0001 0110			PUSH	SS
17	0001 0111			POP	SS
18	0001 1000	MOD REG R/M	(DISP-LO),(DISP-HI)	SBB	REG8/MEM8,REG8
19	0001 1001	MOD REG R/M	(DISP-LO),(DISP-HI)	SBB	REG16/MEM16,REG16
1A	0001 1010	MOD REG R/M	(DISP-LO),(DISP-HI)	SBB	REG8,REG8/MEM8
1B	0001 1011	MOD REG R/M	(DISP-LO),(DISP-HI)	SBB	REG16,REG16/MEM16
1C	0001 1100	DATA-8		SBB	AL,IMMED8
1D	0001 1101	DATA-LO	DATA-HI	SBB	AX,IMMED16
1E	0001 1110			PUSH	DS
1F	0001 1111			POP	DS
20	0010 0000	MOD REG R/M	(DISP-LO),(DISP-HI)	AND	REG8/MEM8,REG8
21	0010 0001	MOD REG R/M	(DISP-LO),(DISP-HI)	AND	REG16/MEM16,REG16
22	0010 0010	MOD REG R/M	(DISP-LO),(DISP-HI)	AND	REG8,REG8/MEM8
23	0010 0011	MOD REG R/M	(DISP-LO),(DISP-HI)	AND	REG16,REG16/MEM16
24	0010 0100	DATA-8		AND	AL,IMMED8
25	0010 0101	DATA-LO	DATA-HI	AND	AX,IMMED16
26	0010 0110			ES:	(segment override prefix)
27	0010 0111			DAA	
28	0010 1000	MOD REG R/M	(DISP-LO),(DISP-HI)	SUB	REG8/MEM8,REG8
29	0010 1001	MOD REG R/M	(DISP-LO),(DISP-HI)	SUB	REG16/MEM16,REG16
2A	0010 1010	MOD REG R/M	(DISP-LO),(DISP-HI)	SUB	REG8,REG8/MEM8
2B	0010 1011	MOD REG R/M	(DISP-LO,(DISP-HI)	SUB	REG16,REG16/MEM16
2C	0010 1100	DATA-8		SUB	AL,IMMED8
2D	0010 1101	DATA-LO	DATA-HI	SUB	AX,IMMED16
2E	0010 1110			CS:	(segment override prefix)
2F	0010 1111			DAS	
30	0011 0000	MOD REG R/M	(DISP-LO),(DISP-HI)	XOR	REG8/MEM8,REG8
31	0011 0001	MOD REG R/M	(DISP-LO),(DISP-HI)	XOR	REG16/MEM16,REG16
32	0011 0010	MOD REG R/M	(DISP-LO),(DISP-HI)	XOR	REG8,REG8/MEM8
33	0011 0011	MOD REG R/M	(DISP-LO),(DISP-HI)	XOR	REG16,REG16/MEM16
34	0011 0100	DATA-8		XOR	AL,IMMED8
35	0011 0101	DATA-LO	DATA-HI	XOR	AX,IMMED16
36	0011 0110			SS:	(segment override prefix)

Table B-3. Machine Instruction Decoding Guide (continued).

1ST BYTE		2ND BYTE	BYTES 3,4,5,6	ASM-86 INSTRUCTION FORMAT	
HEX	BINARY				
37	0011 0110			AAA	
38	0011 1000	MOD REG R/M	(DISP-LO),(DISP-HI)	CMP	REG8/MEM8,REG8
39	0011 1001	MOD REG R/M	(DISP-LO),(DISP-HI)	CMP	REG16/MEM16,REG16
3A	0011 1010	MOD REG R/M	(DISP-LO),(DISP-HI)	CMP	REG8,REG8/MEM8
3B	0011 1011	MOD REG R/M	(DISP-LO),(DISP-HI)	CMP	REG16,REG16/MEM16
3C	0011 1100	DATA-8		CMP	AL,IMMED8
3D	0011 1101	DATA-LO	DATA-HI	CMP	AX,IMMED16
3E	0011 1110			DS:	(segment override prefix)
3F	0011 1111			AAS	
40	0100 0000			INC	AX
41	0100 0001			INC	CX
42	0100 0010			INC	DX
43	0100 0011			INC	BX
44	0100 0100			INC	SP
45	0100 0101			INC	BP
46	0100 0110			INC	SI
47	0100 0111			INC	DI
48	0100 1000			DEC	AX
49	0100 1001			DEC	CX
4A	0100 1010			DEC	DX
4B	0100 1011			DEC	BX
4C	0100 1100			DEC	SP
4D	0100 1101			DEC	BP
4E	0100 1110			DEC	SI
4F	0100 1111			DEC	DI
50	0101 0000			PUSH	AX
51	0101 0001			PUSH	CX
52	0101 0010			PUSH	DX
53	0101 0011			PUSH	BX
54	0101 0100			PUSH	SP
55	0101 0101			PUSH	BP
56	0101 0110			PUSH	SI
57	0101 0111			PUSH	DI
58	0101 1000			POP	AX
59	0101 1001			POP	CX
5A	0101 1010			POP	DX
5B	0101 1011			POP	BX
5C	0101 1100			POP	SP
5D	0101 1101			POP	BP
5E	0101 1110			POP	SI
5F	0101 1111			POP	DI
60	0110 0000			(not used)	
61	0110 0001			(not used)	
62	0110 0010			(not used)	
63	0110 0011			(not used)	
64	0110 0100			(not used)	
65	0110 0101			(not used)	
66	0110 0110			(not used)	
67	0110 0111			(not used)	

Table B-3. Machine Instruction Decoding Guide (continued).

1ST BYTE		2ND BYTE	BYTES 3,4,5,6	ASM-86 INSTRUCTION FORMAT	
HEX	BINARY				
68	0110 1000			(not used)	
69	0110 1001			(not used)	
6A	0110 1010			(not used)	
6B	0110 1011			(not used)	
6C	0110 1100			(not used)	
6D	0110 1101			(not used)	
6E	0110 1110			(not used)	
6F	0110 1111			(not used)	
70	0111 0000	IP-INC8		JO	SHORT-LABEL
71	0111 0001	IP-INC8		JNO	SHORT-LABEL
72	0111 0010	IP-INC8		JB/JNAE/ JC	SHORT-LABEL
73	0111 0011	IP-INC8		JNB/JAE/ JNC	SHORT-LABEL
74	0111 0100	IP-INC8		JE/JZ	SHORT-LABEL
75	0111 0101	IP-INC8		JNE/JNZ	SHORT-LABEL
76	0111 0110	IP-INC8		JBE/JNA	SHORT-LABEL
77	0111 0111	IP-INC8		JNBE/JA	SHORT-LABEL
78	0111 1000	IP-INC8		JS	SHORT-LABEL
79	0111 1001	IP-INC8		JNS	SHORT-LABEL
7A	0111 1010	IP-INC8		JP/JPE	SHORT-LABEL
7B	0111 1011	IP-INC8		JNP/JPO	SHORT-LABEL
7C	0111 1100	IP-INC8		JL/JNGE	SHORT-LABEL
7D	0111 1101	IP-INC8		JNL/JGE	SHORT-LABEL
7E	0111 1110	IP-INC8		JLE/JNG	SHORT-LABEL
7F	0111 1111	IP-INC8		JNLE/JG	SHORT-LABEL
80	1000 0000	MOD 000 R/M	(DISP-LO),(DISP-HI), DATA-8	ADD	REG8/MEM8,IMMED8
80	1000 0000	MOD 001 R/M	(DISP-LO),(DISP-HI), DATA-8	OR	REG8/MEM8,IMMED8
80	1000 0000	MOD 010 R/M	(DISP-LO),(DISP-HI), DATA-8	ADC	REG8/MEM8,IMMED8
80	1000 0000	MOD 011 R/M	(DISP-LO),(DISP-HI), DATA-8	SBB	REG8/MEM8,IMMED8
80	1000 0000	MOD 100 R/M	(DISP-LO),(DISP-HI), DATA-8	AND	REG8/MEM8,IMMED8
80	1000 0000	MOD 101 R/M	(DISP-LO),(DISP-HI), DATA-8	SUB	REG8/MEM8,IMMED8
80	1000 0000	MOD 110 R/M	(DISP-LO),(DISP-HI), DATA-8	XOR	REG8/MEM8,IMMED8
80	1000 0000	MOD 111 R/M	(DISP-LO),(DISP-HI), DATA-8	CMP	REG8/MEM8,IMMED8
81	1000 0001	MOD 000 R/M	(DISP-LO),(DISP-HI), DATA-LO,DATA-HI	ADD	REG16/MEM16,IMMED16
81	1000 0001	MOD 001 R/M	(DISP-LO),(DISP-HI), DATA-LO,DATA-HI	OR	REG16/MEM16,IMMED16
81	1000 0001	MOD 010 R/M	(DISP-LO),(DISP-HI), DATA-LO,DATA-HI	ADC	REG16/MEM16,IMMED16
81	1000 0001	MOD 011 R/M	(DISP-LO),(DISP-HI), DATA-LO,DATA-HI	SBB	REG16/MEM16,IMMED16

Table B-3. Machine Instruction Decoding Guide (continued).

1ST BYTE HEX	BINARY	2ND BYTE	BYTES 3,4,5,6	ASM-86 INSTRUCTION FORMAT	
81	1000 0001	MOD 100 R/M	(DISP-LO),(DISP-HI), DATA-LO,DATA-HI	AND	REG16/MEM16,IMMED16
81	1000 0001	MOD 101 R/M	(DISP-LO),(DISP-HI), DATA-LO,DATA-HI	SUB	REG16/MEM16,IMMED16
81	1000 0001	MOD 110 R/M	(DISP-LO),(DISP-HI), DATA-LO,DATA-HI	XOR	REG16/MEM16,IMMED16
81	1000 0001	MOD 111 R/M	(DISP-LO),(DISP-HI), DATA-LO,DATA-HI	CMP	REG16/MEM16,IMMED16
82	1000 0010	MOD 000 R/M	(DISP-LO),(DISP-HI), DATA-8	ADD	REG8/MEM8,IMMED8
82	1000 0010	MOD 001 R/M		(not used)	
82	1000 0010	MOD 010 R/M	(DISP-LO),(DISP-HI), DATA-8	ADC	REG8/MEM8,IMMED8
82	1000 0010	MOD 011 R/M	(DISP-LO),(DISP-HI), DATA-8	SBB	REG8/MEM8,IMMED8
82	1000 0010	MOD 100 R/M		(not used)	
82	1000 0010	MOD 101 R/M	(DISP-LO),(DISP-HI), DATA-8	SUB	REG8/MEM8,IMMED8
82	1000 0010	MOD 110 R/M		(not used)	
82	1000 0010	MOD 111 R/M	(DISP-LO),(DISP-HI), DATA-8	CMP	REG8/MEM8,IMMED8
83	1000 0011	MOD 000 R/M	(DISP-LO),(DISP-HI), DATA-SX	ADD	REG16/MEM16, IMMED8
83	1000 0011	MOD 001 R/M		(not used)	
83	1000 0011	MOD 010 R/M	(DISP-LO), (DISP-HI), DATA-SX	ADC	REG16/MEM16,IMMED8
83	1000 0011	MOD 011 R/M	(DISP-LO),(DISP-HI), DATA-SX	SBB	REG16/MEM16,IMMED8
83	1000 0011	MOD 100 R/M		(not used)	
83	1000 0011	MOD 101 R/M	(DISP-LO),(DISP-HI), DATA-SX	SUB	REG16/MEM16,IMMED8
83	1000 0011	MOD 110 R/M		(not used)	
83	1000 0011	MOD 111 R/M	(DISP-LO),(DISP-HI), DATA-SX	CMP	REG16/MEM16,IMMED8
84	1000 0100	MOD REG R/M	(DISP-LO),(DISP-HI)	TEST	REG8/MEM8,REG8
85	1000 0101	MOD REG R/M	(DISP-LO),(DISP-HI)	TEST	REG16/MEM16,REG16
86	1000 0110	MOD REG R/M	(DISP-LO),(DISP-HI)	XCHG	REG8,REG8/MEM8
87	1000 0111	MOD REG R/M	(DISP-LO),(DISP-HI)	XCHG	REG16,REG16/MEM16
88	1000 1000	MOD REG R/M	(DISP-LO),(DISP-HI)	MOV	REG8/MEM8,REG8
89	1000 1001	MOD REG R/M	(DISP-LO),(DISP-HI)	MOV	REG16/MEM16/REG16
8A	1000 1010	MOD REG R/M	(DISP-LO),(DISP-HI)	MOV	REG8,REG8/MEM8
8B	1000 1011	MOD REG R/M	(DISP-LO),(DISP-HI)	MOV	REG16,REG16/MEM16
8C	1000 1100	MOD 0SR R/M	(DISP-LO),(DISP-HI)	MOV	REG16/MEM16,SEGREG
8C	1000 1100	MOD 1-- R/M		(not used)	
8D	1000 1101	MOD REG R/M	(DISP-LO),(DISP-HI)	LEA	REG16,MEM16
8E	1000 1110	MOD 0SR R/M	(DISP-LO),(DISP-HI)	MOV	SEGREG,REG16/MEM16
8E	1000 1110	MOD 1-- R/M		(not used)	
8F	1000 1111	MOD 000 R/M	(DISP-LO),(DISP-HI)	POP	REG16/MEM16
8F	1000 1111	MOD 001 R/M		(not used)	
8F	1000 1111	MOD 010 R/M		(not used)	

Table B-3. Machine Instruction Decoding Guide (continued).

1ST BYTE		2ND BYTE	BYTES 3,4,5,6	ASM-86 INSTRUCTION FORMAT	
HEX	BINARY				
8F	1000 1111	MOD 011 R/M		(not used)	
8F	1000 1111	MOD 100 R/M		(not used)	
8F	1000 1111	MOD 101 R/M		(not used)	
8F	1000 1111	MOD 110 R/M		(not used)	
8F	1000 1111	MOD 111 R/M		(not used)	
90	1001 0000			NOP	(exchange AX,AX)
91	1001 0001			XCHG	AX,CX
92	1001 0010			XCHG	AX,DX
93	1001 0011			XCHG	AX,BX
94	1001 0100			XCHG	AX,SP
95	1001 0101			XCHG	AX,BP
96	1001 0110			XCHG	AX,SI
97	1001 0111			XCHG	AX,DI
98	1001 1000			CBW	
99	1001 1001			CWD	
9A	1001 1010	DISP-LO	DISP-HI,SEG-LO, SEG-HI	CALL	FAR_PROC
9B	1001 1011			WAIT	
9C	1001 1100			PUSHF	
9D	1001 1101			POPF	
9E	1001 1110			SAHF	
9F	1001 1111			LAHF	
A0	1010 0000	ADDR-LO	ADDR-HI	MOV	AL,MEM8
A1	1010 0001	ADDR-LO	ADDR-HI	MOV	AX,MEM16
A2	1010 0010	ADDR-LO	ADDR-HI	MOV	MEM8,AL
A3	1010 0011	ADDR-LO	ADDR-HI	MOV	MEM16, AX
A4	1010 0100			MOVS	DEST-STR8,SRC-STR8
A5	1010 0101			MOVS	DEST-STR16,SRC-STR16
A6	1010 0110			CMPS	DEST-STR8,SRC-STR8
A7	1010 0111			CMPS	DEST-STR16,SRC-STR16
A8	1010 1000	DATA-8		TEST	AL,IMMED8
A9	1010 1001	DATA-LO	DATA-HI	TEST	AX,IMMED16
AA	1010 1010			STOS	DEST-STR8
AB	1010 1011			STOS	DEST-STR16
AC	1010 1100			LODS	SRC-STR8
AD	1010 1101			LODS	SRC-STR16
AE	1010 1110			SCAS	DEST-STR8
AF	1010 1111			SCAS	DEST-STR16
B0	1011 0000	DATA-8		MOV	AL,IMMED8
B1	1011 0001	DATA-8		MOV	CL,IMMED8
B2	1011 0010	DATA-8		MOV	DL,IMMED8
B3	1011 1011	DATA-8		MOV	BL,IMMED8
B4	1011 0100	DATA-8		MOV	AH,IMMED8
B5	1011 0101	DATA-8		MOV	CH,IMMED8
B6	1011 0110	DATA-8		MOV	DH,IMMED8
B7	1011 0111	DATA-8		MOV	BH,IMMED8
B8	1011 1000	DATA-LO	DATA-HI	MOV	AX,IMMED16
B9	1011 1001	DATA-LO	DATA-HI	MOV	CX,IMMED16
BA	1011 1010	DATA-LO	DATA-HI	MOV	DX,IMMED16
BB	1011 1011	DATA-LO	DATA-HI	MOV	BX,IMMED16

Table B-3. Machine Instruction Decoding Guide (continued).

1ST BYTE HEX	1ST BYTE BINARY	2ND BYTE	BYTES 3,4,5,6	ASM-86 INSTRUCTION FORMAT	
BC	1011 1100	DATA-LO	DATA-HI	MOV	SP,IMMED16
BD	1011 1101	DATA-LO	DATA-HI	MOV	BP,IMMED16
BE	1011 1110	DATA-LO	DATA-HI	MOV	SI,IMMED16
BF	1011 1111	DATA-LO	DATA-HI	MOV	DI,IMMED16
C0	1100 0000			(not used)	
C1	1100 0001			(not used)	
C2	1100 0010	DATA-LO	DATA-HI	RET	IMMED16 (intraseg)
C3	1100 0011			RET	(intrasegment)
C4	1100 0100	MOD REG R/M	(DISP-LO),(DISP-HI)	LES	REG16,MEM16
C5	1100 0101	MOD REG R/M	(DISP-LO),(DISP-HI)	LDS	REG16,MEM16
C6	1100 0110	MOD 000 R/M	(DISP-LO),(DISP-HI), DATA-8	MOV	MEM8,IMMED8
C6	1100 0110	MOD 001 R/M		(not used)	
C6	1100 0110	MOD 010 R/M		(not used)	
C6	1100 0110	MOD 011 R/M		(not used)	
C6	1100 0110	MOD 100 R/M		(not used)	
C6	1100 0110	MOD 101 R/M		(not used)	
C6	1100 0110	MOD 110 R/M		(not used)	
C6	1100 0110	MOD 111 R/M		(not used)	
C7	1100 0111	MOD 000 R/M	(DISP-LO),(DISP-HI), DATA-LO,DATA-HI	MOV	MEM16,IMMED16
C7	1100 0111	MOD 001 R/M		(not used)	
C7	1100 0111	MOD 010 R/M		(not used)	
C7	1100 0111	MOD 011 R/M		(not used)	
C7	1100 0111	MOD 100 R/M		(not used)	
C7	1100 0111	MOD 101 R/M		(not used)	
C7	1100 0111	MOD 110 R/M		(not used)	
C7	1100 0111	MOD 111 R/M		(not used	
C8	1100 1000			(not used)	
C9	1100 1001			(not used)	
CA	1100 1010	DATA-LO	DATA-HI	RET	IMMED16 (intersegment)
CB	1100 1011			RET	(intersegment)
CC	1100 1100			INT	3
CD	1100 1101	DATA-8		INT	IMMED8
CE	1100 1110			INTO	
CF	1100 1111			IRET	
D0	1101 0000	MOD 000 R/M	(DISP-LO),(DISP-HI)	ROL	REG8/MEM8,1
D0	1101 0000	MOD 001 R/M	(DISP-LO),(DISP-HI)	ROR	REG8/MEM8,1
D0	1101 0000	MOD 010 R/M	(DISP-LO),(DISP-HI)	RCL	REG8/MEM8,1
D0	1101 0000	MOD 011 R/M	(DISP-LO),(DISP-HI)	RCR	REG8/MEM8,1
D0	1101 0000	MOD 100 R/M	(DISP-LO),(DISP-HI)	SAL/SHL	REG8/MEM8,1
D0	1101 0000	MOD 101 R/M	(DISP-LO),(DISP-HI)	SHR	REG8/MEM8,1
D0	1101 0000	MOD 110 R/M		(not used)	
D0	1101 0000	MOD 111 R/M	(DISP-LO),(DISP-HI)	SAR	REG8/MEM8,1
D1	1101 0001	MOD 000 R/M	(DISP-LO),(DISP-HI)	ROL	REG16/MEM16,1
D1	1101 0001	MOD 001 R/M	(DISP-LO),(DISP-HI)	ROR	REG16/MEM16,1
D1	1101 0001	MOD 010 R/M	(DISP-LO),(DISP-HI)	RCL	REG16/MEM16,1
D1	1101 0001	MOD 011 R/M	(DISP-LO),(DISP-HI)	RCR	REG16/MEM16,1
D1	1101 0001	MOD 100 R/M	(DISP-LO),(DISP-HI)	SAL/SHL	REG16/MEM16,1

Table B-3. Machine Instruction Decoding Guide (continued).

1ST BYTE		2ND BYTE	BYTES 3,4,5,6	ASM-86 INSTRUCTION FORMAT	
HEX	BINARY				
D1	1101 0001	MOD 101 R/M	(DISP-LO),(DISP-HI)	SHR	REG16/MEM16,1
D1	1101 0001	MOD 110 R/M		(not used)	
D1	1101 0001	MOD 111 R/M	(DISP-LO),(DISP-HI)	SAR	REG16/MEM16,1
D2	1101 0010	MOD 000 R/M	(DISP-LO),(DISP-HI)	ROL	REG8/MEM8,CL
D2	1101 0010	MOD 001 R/M	(DISP-LO),(DISP-HI)	ROR	REG8/MEM8,CL
D2	1101 0010	MOD 010 R/M	(DISP-LO),(DISP-HI)	RCL	REG8/MEM8,CL
D2	1101 0010	MOD 011 R/M	(DISP-LO),(DISP-HI)	RCR	REG8/MEM8,CL
D2	1101 0010	MOD 100 R/M	(DISP-LO),(DISP-HI)	SAL/SHL	REG8/MEM8,CL
D2	1101 0010	MOD 101 R/M	(DISP-LO),(DISP-HI)	SHR	REG8/MEM8,CL
D2	1101 0010	MOD 110 R/M		(not used)	
D2	1101 0010	MOD 111 R/M	(DISP-LO),(DISP-HI)	SAR	REG8/MEM8,CL
D3	1101 0011	MOD 000 R/M	(DISP-LO),(DISP-HI)	ROL	REG16/MEM16,CL
D3	1101 0011	MOD 001 R/M	(DISP-LO),(DISP-HI)	ROR	REG16/MEM16,CL
D3	1101 0011	MOD 010 R/M	(DISP-LO),(DISP-HI)	RCL	REG16/MEM16,CL
D3	1101 0011	MOD 011 R/M	(DISP-LO),(DISP-HI)	RCR	REG16/MEM16,CL
D3	1101 0011	MOD 100 R/M	(DISP-LO),(DISP-HI)	SAL/SHL	REG16/MEM16,CL
D3	1101 0011	MOD 101 R/M	(DISP-LO),(DISP-HI)	SHR	REG16/MEM16,CL
D3	1101 0011	MOD 110 R/M		(not used)	
D3	1101 001 1	MOD 111 R/M	(DISP-LO),(DISP-HI)	SAR	REG16/MEM16,CL
D4	1101 0100	00001010		AAM	
D5	1101 0101	00001010		AAD	
D6	1101 0110			(not used)	
D7	1101 0111			XLAT	SOURCE-TABLE
D8	1101 1000	MOD 000 R/M			
	1XXX	MOD YYY R/M	(DISP-LO), (DISP-HI)	ESC	OPCODE,SOURCE
DF	1101 1111	MOD 111 R/M			
E0	1110 0000	IP-INC-8		LOOPNE/ LOOPNZ	SHORT-LABEL
E1	1110 0001	IP-INC-8		LOOPE/ LOOPZ	SHORT-LABEL
E2	1110 0010	IP-INC-8		LOOP	SHORT-LABEL
E3	1110 0011	IP-INC-8		JCXZ	SHORT-LABEL
E4	1110 0100	DATA-8		IN	AL,IMMED8
E5	1110 0101	DATA-8		IN	AX,IMMED8
E6	1110 0110	DATA-8		OUT	AL,IMMED8
E7	1110 0111	DATA-8		OUT	AX,IMMED8
E8	1110 1000	IP-INC-LO	IP-INC-HI	CALL	NEAR-PROC
E9	1110 1001	IP-INC-LO	IP-INC-HI	JMP	NEAR-LABEL
EA	1110 1010	IP-LO	IP-HI,CS-LO,CS-HI	JMP	FAR-LABEL
EB	1110 1011	IP-INC8		JMP	SHORT-LABEL
EC	1110 1100			IN	AL,DX
ED	1110 1101			IN	AX,DX
EE	1110 1110			OUT	AL,DX
EF	1110 1111			OUT	AX,DX
F0	1111 0000			LOCK	(prefix)
F1	1111 0001			(not used)	
F2	1111 0010			REPNE/REPNZ	
F3	1111 0011			REP/REPE/REPZ	
F4	1111 0100			HLT	
F5	1111 0101			CMC	

Table B-3. Machine Instruction Decoding Guide (continued).

1ST BYTE HEX	1ST BYTE BINARY	2ND BYTE	BYTES 3,4,5,6	ASM-86 INSTRUCTION FORMAT	
F6	1111 0110	MOD 000 R/M	(DISP-LO),(DISP-HI), DATA-8	TEST	REG8/MEM8,IMMED8
F6	1111 0110	MOD 001 R/M		(not used)	
F6	1111 0110	MOD 010 R/M	(DISP-LO),(DISP-HI)	NOT	REG8/MEM8
F6	1111 0110	MOD 011 R/M	(DISP-LO),(DISP-HI)	NEG	REG8/MEM8
F6	1111 0110	MOD 100 R/M	(DISP-LO),(DISP-HI)	MUL	REG8/MEM8
F6	1111 0110	MOD 101 R/M	(DISP-LO),(DISP-HI)	IMUL	REG8/MEM8
F6	1111 0110	MOD 110 R/M	(DISP-LO),(DISP-HI)	DIV	REG8/MEM8
F6	1111 0110	MOD 111 R/M	(DISP-LO),(DISP-HI)	IDIV	REG8/MEM8
F7	1111 0111	MOD 000 R/M	(DISP-LO),(DISP-HI), DATA-LO,DATA-HI	TEST	REG16/MEM16,IMMED16
F7	1111 0111	MOD 001 R/M		(not used)	
F7	1111 0111	MOD 010 R/M	(DISP-LO),(DISP-HI)	NOT	REG16/MEM16
F7	1111 0111	MOD 011 R/M	(DISP-LO),(DISP-HI)	NEG	REG16/MEM16
F7	1111 0111	MOD 100 R/M	(DISP-LO),(DISP-HI)	MUL	REG16/MEM16
F7	1111 0111	MOD 101 R/M	(DISP-LO),(DISP-HI)	IMUL	REG16/MEM16
F7	1111 0111	MOD 110 R/M	(DISP-LO),(DISP-HI)	DIV	REG16/MEM16
F7	1111 0111	MOD 111 R/M	(DISP-LO),(DISP-HI)	IDIV	REG16/MEM16
F8	1111 1000			CLC	
F9	1111 1001			STC	
FA	1111 1010			CLI	
FB	1111 1011			STI	
FC	1111 1100			CLD	
FD	1111 1101			STD	
FE	1111 1110	MOD 000 R/M	(DISP-LO),(DISP-HI)	INC	REG8/MEM8
FE	1111 1110	MOD 001 R/M	(DISP-LO),(DISP-HI)	DEC	REG8/MEM8
FE	1111 1110	MOD 010 R/M		(not used)	
FE	1111 1110	MOD 011 R/M		(not used)	
FE	1111 1110	MOD 100 R/M		(not used)	
FE	1111 1110	MOD 101 R/M		(not used)	
FE	1111 1110	MOD 110 R/M		(not used)	
FE	1111 1110	MOD 111 R/M		(not used)	
FF	1111 1111	MOD 000 R/M	(DISP-LO),(DISP-HI)	INC	MEM16
FF	1111 1111	MOD 001 R/M	(DISP-LO),(DISP-HI)	DEC	MEM16
FF	1111 1111	MOD 010 R/M	(DISP-LO),(DISP-HI)	CALL	REG16/MEM16 (intra)
FF	1111 1111	MOD 011 R/M	(DISP-LO),(DISP-HI)	CALL	MEM16 (intersegment)
FF	1111 1111	MOD 100 R/M	(DISP-LO),(DISP-HI)	JMP	REG16/MEM16 (intra)
FF	1111 1111	MOD 101 R/M	(DISP-LO),(DISP-HI)	JMP	MEM16 (intersegment)
FF	1111 1111	MOD 110 R/M	(DISP-LO),(DISP-HI)	PUSH	MEM16
FF	1111 1111	MOD 111 R/M		(not used)	

Index

Edited by Brint Rutherford